CW00539804

THE TOWER OF LONDON M⌣⌣⌣⌣
Archaeological Excavations 1995-9

Historic Royal Palaces Monograph No. 1

Graham Keevill

Oxford Archaeology

with

Historic Royal Palaces

Published by Oxford Archaeology, Janus House, Osney Mead, Oxford OX2 0ES on behalf of Historic Royal Palaces, Hampton Court Palace, Surrey KT8 9AU

Text copyright © 2004 Historic Royal Palaces
Pictures copyright © 2004 the copyright holders; see below for details

Picture credits

Aerofilms Photo Library, fig 1; The Board of Trustees of the Armouries, figs 114, 122; Birmingham Library Services, fig 158; Bodleian Library, University of Oxford (Gough Maps 21, fol 40v (lower drawing)), fig 109; By Permission of the British Library, fig 138; © The British Museum, fig 145; The Master and Fellows of Corpus Christi College Cambridge, fig 55; Getty Images, fig 160; The Guildhall Library, Corporation of London, figs 115, 161; The Guildhall Library, Corporation of London/www.bridgeman.co.uk, fig 144; Crown copyright: Historic Royal Palaces, figs 2, 3, 4, 7, 8, 9, 10, 11, 12, 13, 14, 15, 16, 17, 18, 19, 20, 21, 22, 23, 24, 25, 26, 27, 28, 29, 30 (Ian Tyers), 31, 32, 33, 34, 35 (Ivan Lapper), 36, 37, 38, 39, 40, 41, 42, 43, 44, 45, 46, 47, 48, 49, 50, 51 (Ian Tyers), 52, 53, 54 (Edward Impey), 56 (Ivan Lapper), 57, 58 (Rob Scaife), 59, 60, 61, 62, 63, 64, 65, 66 (Ian Tyers), 67, 68, 69, 70, 71 (Ian Tyers), 72, 73, 74, 75, 76, 77, 78, 79, 80, 81, 82, 83, 85, 86, 87, 88, 89, 90, 91, 92, 93, 94, 95, 96, 97, 99, 100, 101 (Jonathan Foyle), 102, 103, 104, 105, 106, 107, 108 (Rob Scaife), 110, 111, 112, 113, 116, 117, 118, 119, 121, 123, 125, 126, 127, 128, 130, 131, 132, 133, 134, 136, 137, 139, 140, 141, 142, 143 (Rob Scaife), 146, 148, 149, 150, 151, 152 (Nigel Cameron), 154, 155, 156, 157, 159, 162, 163, 165, 166, A1.1-A1.12, A2.1-A2.5 (David Higgins); © Jarrold Publishing, fig 6; Courtesy of the Museum of London, figs 5, 147; The National Archives (PRO), figs 84 (MPH 214 (2)), 120 (Works 31/28), 124 (Works 78/1227), 135 (Works 31/36); © Crown copyright NMR, fig 164; Reproduced from the Ordnance Survey on behalf of the Controller of Her Majesty's Stationery Office, figs 2, 3, 7, 8, 9, 22, 78 (AL100005569); RIBA Library Drawings Collection, fig 153; Courtesy of the Royal Brompton Hospital, fig 98; V & A Picture Library, fig 129.

ISBN 0 904220 35 4

Copy editing: Anne Marriott and Christopher Catling
Index compiled by Susanne Atkin

Typeset and printed in Europe by the Alden Group, Oxford, UK

Contents

Figures

CHAPTER 7

CHAPTER 8

CHAPTER 9

CHAPTER 10

APPENDIX 1

APPENDIX 2

Tables

Contributors

The Tower of London moat project was managed for OAU (now Oxford Archaeology) by Graham Keevill, with Duncan Wood and Greg Pugh providing most of the day-to-day on-site supervision.

Historical research was undertaken by Edward Impey and Jeremy Ashbee of Historic Royal Palaces (HRP), with additional work by Todd Longstaffe-Gowan, Ruth Guilding and Stephen Priestley of Elizabeth Banks Associates.

The large environmental programme, including numerous site visits to advise on sampling strategy, was undertaken by the following:

Diatoms: Nigel Cameron (University College London)
Soil micromorphology: Richard Macphail (University College London), John Crowther (University of Wales, Lampeter)
Macroscopic plant and invertebrate remains: Mark Robinson (Oxford University)
Pollen: Rob Scaife (Southampton University)

The dendrochronology programme was carried out by Ian Tyers (University of Sheffield), who also provided wood identifications. Damian Goodburn and Nick Mitchell advised us on timbers and wood technology.

Claire Ingrem and Dale Serjeantson of the Faunal Remains Unit, University of Southampton, analysed the animal bones recovered during the excavations.

Conservation advice and assistance was provided by the following:

David Howell and Caroline Allington (Historic Royal Palaces)
Mike Corfield, Glynis Edwards and Jacqui Watson (English Heritage)
Vanessa Fell (English Heritage/Oxford University Institute of Archaeology)
The fish trap was cleaned by Ronnie Gibbs of HRP's Textile Conservation Studio, under the guidance of Jacqui Watson.

The artefacts were analysed and reported on by the following:

Small Finds: Leigh Allen and Ian Scott (post-medieval and military)
Pottery: Duncan H Brown and Robert Thomson. The initial post-excavation assessment was carried out by Paul Blinkhorn (medieval pottery), Paul Booth (Roman pottery) and Nigel Jeffries (post-medieval pottery)
Glass: Cecily Cropper
Clay Pipe: David Higgins
Leather: Quita Mould
Coins: Venetia Porter and staff of the British Museum's Department of Coins and Medals
Building stone identifications were undertaken by Bernard Worssam.

The methodologies used for the specialist analyses are described in Chapter 3. The results and specialist reports are not separately presented in this volume, but have been integrated into the stratigraphic descriptions in chapters 4–10. An illustrated catalogue of pottery ware and vessel types can be found in Appendix 1. An extended report on clay pipes, with an illustrated catalogue, can be found in Appendix 2. Soil micromorphology data are presented in tabulated form in Appendix 3. Specialists' assessment and analytical reports are available in their original form in the project archive.

Except where otherwise credited, the illustrations in this volume are the work of Steven Cheshire, Anne Dunkley, Amy Hemingway, Sarah Lucas and Amy Tucker at the Oxford Archaeology Graphics Office. The illustration and production programme has been managed by Paul Backhouse.

THE PROJECT ARCHIVE

The archive of records and finds from the moat project is held by Historic Royal Palaces at the Tower of London. A microfiche copy of the records has been deposited with the National Monuments Record Centre at Swindon.

Foreword

In the early 1990s the authority responsible for the Tower of London, Historic Royal Palaces, decided to embark on a scheme to reflood the Moat. Such a potentially controversial project could only be undertaken after the most careful technical and archaeological studies had been completed. This book gives a detailed account of the latter.

Archaeology has caught the public imagination through numerous television programmes. Living, as I did, in the nation's most important historic site throughout the Moat excavations of 1995/97 it is not hard to understand the reasons for this. The enthusiasm of those involved was palpable and the excitement as new and often unexpected finds were made was infectious. Looking at the foundations of what was probably Henry III's entrance to the Tower for the first time since the tower's collapse in 1240 was, even for the layman, a truly amazing experience.

Whether or not the reflooding project ever materialises, the archaeological research it generated has made a major contribution to our understanding of the history of this World Heritage Site. That the research itself proved sufficiently important and interesting to merit a book on the subject is a double benefit. I commend it to the reader and congratulate the project team on its achievements.

Historic Royal Palaces is grateful for the financial support it received for the Tower Environs Scheme from: the Heritage Lottery Fund, the Pool of London Partnership and the J. Paul Getty Jnr Charitable Trust.

Major General G W Field CB OBE
Resident Governor and Keeper of the Jewel House
H.M. Tower of London

Preface

Her Majesty's Palace and Fortress of the Tower of London: the full title of England's most famous historic monument neatly encapsulates its dual role as a medieval royal residence and strategically important castle. Neither aspect is entirely central to the Tower's primary function today as a tourist attraction, but both are fundamental to why the site is an attraction in the first place. Indeed the great historic significance of the Tower of London, and the iconic status of its central feature, William the Conqueror's White Tower, have made the castle a public attraction since the reign of England's first Queen Elizabeth.

The Tower's attractiveness has not always extended beyond the perimeter of its medieval defences, however, and by the 1990s much of the area immediately around it had become a mess of bollards, signs, and poor quality facilities. This was in spite of the fact that the greater part of the inner area had been (and mostly still was) part of the historic Tower Liberties. This important buffer zone around the castle's defences fell within the jurisdiction of the Tower and had been maintained as open ground throughout the medieval period. Encroachment by buildings occurred in several areas during the 17th to 19th centuries, and the historic unity of the Liberties gradually became more and more eroded. Ultimately this led to the unsatisfactory townscape that existed at the end of the second millennium AD, while much of the Liberties had passed beyond the Tower's control by then.

The problems of the area around the castle were widely recognised, and this led to the establishment of the Tower Environs Scheme in the mid-1990s. The Scheme aimed to bring about a radical improvement in as much of the area around the castle as possible, thus providing a setting that would be truly appropriate for a World Heritage Site. The word 'Environs' (defined by the *Oxford English Dictionary* as 'the outskirts, surrounding districts, of a town')

was carefully chosen both to reflect and define the need for change. The full extent of what was achievable was not clear when the project began, but gradually became clearer by the time the fieldwork described in this report had been completed. The first years of the Scheme therefore concentrated on establishing what was, or was not, feasible on both technical and financial grounds. This included detailed assessment of a proposal to re-flood the castle's moat, an element of its defences planned and created as part of Edward I's expansion of the Tower in 1275–81 but drained and backfilled by the Duke of Wellington in 1843–5 while he was Constable. The assessment included a comprehensive archaeological and historical evaluation of the moat, largely carried out during 1995–7 but with some further fieldwork in 1998–9. This report provides a full and detailed description of the results of that evaluation, which provided remarkable new insights into the castle's long history, and especially that of its outer defences.

The Tower Environs Scheme is being implemented as this report goes to press, with new building and landscaping work concentrated along the western side of the castle. The building work has been preceded by detailed archaeological assessment of its impact during the design stage. As a result of this little impact on significant remains is expected, but construction is being monitored with great care by Historic Royal Palaces and Oxford Archaeology. Once again this has led to the discovery (and preservation *in situ*) of important evidence for the outer defences. This will be reported on in due course, but meanwhile this report will be invaluable to all those with an interest in medieval castles and palaces.

Graham D Keevill
July 2003

Acknowledgements

It is a pleasure to acknowledge the very considerable assistance provided by many people during the lifetime of this project, both in the field and during the subsequent analysis and report writing. The historical elements of the text are largely based on research carried out by Dr Edward Impey and Jeremy Ashbee, now of English Heritage but both formerly of Historic Royal Palaces, or on their behalf by Dr Todd Longstaffe-Gowan, Ruth Guilding and Stephen Priestley. Edward and Jeremy also contributed in innumerable ways to the smooth running of the project throughout its lifetime, and we are especially grateful to them for all their help and constant support. We would like to thank Dr Geoffrey Parnell of the Royal Armouries, whose unique knowledge of the Tower's past has enriched the research programme. Dr Parnell also drafted the historical text regarding the Lion Tower and the royal Menagerie. Dr Steven Brindle, Inspector of Ancient Monuments for English Heritage, deserves special thanks for his support and assistance throughout the project; in addition he most generously made available the results of his own research into the past of the Tower environs. We are also grateful to Beric Morley for his advice, especially regarding the possible form of Henry III's western entrance. We also wish to express our gratitude to the many people at Historic Royal Palaces who assisted us in our work, notably Major General Geoffrey Field, Stephen Bond, Dr Simon Thurley, Alison Bailey, David Honour, David Howell, Commander Tim Jones, Clare Murphy, Colonel Hugh Player, Colonel Robert Ward, and all of the Yeoman Warders and other Tower residents who endured the excavations with good humour and great interest. Detailed monitoring of the environmental and soil chemical conditions in backfilled and unexcavated areas was undertaken by David Howell of Historic Royal Palaces. Fondedile Foundations Ltd coredrilled the western foundations of the outer curtain wall. Alister Bartlett undertook resistivity and magnetometry surveys in the north moat during 1995. Subsurface Geotechnical provided a groundprobing radar survey of a 40m square in the west moat during 1995. Finally, Stratascan carried out resistivity and radar surveys of the whole moat circuit and the west end of the Wharf during 1996.

The moat project was very much a team effort, as all such large ventures must be if they are to succeed. Our archaeological team included many specialists, whose contributions at all stages are gratefully acknowledged and whose work has been incorporated in the present volume. For details, *see* Contributors, above.

Inevitably the senior managers of an archaeological unit play a major, if often unseen role in any project. It is therefore my pleasure to thank David Miles and David Jennings, successive directors of the Oxford Archaeological Unit, for their very considerable contribution to the moat project. John Moore, Bob Williams and Simon Palmer provided invaluable, indeed essential logistical support during fieldwork. Anne Dodd, Alan Hardy and Paul Backhouse provided equivalent support during the postexcavation analysis. Finally I am especially grateful to the various illustrators who worked to provide the excellent drawings and maps in the report.

Perhaps the most important people of all, certainly from my perspective as the person in charge of the fieldwork, were the excavation team. They were too numerous to list individually, but I am delighted to proffer my heartfelt thanks to them all. I would be seriously remiss, however, if I did not specifically thank Duncan Wood and Greg Pugh for their magnificent efforts in supervising every aspect of the excavations throughout the main period of fieldwork during 1996–7. Their patience, skill and above all remarkable good humour in often difficult and extremely demanding conditions made my job much easier than I had any right to expect, and I will be eternally grateful to them for their massive contribution to the success of the project.

Summary

Historic Royal Palaces established the Tower Environs Scheme in 1995, in order to carry out improvements to the immediate surroundings of the Tower of London. A major element of the scheme was a proposal to re-excavate and reflood the Tower moat, which had been drained and filled in during the 1840s. A comprehensive archaeological evaluation of the moat was commissioned from Oxford Archaeological Unit (now Oxford Archaeology), mostly undertaken between 1995 and 1997.

This volume presents a full account of the archaeological evaluation of the moat, together with the results of a complementary programme of historical research. Detailed evidence is presented for the development and condition of the moat from the mid-13th century to the present day. This includes the unexpected discovery of the remains of a short-lived entrance to the Tower, which was constructed for Henry III in 1240, but had collapsed irreparably within a year. The evaluations also recovered substantial evidence for Edward I's programme of expansion of the Tower, which saw the construction of the outer curtain wall, the creation of the existing moat, and the establishment of an elaborate western entrance causeway. Significant evidence was also found for the construction of de Gomme's outer moat revetment wall during the later 17th century. The deteriorating condition of the moat is considered in detail, leading to the decision in the 1840s to drain and backfill it.

Finds from the evaluation programme are discussed and illustrated, and these include interesting examples of medieval leatherwork, post-medieval pottery and clay pipes, and a virtually complete wicker fish trap. This volume also reports and discusses the extensive programme of scientific analysis of the moat fills, and a very successful programme of dendrochronological dating.

Abbreviations

ABMAP	Animal Bone Metrical Archive Project
DLR	Docklands Light Railway
ECRC	Environmental Change Research Centre
EH	English Heritage
HPR	Historic Plans Room
HRP	Historic Royal Palaces
LOI	loss on ignition
MNE	minimum number of elements
MNI	minimum number of individuals
NISP	number of identified specimens
OAU	Oxford Archaeological Unit
OD	Ordnance Datum
OIL	oblique incident light
PPL	Plane polarised light
PRO	Public Record Office
rp	rim percentage
SAM	Scheduled Ancient Monument
SF	small find
tdlp	total dry land pollen
TP	total phosphorus
UVL	ultra violet light
XPL	crossed polarised light

Chapter 1:   A Place in History: The Development of the Tower of London and its Environs

INTRODUCTION

No place exists in isolation, and that is as true for the Tower of London as it is for anywhere else. Many factors have influenced the castle's development over the centuries, from the river it sits beside to the varying needs of the people who have lived in and used it. The Tower, like the city around it, has always been a dynamic entity, and this is reflected not only in the many alterations to its fabric but also in its interaction with its surroundings (Figs 1–2). This chapter therefore examines why the site was chosen, and how the Tower of London and its environs became what they are today. The terms city and City of London throughout refer to the area within the Roman city defences and the largely coterminous medieval city. London in the broader sense is usually referred to in terms of suburban development around this nucleus. The term Greater London (ie, today's administrative and political entity) is used only in the context of modern development. As a convention, Roman calendar years have been prefixed with AD for clarity. All other dates are assumed to be AD unless otherwise stated.

THE LANDSCAPE OF LONDON: THE SETTING FOR THE CASTLE

The basics of landform are usually crucial to the establishment and success of any building enterprise, whether it be an entire city or something more specific like an abbey or a castle. Geology, geography and topography go together to provide the physical basis of the chosen site, and the influence of these characteristics is ever-present. The choice of site for the City of London was so successful, and the city has grown so enormously over the two millennia of its history, that the original landform has altered beyond recognition except for one crucial element: the river Thames. Undoubtedly this was the single most important reason both for the choice of site and its success, but why here exactly as opposed to other potential locations up- or downstream? The main reason lies in the river itself, or at least in its prehistoric form, which was much broader and shallower than today. The tidal reach today extends to Teddington Lock, well to the west of the Tower, and in late prehistoric times the river would have been navigable to a similar point. Nevertheless there was no urban settlement in the city area until the Romans arrived; instead, during the late Iron Age there would have been a scattering of farmsteads in a rural environment. The gravel terraces with brick-earth capping on either (but especially the north)

bank were well drained and so attractive to early farmers, although the alluvial margins of the river itself would have been less hospitable (Fig 3). We know very little of the people who lived in the area at this time, although the skeleton of an immature male (13–16 years old) found in the Inmost Ward in 1976 bears witness to their presence (Parnell 1985, 5–7).

ROMAN LONDINIUM

The Roman invasion of AD 43 brought massive changes to the countryside as the invaders exerted an ever tighter grip on the native populace. Military needs were paramount in the first few years, and the army rapidly established its own infrastructure of fortresses, smaller bases and interconnecting roads. The success of the venture (notwithstanding setbacks like the Boudiccan uprising) led to the rapid development of new towns. London was by no means the first of these but its development was under way from around AD 50 and new roads headed towards it from all points of the compass. The site was well chosen, for the area just to the east of the Thames confluence with the Walbrook (an important tributary flowing in from the north) provided the best crossing point on the wide river. A group of islands in the centre of the channel and towards the south bank provided excellent fording and bridging conditions even at high tide (Milne 1985, fig 49).

The city grew rapidly, evidently in a carefully controlled manner, with a regular street grid to the east of the Walbrook; the pattern was somewhat less regular on the west bank, however, partly through the influence of incoming roads (Rowsome 1998). The *insulae* defined by the roads were being developed intensively during the late 1st century AD in at least some parts of the city. The river Fleet would have formed a natural limit to the west as it flowed in from the north to join the Thames, and other streams such as the *Lorteburn* would have fulfilled a similar function to the east (Bentley 1984). Port facilities such as revetted timber quaysides were being built on the north bank of the Thames from the early AD 50s onwards, with warehousing to service the boats using the port (Brigham 1990, 1998). The river edge was gradually pushed further and further outwards as land was reclaimed by the construction of the successive revetments. There was a fort on the north side of the urban area, and major public buildings such as the forum, amphitheatre and public baths were in place by AD 70–80 (Bateman 1998). Even so, at this time and for a century afterwards *Londinium*, in common with most Romano-British towns, did not have any defences.

Fig 1   Aerial view of the Tower of London and its immediate environs. The Bowring Building immediately to the west of the Tower has now been demolished and replaced with the new Tower Place.

The urban area was probably much the same as that later defined by the wall, however, as the distribution of burials around the city shows (Hall 1996; burial within settlements was forbidden under Roman law). Those on the east side of the city were clustered around the road coming in from Colchester and entering at Aldgate; only one burial (a cremation in a cylindrical lead canister) has been found within the walls here, at Fenchurch Street (ibid, fig 9.2 and table 9.3).

Within the Tower (Fig 4), the marshy river edge in what is now the Inmost Ward had been reclaimed by the end of the 1st century AD, and a timber-framed house was built in this area during the subsequent century (Parnell 1985, 8–9). The provision of painted wall plaster shows that this was a building of some pretension despite its basic building materials, but broadly contemporary masonry found around the White Tower clearly relates to something of higher status still. Several rooms were revealed during excavations on the east side of the keep in the 1950s (Parnell 1982, 101–5) and the hypocaust of a heated room was found at the south-west corner in 1899. A foundation discovered under the floor of the White Tower's eastern basement in 1996 may also be of Roman date. We do not know whether these elements belong to several smaller buildings or one very substantial one, but they probably fronted onto a road that ran through the south-eastern quarter of the city at an oblique angle. Today's Great Tower Street is thought to preserve the line of this route as

far as the western edge of the castle. Its Roman ancestry has yet to be proved, but it is scarcely conceivable that such masonry buildings would not have been associated with at least one road frontage.

The city's masonry defences were erected around AD 200 and consisted of a high stone wall backed with an earthen rampart and fronted by a deep, wide ditch (Fig 4). Some buildings (such as the timber-framed one in the Inmost Ward) were demolished in preparation for the new work, but not all suffered this fate: the masonry structure on the east side of the White Tower was left standing. Its retention extremely close to the defensive line was a departure from normal practice and in some way must reflect the importance of the building and its owner. The city wall, meanwhile, had a rubble core with regularly coursed Kentish ragstone facings and tile string courses; parts of this still survive within the Tower, and one of the best-preserved sections in the entire circuit stands on Tower Hill just to the north (Fig 5). It had substantial foundations of flint or ragstone in clay, and culverts were incorporated into the base of the wall at intervals for drainage (Maloney 1983, 98–104). Internal turrets for access to a parapet-level wall walk were probably put up at the same time as the wall itself (ibid, 98), but the bastions on the eastern part of the circuit were added during the 4th century (the western bastions were later still – *see* below). The internal rampart was formed from dumps of brickearth and gravel; on some sites this was built over a road that was

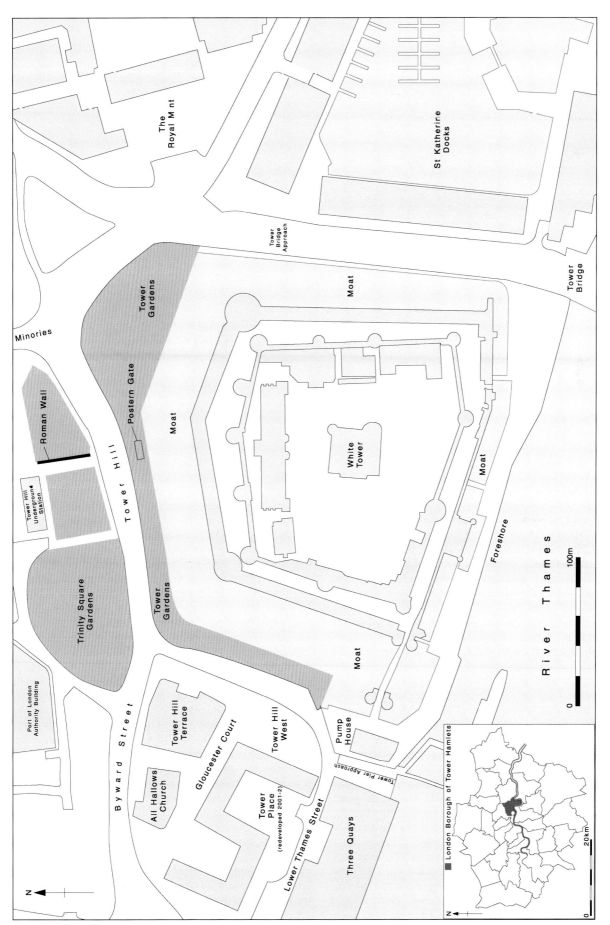

Fig 2   *The location of the Tower of London within its immediate environs.*

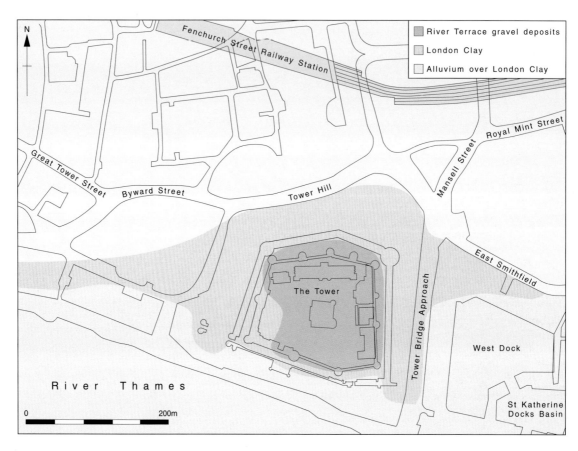

Fig 3   Geology of the Tower of London and its surrounding area.

probably a temporary provision for the building programme itself. The rampart was also built after both the foundations of the wall and the internal turrets had been completed (Whipp 1980, 55–6; Maloney 1983, 101). Much of the upcast earth for the bank seems to have come from the external ditch (Maloney 1983, 101), but it seems unlikely that this could have provided all the material required because the rampart was as much as 9m wide on the eastern circuit. There may have been some general scouring of the natural brickearth surface in the surrounding area to supplement the ditch upcast.

The city wall provided for defence only on the landward sides of *Londinium*. The river itself must have been viewed as the main defence on the south side, while the extensive development of quays along the harbour frontage may have been a constraint on any riverside defences. The changed political climate in the mid-late 3rd century, when Britain was part of the short-lived Gallic Empire, seems to have provided the necessary impetus to over-ride such considerations, and a wall was duly built along London's Thames frontage. This has been excavated at several sites, including the Tower, and the oak piles needed to consolidate the Thames foreshore silts have been dated by dendrochronology to AD 255–70 (Hillam, in Parnell 1985, 45–7). Towards the end of Roman rule the south-eastern

corner of the city defences was completely remodelled when an entirely new wall was built 4m to the north of the old one. About 14.5m west of the corner the new wall turned southwards to join up with the old one, thus forming a sort of bastion at the new corner of the defences (Fig 4). Excavations around the Lanthorn Tower during 1976–9 established that this alteration occurred after AD 388, a decade or two after bastions had been added to the eastern circuit of the landward wall (AD 341–75; Maloney 1983, 108).

The south-eastern quarter of *Londinium* does not seem to have been blessed with major buildings, public or otherwise, though a substantial late 4th-century aisled building found at Colchester House has been claimed as one (Sankey 1998). The masonry structure on the White Tower site must also have been significant, and it continued in use well into the late Roman period; indeed new floors were being laid in the middle of the 4th century, including a tessellated pavement. Early 5th-century coins and the famous stamped silver ingot found near the Lanthorn Tower in 1777 also attest to very late Roman activity in the area, while more ingots were found on Tower Hill in 1898. Elsewhere in the vicinity a substantial stone building with a tessellated pavement was found under All Hallows Barking church during excavations in the late 1920s and 1930s. The date and longevity of this structure

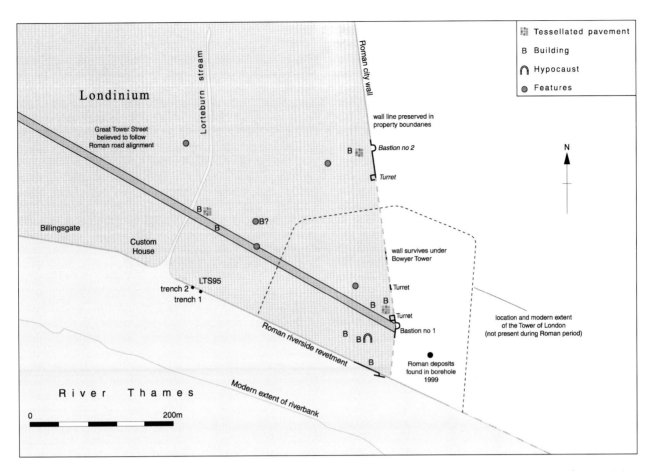

Fig 4   Distribution of the main Roman remains in the area around the Tower of London, showing the surviving stretches of the city defences within and to the north of the castle.

is unclear but it cut a layer of Antonine date and the excavator, Gerald Dunning, thought it belonged to the 3rd century. The excavation (by AoC Archaeology) in 1999 of a small but deep sondage within the churchyard to the south of All Hallows revealed a sequence of mostly timber structures (though mud-brick seems to have been used in one phase) with relatively crude earth floors. The early phases of

Fig 5   An engraving of the Roman city wall on Tower Hill by F W Fairholt, dated 9 July 1852.

the sequence appear to belong to the late 1st and early 2nd centuries AD (eg, earlier than the building under the church if Dunning was correct); box flue and other tiles associated with hypocausts were recovered from these phases, and suggest that the building already had considerable pretensions. The sequence continued into the 3rd and 4th centuries, and by this stage the masonry building would presumably have been dominant. Roman buildings with oak-piled foundations and tessellated pavements were uncovered during the construction of the London Underground across Trinity Square in 1882, but again the date of these buildings is unclear.

Other Roman features have been found to the north and west of the Tower of London. Extensive and apparently late Roman quarrying was found at 41–42 Trinity Square, post-dating a 2-m-deep ditch (Pierpoint 1986). Similar quarry pits were excavated by the Oxford Archaeological Unit on Tower Hill West (where they were dated from the 2nd to the 4th centuries) in 1999–2000. Fragments of painted wall plaster and *opus signinum* (Roman concrete) from these excavations were suggestive of high-status buildings in the vicinity like those under All Hallows Barking church and around Trinity Square. The pits would have been useful sources of gravel and brickearth for local building works. Minor features (eg, gullies, fence lines and isolated postholes) have also been found on sites such as the north end of the subway under Byward Street (Whipp 1980, 50–3).

LATE SAXON LONDON

Remarkably little is known about the Tower and its vicinity in the Anglo-Saxon period. *Londinium* seems to have declined rapidly after the withdrawal of Roman rule in AD 410, and early Saxon activity within the walls was largely confined to 'squatter' occupation and agriculture. It is significant, however, that middle Saxon *Lundenwic* developed outside the Roman walls to the west in what is now the Strand area (Vince 1990, 13–25), though there was some activity at the same time in the city around St Paul's. The 'new' London of the 7th century was among a group of important trading centres set up in Europe at the time. Other English examples included *Eorforwic* (York), *Hamwic* (Southampton) and Ipswich, while equivalents on the Continent included Quentovic (France) and Dorestad (Germany). To that extent the river continued to be the dominant element in London's development.

Evidence for Saxon activity within the city becomes more widespread from the 9th century onwards after the re-establishment of the fortified city under Alfred. The Tower area seems to have been split into three wards – administrative and fiscal units with a defensive function. These were centred on All Hallows Barking (also known as All Hallows by the Tower; Fig 6) and two newly founded churches, St Mary Magdalen by Aldgate and, it now seems likely, St Peter ad Vincula. The latter is generally supposed to be a 12th-century creation, largely thanks to the claim made by Bayley (1821, 118). There is sound evidence associated with the payment of soul-scot (funeral payment) by St Botolph's to St Peter's that it is much older, if not necessarily 9th century (Haslam 1988, 40–1). All three churches remain substantial landmarks within or immediately adjacent to the Tower's environs; the sculptural and structural remains at All Hallows are still the best evidence for the Anglo-Saxon period in the area. They comprise an arch of re-used Roman bricks and rubble at the south-west corner of the church, a quoin also of Roman brick, which might mark the north-west corner of the original nave, and pieces of an elaborately decorated cross-shaft. Current opinion would place both the sculpture and the structural features in the early/mid 11th century. The church is documented in Domesday Book, and so must have been extant by 1086 – tradition would have it as a 7th-century foundation. A few late Saxon or Saxo-Norman burials were recovered during the recent excavations at the church.

In the mid-10th century further fragmentation took place. A new ward called *Portsoken* was established, embracing those areas of St Peter's and St Mary's wards outside the city wall; this time the ward was a civil creation, entrusted or perhaps initiated by a group of citizens collectively known as the *Cnihtengild*. This body probably ceased to exist with the Conquest. The construction of the castle alongside the stretch of wall they were pledged to defend presumably removed its *raison d'être*. Even so the existence of such groups shows very clearly that the old city defences were being maintained, and that this was seen as a communal duty. The property and administrative unit survived, and was granted *en bloc* to the Augustinians of Holy Trinity Aldgate in 1125 (*Cartulary of Holy Trinity Aldgate*, no. 871). More investigation is required into the late Saxon occupation and administration of the area; it should, for example, be possible to plot some of the boundaries mentioned above using later medieval descriptions. Possession and administration of the area was minutely accounted for before the Conquest, and two features of its topography – the churches of All Hallows and St Peter's – were already established.

One should also note the Saxo-Norman ditch found within the Tower as a further indicator of activity (Davison 1967; Parnell 1983a, 111–13), though the significance of the feature and its relationship with the castle defences are difficult to interpret. Dark earth deposits have been found to the north (eg, at 12 America Square), and a group of features containing Anglo-Saxon finds has been excavated at Trinity Square Gardens. Nevertheless, the available evidence scarcely paints a picture of a busy urban environment in the decades before the Norman Conquest, and it is unclear whether the castle was built over a pre-existing tenement pattern as happened at Norwich. Perhaps this has as much

Fig 6   An Anglo-Saxon arch at the south-west corner of All Hallows by the Tower church. The arch was only rediscovered following severe bomb damage suffered in 1940.

to do with archaeological deposit survival and the choice of excavated sites (which has been entirely development-led) as it does with the history of the area.

THE NORMAN CONQUEST: CASTLES TO DOMINATE A CITY

The history of the Tower environs as such begins in 1066, with the implantation of the Conqueror's fortress in the south-east corner of the walled city. How William's appropriation was arranged remains unknown, but it took place as a military expedient in the early months of the Conquest, and was probably based on straightforward expropriation backed by force. The same tactic cleared ground for the same purpose at Wareham, Wallingford, Oxford and elsewhere. The initial foundation took place at the end of the year 1066, shortly after William's encirclement of London and his acceptance of its surrender. According to William of Poitiers, the Conqueror then remained nearby while 'a fortification was put up in the city and preparations made

for his triumphal entry'. After his coronation, the same author tells us that he retired to Barking (Essex), while 'certain fortifications were made in the town against the fickleness of the vast and fierce populace'. William's reasons were plain enough: his castles were not to defend but to control London; his greatest priority was to secure the city, and to do so he required a firm base there to overawe its population. One of these fortresses must have been the Tower of London and the others were probably Baynard's Castle and Montfichet's Tower. Both are known to have existed at the other end of the city in the 12th century, though only the latter's location has been confirmed archaeologically (B Watson 1992).

The 1066 castle at the south-east corner of the city relied on the Roman city wall defences for its east and south sides. Excavations in 1963–5 revealed traces of a bank and ditch (in existence by 1100 but probably before) running westwards from a point on the Roman wall just north of the White Tower (Davison 1967). Further excavations in 1975 identified the likely western arm of this ditch

(Parnell 1983a), thus defining an enclosure in the corner of the city. The ditch could only have been water-filled at its south-western extremity. By the late 1070s the building of the White Tower was already under way, and a reference in the register of Rochester Cathedral priory (the *Textus Roffensis*) shows that Gundulf, their Bishop only after 1077, was 'supervising the king's works on the great tower of London' (Hearne 1720, 212). The building must have dominated its environs very effectively, and the fame of the completed tower, even when more structures of comparable type still stood, implies that it has always been exceptional. It remains at the heart of the castle, the most prominent feature within the environs, and the single best vantage point for observing them.

EARLY GROWTH OF THE CASTLE, AND DEVELOPMENTS IN ITS ENVIRONS

The *Anglo Saxon Chronicle* entry for 1097 records the 'building of a wall around the Tower', which may refer to the replacement of an original timber palisade in stone, but otherwise this line of defence, and the moat/ditch surrounding it, seems to have remained unchanged. So far the story is fairly well established, but the small size of the known castle at this date, given its unique importance, is surprising. There is a reference in 1157 to the church of St Peter 'in the Bailey'. If *de ballio* means within an enclosure and not just an area of jurisdiction, and if this church can be identified with St Peter ad Vincula, the reference implies the existence of a bailey extending at least as far west as Henry III's, but this remains to be proven archaeologically. Indeed there is no archaeological evidence for improvements to the Tower's defences between *c*1100 and the 1190s, and the records from 1155 onwards are sufficiently complete to suggest that nothing major was attempted. If there was an early bailey, therefore, it must have been established in the earlier 12th century if not before. The available evidence suggests that the environs were relatively thinly occupied throughout the 12th century. This is implied by the large size of the Aldgate and Portsoken wards in comparison to those further west such as Bassishaw or Cheap, 'which probably represent more fully settled areas of the city, where property rights were established and respected' (Brooke and Keir 1975, 169). The river edge may have been an exception, for quays were already being established in the 12th century, but expansion would have been a relatively painless exercise.

The most important introduction to the Tower environs in this period came with the foundation of St Katharine's Hospital by Matilda (wife of King Stephen) in 1147 for thirteen poor people (Fig 7). Initially it was administered by the canons of Holy Trinity Aldgate, and its revenues were drawn from theirs. In 1152, however, the patron's additional gift of an annual rent of £20 from Queenhithe and a mill and land 'near the Tower' enabled the canons to move it from its original site, close to their own monastery, to the position due east of the Tower that it occupied until 1824.

Pipe Roll entries in 1190 and 1192–3, passing references to the work by contemporary chroniclers, archaeological excavation and the very substantial standing remains show that the castle defences were enhanced significantly under William Longchamp, Chancellor and Regent to Richard I (1189–99). Expenditure of £2,881 1s 10d is recorded in 1190 (PRS NS i, 4), and £67 2s 6d in 1192–3 (PRS NS iii, 132). The castle was extended westward, as much as doubling its area, with a new or refurbished river wall (the Roman work was ruinous elsewhere along the riverfront) terminating at the Bell Tower. From here a new wall ran northwards to the approximate position of the Beauchamp Tower, before turning north-east to rejoin the Roman wall to the north of the White Tower. The line of this arm may have been chosen to avoid the ancient church of St Peter ad Vincula and its cemetery (but *see* above), while also enclosing a wider strip to the north of the keep. The aim seems to have been to create a wet moat, but two medieval chroniclers suggest that this was not a success. By contrast Gervase of Tilbury, writing *c* 1216, seems to suggest something in better order: 'a palace ... surrounded with the strongest defences; every day the water pours in from the sea at high tide and runs right around it, and on this spot The Tower of London is still standing' (Stevenson 1875, 425). The references are not wholly contradictory: Gervase's description could mean that the north side was dry at low tide. Perhaps this stretch was too shallow, while failure to provide the southern arm with dams and sluices would leave the moat empty at low tide.

THE EXPANSION OF THE TOWER UNDER HENRY III AND EDWARD I

The next major expansion of the castle took place in the successive reigns of Henry III (1216–72) and his son Edward I (1272–1307). The story is taken up more fully in Chapters 4 and 5, and needs only summary treatment here. Henry III pushed the defences further to the north and east, vastly extending the circuit of the curtain wall to take in St Peter's church and, for the first time, moving eastward beyond the Roman wall. The new defences (the inner curtain wall with its mural towers; Figs 7–8) defined an area now known as the Inner Ward, entered through a magnificent new gatehouse on the west side approached along the line of today's Great Tower Street. Written sources for the dating and progress of this activity are disappointing given the mass of documentation that survives for Henry's other building operations. Work to the fortifications seems to have started with the building of the Wakefield Tower in the 1220s, as part of an ambitious enlargement of the Royal Lodgings. Work on the defences began in earnest, however, in 1238, continuing apace through the early 1240s; by the

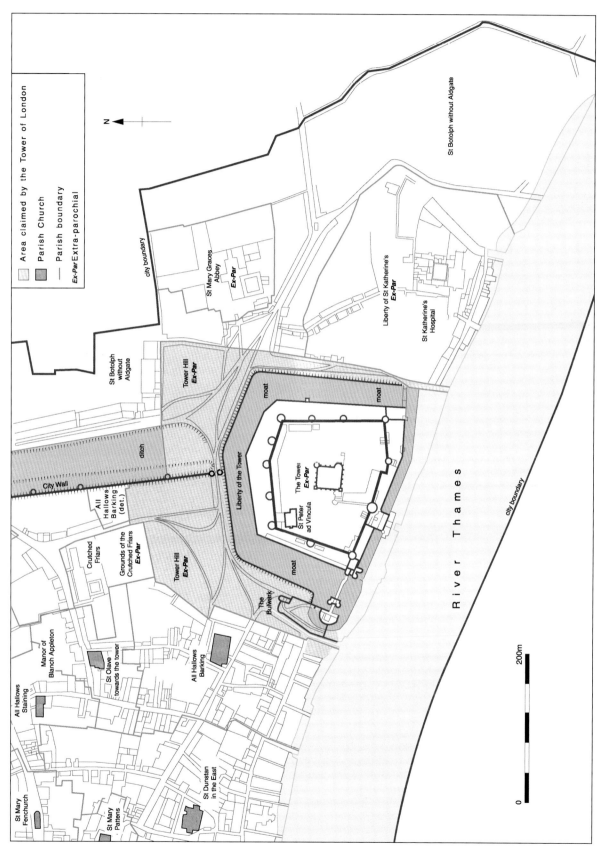

Fig 7 The medieval topography of the Tower environs, showing the parishes and monastic precincts that were such a feature of the area (based on The British Atlas of Historic Towns Volume III: The City of London from Prehistoric Times to c. 1520, Gen. Ed. Mary D. Lobel, 1990). The effectiveness of the Tower of London's control over its Liberties is demonstrated by the fact that most of the area still survives as invaluable open space in the modern townscape.

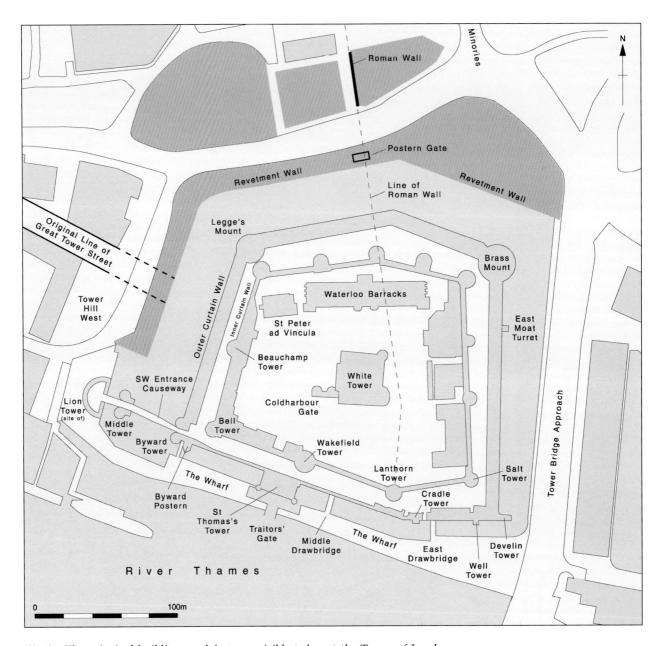

Fig 8   The principal buildings and features visible today at the Tower of London.

1250s the work had slowed down or stopped, payments being made for timber paling to fill gaps in the unfinished curtain wall.

In addition to the costs of labour and materials, the King had to compensate the owners of adjacent land over which the new defences extended. The Liberate Rolls tell us that in 1239 £166 was paid to the Master of St Katharine's Hospital and others in recompense for 'damage they sustained by the wall and ditch [ie, moat] of the Tower of London'. They included the heads or representatives of numerous institutions. Most were local (St Katharine's Hospital, Holy Trinity Aldgate, Southwark Priory, St Paul's Cathedral and St Bartholomew's Hospital); others, such as Oseney Abbey (Oxford), were more distant.

Within three years of Henry's death his son and heir, Edward I, had embarked upon an enlargement of the castle that dwarfed even the scale of his father's achievement. Between 1275 and 1285 Henry's moat was filled in and an entirely new circuit of walls created, enclosing both the landward sides and the river frontage of the castle. The old western gateway was replaced by the south-western complex which, although mutilated, remains the castle's main landward entrance (Figs 7–8). The new walls were ringed by the existing moat, although this has been redefined and much altered since. The impact of this activity on the environs was comparable to that of Henry's expansion. Like him, Edward I was obliged to compensate expropriated landowners. A perpetual annuity was granted to St Katharine's, which had another area sliced off the western side of its precinct including a mill and the greater part of a garden. Others included Dakin de Abingdon, who was to be paid £11 per annum in perpetuity. Edward I also appears to have been responsible for the construction of a new twin-towered gatehouse on the city wall immediately to the north of the Tower. This was known as the Postern Gate, built at some point between 1297 and 1308. Its southern tower had been set up—somewhat precariously, as it turned out—on the sloping outer edge of the castle moat's northern arm. Early in the 15th century the ground gave way beneath the tower and it lurched about 8ft (2.45m) down towards the water before coming to rest; the northern tower was fortunately built on solid ground and continued in use for several centuries more.

THE ENVIRONS IN THE 13TH CENTURY

The years 1211–13 had seen a re-excavation and enlargement of the heavily silted city ditch, to a width approximating that shown in Haiward and Gascoyne's survey (Fig 84; *see* Keay 2001, a major exposition of this key document). In March 1262 Henry III ordered trees to be planted next to the Tower, and pears 'of Cailhou' (*poires de Caillou*, usually used for cooking, were still available in France in the 1930s) to be planted 'in a place which he had lately enclosed near the Tower of London within the City wall'. On 21 January in the following year, the Constable, Richard of Tilbury, bought 10s worth of plants for the 'King's garden outside the Tower'; Henry was clearly concerned with the appearance of the Tower's surroundings, and that they should contain areas for recreation and production for his table. The boundaries of this particular plot were to remain embedded in the local topography until the 1950s: the 'lately enclosed' pear orchard was the Nine Gardens site marked and labelled on the map of 1597 (*see* Fig 84), and progressively built over during the following centuries.

Some commercial and industrial activity within the environs was directly associated with the castle, such as lime-burning for building, which was repeatedly referred to in Edward I's reign. For example, in 1276 'a house of the limeburners towards the city' was built outside the Tower's western entrance (from an account of purchases at the Tower of London and the Palace of Westminster: C47/3/47). Other activity had no particular association with the Tower but was made possible by the open space around it: in 1229, for instance, Henry III granted an annual fair in East Smithfield, possibly on or near the future site of St Mary Graces Abbey (Fig 7). By 1241 open air activity also included the 'tenting' of woollen cloth. This stage in the production of cloth involved stretching it out and exposing it, a local activity that outlived the Middle Ages. Whether the cloth was woven nearby is not clear, but there were certainly dyers active in the locality at the same time. Among the owners expropriated in 1239

were artisans and private citizens such as Hugh le Barber, Payn the Shoemaker, Eustace the Linen-draper, Henry the Cook and Richard the Goldsmith. The length and content of the list implies that the immediate surroundings of the Tower were minutely divided between proprietors, and possibly occupied, to a greater extent than might otherwise be supposed.

River trade continued to have an impact on the Tower's surroundings, particularly in the area immediately to the west of the castle, with the development of wharves and warehouses along the river frontage. The gradual encroachment into the river itself that had occurred in the Roman period also recommenced at around this time. The later 13th century also provides some evidence of the expansion of residential occupation and the definition of the streets that served it. In 1283, for example, the first mention is made of Woodrofe Lane (later called Cooper's Row) running south from Crutched Friars along the western edge of the Nine Gardens (Fig 7). Various properties in the neighbourhood were being walled in the 1280s, possibly along alignments later to be fossilised as street frontages.

The second half of the 13th century saw the refoundation of St Katharine's Hospital by Eleanor of Provence (1261), after a long dispute with the canons of Holy Trinity. Thenceforth it was to be run by a master, three brothers and three sisters, and to provide for ten poor women and six poor scholars. The last decade also saw the establishment of two new religious houses—an abbey for nuns of the Franciscan order of St Clare (Minoresses) in 1293 and the priory of the Friars of the Holy Cross (the Crutched Friars) in 1298. The Minories and Crutched Friars street names commemorate their former presence in today's environs (Figs 7–8).

DEVELOPMENT OF THE RIVERSIDE: THE TOWER, WHARF AND QUAYS TO THE WEST

Edward I's building programme, in full force between 1275 and 1285, slackened off during the remainder of the reign and was completed only under Edward II. Under Edward III, the most important initiative was the extension of the Tower wharf along the whole river frontage. The *Kayum regis* mentioned in 1228 must have lain to the west of the castle and can have had no relation to the existing structure. The curtain walls of both Henry III and Edward I rose straight up out of the Thames, the various gates and posterns being served by jetties planted directly in the water. Neither king is likely to have envisaged the whole river frontage encumbered by a wharf, which would not only have spoiled the visual impact of its buildings but have made it vulnerable to attack—a recurrent worry until the late 19th century. The construction of the wharf as we know it began in the 1330s and was finished by the end of the century. It was prompted by the increasing importance of the Tower's function as a supply depot for the campaigns of the Hundred Years War, at the expense of its own defensive capacity.

Three main stages of building can be identified: those of c1276–1324, 1339, and 1389–91. The earliest part of the wharf may date from Edward I's or the early years of the next reign. Accounts of 1324–5 cover repairs to a bridge between the 'newly built' Byward postern and the *Kayum regis* to the west, showing that it then extended as far east as the Byward Tower. Accounts of 1335 note that the same stretch of wharf needed repair at a cost of £180 13s 4d, and in October 1336 a contract was made with John le Clerk for the work. The second stage, in 1339, probably saw the wharf extended to St Thomas's Tower. In the 1360s the wharf was reconstructed, or faced, in stone. The third and final extension of the wharf as far as the eastern moat came about fifty years later. In 1338, wooden 'brattices' (barriers, or perhaps overhanging galleries) had been set up along the whole length of the riverfront, probably as a defensive response to the threat of French assaults such as those on Portsmouth and Southampton in the same year, but these brattices had not constituted a wharf. However, in 1389 three masons, John Westcote of London, William Janecok of Maidstone and Thomas Crompe of Otham, were contracted to build what clearly was a wharf. It was to have two side walls in stone, and to extend 'from the corner of the east end wall of the Tower facing St Katharine's as far as the Watergate of the said Tower', ie, from the Develin Tower to St Thomas's Tower.

Edward III's other buildings were also largely concentrated on the riverfront. They included the heightening and widening of the wall from St Thomas's Tower to the Byward Tower, the refashioning of Edward I's postern by the Byward Tower and the subsequent demolition and rebuilding of the same in 1342 and 1350 respectively. In 1339 the inner curtain wall between the Bell and Salt Towers was heightened and crenellated, while a new privy water-gate, the Cradle Tower, was built between 1348 and 1355.

During the late 13th century the south edge of [Lower] Thames Street fronted the river, but major changes occurred in this area between c1280 and the early 14th century. The building of the Lion Tower and the wharf immediately to the south of it seems to have altered the flow of the river and caused silting along the foreshore to the west, encouraging encroachment on the river by quays and jetties (Tatton-Brown 1974; 1975). The area to the north of Tower Street seems to have undergone a rapid increase in the density of use at the same time. In the 1270s all the land bounded by Thames Street, Great Tower Street, the western boundary of Tower Hill and the curving north–south street called *Bereward* in the Middle Ages and Beer Lane until obliterated in the 1960s belonged to one man, Jean de la Tour. This suggests that it was not densely populated or developed. By the 1330s the river had been pushed back and the strip of reclaimed ground split between the Stone, Baynings, Galley, Chester and Clares (later

Brewers) Quays, each backed by an elongated tenement extending northwards over Thames Street and de la Tour's former property. The remainder of the area was divided into north-south plots from the late 14th century onwards, these tenements themselves being sub-divided in the 15th and early 16th centuries. The Wyngaerde drawing and 'Agas' plan show the area completely built up, the misalignment of the roofs reflecting the break-up of tenement plots that had occurred in the previous century.

ADMINISTRATION: THE TOWER LIBERTIES, PAROCHIAL AND OTHER MATTERS

The legal status and ownership of the site and surroundings of the Conqueror's castle at the time of its construction remain a matter for speculation, but the later history of its environs suggests that it was surrounded by an enclave under royal control, independent of the city, from its foundation. Evidence for what this may have meant in practice before the 14th century is patchy or non-existent. In 1343, however, the first recorded dispute occurred over the jurisdiction and ownership of the moat's edges and Tower Hill, of a kind that was to recur repeatedly until the 19th century. A royal inquest was held into possession of land in East Smithfield, allegedly acquired in the previous century for the making of the outer curtain. This provoked the citizens to claim that 'the whole of the Tower ditch and all the land of East Smithfield outside the postern in front of the Abbey of St Mary Graces have been time out of mind in and of the Liberty of the City'. The claim was successfully upheld by the City, although the uncertainty as to whether Tower ditch lay within the City or the Tower continued until the mid-17th century.

In 1382 Richard II attempted to clarify the situation by issuing regulations listing the customs and privileges enjoyed by the Constable. These defined for the first time the exact boundaries of his jurisdiction, describing an area known as the Franchise or Liberties that appears to have been co-extensive with the Tower Hill Liberties as defined in 1536 (Fig 7) and as they remain. The Mayor and Sheriffs of London were to allow the Constable to enjoy the customs and profits pertaining to his office. These included the taking of 1d 'for every foot of such beasts feeding in the Tower ditch', and for 'every wain empty or laden which shall fall into the said ditch as forfeit and the constables fee'. The Constable also had all the profits of the grass 'without the outermost ditch of the said Tower'. Nevertheless, differences between the city authorities and the Tower officers continued throughout the century and the next. In May 1465, the Mayor and Aldermen objected to the building of a gallows on Tower Hill by the officers of the Tower as an infringement of the city's liberties. In 1468 certain prisoners arrested in the Tower moat were delivered to the Sheriffs of London 'until it is determined whether the ditch is in the Liberty of the city or not'.

Great Tower Hill formed the greater part of the Liberties, bordered to the south and south east by the Tower Moat, and to the north east by the garden enclosure (Nine Gardens) created by Henry III. By 1358 exclusively horticultural use of the Nine Gardens was being supplanted; an inquisition in that year mentions a brewhouse and the eponymous nine cottages and gardens, which had been leased for a considerable (but unknown) time by the Constables of the Tower. The 14th-century topography of the site is probably represented on Haiward and Gascoyne's plan (Fig 84), as this shows ten buildings, one of which was almost certainly a gate and another the brewhouse. Within about ten years, however, the area had been substantially built over. The open space on the Hill must have been traversed by trackways, although their exact routes are unknown; at least some of the area was evidently grass, as it was used for grazing cattle at least from 1382 onwards and presumably had been since time immemorial. It seems to have been in this period, however, that Tower Hill acquired its best-known and most sinister function, as a place of execution. The first known victims were the Archbishop of Canterbury and his companions, dragged out of the Tower and beheaded there during the Peasants' Revolt of 1381. There may have been a case in Edward I's reign, when 'Lord Herbert de Mora, Knight and Thomas de Bosco esquire, were tried before the Lord Ralph de Sandwich inside the Tower of London, and were later beheaded in the square next to the same Tower' (Stubbs 1882, 148). In 1465 a permanent scaffold was erected in the middle of the open space, and either this or its replacement is shown by Wyngaerde.

An open space known as Little Tower Hill lay to the east of the city wall. This was bounded to the north by the precinct of the Abbey of St Clare (the Minories) from 1293. Before 1350 the area overlooking Little Tower Hill from the east had been open land belonging to Holy Trinity Aldgate. This contained a chapel, and was granted by the canons to a clerk named John Cory in 1348 to serve as a burial ground for victims of the Black Death. In 1350 the cemetery and chapel were bought by Edward III who established a Cistercian Abbey on the site, bringing the first monks from Beaulieu Abbey; the dedication was to *Sainte Marie de Grâce*, soon anglicised to St Mary Graces.

THE LATER MEDIEVAL AND TUDOR TOWER

The late 15th century saw the last extension of the Tower, with the enclosure of the lower half of Tower Hill to protect the western entrance. The new structure was of simple design, consisting of a western wall terminating at its north end in a half-round bastion projecting west, beyond which the wall turned east to a north-facing bastion, the gate itself piercing a southward return from this point. The earliest representation is by Wyngaerde, showing the entire length of the west wall from the

riverside to its termination in a bastion to the north. In Haiward and Gascoyne's projection the western rampart is hidden by the houses built against its inner side, but the basic outline together with the form of the gate and two bastions to the north is clear enough.

Known from the beginning as the Bulwark (Fig 7), the outwork was built by Edward IV in or around 1480 as a response to the increasing effectiveness of artillery. The new work was designed not only to resist artillery but to carry it, and is perhaps the earliest known example of this in England. It was a fittingly impressive and innovative structure to mark the last attempt to keep the defences of the Tower up to date. Within less than a century, however, the military effectiveness of the Bulwark had been lost. Every representation from Wyngaerde onwards shows it choked with houses, encroachments that were to lead to endless litigation and the eventual demolition of its remains in 1668–70 in the wake of the Great Fire of 1666.

By the end of the Middle Ages large areas of land to the north of the Tower were dominated, occupied and largely possessed by prosperous monastic houses. From 1532 to 1540 all this was to change: the monasteries were closed, the religious dispersed and their buildings demolished or put to new uses. Apart from St Katharine's, the monastery most integral to the Tower environs was St Mary Graces (Fig 7). By the end of its existence, the conventual buildings, annexes and enclosures of the abbey extended over a large area to the north east of the castle. The house was surrendered in September 1538, and the site given, in August 1542, to Sir Arthur Darcy. Stow relates that Darcy 'clean pulled down the monastery': in fact complete destruction took much longer, but the associated enclosures were swiftly built over or otherwise used. After Darcy's death the site reverted to the Crown and changed from domestic to official use when taken over by the Queen's Storehouse for Victuals (later known as the Navy Victualling Yard), in turn replaced by the new Mint in 1810.

Henry VIII resided at the fortress occasionally (for a few days only at any one time), most notably in the run-up to his marriage to Anne Boleyn and her coronation as Queen. He was responsible for substantial repairs and upgrading within the palatial accommodation largely in response to this occasion. He had a new wardrobe building put up, running from the Wardrobe Tower east to the Broad Arrow Tower on the inner curtain wall. James I was the last reigning monarch to stay overnight at the Tower.

THE POST-MEDIEVAL TOWER AND ITS ENVIRONS

After Henry VIII's reign the Tower was dominated by various arms of central government such as the Mint and, especially, the Office of Ordnance. Whole areas of the castle were re-arranged or rebuilt at their behest, including the entirety of the palatial accommodation in the Inmost Ward. New buildings were virtually all in brick, sometimes with stone details. They included the New Armouries (1663–4; still in existence) and the Grand Storehouse (1668–91; demolished after a disastrous fire in 1841). The environs, meanwhile, were seriously affected by the Great Fire of London, which started on 2 September 1666 and within five days had destroyed five-sixths of the city. Actual fire damage in the Tower vicinity was fairly limited. All Hallows Barking was saved by the destruction of houses to the west on the orders of Admiral Sir William Penn, seeking to ensure the safety of the Navy Office; only the block immediately to the south and the warehouses on the river were actually burnt. More destruction probably took place on the orders of the Tower officials, anxious for the safety of the castle where magazines of gunpowder were stored. They demolished buildings on Tower dock, against the Bulwark (and ultimately that building itself) and those grouped along the outer edge of the moat and Tower Hill. Many of these would have been timber structures.

The aftermath of the fire saw many schemes devised for the city's rebuilding, but the Tower authorities were also turning their attention to the castle's suitability for contemporary military purposes. Sir Bernard de Gomme, Chief Ordnance Engineer, devised an elaborate project to enclose the landward side of the castle with a bastion trace and less ambitious schemes to reinforce the western entrance and redefine the outer edge of the moat with masonry. In the end only the latter was achieved, although even this was one of the largest building projects ever undertaken at the Tower. Begun in 1672 and completed in 1683, this laid the groundwork for the tidying up of the counterscarp and definition of its outer boundary in the 18th and 19th centuries. It also contributed to the physical and visual isolation of the castle from its surroundings and ended the practice of washing clothes, watering animals and, to a lesser extent, the discharging of waste in the moat.

Until the very end of the 18th century the layout and maintenance of Great Tower Hill was largely haphazard. It was mostly unmaintained open space without defined roadways or any proper barrier at the upper edge of the moat. It was still used as a convenient dumping ground for building rubble and other rubbish, and as a quarry for material needed elsewhere. By the 1790s the contrast between this area and others around the Tower must have been very marked, and in 1797 an Act of Parliament was passed 'for Paving, Lighting, watching, cleaning, watering, improving and keeping in repair Great Tower Hill, and for removing and preventing nuisances and annoyance'. The 'Rhinebeck' panorama of c1810 shows the Hill as a tidy-looking area, well graded and evidently paved, with a row of trees planted along the west edge. A similar impression is given by the Shotter Boys' view across the area in about 1840, showing a broad expanse of paved and drained surface, a lamp post and a row of cannon

bollards continuing the line of Great Tower Street. Elements of this scheme survived until well into the 20th century. Another deliberate improvement of the time, also the result of the 1797 Act, was the laying out of Trinity Gardens to the south of Trinity House. The oval area of grass, ringed by flowerbeds and railings, can be seen in its pristine state in the 'Rhinebeck' view.

VICTORIAN LONDON, AND THE CHANGING FACE OF ITS TOWER

The changing functions of the Tower were never more clearly demonstrated than in the 19th century. The castle had become a substantial barrack centre by then, and Sir Arthur Wellesley, the Duke of Wellington, was a particularly able and active Constable. As commanding officer for the Tower he was ultimately responsible for several major developments. One of these was the clearance of a great deal of clutter on the south and west sides of the castle, most notably along the wharf and around the Lion Tower. Unfortunately this removed some notable buildings, such as the Lion Tower itself and the Spur Guard to its north. It saw too the end of the Royal Menagerie's sojourn at the Tower. Wellington also had the Waterloo Barracks built in 1845 to replace the carcass of the Grand Storehouse, burnt out in 1841. Finally, and after many years of external pressure, in 1843 Wellington ordered that the moat should be drained and backfilled because it had become a health hazard for his garrison. The citizens of London had been saying as much for years. Around a decade later the Lion Tower and virtually all of the buildings around it were demolished; a new pumphouse designed by Anthony Salvin was erected on the site in 1863 (Fig 8).

The environs also felt the effects of overcrowding within the Tower itself, as some offices of state looked outside the walls for alternative accommodation. The Royal Mint had been based at the Tower from the 13th to the 19th century, enabling firm control of its activities and secure storage for bullion; these requirements may have encouraged Edward I's strengthening and expansion of the castle. By the end of the 18th century, however, the Mint's premises, crammed into the narrow lane between the two curtain walls, were too small. Plans for a new building were prepared in 1805 and a site chosen near the Tower, close enough for the administrative and security advantages to be retained. The former site of the abbey of St Mary Graces was then occupied by warehouses and houses in Swedeland Court, Rosemary Lane and Bailey Place. All of these had to be purchased and cleared. Building and equipment costs were estimated at £135,000 in 1805, although far more was spent in the end. In 1807 Robert Smirke took over as Surveyor, and in 1811 the Mint moved in, remaining there until transferred to Llantrisant in Glamorgan in 1967. The rear part of the building was mutilated in the 1980s, but the Palladian façade overlooking Little Tower Hill survives intact.

The creation of St Katharine Docks represented one of the greatest 19th-century enterprises in the Tower environs. Its genesis lay in the massive increase in London's trade after 1800, and the inadequacy of the landing and storage facilities in the Pool of London. From the 1790s onwards the problem was tackled by creating purpose-built basin docks downstream. Early enterprises included the West India Docks across the Isle of Dogs and the docks at Wapping and Blackwall. At St Katherine's an Act of Parliament was passed in 1825, and a consortium raised £1,752,752 for the new docks. Plans were laid in the face of considerable opposition from representatives of the 11,000 people to be displaced, antiquarian interests and the owners of the private quays who feared competition, but the company prevailed. The scheme prepared by Thomas Telford and the architect Philip Hardwick in 1824 was completed in 1828, although the warehouses were finished only in 1852. Financially, the enterprise was a success, being steered through the difficult initial years by the company's able chairman, Sir John Hall.

The new docks were not the only enterprise to affect housing in the Tower environs. A large plot between Tower Hill and All Hallows' churchyard had been in residential use from its grant to St Katharine's Hospital in 1370, after which the plot and tenements were known as St Katharine's rents. In 1860, however, the site was leased for 60 years to a speculative builder, George Myers. He demolished the houses and replaced them with a vast brick and iron warehouse of eight above-ground storeys over basements. It became and remains known as the Mazawattee warehouse, thanks to the gigantic sign raised up over its roof. The building was important not only because it dominated Tower Hill for 80 years, but because it was the first real eyesore to impinge on the environs, and the first to provoke positive action to prevent further blight.

Wheeled traffic increased during the Victorian era, sowing the seeds of a major problem that has worsened ever since, to the incalculable detriment of the environs. At that time all east-west traffic across Tower Hill was funnelled through George Street and the narrow roadway to the north of the moat. Pressure also forced improvements to the Minories, which carried heavy north-south traffic to and from the docks, although this took the less drastic form of repaving and realignment within the roadway. Transport of other kinds had equally dramatic effects in the late 19th century: first the construction of the Underground lines wreaked havoc across the northern margins of the Tower (accidentally exposing Roman remains in the process), and then Tower Bridge rose to dominate the eastern approaches.

Tower Bridge, built in the late 1880s and early 1890s, was strategically vital to London. Unfortunately it was less than beneficial for the Tower.

The ramped approach to the north side of the bridge had to be raised well above the surrounding levels to meet its deck. The approach not only cut into the eastern arm of the moat, reducing its width and effectiveness, but its high level meant that the defences were utterly dominated on the east side. The military value of the Tower as anything other than a garrison must have been questionable for a long time before this, but the construction of Tower Bridge Approach surely destroyed it.

THE MODERN TOWER: DEVELOPMENTS IN THE 20TH CENTURY

There have been various attempts to tackle the problems of the modern setting for the Tower of London. The early years of the 20th century saw an elaborate scheme drawn up to improve the West Gate area, which had been so effectively cleared in the 1850s. In 1913 plans were laid for demolishing the 19th-century pumphouse (now the West Gate Shop) designed by Anthony Salvin and replacing it with a rambling mock-Tudor fantasy, to include a tea-house and ticket office. The scheme also involved the partial re-excavation of the Lion Tower (at least one set of drawings depicts a relentlessly inaccurate treatment of the barbican) and reflooding of the south moat from St Thomas's Tower west to the Lion Tower. The scheme was dropped at the outbreak of the First World War.

Parts of the concept were enacted in the inter-war years. The pumphouse was extended northward by two bays and converted into a restaurant. At about the same time an area of the roadway to the north east of the building subsided, prompting an exploratory excavation. This revealed the drawbridge pit of Edward I's causeway from the Lion Gate to the Lion Tower itself. The Ministry of Works then ordered the re-excavation of the moat to the north of the Middle Tower, exposing the two western entrance causeways and part of the Lion Tower itself. In the 1960s the area was remodelled for more effective display, the existing concrete bridge being positioned over the medieval causeway to echo the original route from Tower Hill. Unfortunately this had the effect of hiding the medieval work from view, and in the absence of any interpretation it seems certain that very few visitors appreciate the subtlety of this routing. The 1960s work also seems to have involved a revival of the plan to re-excavate the whole of the Lion Tower and to flood its moat, along with part of the west moat. Once again demolition of the pumphouse was considered as an option, as part of an associated plan to improve pedestrian and vehicular access through the West Gate area. As with the earlier plans, however, nothing solid seems to have arisen from these designs.

The emergent technology of air flight revolutionised most aspects of modern life, and nowhere more so than in the military sphere. This was apparent even in the First World War, but the effectiveness—and extraordinary destructive power—of airborne warfare was demonstrated very clearly and brutally during the Second World War. Internationally recognised historic monuments were not exempt from the effects of bombardment, as Coventry, Dresden and Monte Cassino (among many other sites) made clear. The Tower of London suffered several direct bomb hits during the Blitz of 1940, although miraculously all the most important buildings remained unaffected. The 18th-century Old Hospital Block, Wellington's North Bastion in the moat and the Main Guard built in 1898 immediately to the south west of the White Tower were not so fortunate, each suffering massive damage from direct hits. The first was rebuilt, but the bastion and guard were subsequently demolished. All Hallows Barking church and the Mazawattee tea warehouse were also extensively damaged. The church was rebuilt after the war, but the above-ground portions of the warehouse were demolished. The warehouse had few devotees, and indeed it had been the subject of concentrated vilification by the Tower Hill Improvement Trust from the latter's inception in 1933. The basements were retained, and form the basis of the existing terrace.

Rebuilding the city: post-war developments

The works around the West Gate in the 1930s were largely the initiative of those entrusted with guardianship of the Tower. Other proposals of more wide-reaching consequence were drawn up by the Tower Hill Improvement Trust in the 1930s, but these were overtaken by the devastation caused by the Blitz. Many bomb-damaged sites in the environs were redeveloped in the post-war years, and this typically involved the construction of medium- or high-rise office blocks to maximise income (Fig 1). This had the effect of diminishing the perceived scale of the Tower itself. Meanwhile larger schemes for environmental 'improvement' were also being developed, including a scheme by the Greater London Council in the 1970s. This involved upgrading the road across the north side of the moat (Byward Street) into a red route, part of strategic

cross-London road planning. The road became a dual carriageway with a changed alignment. It was also raised above its earlier level in places. New pedestrian arrangements had to be set in place to allow for safe crossing, and so the underpass beneath the road immediately to the south of Tower Hill Underground Station was built. Finally, Tower Hill West was remodelled in the mid-1980s, losing its tarmac surface in favour of cobble setts.

Taking the Tower towards a new millennium— the Tower Environs Scheme

The Tower of London attracts approximately 2.5 million paying visitors each year, while at least as many people again pass through the site and use many of the external facilities without entering the castle. Historic Royal Palaces (HRP) was established in 1989 to manage the Tower along with Hampton Court and Kew Palaces, the State Apartments at Kensington Palace, and the Banqueting House, Whitehall. The inadequate nature of the facilities and poor quality of the townscape around the Tower has been recognised for many years. HRP therefore established the Tower Environs Scheme in 1995, its central aim being to address the unsatisfactory presentation of the area around the monument itself. The intention was (and is) to create an appropriate and functional setting for the Tower of London so that visitors and passers-by can more readily appreciate, enjoy and understand the site. One element of the Scheme was a proposal to reflood the moat, effectively reversing the Duke of Wellington's action of 1843–5. The idea was controversial (see, for instance, Parnell 1995), but it was worth considering because of the potential interpretative and presentational benefits to the Tower and its visitors. It was inevitable that extensive research would be required to determine the feasibility of the proposal even in its outline form. The research involved archaeologists, conservation architects, engineers, historians, urban design specialists and many others. This book describes the results of the major campaign of archaeological fieldwork carried out for the Tower Environs Scheme during 1995–9, principally associated with the moat proposal.

Chapter 2:   Past Excavations in the Moat at the Tower of London

INTRODUCTION

There had been a number of excavations within the Tower of London's moat before the Tower Environs Scheme fieldwork started in 1995. Extensive excavations took place in the 1930s to the north and west of the Middle Tower in that part of the moat which had surrounded the Lion Tower (Fig 9). These were not archaeological excavations as we understand the term today, but important drawn and photographic records were made and a brief historical analysis was published (Harvey 1948). A re-assessment of these excavations is under way in 2001 as part of continuing analysis of the Lion Tower area for the Tower Environs Scheme. This work will be published separately in the future.

The first modern excavations in the Tower moat were undertaken by Peter Curnow from 1958 to 1960 (Fig 9). These were essentially small-scale research excavations undertaken to answer specific questions for the publication of volumes 1 and 2 of the *History of the King's Works* (Colvin 1963). Excavations carried out within the Tower during the same period provided information about the former river frontage (eg, at the Bloody Tower and in Water Lane). The exposure of the base of St Thomas's Tower in 1958–9 was by far the most important of Curnow's projects in the moat, but he also excavated a small trench in the angle of the Byward Tower and the western outer curtain wall in 1958. Finally, he dug a series of small trenches immediately to the south of the Brass Mount in 1959–60 to expose the massive battered foundations of three 13th-century towers built in the fastness of the moat. Curnow's work here was followed up by Geoffrey Parnell in 1981 (Parnell 1993, fig 22). He also excavated a small trench at the junction of the outer curtain and Legge's Mount in 1981–2 (Fig 9). Most of the records of these projects are held at the Tower of London. At the time of writing (summer 2001) some drawings were still held by English Heritage in their Historic Plans Room collections at the National Monuments Record Centre in Swindon; these are prefixed HPR in the following text. The drawings are due to be transferred to the Tower archives in the near future.

THE EXCAVATIONS

The junction of the outer curtain wall and Byward Tower in the west moat, 1958

Peter Curnow excavated a test pit in the west moat where the outer curtain wall adjoins the northern drum of the Byward Tower. The excavation was up to 3.47m (11ft 4½in.) long (north–south), 2.24m (7ft 4in.) wide, and 2.21m (7ft 3in.) deep. The work took place from 10 February to 20 June 1958, and was apparently done entirely by hand. The surviving drawings consist of an elevation of the outer curtain wall and the Byward Tower as revealed in the excavation but also including a substantial portion of above ground masonry (HPR 105 FF 48; Fig 10), and a plan of the test pit (HPR 105 FF 49). Both are at a scale of 1:12 (1in. = 1ft) and are dated 19 June 1958, one day before the project ceased. Backfilling must have followed immediately thereafter. Unfortunately the moat fills do not seem to have been recorded. No sectional information was found, and Curnow's own records held in the Tower of London archives do not contain any stratigraphic data.

The excavation revealed the lower portion of the battered faces of the Byward Tower and the outer curtain wall. Digging ceased when an offset foundation was found at the base of the curtain wall. This offset was only 0.23m (9in.) wide, substantially less than was found elsewhere around the curtain during the 1995–7 excavations (*see* Chapter 5). Excavation was only taken to this depth in the north-east corner of the pit, so that the possibility of an equivalent offset under the Byward Tower went unrecognised.

The elevation (Fig 10) has to be examined with a degree of caution. In several cases, for instance, what was drawn as several small stones is actually a single block but partly covered by the crude pointing that typifies much of the curtain wall. It must also be remembered that much of the masonry detail would have been obscured by accumulated dirt. Attempts to record much of the Tower by stereo or rectified photography in the mid-late 1970s were severely hampered by the very dirty condition of the walls, largely from airborne environmental pollutants. The resulting survey drawings, copies of which are also held at EHHPR, confirm this and are of limited value except as a surface condition record. Once this is taken into account the drawing is very valuable. The high-quality ashlar of the Byward Tower is well recorded, and some invaluable details were included. The presence of lead jointing was noted in the lower part of the Byward ashlar, and three different mason's marks were also drawn. The first two (a simple pair of horizontal strokes and a circle) only occurred once, but the other (a cross) was recorded on four stones (three on the Byward and one on a block keying the tower in with the curtain wall). Two other possible occurrences can be seen on the drawing, but are not annotated as mason's marks. The cross mark is especially valuable,

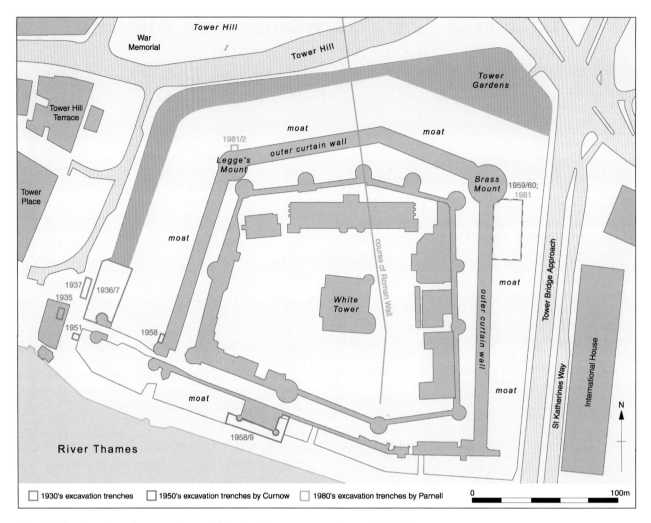

Fig 9   The location of excavations within the Tower moat prior to the 1990s.

because this was also noted on the other side of the northern drum and on the north face of the western causeway during the 1996–7 excavations (*see* Chapter 5). The elevation is also valuable because it seems to confirm that the north drum of the Byward Tower and the battered portion of the outer curtain wall were keyed in together, establishing their contemporaneity. The upper part of the curtain, by contrast, appears to abut the Byward.

The elevation shows a culvert against the outer curtain wall; this is annotated 'approximate position of brick culvert on opposite side of excavations', ie, in the east section. The culvert is not shown on the plan. Presumably the brickwork was removed to allow the excavation to go deeper, and its position therefore had to be extrapolated from the remaining part in the unexcavated section.

St Thomas's Tower, 1958–9

Curnow directed a series of excavations around St Thomas's Tower during 1958/9, starting with a test pit against the east drum in July 1958. This was followed by a major excavation during the rest of

that year and into 1959, encompassing the whole apron now open in front of Traitor's Gate. A large drawing shows the main excavation in two plans and four sections or elevations (HPR 105 S 56). The drawings are unscaled. There is also an archive for this project containing photographs, section drawings at a scale of 1:24, and a notebook including descriptions and sketches of the excavations. The work seems to have been undertaken by hand. The area had been partially lowered under the orders of the architect Anthony Salvin in the middle of the 19th century to create a sloping garden, but this did not expose the battered courses of the turrets (PRO Work 14/2/1 specifies 'Dig out earth to form ha-ha. Repair external masonry').

The 1958 test pit

The test pit measured 2.59m (8ft 6in.) north–south by up to 2.13m (7ft) and was dug to a depth of about 3.2m (10ft 6in.), although the records are somewhat ambiguous about this. The pit was dug at the junction between the eastern turret and the south face of St Thomas's Tower. A detailed 1:24 scale

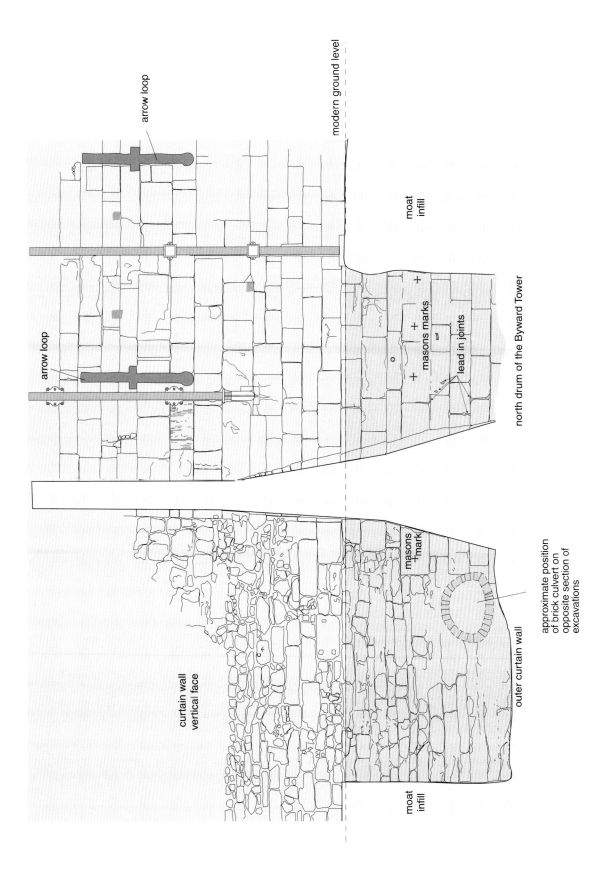

Fig 10 *Elevations of the outer curtain wall (left) and the north drum of the Byward Tower (right) recorded during the excavation at the junction between the two features in 1958. Note the masons' marks and evidence for lead jointing. Individual stones in the lower courses were obscured by calcareous concretions similar to those noted during 1995–7.*

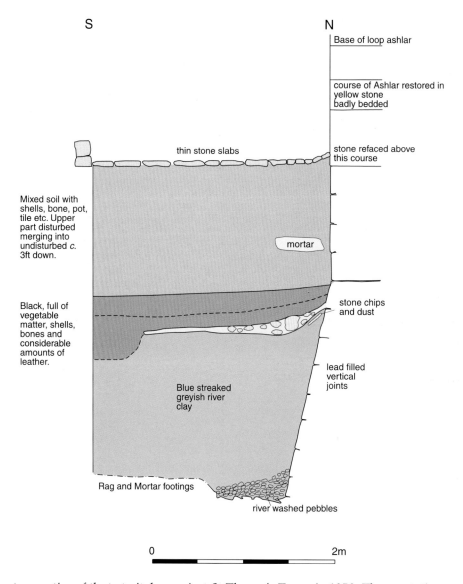

S   N

Base of loop ashlar

course of Ashlar restored in
yellow stone
badly bedded

thin stone slabs

stone refaced above
this course

Mixed soil with
shells, bone, pot,
tile etc. Upper
part disturbed
merging into
undisturbed c.
3ft down.

mortar

Black, full of
vegetable
matter, shells,
bones and
considerable
amounts of
leather.

stone chips
and dust

lead filled
vertical
joints

Blue streaked
greyish river
clay

Rag and Mortar footings

river washed pebbles

0   2m

Fig 11   The western section of the test pit dug against St Thomas's Tower in 1958. The annotations are all transcribed directly from the original drawing.

section in the notebook provides a summary of the stratigraphy in the pit (Fig 11). The most significant discovery was a mortared ragstone footing, which was exposed much more extensively in the subsequent area excavation. Lead filling was also noted in the battered lower masonry of the turret. The lower and middle layers over the footing evidently contained medieval pottery. A 14th-century baluster jug was found in the thick clay layer over the footings, and 15th-century 'Sieburg [sic] etc' was recovered from the organic middle layer, which also contained 'considerable amounts of leather'. A note on the facing page of the notebook appears to contradict this: 'dating evidence from Blue Clay within 18in. of footing. (black glazed plate[?] dated by B.M. [British Museum] to late 17th century (N. Italian)'. The upper fill was a rubbly layer that had evidently been disturbed in the upper reaches, and a brick wall is shown cut into this deposit on the

section. The thin stone slabs of the then existing paving completed the stratigraphy.

The 1958–9 area excavation

Not surprisingly the area excavation (Fig 12) revealed that the stratigraphy was much more complex (Fig 13), although to a degree the basic sequence identified in the test pit was confirmed. Sketch plans in the notebook show that the ragstone footing extended along the whole south face of St Thomas's Tower and around the east turret at least. The situation is not quite as clear for the west turret, although a continuation here is at least implied in one section showing the western half of the excavations: a raft is shown at the bottom of the excavation roughly in front of the west drum. There was a step in the footing 'just forward of the inner chamfered arch order' of Traitors' Gate

Fig 12 View of the early stages of the 1959 excavation around St Thomas's Tower. Note the post-medieval brick wall in the foreground (this can be seen on Works 31/36, Fig 135), and the passage to Traitors' Gate in the background.

(notebook, p 19). Horizontal oak beams were associated with this central part of the raft through the Gate (Fig 14). A layer of 'white silt, stone etc' is shown covering the footing and abutting the battered face of St Thomas's Tower in another section. This layer is not mentioned in the notebook, but similar material found at the base of the outer curtain wall during the 1996–7 moat evaluations has been interpreted as builders' rubble (*see* Chapter 5).

The white silt and the raft were sealed by a thin layer of 'ballast' (river gravel), in turn overlain by a grey clay layer up to 0.84m (2ft 9in.) thick (in effect a foreshore deposit). Figure 13 shows that a series of stakes or piles had been driven through this layer and just into the ballast. Two of the timbers evidently penetrated into the rag footing. A 0.71m-thick (2ft 6in.) layer of mixed buff clay covered the eastern pile, which had protruded some 0.62m (2ft) above the grey clay. The western edge of the latter was cut by the foundation trench for a stone drain or culvert that evidently ran under the wharf. This drain therefore post-dates the construction of St Thomas's Tower and is likely to be either earlier than or contemporary with the extension of the wharf as far as the tower. This provides a date range up to *c*1340. The section appears to show a stake in the edge of the foundation trench, perhaps representing shuttering of what must have been somewhat unstable sides. (A drain similar to this one can be seen in Water Lane in the deep section to the east of

the Wakefield Tower. The section through the inner curtain wall dates from the reign of Henry III and functioned as the main drain of the palace, running south from the south-west corner of the White Tower. The drain was extended during the reign of Edward I to take it through the new outer curtain wall so that it could still discharge into the Thames. The break in construction is very distinct, as can be seen in Parnell 1993, illustration 14. The structure was first exposed in 1899 within the Inmost Ward, and subsequently in Water Lane during another of Curnow's excavations in the late 1950s. It was also revealed in an excavation by Derek Gadd for HRP in 1992. It has now been left exposed to view, though blocked at the breach caused by the excavations.) A fine ashlar chamber had been built over the culvert, presumably to allow access to it for inspection and maintenance (Fig 15). A brick vault extending to the south (Fig 13) appears to have been a later addition. Curnow thought that the chamber might be of Tudor date (annotation to sketch plan at top of notebook p 13). The relationship between the culvert/chamber and a fine ashlar wall built against the west side of the western turret of St Thomas's Tower is unclear. The wall was faced on its south side showing that it was intended to be visible as the river wall, presumably before the wharf extended beyond this point (*see* Chapter 1). The wall clearly post-dated the turret (it butts against it), but it is very difficult to determine how the wall relates to the culvert.

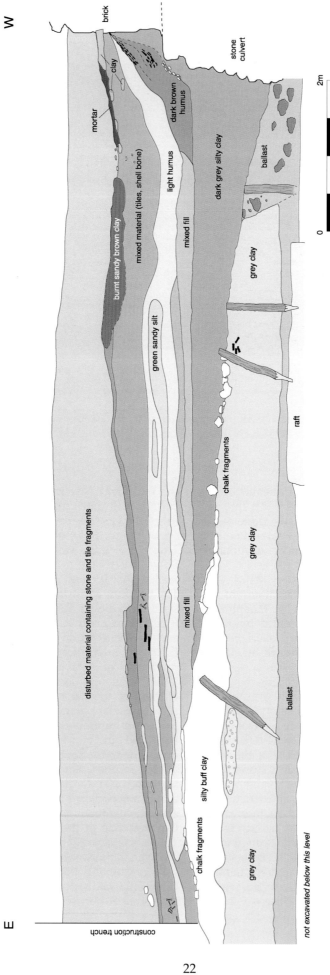

W

E

brick

clay

mortar

burnt sandy brown clay

mixed material (tiles, shell bone)

light humus

dark brown humus

dark grey silty clay

stone culvert

ballast

green sandy silt

mixed fill

grey clay

chalk fragments

raft

disturbed material containing stone and tile fragments

mixed fill

chalk fragments

grey clay

ballast

silty buff clay

chalk fragments

grey clay

construction trench

not excavated below this level

0

2m

Fig 13 The southern section of the 1959 excavation around St Thomas's Tower. This shows the western portion of the section, between the medieval culvert to the right and the former passage under the wharf to Traitors' Gate to the left.

22

Fig 14   View of the timber piles in the apron in front of Traitors' Gate, exposed during the 1959 excavation around St Thomas's Tower.

There is a diagonal cut-back to the north in the wall immediately where the chamber (presumably) sits over the culvert, and it would appear that the chamber was built into this angle. This might imply that the chamber is later than the wall, but it does not establish the relationship between the culvert itself and the wall. This problem is unlikely to be resolvable without further excavation.

The rubble and ballast fill of the foundation trench and the buff clay were overlain by a 'v. black' layer. This seems to have been very similar in character to foreshore layers pre-dating the wharf's construction exposed in test pits along the south moat in 1996 (*see* Chapter 6). The deposit provided a virtually horizontal interface with the layers above, which comprised several mixed deposits of clay and rubble (mortar, chalk, tile etc). Both the black layer and the subsequent deposits butted against the masonry of the culvert and chamber; several of the deposits were distinctively ramped up against the masonry, as though they had been dumped against it. Elsewhere a section shows similar layers abutting the south outer curtain wall.

Curnow's notebook provides important evidence for the foundations of the wharf wall immediately to the east of St Thomas's Tower. He noted '3 periods of stone work in moat wall lowest on a timber sleeper'. His sketch section shows the typical arrangement of a timber pile and beam under the face of the wall as revealed in the 1996 excavations (*see* Chapter 6), but also shows a further pile under the core of the wall

with a tie-back beam linking this to the facing timbers. This suggests that the wharf sat on a substantial raft of interlaced timberwork. The sketch shows the rubble core above this, with a 'change in mortar' perhaps representing one of the three phases of stonework. The third phase was presumably the 19th-century brick facing.

The rubbly fills were cut by a number of later features. The most important was an L-shaped brick wall to the east of Traitors' Gate apparently defining a basin in front of St Thomas's Tower (Fig 12). The masonry started adjacent to (and was probably cut by) the 19th-century abutment at the south end of the east flank wall of the canal under the wharf to Traitors' Gate. The brickwork ran eastwards before turning to the north roughly in line with the east side of the tower's eastern turret. The masonry stood to a height of 0.61m (2ft) here, the foot of the wall evidently lying 1.83m (6ft) below the surface. The northern return was truncated after 1.83m (6ft) by the landscaping that created a sloping lawn in front of Traitors' Gate during the mid-late 19th century. It is likely that the brick wall had joined up with the eastern turret to close off this side of the basin. Curnow's notes suggest that the wall was of 18th-century date.

A second wall of stone rubble ran from the eastern turret to join the wharf wall on the south-east moat. The upper part of the masonry was described as 'squared' while the lower was 'random', perhaps suggesting two phases of construction. The wall was

Fig 15a General view from the south-east of the fine ashlar masonry chamber over the medieval culvert exposed during the 1959 excavation around St Thomas's Tower. Note the brickwork addition to the south.

Fig 15b Overhead detail.

clearly a relatively late insertion, as an elevation on HPR 105 S 56 shows that it rested on 'ballast' foundations (with a levelling course of rubble) cut into clay moat fills. Furthermore the foundation abutted the battered face of the turret well above the rag footing. Curnow's notes make it clear that there was 'no sign of an early wall on E. side', ie, that no equivalent to the river wall abutting the western turret could be found here. Presumably this reflects the later development of the wharf to the east of St Thomas's Tower. Equally, the gap would allow continued access by boat into the south-east moat and thus to the monarch's privy water-gate in the Cradle Tower.

A number of other late features were also identified. Two brick culverts were found immediately to the east of St Thomas's Tower; these had been inserted into the moat by the Royal Engineers *c*1843 as part of the backfilling process (*see* Chapter 10). The 19th-century flank walls of the canal under the wharf leading out from Traitors' Gate were also exposed. Photographs show that the rear faces of the flanks largely consisted of re-used masonry (Fig 16). Several blocks showed characteristic 17th-century horizontal drafting.

The east moat turrets, 1959–60

Curnow also directed the excavation of trenches/pits over the three masonry projections or turrets against the outer curtain wall in the east moat during late 1959 and early 1960 (Fig 17). One drawing contains a plan with three sections/profiles at a scale of 1:96 showing the location of the excavations related to the outer curtain wall, Brass Mount and Tower Bridge Approach (HPR 105 F 41). Another has a set of plans, sections and elevations at a scale of 1:24 of the excavations against the southern and northern turrets (titled Buttress A and Buttress C respectively on drawing HPR 105 F 42). There are also a number of photographs of the excavations in the collections of English Heritage. The work appears to have been undertaken by hand in conjunction with the laying of electricity cables around the moat (Fig 18).

The trench against the southern turret (Buttress A) was broadly rectangular and encompassed the whole base of the standing turret. This is also shown on drawing 105 F 42. Three excavations took place against the middle turret (Buttress B): a T-shaped trench covering the east end and both faces of the structure, and two test pits to assess its relationship with the outer curtain wall. Three excavations were also carried out on the northern turret (Buttress C): a test pit at each of the north-east and south-east corners, and a pit to assess the junction of the north face of the turret with the Brass Mount.

The northern and southern turrets both lay at a reasonably true perpendicular to the outer curtain wall. The middle turret, however, was skewed at an angle of about 5° to the north of the perpendicular. Otherwise the foundations seem very similar formally, running horizontally for 7.32–7.62m

Fig 16   The rear face of the eastern wall passage to Traitors' Gate exposed (and removed) during the 1959 excavation around St Thomas's Tower. Note the horizontal tooling on several stone blocks.

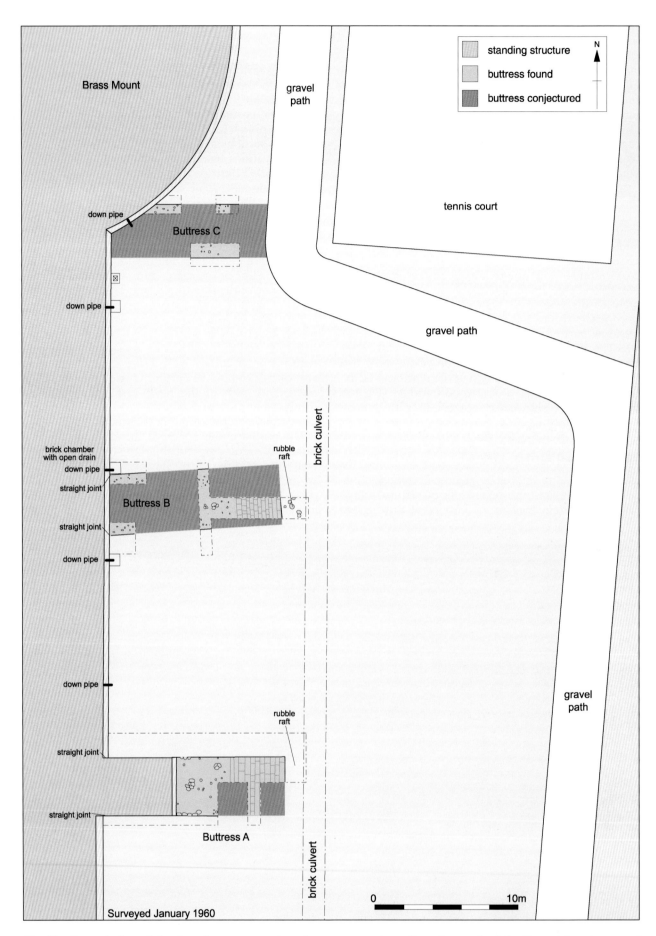

Fig 17   General plan of the three buttresses against the outer curtain wall to the south of the Brass Mount, exposed during the 1960–1 excavations in the east moat. The southern buttress is still visible above ground. Its foundations were re-examined in 1997.

Within the figure:

- standing structure
- buttress found
- buttress conjectured

N

Brass Mount

gravel path

tennis court

gravel path

down pipe

Buttress C

down pipe

down pipe

brick chamber with open drain

down pipe

straight joint

Buttress B

straight joint

down pipe

rubble raft

brick culvert

gravel path

down pipe

rubble raft

straight joint

straight joint

Buttress A

brick culvert

straight joint

0   10m

Surveyed January 1960

Fig 18   General view of the 1960–1 excavations in the east moat.

(24–25ft) from the curtain wall 0.3–0.46m (1ft–1ft 6in.) below ground level. Then the foundations battered downwards. The plan is annotated to show a straight joint between the southern and middle turrets and the outer curtain wall, establishing that the former were additions to the latter. No such annotation is present for the northern turret, though this is also dealt with on drawing 105 F 42 (*see* below).

The more detailed drawings are very valuable, although they contain no information about the moat fills. The trench against the southern turret (Buttress A) is recorded in plan, a profile of the masonry, and an elevation of the north face of the turret (Fig 19). The latter still stands above ground (the other two survive only below grass level), and work was no doubt concentrated here because of this. A 14.17m-long (46ft 6in.) trench was excavated at right angles to the outer curtain wall on the north side of the turret. The west end of the trench was 1.52m (5ft) wide against the standing masonry and was then offset to the south with the north face of the turret

running just within the excavation. Two extensions were dug southwards from the main trench to establish the position and alignment of the south face of the masonry. This proved that the structure was continuous at the same width (3.4m/11ft 2in.) above and below ground.

The east face of the standing turret continued down for 0.46m (1ft 6in.) to the foundations, which extended eastward for 3.05m (10ft), with a single step down about halfway along. The batter then continued for a further 3.35m (11ft) in length, the upper surface being covered with coping stones. Some of these were missing (thus exposing the rubble core) or dislodged, usually having been turned through 90°. The batter terminated in a 0.53m-high (1ft 9in.) face either resting on or dug through a raft of unidentified material apparently forming the base of the moat (*see* Chapter 5). The 'raft' continued to slope slightly away until it was truncated by the Royal Engineers' culvert, inserted in 1843. The excavation reached a maximum depth of

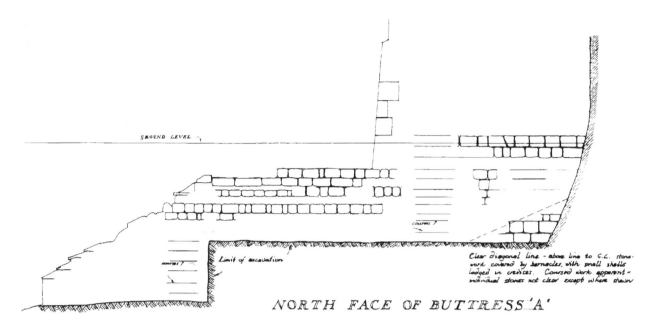

Fig 19 *The north face of the southern buttress seen in profile. This is a transcription of the original annotated drawing made in 1960–1.*

3.5m (11ft 6in.) here. The raft was also found under the middle buttress, apparently consisting of stone rubble there.

The elevation of the turret's north face depicts 16 courses of ashlar below grass level. The upper two courses represented the continuation of the standing turret while the lower 14 comprised the foundations. The drawing shows most of the coursing conventionally as ruled horizontal lines, with details of the individual ashlar blocks where these were visible (Fig 19). The reason for this is noted on the drawing in relation to a dashed line where the elevation of the turret adjoins the outer curtain wall. The line starts against the latter 1.07m (3ft 6in.) below grass level and then runs diagonally down to the base of the excavation at 1.83m (6ft) below the surface (still above the base of the moat here). The annotation reads: 'Clear diagonal line – above line to G.L. [ground level?] stonework covered by barnacles with small shells in crevices. Coursed work apparent – individual stones not clear except where shown'. Evidence for similar concretions was found in several of the 1996–7 excavations and is dealt with in Chapter 8. The elevation also confirms that the turret foundations abutted the outer curtain wall.

The outer curtain wall, Legge's Mount and Brass Mount, 1981–2

The laying of new electricity cables in the moat in 1981 gave Geoffrey Parnell the opportunity to re-examine the northern of the three turrets, where Curnow's 1959–60 excavations had been least useful. The 1981 work exposed the entire upper surface of the turret and the upper part of the facing as well (Parnell 1993, fig 22). Only the upper moat fills could be examined within the scope of the electrical works. The excavation confirmed that the Brass Mount was an addition to the outer curtain wall while the latter was still at its low level (ie, before it had been heightened over the battered segment). The base of the Mount also butted against and rode over the north side of the northern turret. Several cross-shaped mason's marks were found on the coping stones of the battered face (annotation on a plan in the Tower archive). Parnell also excavated a test pit at the junction of Legge's Mount and the north-west outer curtain wall. This established that the base of the Mount and the wall were contemporary, and that only subsequently had they been raised to their full height (excluding the Victorian tops of the walls).

Chapter 3: Archaeology in the Tower Environs Scheme

INTRODUCTION

The Tower of London is recognised as being one of Britain's most important historic sites. Indeed, its universal significance is acknowledged in its designation as one of only 13 cultural properties among England's World Heritage Sites (as at 2001). This recognition does not afford any additional protection to the site, but the castle and its environs already enjoyed a high degree of statutory protection before becoming a World Heritage Site in 1988. The Tower was one of the first sites in Britain to be designated as a Scheduled Ancient Monument (Greater London No. 10). The Scheduled area currently extends to the railings on the outer edge of Tower Gardens on the north and west sides (taking in the Lion Tower and West Gate shop area at the south-west corner), Tower Bridge Approach on the east side and the river wall along the Thames foreshore to the south. These boundaries were adopted for the World Heritage Site. The adjoining area of Tower Hill West is also a Scheduled Ancient Monument (Greater London No. 158) contiguous with the west side of the Tower SAM.

The Tower is Crown property managed by Historic Royal Palaces (HRP), who have also assumed responsibility for the management of Tower Hill West, an important element of the historic Tower Liberties. Proposals for work on Scheduled sites require the formal permission of Her Majesty's Secretary of State for Culture, Media and Sport, advised by English Heritage; permission is usually granted on the basis of an application for Scheduled Monument Consent. HRP is a charitable trust established by Her Majesty's government specifically to preserve and conserve the sites under its management for future generations. The sites managed by HRP have Crown exemption from statutory Scheduled Monument Consent controls under section 50 of the *Ancient Monuments and Archaeological Areas Act (1979)*. HRP recognises and fully accepts its fundamental duty of care over the monuments, however, and consequently follows the parallel procedure of application for Scheduled Monument Clearance.

THE MOAT EVALUATIONS: APPROACH AND STRATEGY

The Tower Environs Scheme's bold, even controversial, proposal to reflood the Tower moat inevitably raised archaeological concerns. Despite the long history of cleaning and dredging that stretched back even to the late 13th century, past excavations (Chapter 2) had shown clearly enough that archaeological remains might be present virtually anywhere around the moat's 850m circuit. Furthermore, Curnow's excavations around St Thomas's Tower had demonstrated that organic material such as wood and leather might survive in exceptional condition due to the anaerobic (oxygen-free) waterlogged conditions in the lower levels of the ditch.

It was, therefore, inevitable that the feasibility of the reflooding proposal would have to be tested from a variety of angles. The engineering and conservation consequences of removing soil that had lain against the outer curtain, revetment and wharf walls for more than 150 years had to be examined, for instance. Equally, the potential effects of reintroducing water both to the masonry and to any soil left in place had to be assessed. Most fundamentally of all, however, the archaeological impact of reflooding had to be measured. First and foremost the question had to be asked: was the proposal acceptable at all on archaeological grounds, or would the remains in the moat be so sensitive as to preclude the very concept of reflooding? Going on from this, the extent of excavation which might be acceptable if reflooding could go ahead had to be addressed.

The reflooding concept was introduced early in 1995, before the Tower Environs Scheme had been formally established. Discussions soon commenced between HRP, English Heritage and the Oxford Archaeological Unit (OAU). HRP had appointed OAU as their archaeological consultants in 1993, and the Unit had thus already gained considerable experience of working at the Tower by 1995—it soon became clear, however, that the moat was likely to be the largest project undertaken for HRP to date, even if many of the individual excavations might be on a small scale (Fig 20). The first of many Scheduled Monument Clearance applications was applied for and granted in the second quarter of 1995. This was for geophysical survey in the north moat, an auger survey of the moat's profile across a series of transects distributed around it, and 11 trial trenches and test pits mostly located close to the auger transects. The latter factor was to become crucial to the development of the archaeological strategy in the following two years. This first phase of work was carried out during the late spring and early summer of 1995.

The strategy had been for progressive investigations from the very beginning, moving from non-intrusive and minimally invasive techniques such as the geophysical and auger surveys up through successive stages of excavation from small test pits to large trenches. Each main phase of work required a new Scheduled Monument Clearance (or Section 42 Licences under the *Ancient Monuments and Archaeological Areas Act (1979)* for the geophysical surveys), and the various applications all contained

Fig 20   General view of excavations in progress during 1996. This photograph taken from the Byward Postern shows test pits in the south moat on the west side of St Thomas's Tower. There is no direct vehicular access to this area, so the mechanical excavator had to be lifted in by crane.

a series of research aims that formed the basis for the methods employed. At all stages the intention was to excavate as little as was necessary to achieve the aims, therefore leaving the majority of the archaeological remains intact and in place. This basic approach persisted throughout the remainder of the programme, which ran through most of 1996 and 1997. A few further related excavations occurred during 1998 and 1999. The main phase of work from 1995 to 1997 comprised three separate geophysical surveys, one manual and three powered auger surveys, and no less than 71 separate excavations. The latter covered approximately 2,100m², representing a little over 8 per cent of the moat's surface area. The cubic percentage was significantly less than this because all the larger excavations were stepped in by just over 1m at each 1.2m stage of excavation for safety reasons.

Technically the entire programme was an exercise in archaeological evaluation, the type of project that usually precedes commercial or other developments as part of the planning process. In a few cases, however, the excavations grew both in scale and intent to such an extent that they could be (and were) regarded as research work in their own right. The trenches at the south-eastern and south-western corners and in the middle of the western arm of the moat were therefore conducted not only to provide the planning and feasibility information required for the Scheme, but also to acquire adequate research data for purely archaeological purposes.

The goal was still to retain and preserve as much as possible of the stratified archaeological deposits *in situ*. Virtually all of the medieval timberwork was left in place rather than removed, for instance. Furthermore, in one case (trench 30) an important and complex timber structure of late 18th-century date was discovered. This had to be left untouched, and so there was minimal excavation into earlier levels below it. Inevitably this reduced the potential for interpreting the medieval and early post-medieval archaeology there. The results from the major trenches necessarily dominate this account of the excavations, although the amount of useful information derived from every one of the excavations, even the smallest, was gratifying. Further information on the reasons for and strategy of specific excavations is provided where relevant in the following chapters, and full details are available in the project archive.

METHODS

The geophysical surveys

The first geophysical survey was conducted by Alister Bartlett and covered an area of approximately 1,600m^2 in the middle of the north moat. The techniques used were earth resistance and magnetometry. The aims were to locate three documented structures. These were a weir shown across the north moat in several late 18th- and early 19th-century illustrations, an underground reservoir built as part of the backfilling in the 1840s and the Victorian North Bastion. The two 19th-century structures were located very clearly (Fig 21), but the weir to the west proved more elusive. A weak alignment of positive resistance readings corresponded with its approximate position as shown on 19th-century illustrations, but the response was not particularly convincing, especially in comparison with the strong readings from the North Bastion and reservoir.

This work was followed by a ground-probing radar survey of a 1,480m^2 area in the west moat by John Glover of Subsurface Geotechnical. This was done in October 1995 using a 100 MHz survey antenna to assess the extent of the masonry structure that had been unexpectedly revealed in trial trench 2 earlier in the year (see Chapter 4). Radar was chosen

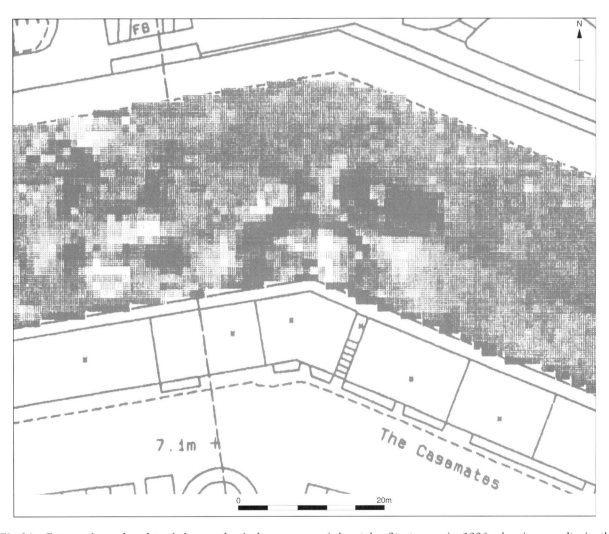

Fig 21 Extract from the plot of the geophysical survey carried out by Stratascan in 1996, showing results in the northern arm of the moat. The North Bastion and the below-ground reservoir immediately to its north-east are clearly visible. Both buildings suffered severe bomb damage in 1940, and the remains of the bastion were subsequently demolished.

because of its theoretical ability to penetrate to greater depths than earth resistance and magnetometry surveys. The results were inconclusive; masonry seemed to be present in the east half of the survey area, but later excavation showed that there was little correlation between the radar results and the structure that was completely exposed in trench 27.

The main survey was undertaken by Peter Barker (Stratascan) during May 1996 using earth resistance and ground-probing radar. The work covered the entire moat using both techniques, and a substantial area on the wharf between the Queen's Steps and the Salvin pumphouse (now the West Gate shop) using the radar only. A major advantage of radar is its ability to provide information about layers underneath solid surfaces, such as paving slabs and cobble setts, which are impenetrable to other archaeological survey techniques. The 1996 survey used a 300 MHz survey antenna, as this mid-range frequency offered a good compromise between depth penetration and detail resolution for archaeological purposes. The depth of penetration was expected to be up to 3.2m, although in practice it was mostly between 1.5m and 2m.

The two survey methods were largely complementary within the moat. Features such as the medieval masonry turrets against the outer curtain wall at the north end of the east moat (Chapters 2 and 5), the North Bastion and the underground reservoir (Chapter 10) were located as strong anomalies. Both the radar and resistivity surveys suggested that there was an opening in the top of the reservoir. The 19th-century Royal Engineers' culvert also showed up in places, but neither technique could follow the culvert around its complete circuit or locate the many secondary culverts feeding in to it at various points. More seriously, perhaps, the surveys again failed to give a good result over the mid-13th-century structure in the west moat. Extremely weak radar reflections were noted here but, in the words of the Stratascan report, 'had the excavation information not been available at the time of interpretation, it is doubtful whether any anomalies would have been identified in this area such is their general weakness'. Equally, a masonry causeway at the south-east corner of the moat (*see* Chapter 5) was located only after extremely careful study of the radargrams, probably because the extensive spreads of rubble above the structure presented a confused radar response. The high water table and the extreme waterlogging of the lower levels in the moat seem to have combined frustratingly to limit the radar signal response.

The radar survey on the wharf and the earth resistance survey on the lawn to the south of the Middle Tower were rather more successful. In particular, the radar located a large sub-rectangular building at the south-east corner of the Lion Tower, a cross-wall to the north of this and the revetment wall on the south side of the Lion Tower moat. The radar and resistivity surveys also located the position of a building range on the Middle Tower lawn, although

no internal detail was evident. The plan of these responses corresponds reasonably well with the distribution of buildings and walls in and around the Lion Tower as shown on later 17th- and early 18th-century surveys.

The auger surveys

The initial intention had been to sink a series of augers manually in transects at regular intervals around the moat. This proved to be impossible because the coarse rubbly fills in the top metre or so proved to be utterly impenetrable using a hand auger. Indeed, one auger bit was broken before the method was abandoned in favour of powered augering. This used a small pneumatic drill to drive a core down into the moat fills, resulting in the removal of a virtually continuous sample at each auger location. It was still exceedingly hard physical work, especially during rain, but a team led by Dr Rob Scaife carried out three sampling operations. These took place during late 1996 (three transects comprising ten augers and a further two single cores), December 1997 (three transects, 12 augers) and February 1998 (three transects, 11 augers). The west, north and east arms of the moat were sampled in this way, but the southern arm was omitted. It was not felt that the augering would add significantly to the test pit data there. Further information on the moat profile is provided in subsequent chapters as appropriate.

The excavations (Fig 22)

The excavations mostly followed a common methodology combining machine and manual work. There were some exceptions, chiefly in test pits at and just outside the south-western entrance to the castle, where operations had to be entirely by hand because the relevant locations were not accessible by machine. Elsewhere mechanical excavation was generally restricted to the removal of thick layers of 19th- and 20th-century fill in the middle and upper sections of the soil profile, though some post-medieval layers were also removed by machine where this could be achieved without the loss of significant archaeological information.

Most excavation in the lower levels was carried out by hand with mechanical support for removing the excavated soil from the trench. Even here, however, it was occasionally appropriate to use machines for excavation where the fills were not important. There were very few finds from the lowest levels, for instance, and the machine operators were extremely skilful in removing very thin slices of soil under the close control of the archaeological team. Extreme care was always exercised whenever the machine was used irrespective of the physical level involved because there was always the potential for unexpected discoveries. In the trenches on either side of Edward I's south-western entrance causeway, for instance, 18th- and 19th-century timberwork was found at quite high levels.

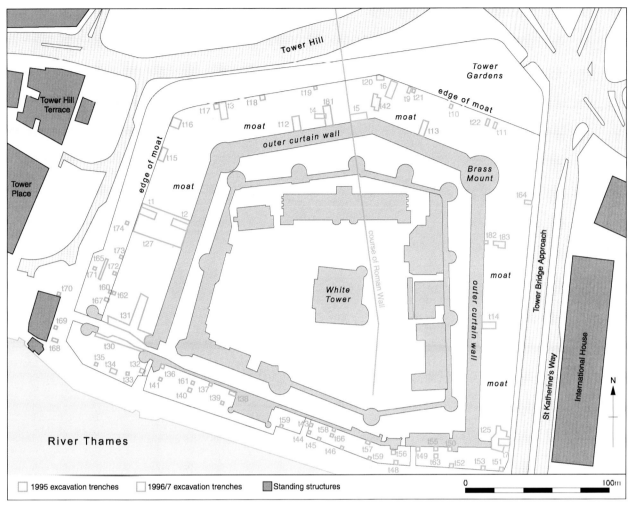

Fig 22   Location of the 1995–7 excavations in and around the moat.

The majority of the pits and trenches were aligned at right angles or parallel to the outer curtain and revetment walls or some other obvious structure (eg, the south-west entrance causeway). Compass points were then used conventionally within each excavation rather than magnetically or according to Ordnance Survey orientation. This convention is maintained throughout the descriptive text in subsequent chapters. Every individual excavation was given a separate number for ease of identification. This number was also used as the prefix for the four- or five-digit numbering system used throughout OAU excavations. In this way blocks of 100 plan, section and soil (context) numbers were allocated; for example the first plan, section and context from trench 81 were numbered 8100. Extensive drawn, written and photographic records were made of every trench and pit, though in one or two cases health and safety considerations prevented access for detailed drawings to be made. Digital surveying and recording was also used to aid in the accurate three-dimensional location of the works. The stratigraphy (the sequence of soil deposits, structures and features) was analysed in detail both during and

after the excavations, and a number of reports were written describing the results.

Several purely practical matters affected the progress of the excavations at various stages. The main ones concerned the safety of the excavations and the ability to keep them drained. Most of the pits and trenches were taken to depths of between 2m and 3m, with a maximum of approximately 5m in trench 27. This is well beyond the limits of safe working in normal circumstances, and the problem was exacerbated by the tendency of the silt- and clay-rich moat fills to shrink, crack and even collapse as they dried out. Such conditions are commonplace in deep, waterlogged urban excavations, and there are a number of approaches that can be adopted to make the work safe. The trench sides can be cut to a slope (batter) of around 45°, for instance, or continuous sheet piling and shoring can be inserted to retain the soil. Another method involves cutting steps at stages within an excavation so that it becomes progressively more narrow as it gets deeper. Battered edges were discounted from the beginning because it is extremely difficult to record sectional information adequately in such conditions.

Shoring was used in most of the smaller excavations, with frames and sheets being inserted as necessary. It was always possible to avoid significant archaeological remains such as timber structures in the smaller pits and trenches, while careful placing of the sheets also left parts of the soil section available for recording. The larger trenches provided a different challenge, however, as the greater physical areas involved required much more safety planning in advance. It was decided at an early stage that continuous sheet piling and de-watering such as is often used in these conditions were inappropriate in the Tower moat. This was because of the inherent likelihood that important historical timberwork might be encountered in the lower levels of excavation. The sheet piling would have to be driven 'blind' into these levels, presenting an obvious risk of severe damage to timbers (and indeed other remains). Ground de-watering was also discounted because this would run the risk of drying out organic materials such as timber and leather, the condition of which could then deteriorate rapidly. The stepped option was therefore chosen for all the larger excavations (Fig 23).

Ground water was both a major operational problem and, paradoxically, an important benefit during the excavations. On the one hand even the smallest test pits had a tendency to become inundated by water seeping in through the sides of the excavation once a depth of around 1.5m had been reached (sometimes much less). In the larger trenches this could have serious consequences, both creating unworkable conditions and affecting the stability of the trench edges. Pumps were used to manage this problem, for the most part successfully. The main reason for this was the culvert inserted in a continuous ring around the moat by the Royal Engineers during the draining and backfilling of the moat in the 1840s. This continues to drain water that accumulates in the moat out into the river Thames at low tide through outfalls above the low tide level. We were able to pump standing water out into the culvert, and this could then be released into the river on the ebb tide. At times, however, various operational factors meant that the culvert could not be drained. In these circumstances the water could not be removed from the excavations and, indeed, water backing up in the culvert might seep back out into the trenches. There would then be no alternative but to halt operations until drainage was possible again.

By contrast the standing water often acted as a ready-made preservative for the *in situ* conservation of timbers and other organic materials found in many trenches. These frequently had to be exposed for a considerable time so that recording could be carried out and because of the strategy specific to the relevant excavation. Water accumulated in the excavations as soon as the pumps were turned off, soon rising to cover the timbers. This, allied to coverings of capillary matting to retain water, meant that the wood

Fig 23 This photograph of trench 27 shows the extreme waterlogging encountered in the lower levels of most excavations. This required constant pumping to keep water levels down during the day, but the trenches and pits were allowed to re-flood during the night. This helped to preserve the timberwork while the excavations remained open.

could be kept permanently wet. The natural processes of drying and decay were therefore kept at bay. The backfilling process was also carried out extremely carefully in an attempt to recreate the buried environment that had existed around the timberwork before the excavations had begun. The same silty clays that had surrounded the timbers were packed around them firstly by hand, and then by machine. The aim was to replicate the original burial environment and therefore ensure the long-term preservation of the organic remains. Subsequent monitoring suggests that this aim has been fully achieved.

FINDS

The artefacts recovered during the excavations were perhaps rather disappointing both in date range and quality given the extent of the work and the type of site being studied. Medieval finds made up only a very small percentage of the material recovered, while there was a real dearth of early post-medieval artefacts. Dr Higgins' comments on the virtual absence of early clay pipes are especially relevant here. The wide geographical spread of the excavations means that these are real factors rather than being something caused by a bias of excavation in one area or another.

Despite this, the finds have been used wherever possible to provide dating for the soils in which they were found. The small quantities recovered from the lower levels inevitably cause problems with such an approach as the evidential basis is relatively slight. Fortunately, the excellent dendrochronological evidence from several trenches gives a firm basis for the commencement of the overall stratigraphic and structural sequence. This has helped considerably in defining the relative chronology in all trenches. The historical background to the work has also been valuable in this respect. Edward I's enlargement of the defences, Sir Bernard de Gomme's construction of the revetment wall in the 1670s and, of course, the draining and infilling of the moat in the 1840s provide the most significant 'anchors' in this respect, but there are others. These are noted where relevant in subsequent chapters.

The dating of individual contexts and stratigraphic groups has also had to take account of two problems that bedevil many archaeological excavations. In the first instance, some artefacts may be earlier in date than the layer in which they were found; this is known as residuality. Secondly, some layers may contain intrusive finds of a later date, perhaps introduced during the insertion of features such as mains services. Where such problems have been apparent, dating has usually been resolved by reference to the soils around, above and below the relevant context. To a considerable degree this has been a matter of pragmatism mixed with experience of site conditions during excavation, which—in terms of waterlogging at least—often seemed close to replicating the original conditions within the moat.

The following sections describe any methodological considerations thought to be relevant by the specialists. In each case the author identified here also provided those sections on the relevant finds materials that have been incorporated into the descriptions in subsequent chapters. The same applies to the environmental specialists and their contributions.

Pottery
Duncan H Brown and Robert Thomson

During the excavations 1,977 sherds of pottery (95.14kg) were recovered. Not surprisingly, given the Roman background of the Tower, a small quantity (27 sherds, 467g) of Romano-British pottery was recovered. This included black-burnished ware, mortaria, Samian and greyware. There was also a single small sherd (4g) of early medieval flint-tempered ware in a 19th-century context. Small but significant quantities of 13th- to 16th-century pottery were recovered, but the assemblage is dominated by later 17th- to 20th-century products.

All sherds were recorded and catalogued with reference to existing type series. Appendix 1 provides a catalogue of ware and vessel types. This is set out with English wares described first, then imported types, in chronological order. English wares are ordered according to increasing distance from London—thus London products are described before those from Surrey and so on. The quantities of each ware type are given by rim percentage (rp), weight in grams and sherd count. Detailed fabric descriptions are not necessary for most of the wares in this assemblage, as they are familiar post-industrial types such as Creamware or Transfer-printed ware, or else medieval or post-medieval types that have been described elsewhere. The purpose of the catalogue is to introduce the range of types present. Analysis of the quantification is incorporated in the following chapters.

Clay pipe
David Higgins

A total of 996 fragments of pipe were found, comprising 441 bowl, 537 stem and 18 mouthpiece fragments. The fragments have been individually examined and details of each piece logged on to record forms developed at the University of Liverpool (Higgins and Davey 1994). A context summary giving the overall numbers and date range of the fragments from each context has also been produced. Bowl forms have been recorded with reference to the London typology published by Atkinson and Oswald (1969) although the dating has been modified according to the form and attributes of the individual fragments. Variants of the basic London shape illustrated in the 1969 typology have had the letter 'v' placed after their type number. Unless otherwise stated the earlier makers have been identified using the national list provided in

Oswald 1975, and the later makers by reference to an unpublished list of later 18th- and 19th-century London makers provided by Peter Hammond of Nottingham from his current research.

An assessment of the likely date of the stem fragments has been provided. The stem dates should be used with caution, however, since they are much more general and less reliable than the dates that can be determined from the bowl fragments. All of the pipes were recorded and dated before the historical background, excavation summary or site matrices were examined. This avoided any preconceptions being formed as to the possible date or nature of the various pipe groups while they were being examined and catalogued.

Metal, bone and other materials
Leigh Allen

The vast majority of artefacts originated from post-medieval contexts, especially those dating to the 18th and 19th centuries. Remarkably few finds of any material were recovered from the lower, medieval levels. This is especially notable as manual excavation was the norm in these levels (*see* above). The lack of finds can therefore be taken as a real reflection of the situation in the moat (or at least in those parts of it which were excavated).

A total of 240 objects of metal or bone were recovered from the moat excavations, along with numerous unidentifiable fragments and nails. The latter are not included in this report but they will appear as a list in the archive. The remaining 228 metal objects, 11 bone items and single wooden object are discussed in subsequent chapters. The illustrated objects are described in the relevant figure captions. The prefix 'SF' (for small find) is used for all finds (including leather etc).

Glass
Cecily Cropper

The glass assemblage comprised 395 fragments with similar proportions of window glass, bottles and phials. A small quantity of vessels and glass objects were also represented. All of the glass was post-medieval in date, ranging from the mid-late 17th to the 20th centuries.

Leather
Quita Mould

Seventy-seven items of leather were recovered during the moat investigations. Every item recovered has been fully catalogued in the archive. Most of the leather was found in the west moat. Two components from soles of post-medieval welted construction were found in test pit 16 in a context (context 1632) immediately pre-dating the construction of the revetment wall in the 1670s. A piece of secondary waste was found unstratified in trench 15. Approximately 23 objects were found in trench 27,

representing a minimum of 14 shoes, a patten, a possible mitten fragment and two straps. Trench 31 contained approximately 39 objects representing a minimum of 20 shoes, 3 straps and 3 unidentified items. This material is considered in more detail in subsequent chapters. Leather was recovered, but in much smaller quantities, from the north (trenches 13, 21 and 22), east (trench 64) and south (trenches 35, 38 and 45) sides of the moat. The turnshoes dated from the later medieval period to the early 16th century, while those of welted constructions dated to the post-medieval period.

Stonework

Dr Bernard Worssam visited the excavations on several occasions to provide details on the geological source of the building stones evident in the trenches. His report was based on observations made during these visits. The lithology of excavated architectural fragments and masonry structures (above and below ground) was assessed visually and, where relevant, stone samples were taken for more detailed analysis. Jeremy Ashbee has examined the assemblage of architectural fragments recovered during the excavations, and has provided the comments and comparative information used in later chapters.

DENDROCHRONOLOGY
Ian Tyers

Tree-ring dating (dendrochronology) samples were taken from 164 waterlogged timbers in three separate trenches, and advice was given on the (negative) potential for dating timbers in many of the smaller pits as well. The timbers from a structure found in pit 38, for instance, were all elm; this species cannot be dated by dendrochronology. Most (85) samples were beech, with 22 oak, 19 pine, 24 spruce or larch, 6 other softwoods too badly degraded to be identified by genus and 8 elm. None of the timber types is especially unusual or unexpected, although the softwood fragments are probably derived from imported timbers. Fifty-five samples had too few rings for analysis. These were identified to species or genus where possible. Analysis then concentrated on beech (*Fagus sylvatica* L.) and oak (*Quercus* spp), although some softwood timbers (*Pinus* spp and *Picea* spp) were also sampled as part of a wider research programme supported by English Heritage. The main aim of the analysis was to provide accurate and independent dating evidence for structures revealed during the excavations. A secondary aim was to assist in the strengthening of the beech tree-ring chronology for London.

The general methodology and working practices used at the Sheffield Dendrochronology Laboratory are described in English Heritage (1998). Tree-ring dating methods can only date the rings present in the timber. The interpretation of any dates obtained relies upon the nature of the final rings in the sequence. A precise felling date can be determined from the date of the last surviving ring if the sample survives to the bark-edge (ie, to the point at which the tree stopped growing/died). One cannot be sure how many tree rings have been lost if the bark-edge does not survive, however, and in these circumstances the last surviving ring defines the date after which (*terminus post quem*, or *tpq*) the tree must have died or been felled. This *tpq* may be many years or decades earlier than the real felling date because there is no way of knowing how many rings (and thus years' growth) have been lost. Fortunately, most of the viable samples from the Tower moat, and all of the beeches, retained their bark and thus provided precise felling dates. In the absence of the outer rings of oak, the analysis assumed that a minimum of 10 and maximum of 46 sapwood rings would have been present. These figures provide 95% confidence limits (Tyers 1998) and appear to be applicable to archaeological material excavated from England. They are a refinement of the values applicable to oaks from the British Isles as a whole (eg, Hillam *et al* 1987). It is generally believed that timbers were used shortly after felling (eg, Charles and Charles 1995, 46; Rackham 1990, 69; Schweingruber 1988, 146).

Full technical details of identification and size of the samples as well as the correlation between individual beech timbers from the site and the dating evidence for the three oak sequences are provided in the archive report (Tyers 2000). Further details of the softwood samples are provided by Groves (forthcoming). Most (78) of the beech samples, 12 of the oaks and 19 softwoods were suitable for analysis. Chronologies were constructed from different groups of material and combined to create a single site master sequence (Table 1). This was then compared to dated reference chronologies (Table 2). Absolute dates were successfully achieved for 66 beech and 3 oaks, but none of the softwoods. Therefore 40 of the 109 samples analysed could not be dated. More than half of these were from later post-medieval structures largely built from softwoods. Even though many of the undated samples are smaller fragments, each was re-examined to ensure there had not been any measurement errors. The data was compared with both the rest of the dated and undated material from the site, as well as with

Table 2   Correlation between the Tower moat composite beech mean and reference beech and oak chronologies, t-values calculated using the CROS algorithm of Baillie and Pilcher (1973)

Reference chronology	Tower moat Composite 66 samples 1126–1277
Oak reference data	
Bedfordshire Chicksands Priory (Howard *et al* 1998)	6.08
Essex Belchamp St Pauls Barn (Tyers and Hibberd 1993a)	6.34
Kent master sequence (Laxton and Litton 1989)	5.13
London Billingsgate BIG82 (Hillam 1992; Tyers 1996)	5.23
London Thames Exchange TEX88 (Nayling 1991)	5.48
London Mermaid Theatre THE79 (Hillam 1979)	5.34
London Fleet Valley VAL88/PWB88 (Tyers and Hibberd 1993b)	6.48
Beech reference data	
London Fennings Wharf FW84 Beech (Tyers forthcoming)	8.00
London Lafone St LAF96 Beech (Tyers and Boswijk 1996)	10.99
London Millennium Bridge City MBC98 Beech (Tyers 1999)	6.73
London Fleet Valley VAL88 Beech timber 13365 (Tyers and Hibberd 1993b)	7.41

reference chronologies from throughout Britain and elsewhere in Europe. This exhaustive checking failed to provide any dating evidence for these timbers.

ANIMAL BONE
Claire Ingrem

Most of the animal bones were found in post-medieval contexts, although some (especially fish) bones were recovered from medieval layers. When recording the bones, all anatomical elements were identified to species where possible except for ribs and vertebrae, which were assigned to size categories. Mandibles and limb bones were recorded using the zonal method developed by Serjeantson (1996). This produced a basic count of the number of identified specimens (NISP). The minimum number of elements (MNE) was calculated by adding together the most numerous left- and right-sided zones for each element. The minimum number of individuals (MNI) was estimated as the highest MNE score obtained from one side of the body. The presence of gnawing, butchery and burning was also recorded. Measurements were taken according to the conventions of von den Driesch (1976) and

Table 1   Correlation between the beech composite sequences made from each trench at the Tower, t-values calculated using the CROS algorithm of Baillie and Pilcher (1973)

Trench group No of samples And dates	Trench 27 24 samples 1150–1240	Trench 31 30 samples 1132–1277
Trench 25 12 samples 1126-1276	6.92	13.17
Trench 27 24 samples 1150–1240		7.30

compared with data held on the Animal Bone Metrical Archive Project (ABMAP) at the University of Southampton. The wear stages of lower cheek teeth were recorded using Grant's method (1982). Age attribution followed Payne (1973) and Halstead (1985). The fusion stage of post-cranial bones was recorded and age ranges estimated according to Getty (1975).

All fragments representing less than 50% of a zone, but over 10mm, were counted. Where possible these were ascribed to size categories and noted as either long bone, vertebral or skull fragments. Those fragments categorised as large mammal are likely to be from cattle and horse. Medium-sized mammal fragments probably represent sheep/goat and pig. For this reason they have been included in the count of identifiable fragments. Despite careful analysis using the methods of Boessneck (1969) and Payne (1985), no bones were positively identified as goat. Elements assigned to the sheep/goat category have therefore been treated as sheep.

Fish bones were identified with the aid of the comparative collection at the University of Southampton. All fragments which could be identified to species or family level were recorded. Indeterminate fragments, including ribs and fin rays, were not quantified. Where possible elements were ascribed to a side of the fish. The MNI calculation is based on the most frequently occurring element from one side of the body. Size was categorised visually as very small (less than 150mm), small (150–300mm), medium (300–600mm), large (600–1200mm) and very large (1200–c2000mm).

ENVIRONMENTAL EVIDENCE

It was clear from the earliest days of planning the excavations that environmental archaeology would be crucial to the success of the moat project. Such studies had not formed a part of any of the past excavations in the moat, but such evidence as was available from the photographs and drawings demonstrated that waterlogged soils should be present in the lower levels at least. Drs Richard Macphail, Mark Robinson and Rob Scaife took part in the planning and execution of the excavations from 1995 onwards, helping to devise soil sampling strategies and often carrying out the sampling themselves during their regular site visits. Subsequently Dr Nigel Cameron joined the environmental team, working especially closely with Rob Scaife, while Dr John Crowther collaborated with Richard Macphail during the post-excavation stage.

As anticipated, sediments of high environmental potential were present in many of the trenches and pits, large and small. Indeed, the potential was often demonstrable with the naked eye in the case of larger (macroscopic) plant remains and mollusc shells, though the microscopic remains of, for example, pollen and diatoms had to wait for laboratory testing before the potential could be confirmed. Rich sequences of environmental evidence were recovered from each of the major periods encountered in the moat from the mid-13th century onwards, continuing through into the late 18th to early 19th centuries. The greatest potential was clearly concentrated in the largest excavations (trenches 25, 27, 30 and 31), especially as these traversed the whole width of the moat, and the greatest environmental effort was concentrated on these during the fieldwork (Fig 24) and in the subsequent specialist analyses. Several of the smaller trenches and even the test pits also contained sediments of obvious environmental potential, however, and samples were taken from these wherever and whenever merited. The following sections describe the specialists' methodologies.

Macroscopic plant and invertebrate remains
Mark Robinson

Sequences of samples were taken from the water-lain and dumped clay sediments for analysis of macroscopic plant and invertebrate (mollusc and beetle) remains where they had been exposed in the major trenches (25, 27 and 31) and from many of the smaller excavations in various locations. Laboratory analysis showed that the plant remains (seeds etc) and molluscs were generally well preserved as a result of waterlogged and calcareous conditions respectively. The number of Coleoptera (beetle) fragments was insufficient for general interpretative purposes but some useful results were obtained for some species that live in close association with humans or their structures. Useful results were also obtained for caddis fly (Trichoptera) larval cases and pupae/puparia of flies (Diptera).

Long column sequences of samples were taken from trenches 1, 27 and 31 (Figs 25–27). Shorter sequences or individual samples were taken from trenches 2, 6, 13, 14, 16, 25, 37 and 39. In each case, 150g of the sample was washed through a stack of sieves down to 0.2mm and sorted in water with the aid of a binocular microscope. The macroscopic biological remains recovered were identified and the results given in Robinson (1995) and Robinson (1998). A total of 53 samples were analysed.

Pollen
Rob Scaife

There have been few pollen studies carried out on the sediment fills of moats. This is perhaps because of the complex taphonomy of pollen coming from different sources (both natural and of secondary origin) and the problems caused by the periodic cleaning out of sediments. However, given that there are often waterlogged sediments remaining even where sites have been backfilled, moats can have enormous potential for the study of environmental change over the past 1000 years. The few studies previously carried out have demonstrated that useful information can be gained from pollen analysis of such sediment fills, especially when related to other

Fig 24 Drs Richard Macphail (left) and Mark Robinson taking soil samples in trench 27 during 1996 for subsequent laboratory analysis. The examination of the past environment in and around the moat was a major aim of the excavations.

environmental studies. For example, pollen and plant microfossil studies of the moat of Hampton Court Palace elucidated the character of the local parkland and gardens and the tree species planted locally as well as the more regional vegetation (Robinson 1996; Scaife 1996). Evidence for local vegetation changes has also been forthcoming from the study of the moated manor at Yaxley Manor Farm, Cambridgeshire (Scaife 1990).

Column and individual samples were taken for pollen in trenches 1, 2, 6, 27 and 31, and all of these were assessed. Preliminary analyses of the sediments demonstrated the preservation and marked diversity of pollen and spores present (Scaife 1995a). Subsequently, full pollen analysis has been carried out on sections A (trench 27, Fig 25), C (trench 31, Fig 27) and D (trench 6). It was anticipated that analysis of sub-fossil pollen and spores would provide data on

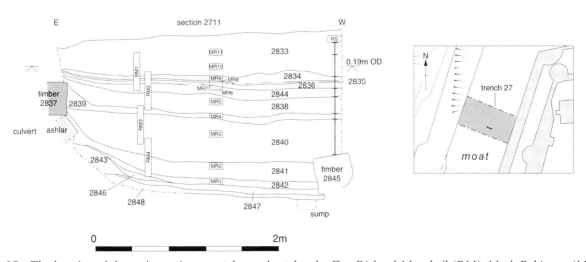

Fig 25 The location of the main environmental samples taken by Drs Richard Macphail (RM), Mark Robinson (MR) and Rob Scaife (RS) in trench 27.

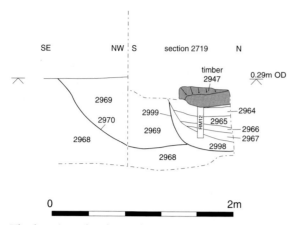
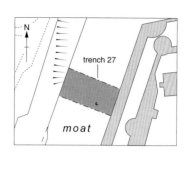

Fig 26   The location of soil sample 12 taken by Dr Richard Macphail in trench 27.

the local environment of the Tower. This would include exotic plant introductions (gardens?), regional vegetation, local vegetation growing in and around the moat, possible evidence of water input from the Thames and human food resources from faecal and domestic debris disposed of in the moat directly or via garderobes.

Samples were taken sequentially from the faces of excavation trenches either directly or by using overlapping plastic monolith samples (100mm by 100mm by 500mm or 750mm). Pollen and spore extraction and concentration followed those procedures outlined by Moore *et al* (1991) but with the addition of micro-mesh sieving (10μ) for removal of the clay fraction. Samples were decalcified with 10 per cent hydrochloric acid and deflocculated with 8 per cent potassium hydroxide. Coarse debris was removed through sieving at 150μ and clay by micro-mesh (10μ). Remaining silica was digested with hydrofluoric acid. Erdtman's acetolysis was carried out for removal of cellulose. The concentrated pollen and spores were stained with safranin and mounted in glycerol jelly.

Pollen was identified and counted with an Olympus biological research microscope equipped

with Leitz optics and phase contrast facility at magnifications of × 400 and × 1000. A pollen sum of 400 grains per level was counted where possible plus extant spores and miscellaneous palynomorphs, dinoflagellates and *Pediastrum*. Taxonomy used follows that of Stace (1991) for plant names and for pollen, generally that of Moore and Webb (1978) and Moore *et al* (1991) and modified according to Bennett *et al* 1994. Data obtained are presented in standard pollen diagram form (Figs 58, 108 and 143) with percentages calculated as follows:

Sum = % total dry land pollen (tdlp)
Marsh/aquatic = % tdlp+sum of marsh/aquatics
Spores = % tdlp+sum of spores
Misc. = % tdlp+sum of misc. taxa

All of the pollen profiles exhibit a very diverse range of taxa, including herbs, shrubs and trees. The herbs are markedly dominant, primarily through grasses and cereals. The trees and shrubs also show a substantial range of taxa, but in many cases occur only sporadically. Pollen zonation is not especially distinctive because of the substantial degree of homogeneity caused by herb dominance. Nevertheless, pollen assemblage zones have been drawn

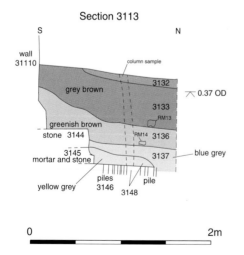
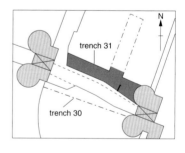

Fig 27   The location of the main soil samples taken by Drs Mark Robinson and Rob Scaife in trench 31.

based on the inherent changes in the microfossil content, both of the pollen and also algal *Pediastrum*, and derived palynomorphs. These changes are also clearly linked to changes in the stratigraphy and sediments, and thus the depositional environment.

Diatoms
Nigel Cameron

Diatoms are microscopic algae (plants) that live in water and are characterised by their ornamented silica shells (frustules). They grow as single cells or in groups, which may be living in the water (planktonic), attached to submerged surfaces, or mobile in and on underwater surfaces. After the death of the diatom, the shells are often preserved in the sediments of ditches, ponds, lakes, rivers and coastal or oceanic sediments. There are many thousands of species, and their characteristics are dependent upon water quality factors such as the level of acidity, phosphate (eg, from sewage inputs) and salinity. The range of species present can provide important information on water quality and other aspects of the past environment.

The purpose of applying diatom analysis to sediments from the moat was to reconstruct past water quality, with particular reference to qualitative reconstruction of broad salinity levels and quantitative reconstruction of total phosphorus (TP). In the latter case, few attempts have been made so far to reconstruct aquatic nutrient levels on archaeological sites (Cameron 2000a, 2000b). It was also hoped that the diatom habitats, source communities and the quality of valve preservation would assist in other aspects of environmental reconstruction for the site.

A pilot study was carried out on six sub-samples from a sediment sequence retrieved by Dr Scaife during core sampling in 1998. The samples were found to have a high quality of diatom preservation. Diverse floras were present, suggesting that diatom analysis would make a major contribution to the study of the past environment. Therefore a rapid assessment was made of diatoms from 37 sub-samples from three pollen columns (sections A and B from trench 27, and section C from trench 31) collected by Dr Scaife and the excavation team during 1996. Diatoms were again well preserved and concentrated in many of the sub-samples from sections A and C, and these sections and levels were selected for more detailed analysis. Section B contained only a single valve of *Thalassiosira* sp., however, so no further analysis was carried out.

Diatom preparation and analysis followed standard techniques. Slides were counted using a Leitz research microscope at magnifications of × 1250 or × 1000 under phase contrast. Approximately 125 diatom valves per sample were counted in order to make the best use of available resources. This sum is low, especially where the diatom assemblage is diverse, but it was adequate and allowed the maximum coverage of samples for diatom-based environmental reconstruction. Where necessary,

diatom identifications were confirmed using diatom floras and taxonomic publications held in the collection of the Environmental Change Research Centre (ECRC), University College, London. The floras most commonly consulted were Cleve-Euler (1951–1955), Hendey (1964), Hustedt (1930–1966) and Werff and Huls (1957–1974). The principal source of data for species ecology used was Denys (1992).

Diatom species' salinity preferences were classified using the halobian groups of Hustedt (1953; 1957, 199):

1. Marine (polyhalobian).
2. Brackish (mesohalobian).
3. Brackish to fresh (oligohalobian-halophilous), optimum in slightly brackish water.
4. Freshwater (oligohalobian-indifferent), optimum in freshwater but tolerant of slightly brackish water.
5. Exclusively freshwater (halophobous), intolerant of brackish water.
6. Unknown salinity preference.

Diatom groups are indicated above the percentage diagrams and the water (halobian) group composition is summarised at the right-hand side of each diagram.

Diatom-based total phosphorus (TP) reconstructions were carried out using a Europe-wide diatom-TP training set (Bennion *et al* 1996). The program TRAN was used to harmonise diatom taxa in the moat fossil assemblages with those in the diatom-TP training set. The program CALI was used to model the diatom-TP data; modelled species data was $\log_{10}$ transformed and an inverse regression was used. Simple weighted averaging was used to reconstruct total aquatic phosphorus.

Sediment micromorphology, particle size, chemistry and magnetic properties
Richard Macphail and John Crowther

The study of sediments in thin section is a standard technique in geology (Reineck and Singh 1986). A number of reconstructions of past environments based upon soft sediment and anthropogenic deposit analysis have also been carried out in an archaeological context. Databases relevant to the Tower moat include those on intertidal sediment deposition and ripening (sub-aerial weathering), alluvium, and anthropogenic materials, such as building debris and coprolitic wastes (Kooistra 1978; Courty *et al* 1989; Macphail 1994; Bell *et al* 1999). In addition, floor deposits and underlying ripening Thames sediments at the Rose Theatre, Southwark (Macphail nd) provided a local sedimentary comparison for this study.

The moat sediments were studied to complement the stratigraphic and other environmental investigations. The methods employed were soil micromorphology on undisturbed monolith samples and particle size, chemistry and magnetic susceptibility assays on bulk samples. These were used to gain additional insights into the character of the sediments, their origin and mode of formation, and to identify any post-depositional transformations that may have occurred over the centuries. Samples were taken by Dr Macphail on four occasions (19 August, 3 September, 1 October and 11 November 1996). Work concentrated on trenches 25, 27 (sections A and B; Figs 25–6) and 31 (section C; Fig 27). Thirteen undisturbed monolith samples varying in length from 80mm to 400mm were collected, alongside 25 bulk samples from the contexts sampled by the monoliths. All samples were assessed through phosphate and magnetic susceptibility analyses in 1996/7.

During 1999–2000 25 bulk samples and 15 thin section samples selected during the assessment were processed in order to investigate 25 archaeological contexts. The laboratory investigation comprised two different approaches, namely analysis of bulk samples and investigation of sediment (soil) micromorphology of undisturbed moat deposits in thin section. The approaches focused upon recovering standard geoarchaeological data and information specifically pertinent to a study of moat sediments that could have been influenced by brackish river flow. Analysis focused on the following properties, most of which are routinely determined in archaeological site investigation.

Calcium carbonate ($CaCO_3$): The London Clay contains relatively little carbonate, and the latter's occurrence in this environment is likely to reflect deposition of carbonate from water entering the moat. The River Thames, for example, contains quite high concentrations of dissolved carbonate derived primarily from chalk within its catchment. Other potential sources include fragments of mollusc shells and/or mortar used in building construction. Soil pH is also an important indicator. In a moat environment higher pH values are likely in carbonate-rich or saline sediments. Soil pH (1:2.5 in water) and carbonate content (by calcimeter) were determined using the methods presented by Avery and Bascomb (1974).

Specific conductance: This provides an indication of the concentrations of soluble salts present. Higher values could indicate periodic inundation of the moat by sea water. Specific conductance was measured on the soil solution used in the pH analysis.

Loss-on-ignition at 375°C (LOI): This is used to provide an approximate measure of the organic matter concentration within the sediments. High LOI figures might be attributable to inputs of organic-rich sediments (eg, cess or organic topsoil) or to plant growth and decay within the moat. LOI was determined by ignition at 375°C for 16 hours (Ball 1964). Previous experimental studies have shown that there is no significant breakdown of carbonate at this temperature.

Total phosphate (phosphate-P): Phosphates are present in all organic material (plant tissue, excreta, bone, etc). They tend to form insoluble compounds when released by organic decomposition processes, and thus become 'fixed' within the mineral fraction of soils and sediments. Phosphate enrichment in sediments is therefore normally indicative of substantial organic inputs (see Hamond 1983; Bethel and Máté 1989). Relatively high concentrations of phosphate-P in the moat sediments might be associated with cess inputs. Phosphate-P was assessed by alkaline oxidation with NaOBr (Dick and Tabatabai 1977).

Particle size: This provides an indication of the nature of the sediment sources and depositional environment. Silts and clays are associated with low-energy (generally slow) water flows, whereas sands are associated with deposition under higher energy conditions (faster water flow). Measurement was carried out by the pipette method.

Magnetic susceptibility (low frequency mass-specific magnetic susceptibility, χ): This largely reflects the presence of magnetic forms of iron oxide (eg, maghaemite), and is dependent on the occurrence of iron and alternating reduction-oxidation conditions that favour the formation of magnetic minerals. Enhancement is particularly associated with burning, but is also caused by microbial activity in topsoils (see reviews by Clark 1990; Scollar et al 1990). χ_{max} is a measure of maximum potential magnetic susceptibility, determined by subjecting a sample to optimum conditions for susceptibility enhancement in the laboratory. In general it will tend to reflect the overall iron concentration of a sample. χ_{conv} (fractional conversion), which is expressed as a percentage, is a measure of the extent to which the potential susceptibility has been achieved in the original sample, viz: $(\chi/\chi_{max}) \times 100.0$ (Tite 1972; Scollar et al 1990). In many respects this is a better indicator of magnetic susceptibility enhancement than raw χ data, particularly in cases where soils or sediments have widely differing χ_{max} values (Crowther and Barker 1995). A Bartington MS1 meter was used for magnetic susceptibility measurements. χ_{max} was achieved by heating samples at 650°C in alternate reducing and oxidising conditions. The method used broadly follows that of Tite and Mullins (1971), except that household flour was mixed with the soils and lids placed on the crucibles to create the reducing environment (after Graham and Scollar 1976; Crowther and Barker 1995).

Lead (Pb), zinc (Zn) and copper (Cu): Enrichment with heavy metals is likely to be associated with human activity, particularly with industrial waste. Measurements were achieved by atomic absorption spectrophotometry.

The 15 thin section samples (listed as A–T) were impregnated with crystic resin, cured, cut into blocks and manufactured into 75mm by 50mm thin sections (Murphy 1986). Soil micromorphology employed standard description methods (Bullock et al 1985). Plane polarised light (PPL), crossed polarised light (XPL), oblique incident light (OIL) and ultra violet light (UVL) were used as recommended by Courty *et al* 1989 in order to aid identifications and interpretations. For example, slides were scanned under UVL to search for fine bone and calcium phosphate-cemented coprolites. The micromorphology of each context was analysed to produce a microfabric type based upon descriptions and counts (Tables A3.7 and A3.8, Appendix 3).

Features and inclusions were grouped as indicative of the following factors:

Sedimentary composition	clay, silts and clay and calcitic (finely (less than 10µm) crystalline micrite, pellety micrite and more coarsely (10–50µm) crystalline micro-sparite).
Sedimentary feature type	laminated (bedding), massive and heterogeneous (mixed material).
Included natural materials	pyritised wood (relic of the London Clay), clasts of gypsum introduced from some distance off-site (reworked grains), coarse mollusc shell (eg, bivalves more than 0.5mm), ostracods and detrital organic matter.
Included anthropogenic materials	grouped as anthropogenic inclusions (including coarse wood charcoal, bone, likely coprolitic yellow stained bone, and nodules of cemented charcoal, ash and bone with vivianite) or grouped as mortar (including coarse-grained mortar, finer grained plaster and associated glauconitic sandstone and limestone fragments).
Biological activity	roots and root traces, root channels, very thin (less than 100µm) excrements and earthworm features (biogenic calcite, calcite granules, broad (more than 2mm) mammilated excrements).
Secondary mineral formations	gypsum (calcium sulphate), pyrite (iron sulphide), vivianite (iron phosphate) and secondary iron hydroxide as impregnative staining, void hypocoatings and organic matter replacement.

Dominant features were assigned a value on a frequency scale (after Bullock *et al* 1985, 23), and those which occurred in small amounts were assigned a value on a scale of abundance (ibid, 112). Such semi-quantitative estimations were only made after considerable time had been spent studying the thin sections so that no important soil microfabric types, inclusions and pedofeatures (*sensu lato*) would be missed during counting (Acott *et al* 1997; Simpson 1997; Ponge 1999). Other uncounted aspects described are, first, sandy clasts natural to the London Clay, second, fine carbonaceous spherules indicative of high-temperature burning of charcoal and fossil fuels and, third, detrital organic matter that is indistinguishable from natural detrital organic matter but a likely component of which is cess.

Chapter 4: Period 1: The Mid-13th Century (Henry III)

INTRODUCTION

It is conventional in archaeological reports to describe excavation in sequence, starting with the earliest remains to be discovered and working steadily forwards in time towards the present day. This is particularly appropriate for the Tower moat, because the earliest features and structures were also by far the most important for our understanding of how the castle and its defences developed through time. These discoveries were largely fortuitous, and certainly unexpected, although at least they were the result of the carefully devised programme of investigations described in Chapter 3. As we have seen, the initial trial trenching in 1995 had been designed to fit in with the hand auger transects. These had been laid out on a regular pattern around the moat, with the main sample rows spaced at 100m intervals. One of the transects happened to be in the middle of the west moat; the locations of trenches 1 and 2 were therefore fixed relative to this (Fig 22). The main aims of the two trenches—as with most of the others dug in 1995—was simply to assess the moat fills and examine the foundations of the defensive walls around its sides.

As with all of the larger excavations, the sides of trench 2 had been stepped in at a depth of 1.2m, and the presence of service cables at the east end of the trench further constrained the work. Indeed, deeper excavation was restricted to an area of c3m (east-west) by 1.6m and the early results were only mildly promising: the lower moat fills contained few finds but there seemed to be better potential for environmental archaeology. Even so there was a slight but quite distinct sense of disappointment on all sides with what we were finding. We should have known better: it is a truism among archaeologists that the best and most exciting discoveries are always made at the very end of an excavation, usually when there is little or no time (and money) left to deal with them.

So it proved in 1995, when masonry was discovered roughly 3m down at the bottom of trench 2 in the last few days of that year's intended excavation season (Fig 28). The stonework was exceptional, both in terms of its quality and its preservation, but its position was the most surprising thing of all. It lay underneath all the fills in and the cut for Edward I's moat. It therefore self-evidently pre-dated that King's extension of the Tower's defences from 1275 onwards. Of course, the limited nature of the excavation meant that we could see only a very small part of what was likely to be a substantial structure. Even so there was a general consensus that the masonry probably belonged to the earlier 13th century because of the building stones and techniques used. There was also complete

agreement that a much larger excavation was needed if we were to make proper sense of the discovery. Initially it seemed likely that this could happen straight away in 1995 under the terms of the existing Scheduled Monument Clearance. That year, however, was also the 50th anniversary of Victory in Europe (VE) day, the celebrations for which included a major event at the Tower. A massive marquee had to be erected in the west moat during the summer—and an enlarged excavation was scarcely compatible with this.

Accordingly trench 2 was backfilled in 1995, and the various parties to the project withdrew to consider the excavation strategy in more detail. Thus an application for Scheduled Monument Clearance was submitted in spring 1996 for a new trench (27) spanning the full 38m width of the west moat. The intention was to expose the whole of the masonry if at all possible and to see whether there were any other features associated with it. The known depth of the masonry from ground level dictated that at least two steps would be needed along both sides of the trench, which would take up 4.8m in all. The masonry building was fully exposed in the initial stages of excavation, but it soon became clear that we were dealing with substantial areas of timberwork as well. What was perhaps even more of a surprise, however, was the existence of a massively deep moat to go with the structures. All three elements—stone, timber and moat—underlay Edward I's moat, as we had seen in 1995. In the end the excavation bottomed out at approximately 5m from the existing grass level. Three steps had to be cut, and the excavation therefore ended up being 18m wide. The excavation strategy evolved gradually throughout 1996/7 in consultation with Historic Royal Palaces and English Heritage to take account of the emerging evidence for the pre-Edwardian stratigraphy.

It subsequently became apparent that more elements of the earlier moat were present in several other trenches as well. Once again most of these discoveries were unexpected and in trenches being dug with other aims in mind. An extension to the north of trench 31, for instance, had been intended to examine the bottom of Edward I's moat and the possibility that the Roman riverside defences might be encountered here. The earlier and deeper moat was found instead, along with more timberwork. Trench 81, in the north-west arm of the moat, was designed to examine Edward I's outer curtain wall and also to look for a well documented post-medieval weir across the moat. This structure was not found, but the north edge of the earlier moat was discovered underneath its late 13th-century successor. Ultimately we were able to build up a consistent

Fig 28   The upper, Reigate course of masonry exposed in the base of trench 2 in 1995.

picture of a previously unsuspected element of the Tower's early defences from these three trenches. The dating of the timberwork and masonry has been established with reasonable certainty on a number of grounds, but the origin of the moat is less clear. These issues are discussed in detail below.

Inevitably the pre-Edwardian discoveries were not only an exercise in archaeological practice but also the subject of extensive historical research. Students of the Tower are fortunate in having an exceptional range and quality of documentary evidence for the site. This is to be found in primary sources such as the Liberate and Pipe Rolls, which present a relatively dispassionate account of expenditure, as well as in contemporary chronicles, which provide more partial but equally important witness to events. Even in 1995 it was apparent that certain events in the reign of Henry III offered a possible and

plausible context for the archaeological discoveries. In particular, well-known entries in the Great Chronicle (*Chronica Majora*) of Matthew Paris described a sequence of catastrophic events that befell Henry III's work on the defences at the Tower in 1240/1 (Parnell 1993, 34). Historical research therefore concentrated on this period both while the excavations were still in progress and afterwards. Eventually there was a remarkable conjunction of the two strands of evidence, centring on the absolute dating method of dendrochronology. Some of this evidence has been rehearsed in print already (eg, Impey 1997), but this chapter presents the data in full. The early moat is described first, with masonry and timber structures being considered thereafter. The historical research by Jeremy Ashbee and Dr Edward Impey is fully integrated with the archaeological analysis.

STRATIGRAPHY OF THE MID-13TH-CENTURY MOAT

The junction of the moat with the river Thames: evidence from trench 31 (north extension)

Trench 31 had been excavated primarily to examine Edward I's south-western entrance causeway, but in the later stages of work here it became apparent that important evidence for the earlier moat was present as well. This was especially so in the northern extension dug during 1997. Meanwhile work in the centre of the original trench also provided very important information on the pre-Edwardian topography of the Tower. In this case, though, the data related more to the river Thames and its foreshore than the earlier moat (Fig 29).

The highest point at which the natural London Clay was identified lay 9.6m north of the 1270s causeway, where the clay (31180) was found at −0.65m OD. Some 4m to the south of this (ie, moving towards the causeway), the clay (31174) lay at −1.1m OD, evidently having sloped slightly downwards in the intervening distance. The surface was level at this point for 1.5m southwards, at which point it sloped down at a shallow and irregular angle for 2.3m to a depth of −1.8m OD, where the foundations of the Edwardian causeway cut into the clay. This was interpreted as the original edge of the Thames foreshore.

As we have seen, the highest level for the clay was −0.65m OD, but immediately to the north of this point it was truncated by a cut (31207) that sloped down at an angle of 60° to form a slightly undulating base at −1.75m to −2m OD. The cut itself was excavated only within the very narrow confines of the northern extension's lowest level, which hampers detailed interpretation. Nevertheless it appeared to be linear, running east–west, and the bottom certainly continued beyond the northern limit of the excavations (ie, towards trench 27). For reasons which will become apparent this was interpreted as

the southern end of the same moat revealed in trench 27 (see below).

The undisturbed London Clay (31210) between the moat cut (31207) and the sloping edge of the Thames can be seen as a natural bank separating the two. Unfortunately, detailed investigation of the alignment and characteristics of the southern edge of the bank could not be undertaken because of truncation by a Victorian feature. Five timbers (31211–5) were identified on the north edge of the bank, however, in an east-west orientation. Four of the timbers (31211–4) were roughly circular unconverted beech tree piles, set at 0.4m centres. All four retained their bark and dendrochronology samples were taken. The fifth timber (31215) was a small oak stake, rectangular in shape, set between piles 31211 and 31213; this was unsuitable for dendrochronology sampling. The beech samples were all dated to the year 1240/1 and share a similar age-range, between 45 and 60 years (see Fig 30).

The London Clay (31174) of the Thames edge was overlain by a deposit of grey silt and gravel (31226) sealed in turn by redeposited natural clay (31225). This only extended 0.4m into the trench and was 0.44m thick. A deposit of mixed silty clay (31224) containing fragments of limestone and chalk filled the remaining depression in the natural at the southern end of the northern extension. This silty deposit was covered at its southern end by a layer of what appeared to be redeposited London Clay (31223). This extended for 0.9m where it became a considerably more silty clay (31221) over the rest of the southern sondage to a level of −1.02 m OD. Two clay deposits (31173 and 31222) filled the trench to a level of −0.65 m OD. These layers seemed identical to foreshore deposits identified in the south moat in 1996. Similar material had been seen during an excavation against the exterior of Henry III's inner curtain wall in Water Lane immediately to the west of the Salt Tower (Parnell 1983b, 97).

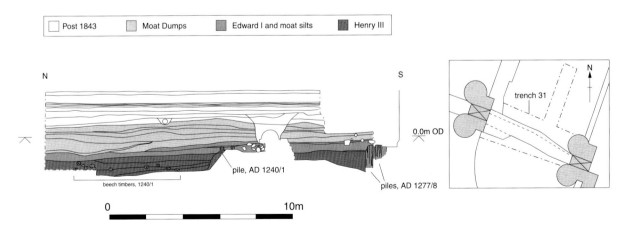

Fig 29   The eastern section of the northward extension of trench 31, showing the sequence of layers in the Henry III and Edward I moats.

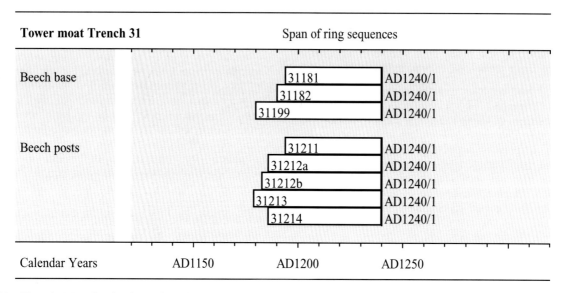

Tower moat Trench 31   Span of ring sequences

Beech base	31181 AD1240/1
	31182 AD1240/1
	31199 AD1240/1
Beech posts	31211 AD1240/1
	31212a AD1240/1
	31212b AD1240/1
	31213 AD1240/1
	31214 AD1240/1
Calendar Years	AD1150 AD1200 AD1250

Fig 30   Trench 31 – dendrochronology bar diagram showing the dated position of mid-13th-century samples. All the bars are beech.

A single residual sherd of Roman pottery was found in layer 31222, but the most important finds came from contexts 31223 (SF230; Fig 31) and 31224, where the remains of two turnshoes were recovered. Each had been deliberately cut to salvage re-usable leather and are thus likely to be cobbling debris. They were of mid- to late 13th-century date, consistent with the stratigraphically pre-Edwardian position of these contexts.

The moat in trench 27

The natural fissured London Clay (2997, 8011 and 8044) had been cut away (8052) to a very significant depth (Figs 32–3). The cut formed two sloping edges or banks approximately 9m apart (8022 and 8024); these were 1.3m deep and sloped at 30° to form a 5.6m-long flat base at −2m OD. The cut extended flat for 8m from the west bank (8024) at −0.6m OD.

The London Clay was sampled for soil micromorphology analysis in two places in trench 27 (Figs 25–6). It was a very poorly calcareous (0.62 per cent carbonate) clay (3.8 per cent sand, 36.8 per cent silt, 59.4 per cent clay) with very low organic matter (2.54 per cent LOI) and total phosphate (0.544 mg g^{-1}) contents. It had a moderately high magnetic susceptibility (44.6 × 10^{-8} m^{3}kg^{-1}) and high

χ_{conv} (20.4 per cent). In thin section J it was yellowish brown (plane polarised light), massive with fine bedding, and uni-strial b-fabric (crossed polarised light). The silt and sand were composed of very dominant (more than 70 per cent) quartz, with very few (less than 5 per cent) mica, glauconite and opaque minerals (eg, limonite). In addition, a few coarse 0.4mm by 0.8mm rounded nodular concretions of black pyrite/pyritised wood (brassy under oblique incident light) were present. Many fine to coarse (80–800µm) secondary lenticular and septaric crystal growths of gypsum impregnated the pyrite nodules and clay matrix. The pyrite supplied sulphur for gypsum formation. One source of copper would be decomposing organic matter and shell in brackish river water (Kooistra 1978; Bullock *et al* 1985). Gypsum is present locally in estuarine sediments below the Rose Theatre.

A borehole from the south bank of the Thames found London Clay at −5.35m OD, beneath 5.6m of Terrace Gravels, 0.88m of fine alluvium and 2.27m of made ground (top at 3.4m OD). Described as a very stiff closely fissured grey brown clay, the London Clay includes small (15mm by 5mm) pockets of partly pyritised fine sand, fine sandy and silty partings and lignite. Dr Jackie Skipper has also noted the presence of silts, fine sands, pyrite and

Fig 31   Leather shoe of turnshoe construction for the left foot comprising sole, rand, one-piece upper and heel stiffener. Sole complete, torn in two across the waist, with pointed toe, medium tread, waist and seat. Worn through at great toe, centre of tread and exterior seat. Edge/flesh seam around perimeter. Tunnel stitching on grain side to attach clump repair pieces to forepart and seat. Four fragments of rand. One-piece upper, much of right side and seat area torn away. Throat and top edge have been cut away so that the style of the shoe is unknown. Lasting margin double stitched at waist from repair. Leather worn calfskin. Small triangular heel stiffener whip stitched to the interior at centre back, top edge also cut away. Sole length 275mm, width at tread 94mm and at waist 42mm. Adult size 7, size 9 with 10% allowance for shrinkage. SF 230, context 31223.

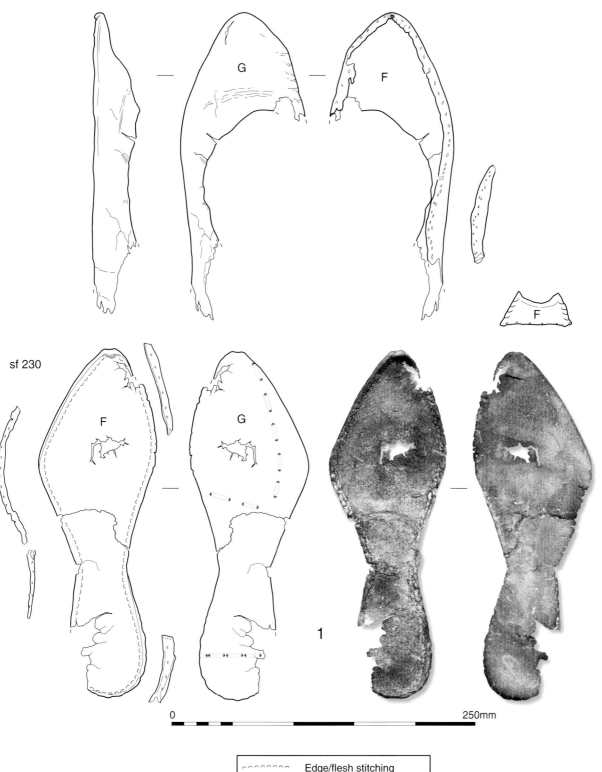

sf 230

1

0   250mm

∩∩∩∩∩∩∩∩	Edge/flesh stitching
○ ○ ○ ○	Grain/flesh stitching
←→ ←→	Tunnel stitch
⊤⊤⊤⊤⊤⊤	Whip stitch
⊩⊩⊩⊩⊩⊩	Whip stitch for attachment of strengthening cord

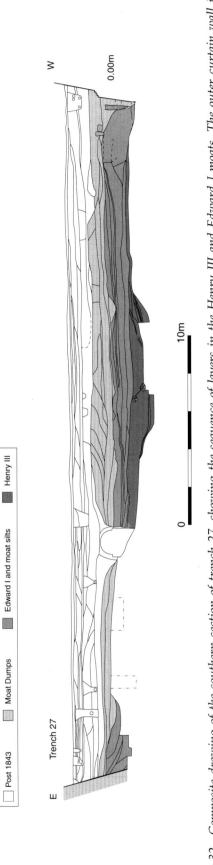

W

0.00m

10m

0

Trench 27

E

□ Post 1843 ▨ Moat Dumps ▨ Edward I and moat silts ■ Henry III

Fig 32 Composite drawing of the southern section of trench 27, showing the sequence of layers in the Henry III and Edward I moats. The outer curtain wall is to the left, and the revetment wall to the right.

gypsum in the London Clay. The descriptions of field exposures are consistent with the findings from the moat (Bone 1999; Skipper pers comm).

The London Clay at the base of Henry III's moat was silt-rich clay containing fine sand pockets and pyrite. The particle size and chemistry of this geological substrate influenced the character of the moat sediments. For example, the gypsum that is found in the sample of London Clay and the redeposited London Clay of the coffer dam (below) is a breakdown by-product of pyrite, the latter being a source of sulphur (Bullock *et al* 1985). Silty clay moat sediments at the Tower probably originate from reworked London Clay, while the presence of gypsum in such deposits also seems to lower pH but raise specific conductance. Reworked London Clay, for example, seems to have strongly influenced medieval sedimentation in Edward I's moat (Chapter 6) and sediment formation after works in 1680 at the Iron Gate causeway (trench 25; *see* Chapter 7).

A possible early moat cut in trench 81

Trench 81 was excavated in the north-west arm of the moat in May 1997 to identify the supposed position of a documented 18th-century batardeau or weir within the area. The trench was 4.8m wide and 13m long (north–south), running up to the outer curtain wall at its south end. The weir was not found, but a possible north edge for the early moat was located at the base of the excavations instead. The *in situ* London Clay was identified at *c*0.8m OD in the centre of the trench. At the south end, however, the clay had been cut away by a substantial feature (8138) that sloped down to −0.59m OD before being removed in its turn by the foundation trench (8149) for Edward I's outer curtain wall (Fig 34). Feature 8138 therefore demonstrably pre-dated the 1275–81 extension of the castle's defences.

Several fills were recorded within the early feature, mostly consisting of clays including variable amounts of gravel. One of the middle fills (8148) contained a high proportion of organic material (40 per cent) and a single sherd (13g) of London-type ware with a date-range from the mid-12th to the early 14th centuries. This was the only potsherd recovered (by hand excavation) from the lower levels of this trench, and it is significant given that the feature obviously cannot post-date the 1270s. It therefore seems likely that feature 8138 was the outer edge of the northern arm of the moat already revealed in trenches 27 and 31. Unfortunately, it is abundantly clear that the majority of the northern part of the feature—whatever its date and nature—must have been removed by the foundations for Edward I's outer curtain wall.

The early moat: who created it?

When was the earlier moat dug out, and on whose orders? At first sight it seemed reasonable to suggest

Fig 33   View of the central area of the southern section, trench 27. Compare this with Figure 32. Note the clear change in the nature of the moat fills half-way up the scale on the lowest step in the excavation, marking the interface between the Henry III and Edward I moats.

that the feature was at least broadly, and perhaps absolutely, contemporary with the structural remains found in trench 27. This could not be anything more than a hypothesis, however, as there was no absolute proof (or indeed disproof) in purely archaeological terms. Stratigraphically the masonry and timber structures overlay or were dug into the same natural London Clay that formed the bed of the earlier moat, and so technically one could say that the former post-dated the latter. This is of little use to us because there is no time value in archaeological stratigraphy: in other words the structures might post-date the moat, but the time lag could be a matter of hours, days or many years. The observed relationship was more to do with sequence than time as such. The remarkable dendrochronology results from the beech timbers in trenches 27 and 31 (*see* below) provided a very clear latest date (*terminus ante quem*) for the excavation of the earlier moat, but they could not give us an earliest date. Other finds were of limited value because there were so few of them, but the single London-ware sherd from trench 81 at least suggests that the ditch could not have been dug any earlier than the mid-12th century.

Excavations in the 1960s and 1970s showed that William the Conqueror's White Tower sat within a defensive enclosure formed by the old Roman city defences on the east and south sides, and by newly dug ditches on the north and west (Parnell 1983a). The area thus enclosed is notably small given the massive scale of the great keep itself, and this has led

to some suggestions that there might have been an outer defensive work as well (Parnell 1993, 19; Impey and Parnell 2000, 16). No hard archaeological evidence for this has been found to date, but there are some historical references which might support the hypothesis. Those relating to the Chapel of St Peter ad Vincula have already been mentioned (Chapter 1), but there are others referring to the overall area under the Tower's jurisdiction—what became known as the Tower Liberties.

There is a fairly substantial body of information from the 12th century which suggests that even then the influence of the Tower of London stretched beyond the immediate enceinte of the castle to encompass the local area. Whereas in the 14th century (and perhaps slightly beyond) some of the focus of this seems to have been on the western side of the fortress, the earlier evidence rather indicates contested land ownership on the northern side. This is most manifest in a long-running dispute between the Tower and the Priory of Holy Trinity Aldgate over the possession of land within the *soke*, defined as the territory of a pre-conquest institution, the *Cnichtengild*. We read about appropriations of land by early *custodes* of the Tower, and of churches and ecclesiastical benefices by the Tower's chaplains. As early as 1128–34 the Tower authorities were urged to 'do justice to the canons of Holy Trinity concerning the parish of Saint Botolph of whom Dermannus the priest of the Tower [*sacerdos de turre*] has unjustly deprived them' (Hodgett 1971, 191).

A few years later, in 1136–7, a plea *coram rege* was entered between the Prior of Holy Trinity Aldgate and the castellan of the Tower of London over the possession of land in the *soka appellata Englysch-knyctengylda*. Othuer, *quondam regie turris custos* (formerly custodian of the King's Tower), had allegedly appropriated by force a part of the land in this soke from the possession of the church. *Aschuillus etiam successor Otheri in turris custodia eandem partem vi tenuit* (Aschuillus, Othuer's successor as custodian of the Tower, also held this area by force). Aschuillus was evidently the *custos* some time in Henry I's reign (after Othuer's death in 1120), but the case was only resolved under Stephen, during a hearing in Westminster. Aschuillus, evidently still in post, was called to give evidence. The dispute was decided in favour of the church (Cronne and Davis 1968, 189).

There are further references later in the 12th century, but perhaps an early 13th-century one is more telling. This document purports to be the definition of the boundaries of the *soke* as granted by Queen Matilda in the 12th century (Hodgett 1971, 2 and 228–9), but some of the topographical terms evidently relate to early 13th-century tenure. *Preterea sciendum est quanta sit ista soka cuius fines tales sunt: a porta de Algate usque ad portam Ballii Turris que nuncupatur Tungata et tota venella vocata Chykenlane versus Berkyngchirche usque ad cimiterium* (Furthermore, be it known that the size of the soke is this and that these are its boundaries: running from the gate of Aldgate to the gate of the bailey/bailiwick of the Tower which is called *Tungate* and all along the lane called Chicken Lane towards All Hallows Barking as far as the cemetery). The name *Tungate* is interesting, while the reference to the All Hallows cemetery, if taken at face value, would suggest that the Tower's influence stretched out to the westernmost extent of the later Liberties even at this early date.

None of this is conclusive evidence of the castle's earlier extent, as the jurisdictional area need not have been the same as the physically defended one. There are only two likely historical contexts for an extension of the defences, if William had not created an outer enclosure of some sort. One is the documented attempt by William Longchamp to establish or improve the castle's moat at the end of the 11th century (Fig 35). Matthew Paris states that Longchamp's work did not succeed because the inadequate sluices failed to retain water at low tide (Parnell 1993, 25). One may doubt whether the work was as unsuccessful as Paris suggested, but it seems unlikely that the deep moat found in trenches 27, 31 and 81 could ever have suffered problems of retaining water irrespective of sluices. The other historical context is the extension of the castle's defences by Henry III in the middle decades of the 13th century. This seems more plausible given the overall extent of the discoveries during 1995–7, and it is considered in detail below.

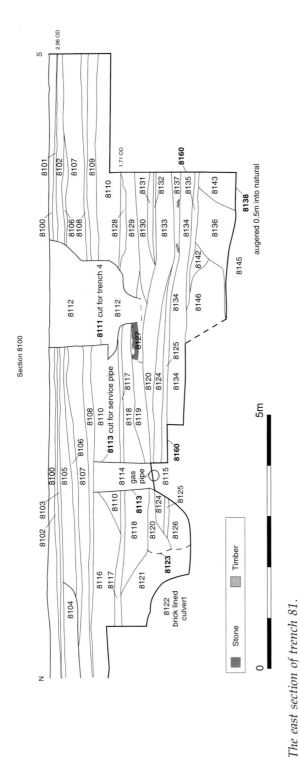

Fig 34 The east section of trench 81.

52

Fig 35 An aerial view of the Tower of London from the south west, as it might have looked following the improvements of 1190 and 1192–3. The castle has still not expanded eastwards beyond the Roman city wall, or encroached on the river, but has taken in new land to the west. Surviving elements of Longchamp's work include the Bell Tower at the south-west corner and a stretch of curtain wall to the east. (Painting by Ivan Lapper, with advice from Beric Morley.)

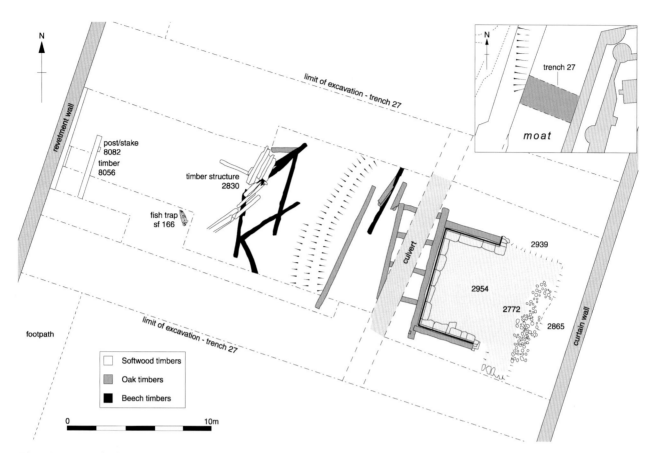

Fig 36   General plan trench 27, showing the relationship of the Henry III structure to Edward I's outer curtain wall. The 13th-century oaks and beeches are shown in tone and black respectively. The post-medieval timbers against the revetment wall and the softwood raft are shown in white.

THE MASONRY STRUCTURE AND ASSOCIATED TIMBERWORK

The discovery of a previously unsuspected masonry structure in trench 2 during 1995 led on to the excavation of a much larger trench (27) in the centre of the west moat during 1996/7 (Figs 36–7). This exposed not only the full extent of the masonry but also numerous oak and beech timbers. Many of these were structural and related to the masonry, but

Fig 37   General view of the masonry structure in trench 27 under excavation in 1996. Note the horizontal water level relative to the sloping masonry.

others had more to do with the last days of the building. The results of the excavations were extremely complex and fully justified the time and effort expended. The following description and discussion move successively through the evidence for the construction of the building, its purpose and the sequence of and reason for its abandonment.

The construction cut on the east edge of the moat

A construction trench (2939, 2970 and 2996) had been cut into the London Clay on the eastern side of the moat and a substantial masonry structure (2954) erected within it. The construction trench was seen in three sondages. The cuts to the north and south were nearly vertical and up to 1.6m deep. The trench to the west had been cut at 45°. Together these provided a flat base for the structure's foundation. This base seemed to be covered with a raft of rubble comprising a 0.12m-thick mix of tenacious brown clay with 50–60 per cent limestone rubble (2952). This appeared to form a foundation raft for a timber framework (2951) and limestone structure (2954). There was no question of attempting to excavate beneath the great mass of the masonry (*see* below), so the raft could be observed only around the edges of the structure. Nevertheless angled and horizontal probing with metal rods for 1m or more did not reveal any more substantial foundation course or material around the edges of the building. Equally significantly, there was no evidence for piles having been inserted below the masonry.

The masonry structure

The masonry structure (2954) lay between 2.75m and 3m out (west) from the outer curtain wall and at a slight angle to it. The main part of the structure formed a square, with 6.85m-long sides (Figs 38–9). It survived to a maximum height of 1.6m, with the upper surface lying at 0.24m OD. The north-east and south-east corners both turned outwards, creating an irregular 'T' shape. The southern return extended for a further 1.7m beyond the face of the building, while the northern return extended for only 0.75m.

The structure consisted of two basic elements: a Kentish Rag rubble core, with ashlar facing (Figs 40–41). The ragstone (2872) seemed to have been poured in distinct rises or courses; at least four such bands were evident where the corework was exposed at the ends of the two corner extensions (Fig 41). The stone was bonded with a grey/white lime mortar (2871) containing shell and angular gravel inclusions, and was of regular size throughout the core (pieces normally 250mm by 220mm by 8mm). There were four courses of ashlar surviving fully on all three faced sides (the north, west and south; the east side had been built into the clay bank). A fifth course survived only on the south face.

Two stone types had been used (Figs 40–41). The bottom three courses consisted of grey-blue Purbeck marble (2870). The ashlar blocks ranged in size from 0.54m to 0.85m in length and 0.15m to 0.18m thick and had been expertly laid to give only the slightest of gaps between stones all round. The interstices had been bonded with lead. They had been hand-cut or sawn and retained vertical combing marks in virtually perfect condition. The lowest of the three Purbeck courses was chamfered; this stopped against the two corner returns, both of which used exactly the same materials as the main block and in the same course beds. None of the upper faces of the Purbeck blocks was visible in the main structure as they were all overlain by further coursework. The end blocks of each course were exposed at the termination of the corner returns, however, and empty cramp holes were present on the second and third (but not bottom) courses. The holes were 240mm long, 40mm wide and up to 50mm deep. They suggested that most of the masonry had been cramped together for solidity.

The upper two courses of ashlar consisted of green Reigate stone (2869), providing a stark contrast with the grey-blue Purbeck in two distinctive bands (Figs 40–41). The Reigate courses comprised very large blocks, ranging from 0.85m to 1.1m in length and from 0.5m to 0.65m thick. However, the same vertical combing was observed as on the lower courses. The basal Reigate course was chamfered like the lowest Purbeck, but in contrast to the latter the Reigate course turned and continued onto the two corner extensions. The original extent of this chamfer is unknown as no Reigate courses survive on either of the returns, but the cramps on the corner blocks suggest that it was meant to continue onto the extensions. Indeed, all the exposed blocks had cramp holes (Fig 42). These had suffered noticeably more erosion than their Purbeck counterparts, a reflection on the relative hardiness of the two stone types. The Reigate cramp holes were 230mm long, 40mm wide and up to 50mm deep.

Once again lead bonding (SF 138) was observed between the Reigate blocks in the upper courses of the structure, while irregularly shaped fragments of lead (SF 67) were also recovered. Lead was occasionally used as a jointing compound in medieval structures, poured between the masonry blocks; it made strong joints and set instantly (Alexander 1996, 231–4, fig.17.13), but critically it provided a water-tight joint. Lead can be seen in many of Edward I's structures (eg, St Thomas's Tower and the south face of the south-western entrance causeway, both originally exposed to the Thames). The irregular fragments were probably used to secure the iron cramps to the masonry blocks.

The oak timber structure and its relationship to the masonry

Structure 2951 consisted of 11 large oak timbers integrated at the east end into the construction of the masonry building 2954 (Figs 38–9, 43–8). The existence of a twelfth timber can be assumed both

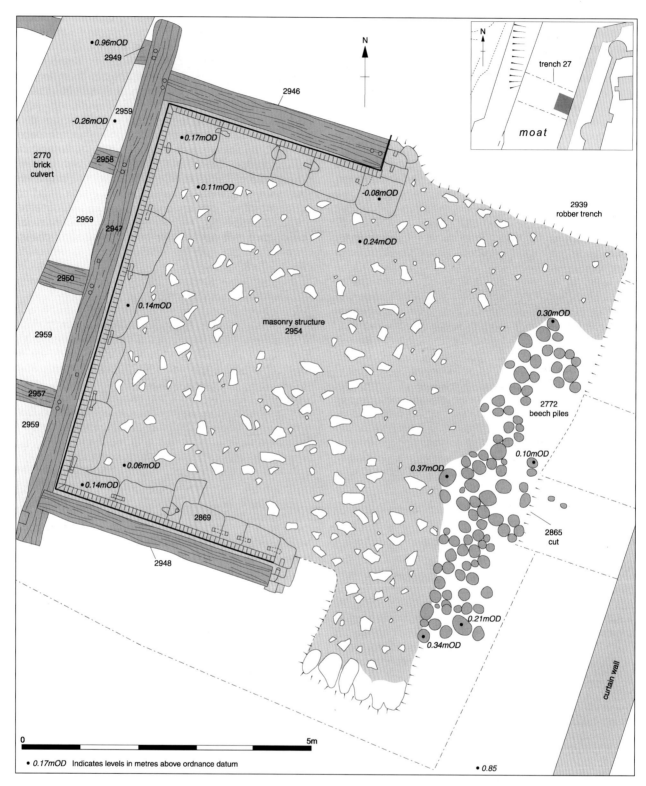

Fig 38   Detailed plan of trench 27: the Henry III masonry structure and associated timbers to the east of the culvert built in 1843–5.

circumstantially and from the presence of voided jointing. The structure in its excavated form was approximately 11m long (east–west), while two complete transverse timber plates (2845 and 2947) defined a width of 8.9m. All the timbers were of boxed (squared) cross-section with a typical scantling of 0.31m.

Two east–west timbers (2946 and 2948) had been jointed by double-pegged mortice and tenons to the east face of transverse plate 2947. These three timbers

Fig 39   The east end of trench 27 viewed from the top of Edward I's outer curtain wall. The square base of the Henry III masonry is clearly visible, with the stub-like projections at the bottom left and right corners. The three oaks which surround the main structure can be seen emerging from the water, with the cross-members continuing westward until cut away by the brick culvert which runs across the top of the photograph. The beech piles against the east side of the masonry run across the bottom of the picture.

formed a frame around the three sides and flush against the faces of masonry structure 2954 and sat within the construction trench surrounding it (Figs 38–9). Indeed, the rubble raft was visible under the northern and southern timbers (2946 and 2948; Figs 40–41). The east ends of these had been seated beneath the coursed stone returns at the north-east and south-east corners respectively of the masonry structure and were thus obscured. A mortice had been cut in the outward face of each timber immediately west of the returns (Fig 43). This suggests that the design intention had been to extend the timber frame outwards parallel with the masonry returns. The mortices were empty, however, showing that this had not been achieved. There was no sign that they had ever been used since the peg-holes remained empty with no evidence for pegs having been drilled out or broken. The evidence for the seating of the oaks under the returns was crucial, because it established beyond doubt that the masonry and timberwork were part of a single, unified building campaign. It would have been virtually impossible to insert the timbers after the masonry had already been built.

The west face of transverse plate 2947 was joined to a further four east-west timbers (2949, 2950, 2957 and 2958) at 2m intervals although originally there would have been five. The southern timber was missing, but a void mortice was found in its place (Figs 38–9). It may have been removed when the culvert was inserted into the moat in 1843 (*see* Chapter 10); certainly the four remaining oaks had been interrupted by the culvert. They were again joined to plate 2947 by double-pegged mortice and tenons. At their west ends the four longitudinal beams were also tenoned and pegged into a second transverse plate, 2837, the southern end of which has been cut away by the culvert (Figs 44–5). The northernmost beam, 2949, had withdrawn halfway from its original position within the mortice and the oak pegs securing the joint had sheared.

A further mortice was found almost opposite this on the west face of plate 2837. In this instance half of a tenon remained *in situ* within the mortice. The tenon had broken from timber 8001, which lay detached to the west, aligned north to south (Figs 44–5). The two timbers would have met with a chase-mortice and tenon designed to join beam 8001 to the transverse plate at an angle of 45°. Timber 8001 would thus have extended north west externally away from the main ground-frame. A second and identical chase-tenoned beam (8002) lay 0.5m to the west of 8001. It was also detached from its mortice in the east face of a third transverse plate (2845; Figs 44–7), but here the mortice had been ruptured as the tenon broke through its upper 'lip'

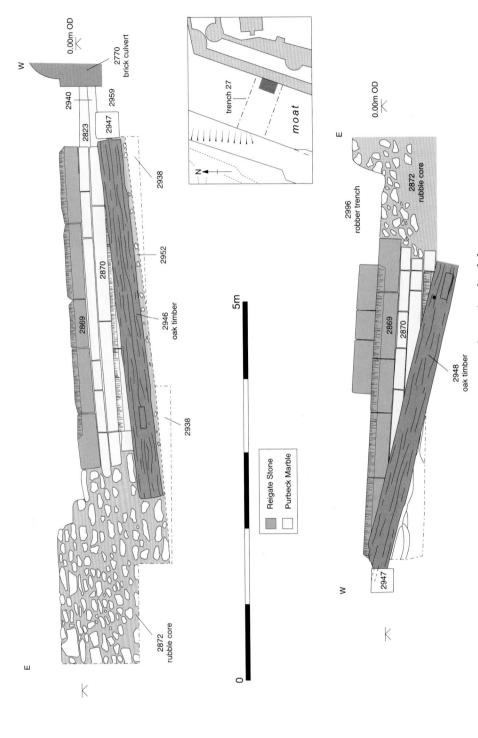

Fig 40 The north (upper) and south (lower) elevations of the Henry III masonry and associated oak beams.

Fig 41   The north elevation of the Henry III masonry. The bottom three courses are in Purbeck Marble, with a chamfered Reigate course above. Three Reigate ashlar blocks, all that survived of the fifth course, can be seen on the far side of the structure. Note that the oak beam along the northern face is seated under the northern projection. The latter's coursed Kentish Rag core is also apparent. The beech piles seen on Figure 38 can also be seen on the left of this photograph. Note Edward I's outer curtain wall rising behind the piles.

(Fig 48). A chase-mortice was also cut at the southern end of 2845, again in the east face and similarly intended for a timber extending externally, but to the south, at an angle of 45°. This and a presumed equivalent chase-tenoned timber at the (lost) southern end of plate 2837 were not present within the confines of the excavation. There were five empty and apparently unused mortices in the west face of transverse plate 2845 (Fig 47), closely paralleling the positions of the five mortices in plates 2837 and 2947 (and the timbers lining them).

The area between the small oak cross-beams and the two north–south beams had been filled in with yellowish white mortar and Kentish ragstone (2959). This formed an even if slightly rough surface. Like the masonry and the main timber frame, this rested on the clay and limestone raft.

Timber selection

At a little under 9m long (just under 30ft) and 0.3m thick the transverse plates were large timbers but would certainly not have been the largest available to the King in the 13th century (Salzman 1997, 238). Ideally they would have been cut from straight-grained oaks from which the soft and beetle-prone sapwood could be removed. The joints would be cut directly into the tough heartwood. The two western

plates, however, had been cut from relatively knotty and curved trees that could not be squared by saw for their whole lengths without giving way in part to sapwood and the 'wane' (the rounded outside part of the tree). Several of the mortices had been cut beneath slender and deficient sections of waney sapwood. In the case of the north-eastern chase-mortice of soleplate 2845, this had sheared, setting free the chase-tenoned timber 8002 (Fig 46). In contrast, the four mortice-and-tenon joints on the east side of transverse plate 2947 had been cut into full sections of heartwood and have survived the trauma intact.

This might suggest a 'use what you can' approach, but other features indicate a more careful selection of the timbers to be employed. Fast-grown oaks were used, for instance, and such trees are acknowledged as making stronger timber. This may have been a desired and even requested quality, especially in the context of the type of structure being erected (*see* below). Unfortunately such a selection can be frustrating archaeologically because fast-grown timbers are notoriously difficult for dating by dendrochronology.

There is also some evidence that the timbers were not used in their freshly cut 'green' state. The sapwood of timbers 2837, 2950 and 2958 showed some limited signs of woodworm, which would have

Fig 42   Detail of the cramp holes between two of the Reigate blocks.

Fig 43   Detail of the oak beam embedded under the northern return wall.

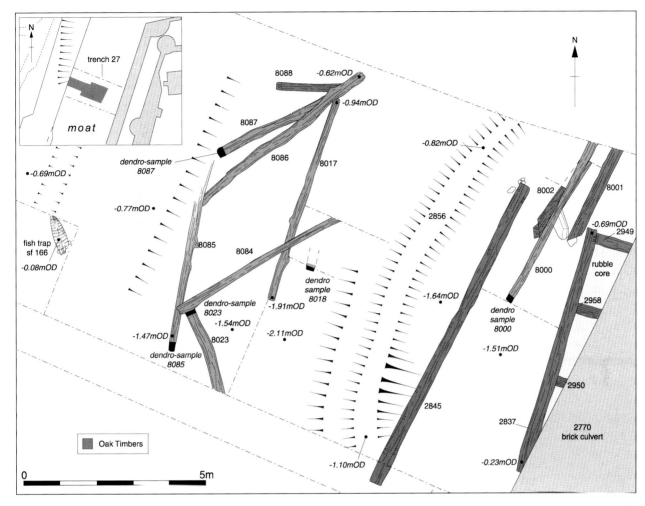

Fig 44 Detailed plan of trench 27: the Henry III timberwork to the west of the culvert, also showing the location of the late medieval fish trap.

occurred between the death (felling) of the tree and its submergence below water. This, together with the presence of shakes or drying splits along the grain, which occur when oak is left to season, suggests that the timbers had been laid up after felling and were waiting to be used. The use of seasoned oak is also a quality which could have been specifically requested for its added strength and because the tendency of oak to warp and distort as it 'seasons' can add an unknown and unwanted quantity to green-oak construction (Salzman 1997, 239). The degree to which such timbers would have warped at the bottom of a moat may, however, have been negligible.

There were many fine cut-marks on a single surface of several of the timbers (2837, 2947, 2949, 2958 and 2950). These were very fine (50–120 mm long) and occurred in concentrations, with some on timber 2950 being curved. Assuming that these timbers had been stockpiled at a timberyard it is possible that they had been used as temporary work surfaces, when the use of axes and knives could have resulted in these marks.

Conversion

Where tool-marks were visible, it was clear that all surfaces of both the outer sides and the inner parts of the tree had been sawn. The marks show different directions of sawing from each end and indicate the 'see-sawing' style of conversion commonly practised in the 13th century (Goodburn 1992, 114). Two of the shorter timbers (2950 and 2958) had been squared into quarter-sections, probably enabling more than one timber to be created from a single section of tree. The long transverse plates, however, had been sawn to a boxed heart, which would have been necessary in order to counter the curves of the tree.

The southern ends of two transverse plates, 2947 and 2845, both showed axe-marks cutting two opposing faces at approximately 45° to the main stem of the timber. This is almost certainly the direct result of the felling of the tree and the jagged break of 2947 shows that it fell, or was pulled over, when a substantial portion of the tree remained uncut.

Fig 45   The oak timbers and unconverted beeches to the west of the 19th-century brick culvert. Three of the empty mortices can be seen just above the water in the nearest oak beam, with the curving bank of redeposited clay immediately in front of it. The single empty mortice and the diagonally-butted oak which fitted into it can be seen at the top left, just in front of the culvert.

The joints

All the mortices of this structure conformed to the standard practice developed by this date of cutting broad tenons to the full width of the timber itself with their thickness being approximately one third of the timber's section. The use of the chase-mortice in the lateral plane is interesting since it is normally employed upright to join a brace to a baseplate or other member. Its use suggests that it was expected

Fig 46   A block of Purbeck Marble ashlar, originally part of the Henry III structure but found embedded in the silts at the bottom of his moat. The block is upside-down, but the chamfered upper surface can just be seen at its bottom right-hand corner. Note also the 45° angle of the external face, critical to our interpretation of the superstructure of the Henry III masonry. The keel moulding can also be seen on its left-hand side. The block lies between an unconverted beech on the left and one of the diagonally-butted oaks on the right; note the latter's broken tenon.

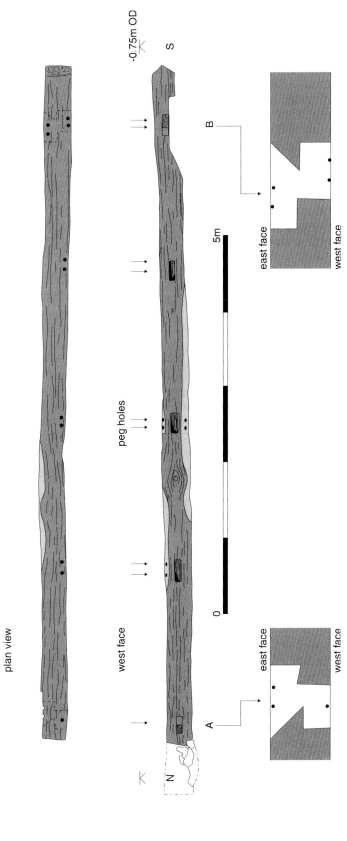

Fig 47 Plan and west elevation views of oak beam 2845 with details of the angled mortices at either end.

Fig 48   Oak beam 2845: detail of the ruptured mortice at the north end of the east face.

to resist only the north-south flow of the tidal moat waters.

The backs of the mortices bore the marks of first having been augered with a spoon bit at both ends of the joint and then blocked out by axe or other hewing and levering tools. The pegholes showed the reverse in that they were first marked out square with a chisel before being augered. The positions of the mortices were marked on the upper surfaces of the timbers by groups of three or four parallel axe-chops before they were cut. Although the mortices themselves were not cut in the upper surfaces, the markings were directly in line with them. They could not have marked out the position of further mortices for the upper surface as this would have rendered the timber too weak. There were three mortices in the west face of the western transverse plate 2845 that had been begun and not completed. These were probably the aborted first attempts at cutting the joints before the design and the interval of the adjoining timbers had been finalised.

Two unusual rectangular 'pegs' were found, one each in the upper surfaces of plates 2837 and 2845. They were tightly inserted midway along the timbers and measured 80mm by 30mm. Their upper surfaces were level with the main timbers and their function is unknown. They served no obvious purpose for the nearby mortices. It is possible that they derive from a period of lying in the timberyard, waiting to be used.

THE NATURE OF THE STRUCTURES (ABUTMENT OR TOWER?) AND THE FORM OF THE BRIDGE

The evidence from the masonry and timber structures

There is no doubt that the masonry and timber structures were planned together, and any interpretation of them must necessarily take account of this. The disposition of the oaks and especially the lack of evidence for a timber superstructure rising from them demonstrates that the timberwork does not conform to the conventional method of spanning a castle moat, already well established by the mid-13th century (Rigold 1975). With no exact parallel for the structure from either moat or river bridges excavated so far, its form is open to interpretation. A construction more akin to that employed for the building of large river bridges is suggested here (*see* below).

Much the same can be said of the masonry, physically bonded as it was with the oaks. There are two main interpretations for the function of this building, though these are by no means mutually exclusive. There seems to be every likelihood that the stonework acted as an abutment where the oak base of the bridge met 'dry' land. At the same time it seems inconceivable that it could have been left as a simple abutment given its position on the inner edge of a moat surrounding one of the most important castles of the realm. It seems inherently likely that a protective gate-tower would have risen from it. This prospect is increased both by the combination of stones used in its construction and the fineness—even ostentation—of its finishing. It is scarcely conceivable that the polychrome effect of the Purbeck marble and Reigate stones was in any way accidental (*see* below), especially as they were so perfectly coursed. The continuation of the coursing onto the corner returns seems particularly important here. It is also notable that the building faced westwards towards the city, and this was the side of the defences upon which successive kings would choose to lavish the greatest expense. Henry III built the Coldharbour Gate and Beauchamp Tower on this side of the castle, for instance, while his son Edward I threw out the massive Lion Tower barbican in front of his own Byward and Middle Towers (impressive enough structures in their own right). In all these cases the major structures were characteristically more impressive in outlook and exterior finishing in comparison to the curtain walls to which they were attached, particularly in their use of top-quality ashlar dressings.

The core work also survived to a greater height towards the rear (east) of the structure, suggesting that it had risen further from the excavated level. Several stray blocks of ashlar (both Purbeck and Reigate) were found in the fills of the moat around the building, tending to support the contention that it had been planned as a tall rather than flat structure. Indeed several of the stray Purbeck blocks were chamfered, but the surviving chamfered course in the structure was clearly complete. These blocks must therefore have come from some other structural element, and it seems likely (though not certain—*see* below) that this was an upper element of a tower rising from the platform. The east edge of the building was largely hidden behind a line of piles associated with it. Despite this no evidence could be found for a masonry face on this side of the structure, and it seems probable that it had been terraced into the clay 'bank'. Clearly there must have been an east face to the masonry above this level if there had been a tower or similar structure above the base.

The projecting returns or 'wings' extending from the north-east and south-east corners of the stonework are enigmatic features. Once again it seems clear that they were incomplete. The empty cramp-holes in the upper two courses of Purbeck in each return certainly imply an intention to extend these courses outwards at least. The lower Reigate course was also supposed to turn onto the projections, complete with its chamfer. Curiously, however, the last stone in the bottom Purbeck course on each extension did not have cramp-holes. The relevant blocks were fairly tight to the edge of the foundation trench. Perhaps the projections would originally have stepped up over or even terminated on the edge of this trench. The void mortices in the external faces of oaks 2946 and 2948 scarcely help to clear up this picture, in that they imply an original intention to lay further timbers (admittedly of unknown length) to the north and south parallel to the masonry returns.

What purpose did those returns serve? This is perhaps the most difficult of the many questions relating to the discoveries in trench 27. They might have been the bases of stair turrets providing access to the upper levels of the putative tower. This was certainly the interpretation that gained the most immediate acceptance during the excavations. Alternatively, they may simply have been intended to buttress the structure or key it into the clay bank. There is no doubt that the building would have had to withstand many engineering forces, but most of these would probably have been around the vertical and/or east—west horizontal axes. The projections, aligned north–south as they were, would seem to be very poorly placed to counteract these, and so can perhaps be discounted as buttresses. Probably the most intriguing interpretation of all, however, is that

the projections were no more than the intended links into a planned curtain wall. In other words, the abutment and tower were meant to be part of and sit forward from an outer curtain wall pre-dating that of Edward I. If this was the case, the lack of any masonry extending to the north and south within the excavations (which admittedly were more restricted there) might suggest that such a plan was aborted at an early stage.

A further possibility is that the masonry 'returns' were associated with walls returning eastwards to the foot of the main gateway on the inner curtain wall, guarding a roadway between the two structures. This practical arrangement was arrived at in stages at Portchester. Twelfth-century examples are known at Framlingham (Suffolk) and Conisborough (Yorkshire), and from the 14th century at Alnwick (Northumberland) and Lincoln. At the Tower, the major question must be the position of the 'noble gate' described by Matthew Paris (*see* below), to which we are assuming it was linked. If this was on the site of the Beauchamp Tower, as suggested by Colvin in the 1960s, the defended causeway would either have been at a diagonal to the inner curtain or must have contained a right-angled bend. Such arrangements might have provided extra security, but they would have been architecturally clumsy. It is tempting to suggest that the 'noble gate' was in fact a little further north than the Beauchamp Tower, more or less due east of the barbican and linked to it by a straight causeway. If so, it is worth noting that the complex would have been almost directly aligned on the east–west Great Tower Street, facing it across the moat. Such an arrangement would have made it all the more imposing.

Turning to the bridge running west from the structure found in trench 27, the masonry would provide the stable ground off which a timber-framed bridge would be constructed. The usual medieval form would consist of trestles rising from baseplates laid at intervals on the base of the moat. Rigold demonstrated that this standard baseplate and trestle model for spanning castle moats was developed early in the medieval period and that there was very little variation from, or within, this formula throughout the period (Rigold 1975). The Tower moat structure varies from the model in many ways, the most obvious of which is the complete lack of mortices in the upper surfaces of the timbers from which a superstructure could rise to carry a walkway above. It seems inconceivable that the joints for this were yet to be cut when the timbers were placed in the moat, particularly in the difficult working conditions that must have prevailed in the moat even if temporary drainage schemes had been engineered. This is especially so as medieval timber-frame construction is known to have worked consistently from prefabrication in the timberyard.

It is clear from the intact empty mortices and pegholes of several of the timbers that the moat bridge remained unfinished. A reconstruction of the timber frame as far as it was completed would show a pointed 'cut-water' shape extending from both the north and south sides by means of angled timbers secured by chase-tenons. Such a shape is reminiscent of many medieval bridge pier bases with cut-waters to encourage the smooth flow of water between the piers.

At Kingston upon Thames the original late 12th-century bridge across the river was built on timber baseplates near the banks, and within rings of piles where the bridge was in mid-river. At least part of a 13th-century masonry causeway at Kingston was constructed, or retained, behind a large horizontal timber and piles (Potter 1991, 141). The latter form of construction is also seen at Hemington Fields (Leicestershire) on at least one side of a pier base, also in mid-river and dated to 1240 by dendrochronology (Cooper and Ripper 1994, 160). The horizontals at both sites have no joints from which a wooden structure could rise. The use of timber surrounds at the bases of these bridges when in mid-channel suggests that they performed a function of retaining the pier foundations and protecting them from the scouring action of the flowing water, perhaps both during and after construction.

It seems likely that this is at least part of the function of the Tower moat timber frame. It would also have had the effect of setting out the form of the structure with straight lines within which a masonry pier base could be built. A chamfered Purbeck marble ashlar block with an outer angle of 135° (Fig 46, and *see* below) was found in close association with the chase-tenoned angled timbers. This could support the hypothesis that the timberwork here was indeed intended to be a frame compartment of cut-water shape to accommodate a masonry pier. Some (or all) of the stray chamfered Purbeck ashlar blocks referred to above could perhaps have derived from such a pier. The Purbeck pieces could have belonged to the superstructure of the main masonry feature, as suggested below, but this would not invalidate the interpretation of the timberwork advanced here. The use of five longitudinal timbers linking the transverse plates and the anchoring of the frame to the masonry abutment suggest that these timbers were also to perform a structural role. However, with only two pairs of chase-tenons connecting the timbers around the proposed masonry pier base, the strength of this design is minimal.

A bridge design with masonry pier bases does not necessarily indicate masonry arches, while the oak frame at the base demonstrates that a timber walkway could easily span the gap between the masonry abutment and the proposed pier base. Such a combination of masonry pier and timber walkway is suggested for Mordiford Bridge in Herefordshire. Corbels just above the water level there indicate that angled timber braces may have originally supported the carriageway above (Cook 1998, 22).

The variations employed in spanning the moat at the Tower of London may stem from a combination of factors. Unlike most moats it was tidal, subject to flowing (if slow) water yet not to river traffic. In contrast to most river bridges, therefore, the interval between piers at the Tower moat would not have to accommodate bulky waterborne traffic. The design of short intervals, the first being approximately 3.5m, would allow easy timber construction without the use of braces (and presumably with a drawbridge at some point). The lack of traffic around the moat may also have enabled the eccentric inclusion of the baseframe with its longitudinal timbers connecting the pier to the abutment. The use of piles beneath bridge pier bases for stability (a 'staddle'), and around the edges (often around an outer platform or 'starling') to protect the masonry from the water's scouring action, is well known in the construction of early medieval bridges, including Old London Bridge (Cook 1998, 28). The addition of a large horizontal timber frame in conjunction with the piles, as seen at Hemington Fields and Kingston upon Thames when building in mid-river, may be a 13th-century variation. The omission of the piles from this formula for the Tower moat bridge may have been directly responsible for its downfall.

Consideration of the rubble raft

One related element of the construction remains to be considered: the rubble found between the oak beams immediately to the west of the masonry. The rubble had clearly been packed in after the timbers had been laid down, though it is much less clear when this took place. At first sight it would seem reasonable to suggest that there would have been little if any time-lapse between the two stages, and on balance this seems to be the most likely case. It must be admitted, though, that the rubble was found at the same height as the upper surface of the oaks in each of the 'bays' marked out between timbers 2837 and 2947 by the cross-members joining them. We will shortly see how these beams had suffered severe twisting and lifting stresses, however, and these place some equivalent strain on the interpretation of the rubble raft. Either it must have moved with the timberwork or it was inserted after the movement had taken place.

Two pieces of circumstantial evidence relate to this question, though neither of them necessarily solve it. Firstly, a block of Purbeck marble ashlar was found resting on the surface of the raft between timber 2947 and the Victorian culvert. Presumably this piece must have come to rest there during or after the problems suffered by the masonry. Secondly, there was a distinct gap between the oaks and the raft in places, similar in width to the displacement oak 2947 and the cross-member 2948. If anything, this probably supports the argument that the rubble was integral to the planning of the timber structure rather than a response to later problems.

Comparisons for the masonry

The large piece of Purbeck marble found between timbers 8001 and 8002, when considered in its structural context, defines a relatively simple feature: the corner of a building set at approximately 45°, at the level of a simple chamfered offset in its wall-face. The implications of this fragment for the reconstruction of the building, however, are considerable. Moreover, the stone also bears evidence for an earlier and quite different design.

On the lower face, the fragment bears a broad wave moulding, interpreted here as a keeled shaft left unfinished. In view of the use of Purbeck marble, this is likely to be a decorative detail for a project of very high status at a major church or palace—the stone may even not have been intended for the Tower. Architectural fragments excavated in the vicinity of Corfe (Dorset) have suggested that there was a local industry involved in the creation of finished mouldings before shipment to their final destination (Blair 1991, 41). It is therefore conceivable that this fragment was not intended for the Tower at all, but for one of any number of projects (particularly ecclesiastical) throughout the country.

The use of Purbeck does receive some mention in the documentation of the Tower, particularly in the instruction by a writ of *Liberate* issued on 28 November 1239 to the sheriff of Dorset, for the dispatch to the Tower of four shiploads. The same writ specifies that a mason had been sent from the Tower to Dorset to select the stones on site (*Calendar of the Liberate Rolls of Henry III, 1226–1240* (London 1916), p 433). A further shipload was ordered in August of the following year (ibid, p 488). In December of 1240, Henry III also ordered the keepers of the works to procure a 'marble' font for the Chapel of St Peter ad Vincula standing to 'marble columns, well and fittingly carved', almost certainly also in Purbeck (PRO C62/15/m19). The evidence that the Tower's mason was being selective about stone in 1239 should be set against the clear indication from other writs that the pace of work became more frenetic over the next two years. The use of a stone on which work had already started comes as little surprise.

The eventual use of the fragment, with the chamfers facing upwards and with sinkings for cramps on the upper faces, allows certain conclusions to be drawn regarding the structure from which it came. It was clearly a masonry structure incorporating chamfered offsets, either partly or wholly planned around an octagon or half-octagon. The similarity of tooling (vertical striation without claw) and of material (Purbeck marble) to the masonry of the main stone structure demonstrates unequivocally that the two were made at the same time. As pointed out above, it is possible to interpret the piece as a component of a bridge running westwards from the Tower towards the City of London. Nevertheless the favoured hypothesis here is that the fragment originated in the sub-square structure; this is supported by the identical tooling, materials and the profile of the chamfered offsets.

The function of this structure has proved controversial. It has been suggested, for example, that it formed the eastern abutment and landing of the bridge. However, several arguments would support a reconstruction as a larger element. These include its impressive dimensions (roughly a square with 6.85m-long sides) and the evidence for its having slumped and rotated out of its original position (*see* below). It was the opinion of Professor John Hutchinson (Emeritus Professor of Engineering and Geomorphology, Imperial College, London) that the evident displacement of the structure had been the result of an excessive weight being placed upon it. Such weight would be applied most convincingly by a tall masonry superstructure. For this reason, several graphic reconstructions by Edward Impey and by Ivan Lapper have shown the building as a tower.

Even before the excavation of the angled fragment, Beric Morley had suggested that a mid-13th-century gateway tower in this position might take a more elaborate form than a simple square plan. This took on particular significance in the light of Matthew Paris's comment in the *Chronica Majora* that the gate which collapsed in 1240 was 'noble' (Luard 1876, 80), though it must be acknowledged that this may be more of a literary *topos* than an architectural comment. Comparable architectural examples suggested at the time included the Water Tower at Kenilworth castle (not precisely dated but likely to have been constructed *c*1240) and the dams and main outer gatehouse at Caerphilly castle (conventionally dated to the later 1270s; Renn 1997, 13, 28–9 and plan). The method of placing a non-square superstructure (specifically in these cases a half-octagon) might vary between two solutions: either to construct pyramidal spurs projecting upwards (as at Caerphilly) or to taper the diagonal faces downwards to form points at the corners of the square bases. The latter form can be seen in numerous castles, including Dover (Colton's Gate and the Treasurer's Tower, partly rebuilt), Ludlow (Garderobe Tower) and Trim (West Gate; McNeill 1997, 24). Of the two types, the latter would have a comparatively early date range: none of the examples cited here is precisely dated, but all are likely to lie within the last quarter of the 12th century or the early years of the 13th.

It seems likely that the surviving masonry represents one of the lowest portions of the base, levelled off at some point before 1275. The attached oak timbers for the bridge structure seem to represent a level corresponding to the baseplates of the bridge piers, implying that the carriageway was situated at a considerably higher level. This makes it unclear whether the tower was square or polygonal at the point at which the carriageway ran through it. The examples of gateways from Dover and Trim cited above are both square at the level of the passage floor, only becoming polygonal at approximately the height of the springing of the arch. Such a design would perhaps be slightly archaic by the 1240s, but it would at least allow for a wider carriageway, ideally not much less than 3m. The maximum width of the base is 6.85m, allowing only limited space for the side-walls of the passage even without the narrowing that a change to a polygonal superstructure would impose.

As was observed from the surviving courses of the structure, and as was inferred from the architectural fragments located in the immediate vicinity, the structure was faced in two visually distinctive types of stone: Reigate stone and Purbeck marble. The chamfered fragment of Purbeck with an obtuse angle therefore has several important implications, principal among them being the possibility that the building was constructed with variegated horizontal bands of masonry. In other contexts, it has become common to interpret this as iconographic. By far the best-known example is that of Caernarfon castle, begun by Edward I in 1283 with walls incorporating bands of darker carboniferous sandstone against a ground of limestone. Arnold Taylor has famously suggested that this feature (and specifically its use on polygonal towers) constituted an architectural reference to the origin myth for the castle extracted from the *Mabinogion* and inspired (directly or indirectly) by the banded masonry of the Theodosian walls of Constantinople (*History of the King's Works*, 1, pp 368–71). However, the construction of castle walls in banded masonry is of a far longer pedigree: 12th-century examples can be found from the reign of Henry II at Dover (the lower storeys of the keep, under construction in the early 1180s) and Richard I at Château Gaillard (on the south-western bailey and the polygonal garderobe tower, built at great speed in the 1190s). One of the most accomplished essays in the genre was constructed at Angers in the second quarter of the 13th century by Louis IX of France, with multiple bands of light-coloured masonry in the round turrets of the curtain wall. It should also be noted that the motif is not confined to secular structures, existing in numerous churches well before the 1240s (as varied as the crypt of St Mary's church, Warwick and the Romanesque western façades of cathedrals in France and Italy, such as Arles and Ferrara).

If, as has frequently been assumed, horizontal banding of masonry was employed in the Middle Ages in imitation of a previous architectural practice, the most plausible suggestion is that it was inspired by the tile coursing visible in masonry walls of the Roman Empire. Without necessarily invoking the precedent of Constantinople, many large examples of banded Roman walling existed beside and even within the Tower of London during the early reign of Henry III. Examples can still be seen to the north of the Tower beside Tower Hill Underground station and inside the castle in the footings of the Wardrobe Tower. The hypothesis may be drawn that in the late 1230s these ancient walls were recognised as the work of a former great civilisation—the Romans or, conceivably in the 13th century, the Trojans, to whom the foundation of the Tower and the City of London was sometimes ascribed (Wheatley forthcoming). Henry III's masons may well have built their new work in horizontal stripes in an attempt to

harness some of the imperial associations to the King's cause.

EVIDENCE FOR STRESS AND COLLAPSE

Tilting and distortion

It was obvious that both the masonry and the timberwork had suffered severe structural problems. The stonework, for instance, did not sit horizontally within the excavation but sloped in two different planes (Figs 38, 40). This was most clear from west to east (ie back into the London Clay), where the structure dropped 0.3m in little more than 4m. There was also a slight tilt from north west to south east. This must have put great stress on the masonry and some distortion of the course beds was evident on the north face (Fig 40). These did not describe straight lines, but were instead distinctly bowed. This is particularly apparent in the Reigate course, but the same phenomenon can be seen in the upper course of Purbeck as well.

While the masonry exhibited clear enough signs of structural difficulty, the evidence from the timberwork was yet more dramatic. The frame of three oaks around the stonework had suffered even greater distortion, not least because the eastern ends of oaks 2946 and 2948 were so solidly locked underneath the corner returns. The junction of the northern and western beams (2946 and 2947) lay just above the bed of the middle course of Purbeck, representing a lift of approximately 0.2m in comparison with the coursing or, more dramatically, almost 0.5m from the horizontal. The western timber (2947) continued to rise, being virtually level with the top of the first Reigate course at the south-west corner (ie a further 0.5m lift). This understates the true extent of the problem, however, for the southern end of oak 2947 had clearly been truncated at a later date, perhaps during one of the periodic attempts to clean the moat out. The upper half of the oak had been cut away, completely exposing the tenon of beam 2948 within its mortice.

Similar lifting was evident in beam 2837, but at a lower level. Where oak 2947 sloped from −0.28m OD up to 0.22m OD at its southern end, the equivalent levels for 2837 were −0.69m and −0.23m OD. The latter height, admittedly, was at the point where the beam had been cut by the Victorian culvert rather than its south end, but the difference in levels is still clear enough. This had a knock-on effect for the four linking oaks, which thus sloped down severely from east to west (Figs 38, 44). Remarkably, most of the joints remained intact (if somewhat distorted), although as already noted the tenon of 2949 had been pulled almost clear of its mortice in 2837 and the pegs had sheared.

Perhaps the most telling evidence came from the two angled beams, 8001 and 8002, and their mortices at the northern ends of plates 2837 and 2845 respectively. As described above, half of the tenon from 8001 remained *in situ* within the mortice in 2837 with the remainder still on the beam. In the case of beam 8002, the tenon was intact but the mortice in the east face of plate 2845 had been ruptured as the tenon broke through its upper surface. Presumably this occurred before any timbers were set in the five void mortices in the western face of 2845.

An attempt to support the structure?

An attempt seems to have been made to support the east side of the masonry by driving 95 roundwood beech piles (2772) against it (Figs 38–9, 49). These ranged in diameter from 0.1m to 0.28m and had been driven in at raking angles from 5° to 20° down the back of the corework. Their tops had been sawn and the edges of most of the tops had been chamfered to prevent splitting during the pile-driving process.

Some had clearly been truncated at a later date, probably during one of the regular attempts to clean Edward I's moat. The piles were spread irregularly over a 5.6m-long (north-south) and 1.2m-wide area. This was not central to the eastern face of the structure, but was offset to the south. The southern-most pile aligned with the south face of timber 2948, while the opposite end lay 1.5m back from the north face of the masonry. A whitish fungal growth was recorded on about 10 per cent of the piles; this growth formed no spatial pattern but was most noticeable on the highest protruding piles. The piles were surrounded by a blue-grey gravel and lime mortar (2824/5) including 10 per cent limestone rubble.

Dendrochronology samples were taken from 19 of the piles (Fig 50), in four or five groups across to test both whether they were all of the same phase and if

Fig 49 Detailed view of beech piles 2772, seen from the south. The intact bark surfaces so crucial to the accurate dendrochronological dates can be seen clearly on several piles.

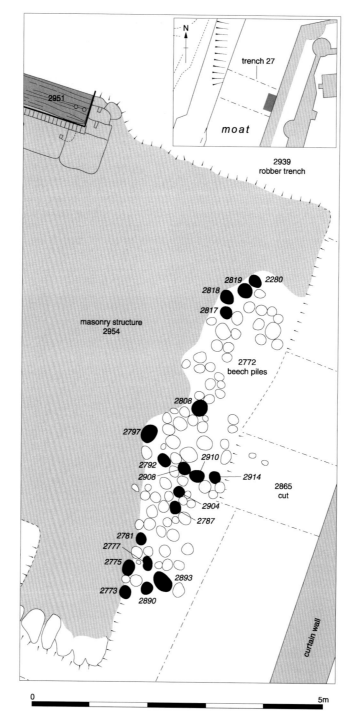

Fig 50   Plan showing the location of dendrochronological samples in the beech piles (2772).

groups of piles had been cut from the same tree. All of the samples were complete to the bark-edge and all included a ring for 1240 directly under the bark surface (Fig 51). This last ring appears to be complete, indicating that felling of these trees occurred in the winter of 1240/1. The trees were shorter-lived and faster growing than those used at the south-east corner of Edward I's moat a generation later; neither was the material as internally consistent as the latter

group (*see* Chapter 5), suggesting that a more diverse source of trees was exploited.

Rescuing materials? A possible coffer dam

The area between the Victorian culvert and the east side of the moat cut (8052, 'bank' 8022) contained a series of localised deposits. The earliest of these was a mortar floor surface (8090) lying at −1.55 OD.

Tower moat Trench 27   Span of ring sequences

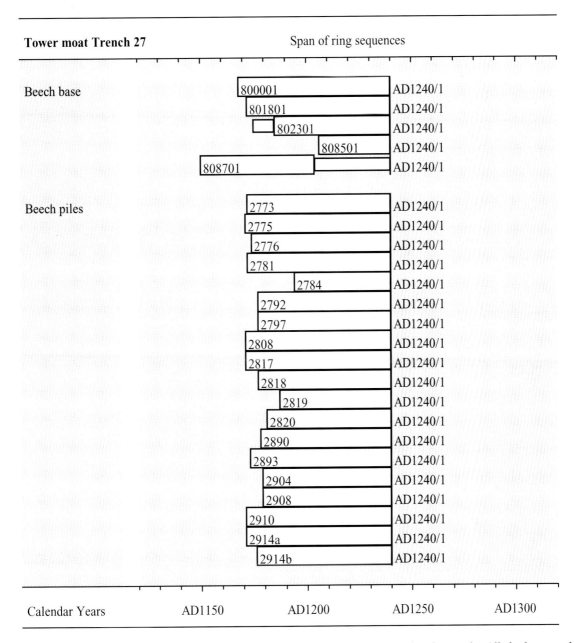

Fig 51   Trench 27 – dendrochronology bar diagram showing the dated position of each sample. All the bars are beech. Narrow bars represent counted but unmeasured rings.

The extreme waterlogging of the excavations made it difficult to examine this in detail. It was notable, however, that this floor provided a firm platform for the excavators to work on, in very distinct contrast to all the other 'soft' deposits in the base of the moat. Layer 8090 was between 10mm and 40mm thick and contained 20 per cent limestone pieces and occasional shell fragments. The extent was defined by timber 2845 to the west, while the floor extended c0.5m over the eastern bank.

The mortar floor was partially enclosed by a distinct bank of redeposited London Clay (2856; Figs 44–5) that extended virtually onto the east bank of the moat. The redeposited clay was extremely compact and of a slightly different colour (grey-brown) to the natural

material. It also contained fragments of degraded mortar and sand perhaps derived from 8090. The clay mound was 1.5m wide and 0.5m high. The remainder of the mortar surface was covered by a 40mm-thick layer of tenacious mid-brown to grey sandy clay (2848). Oak plate 2845 rested on this, and its southern end was abutted by the clay bank (2856). There was no stratigraphic link between the latter and sandy clay 2848 but their relative relationships with timber 2845 showed that 2848 must already have been deposited by the time the bank was established. It seems highly unlikely that any significant length of time had elapsed in the meanwhile.

The clay employed in the coffer dam was studied essentially micromorphologically. It was no different

71

from the natural London Clay substrate, although amounts of calcium carbonate, the loss on ignition and total phosphate were all slightly higher. On the other hand in thin section K the deposit was no longer a homogeneous laminated deposit but a heterogeneous one composed of fragmented London Clay elements (table A3.8, Appendix 3).

It seems likely that the mortar floor was broadly contemporary with the construction of the timber and masonry structures. It was similar in character to the foundation raft under the masonry and the rubble infill between the oak timbers. It is easy to imagine the benefits such a surface would have presented to the builders. Clay bank 2856, by contrast, clearly post-dated the construction campaign and appeared to be part of the response to

the problems being suffered by the buildings. The bank has been interpreted as a coffer dam, established to assist in attempts to keep the area around the masonry dry while attempts were made to salvage material from it. The discovery of several blocks of Purbeck marble ashlar in moat fills suggests that the dam was only partially (if at all) successful.

Moat fills and their relationship with further timbers

Trench 27 (Figs 32–3, 44–5)

The earliest moat fills lay against the sloping western bank (8024; *see* above) of the moat. These

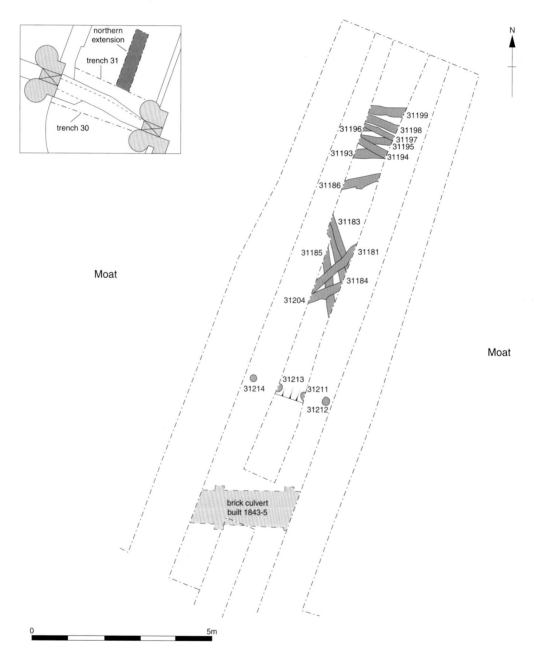

Fig 52   Detailed plan of 13th-century beeches in the northern extension of trench 31.

Fig 53   A group of unconverted beeches exposed in a narrow trench running north from the Edward I causeway at the south-west corner of the moat.

comprised a series of sandy silt and silty clay layers (8038–8043) containing shell fragments and sub-angular gravel and ranging in thickness from 40mm to 0.42m. The base of the moat between the two banks was filled by fine-grained brown silty clay (8021) up to 0.3m thick. The constantly waterlogged conditions at the bottom of the excavation militated against extensive excavation of this deposit. Despite this, two north–south aligned beech timbers (8017 and 8018) were found within layer 8021. They were unconverted trunks 0.2m and 0.26m in diameter respectively. The only evidence for tool-marks was found at the ends and at former branch positions, which carried saw- and axe-marks. Timber 8017 was 5.7m in length and sloped down at 10° from north to south. Beech 8018 was only exposed in section but appeared to be horizontal. Both retained their bark.

Five further unconverted beech poles (8023 and 8084–7) lay at or just above the interface between layer 8021 and the subsequent moat fills. The latter consisted of two micro-laminated bands of black organic silty clay (8020 and 8025). Each was 40mm thick and 7.6m in length between the two moat banks (8022 and 8024). The timbers range from 0.18m to 0.29m in diameter and were up to 5.5m long. Two of them were not fully exposed. The first (8023) was aligned north–west to south-east and sloped at an angle of 25° for 3.5m before entering the southern baulk of the excavations. The second (8087) was aligned north-east to south-west at an angle of

10° and extended for 3.2m before entering the northern baulk.

In common with all the *in situ* medieval timbers described in this report, the beeches were left undisturbed in the trench but samples were taken from five of this beech group for dendrochronological analysis. Like the piles behind the masonry they were complete to the bark-edge and included a complete ring for 1240 directly under the bark surface (Fig 51), indicating the same felling season in the winter of 1240/1. Both groups were therefore clearly of the same date, but the five poles had a greater age-range (from 45 to 90 years) and a much lower degree of intercorrelation in their ring sequences than the pile group 2772. Although the dating might suggest at first glance that all the beeches were from the same batch of timber, it therefore seems more likely that they were taken from diverse sources during a single campaign of requisitioning.

Trench 31 (northern extension; Figs 29, 52–3)

The primary fill of the moat cut (31207) in trench 31 was a layer of tenacious light-brown clay (31208). It resembled redeposited or disturbed London Clay and directly overlay the sloping edge of the moat to a depth of 0.3m. The clay also butted against the timber piles (*see* above). Three unconverted beech poles (31183–5) with branches removed overlay the London Clay to the north of the bank. All three

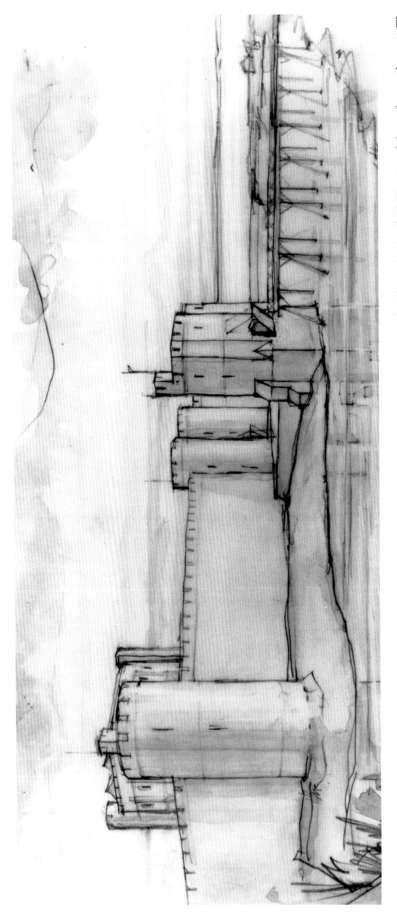

Fig 54   Henry III's short-lived western entrance to the Tower, as it might have looked on the eve of the second collapse in April 1241, viewed from the north west. The reconstruction of the barbican and bridge is based on the archaeological evidence; the twin-towered gatehouse, on the site of the later Beauchamp Tower, is conjectural. Although inadequately executed, the design was sophisticated and formidable: an assailant would have had to cross the moat on an exposed timber bridge, negotiate the barbican drawbridge, take the barbican and survive raking fire from the main curtain before breaking through the main gate. The wet moat would have prevented mining and kept siege engines at a distance. (E Impey, with advice from Beric Morley and Geoffrey Parnell.)

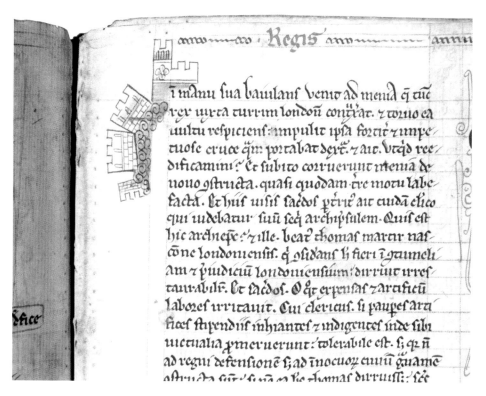

Fig 55 A marginal illustration from the Chronica Majora by Matthew Paris, showing collapsing masonry.

timbers measured 0.18m in diameter and were aligned north-west to south-east. Although the bark was present on all three timbers no free ends were present within the confines of the excavation and therefore no dendrochronology samples could be taken. Two clay layers overlay the three timbers and deposit 31208. The first (31179) was a tenacious bluish grey clay 0.2m thick. This was overlain by a brown clay (31178) 0.3m thick containing up to 15 per cent organic material (mostly bark fragments). A leather clump sole repair for a turnshoe (SF212) was found in layer 31178. This piece was probably contemporary with the timbers.

A further 11 unconverted beech trees (31181/2, 31186, 31193–9 and 31204) were found within the two clay layers, no more than 0.6m above the base of the cut. The timbers were all beech and were similar in dimensions to the three timbers at the base of the cut. Eight of the beeches were aligned east–west, two were aligned north-east to south-west and one was aligned north-west to south-east. The timbers appeared to form a crude structure and were assigned the structure number 31200. Where timbers overlay others jagged cracks or breaks were evident (also seen in trench 27). All of the timbers were excellently preserved with their bark intact. Only three of the timbers (31181/2 and 31199) could be sampled for dendrochronology (Fig 52). They were also dated to the year 1240/1 and share a similar age-range, between 45 and 60 years (Fig 30). This suggests that they were brought in to be used

as part of the piling along the top edge of the sloping bank. Presumably they were surplus to requirements and were simply dumped in the base of the moat. The varying alignments did not suggest that much care had been taken over this process, but there may have been an intent to retrieve the poles and use them elsewhere. The fact that the timbers were found within the clay deposits suggests that the latter either accumulated gradually or were dumped around the timbers. There was insufficient evidence to determine which was the case.

THE HISTORICAL CONTEXT FOR THE DISCOVERIES (FIGS 54–6)

Any historical discussion of the dramatic events at the Tower of London in 1240/1 must necessarily commence with the words of the *Chronica Majora*, written by the monk Matthew Paris shortly after the event. The whole content of both passages is in some way relevant, and deserves quoting in full. The earliest (Luard 1876, 80), firmly placed in 1240, states that:

Structura lapidea nobilis portae novae cum suis antemuralibus juxta turrim Londoniarum constructis corruit.

Eodemque anno, structura lapidea cuiusdam nobilis portae, quam sumptuoso nimis labore rex construxerat, quasi quodam terrae motu concussa, cum suis antemuralibus et propugnaculis nocte sancti Georgii corruit.

Fig 56 Reconstruction of the Tower of London immediately prior to the collapse of April 1241, showing Henry III's enlargement of the castle and the excavation of the new moat in progress. The order in which the works are shown being carried out and much of the detail is conjectural, but the general picture must be largely correct. The south-western corner of the curtain wall has been retained, but the northern curtain wall, built or extended by Longchamp (Fig 35), has been cleared away. The wall that replaced it, further to the north, is shown here under construction. To the east (right), beyond the line of the Roman wall, an entirely new rampart is being set out. The twin-towered gateway and the barbican tower on the west side (lower left) are the ill-fated structures illustrated in Fig 54. (Painting by Ivan Lapper.)

Quo audito rex, multiplicatis sumptibus, jussit illud ruinosum restaurari et in melius redintegrari.

The stonework of a noble gate newly built next to the Tower of London collapsed together with its forebuildings.

In that same year on the evening of the Feast of St George, the stonework of a certain noble gateway which the king had constructed in the most opulent fashion collapsed, as if struck by an earthquake, together with its forebuildings and outworks. When the king heard of this he gave orders that the ruined building should be rebuilt, more soundly this time and at still greater cost. (Translation by Jeremy Ashbee.)

The second (Luard 1876, 93–4), equally firmly dated to 1241, is as follows:

De quadam visione cuidam presbitero facta Londoniis mirabili.

Circa dies illos, cuidam presbitero viro sancto et prudenti in nocturna visione revelatum est, quod quidam archipraesul pontificalibus ornatus, crucemque in manu sua bajulans, venit ad moenia, quae tunc rex iuxta Turrim Londoniarum construxerat, et torvo ea vultu respiciens, impulit ipsa fortiter et impetuose cruce quam portabat dextra, et ait; 'Ut quid reaedificamini?' Et subito corruerunt moenia de novo constructa, quasi quodam terrae motu labefacta.

Et his visis sacerdos perterritus ait cuidam clerico, qui videbatur suum sequi archipraesulem, 'Quis est hic archiepiscopus?' Et ille; 'Beatus Thomas martir, natione Londoniensis, qui considerans haec fieri in contumeliam et praejudicium Londoniensium, diruit irrestaurabiliter'. Et sacerdos; 'O quot expensas et artificum labores irritavit'. Cui clericus; 'Si pauperes artifices stipendiis inhiantes et indigentes inde sibi victualia promeruerunt, tolerabile est; sed quia non ad regni defensionem, sed ad innocuorum civium gravamen constructa sunt, si non ea beatus Thomas diruisset, sanctus Aedmundus, confessor et successor eius, crudelius ea funditus evertisset'.

Et his visis memoratus sacerdos expergefactus a sompno, surrexit, et in medio noctis conticinio palam, quae sibi videbantur, omnibus in domo existentibus enarravit. Mane autem facto, per totam civitatem Londoniarum rumor increbuit, quod moenia Turrim aedificata, pro quibus construendis rex plus quam duodecim milia marcarum effuderat, irrestaurabiliter corruerunt, multis admirantibus et quasi pro malo praenostico praeconantibus, quod eadem nocte, immo eadem hora noctis anno praeterito, scilicet nocte sancti Georgii, ipsa muralia cum suis propugnaculis corruerunt. Pro quo casu cives Londonienses minime dolentes, vehementer obstupuerunt. Erant autem eis quasi spina in oculo. Audierant itaque minas objurgantium, quod constructa erant memorata moenia in eorum contumeliam, ut si quis eorum pro libertate civitatis certare praesumeret, ipsis recluderetur, vinculis mancipandus.

Et in plures pluribus includerentur carceribus, multa in eisdem distinguebantur diverticula, ne quis cum alio haberet confabulationem.

Concerning a wondrous apparition to a priest of London.

At about this time, a night-time vision appeared to a certain wise and godly priest, in which an archbishop, wearing his full vestments and brandishing a cross in his hand, came up to the walls which the king had then raised next to the Tower of London, and looking at them with an angry expression, he boldly struck the walls hard with the cross in his right hand and said 'to what end are you being rebuilt?' Suddenly the walls collapsed as if they had been struck by an earthquake, although they were only recently built.

At this a clerk appeared following the archbishop. The priest, terrified by what he had seen, asked him 'who is this Archbishop?' He replied 'This is the Blessed martyr Thomas, a Londoner by birth, who sees these buildings as an insult and a danger to the Londoners; that is why he has destroyed them irreparably'. The priest replied 'but what about the cost and effort of the workmen? He has ruined it all'. The clerk answered him 'if the poor needy workmen were able to buy food with the wages they earned, that is indeed a good thing, but these walls were built not for the defence of the realm but to harm innocent citizens and if the Blessed Thomas had not destroyed them, his successor Saint Edmund the confessor would have uprooted the foundations even more violently'.

When the priest awoke from his sleep, he remembered what he had seen and though it was still the middle of the night, he openly told the story to everyone in the house. Early next morning, a rumour spread through the whole city of London, that the walls which had been built around the Tower, on which the king had spent more than twelve thousand marks, collapsed irreparably. Many people wondered at this and declared it was an evil omen, because at exactly the same time, that is to say, Saint George's night, but in the previous year, the same walls fell down together with their outworks. The citizens of London were completely amazed at this and not at all sorry. The walls were like a thorn in their eye. They had heard people taunting that the building of the walls was an insult to them, because if anyone dared to stand up for the rights of the city, they could be clapped in irons and imprisoned inside. Many cells could be seen in the buildings for the imprisonment of large numbers separately, so that none of them could speak with another. (Translation by Jeremy Ashbee.)

The chronicle's tale has of course been familiar to historians ever since its writing, but advances in the study of castles and the Tower of London over the last 150 years (particularly the realisation that the existing outer curtain wall and main entrance date from no earlier than the 1270s) have raised a wide range of questions. Where, if this tale was to be believed, did the noble gateway and its 'forebuildings and outworks' stand? What form did the complex take? Was it really, as the chronicle goes on to suggest, rebuilt 'more soundly this time and at still greater cost'? How should we interpret a subsequent passage that suggests a second collapse, exactly a year later? What then happened? Some of these issues were addressed as early as c1600, and most importantly since then by Sir Howard Colvin, who, in the 1960s, firmly identified the main developmental phases of the castle's construction. Nevertheless the chronicle text, even with the support of other documentary material, could only lead the investigator so far. Further progress would have to depend on structural and archaeological discoveries. The excavations during 1995–7 at last provided solid evidence for the fabled but so far unlocated dramas of the 1240s (Fig 55).

A combination of structural detail, its situation on the west side of the castle, irrelevance to the Edwardian defences and the obvious signs of structural failure were enough to affirm the association of the platform with the collapse of 1240. Should there be any doubt that this event really occurred, it is confirmed by an order to the Constable of the Tower on 23 September 1241, 'to pull out the lead and boards which lie under the tower recently fallen, to bring together the timber and freestone and put them in a suitable place' (*Calendar of the Liberate Rolls of King Henry III, 1240–1245* (London 1930) 74).

That there was collapse in 1240 is at least unambiguously stated in Paris's text. He then explains, equally clearly, that 'when the king heard of this he gave orders that the ruined building should be rebuilt, more soundly this time and at still greater cost'. The suggestion of a second collapse, a year later to the day, is contained in the later passage of the *Chronica* relating the priest's dream on St George's Eve (23 April) 1241. Many historians have read this as reference to a second disaster that actually occurred, but close scrutiny of the passage and its context suggests an alternative interpretation. The priest dreamed of a collapse, and in the morning a rumour circulated in London that this had happened, fuelled by its timing on the anniversary of the last collapse. Nowhere, however, is there a specific reference in the *Chronica* to an actual physical event. A second collapse in 1241 is mentioned in the *Flores Historiarum* (Luard 1890, 245), but this is interpolated from the *Chronica* and to some extent must be regarded as a second-hand version of events. The author may still have had access to a first-hand source, however, and so attribution of the failure of the known structure to either 1240 or 1241 is still an open issue. In either circumstance the dendrochronological evidence can be accepted as an absolute link between the historical text and the archaeological remains (Figs 54, 56).

HOW LONG WAS THE STRUCTURE KEPT 'OPEN'?

Evidence from the masonry

There was little evidence from the masonry itself to suggest how long it had been kept in use. The combed surface finishes were in virtually perfect condition, but it is difficult to assess the significance of this because one would not necessarily expect to see much (if any) surface erosion even if the building had remained operational right through to the Edwardian extension of the defences from 1275 to 1281. Equally, the greater degree of erosion noted on the cramp-holes in the upper Reigate ashlar may reflect little more than the different properties of the stone compared to the Purbeck marble. Nevertheless, the erosion is at least direct evidence that the masonry remained exposed for some time after 1240/1, even if this cannot be taken as firm evidence for continued use. Similarly, the whitish fungal growth seen on some of the piles along the east side of the structure shows that they must have remained exposed long enough for decay processes to begin.

Evidence from the moat fills and their relationship with structural elements

The construction trenches (2939, 2970 and 2996) around the masonry were filled with a mixture of clay and mortar deposits. To the west and to the south, the bulk of the cut was filled by a tenacious brown clay (2969 and 2995 respectively) containing flecks of whitish mortar. The deposits were excavated to a depth of 1.3m. Separate bands of mortar and clay (2941–5) were found on the north side and around the north-east corner of the masonry. The lowest (2945) was a 50mm-thick light-green deposit and appeared to be mortar or crushed Reigate greenstone. This was overlain by two thick bands of brownish grey heavy clay (2943 and 2944) up to 0.75m thick. A 0.34m-thick yellowish white sandy mortar (2942) sealed the clays. It contained 20 per cent gravel and occasional fragments of limestone. The mortar was similar in colour and composition to the flecking seen in the main clay backfills. The final fill was a reddish brown clay (2941) up to 0.6m thick. These deposits reached the level of the masonry's second chamfer but did not cover the structure.

The clay fill (2969) of foundation trench 2970 had been truncated around the southern end of oak plate 2947 by a second cut (2997). This contained a sequence of five fills (2964–7 and 2998). These sediments were sampled by Dr Macphail, and subsequently layers 2964–7 were studied in detail by Drs Macphail and Crowther. The lowest of these (2967) comprised about 15 thin (1–2 mm) sloping (c10°) white (calcareous) and brown (organic clays) lenses (thin section S). The calcareous lenses were either massive micrite or a spongy micrite composed of very thin excrements, whereas the organic clays contain likely London Clay, fine to coarse (0.8 mm) partially iron-replaced plant fragments, fine charcoal, and *in situ* roots (width 0.2–0.5 mm). The calcareous lenses also exhibited iron replacement of organic matter and pyrite formation. The lenses combine as a highly calcareous (33.9 per cent carbonate) silt loam (16.7 per cent sand, 56.3 per cent silt, 27 per cent clay) with very low organic matter (2.69 per cent LOI), low total phosphate (0.761mg g^{-1}), moderate magnetic susceptibility (20.1 × 10^{-8} m^{3}kg^{-1}) and χ_{conv} (16.5%) and high lead content.

The context above (2966) was a calcareous (15.1 per cent carbonate), poorly humic (4.28 per cent LOI) silty clay (7.3 per cent sand, 50.6 per cent silt, 42.1 per cent clay) with inclusions of sand pockets from the London Clay (thin section S). It had a higher total phosphate content (0.983mg g^{-1}) but a lower χ_{conv} (9.81 per cent). The upper contexts (2964 and 2965) comprise a series of coarsely laminated (1–5mm) steeply sloping (*c*40°) calcareous (15.4 per cent carbonate) silty clays (2.4 per cent sand, 50.9 per cent silt, 46.7 per cent clay). They became more sandy (silty clay loam, 13.2 per cent sand, 54.4 per cent silt, 32.4 per cent clay) and calcareous (26.3 per cent carbonate) in thin section Q. Although similarly low in organic matter (3.04–4.14 per cent LOI), they contain more total phosphate (1.12–1.18mg g^{-1}). Secondary gypsum and pyrite were present but rare, with rare secondary microsparite infilling voids. Some lenses were rich in fine charred organic matter.

The first 15 or so lenses (2967) included calcareous layers that were spongy (algal weathering/very thin excrements?) and also finely rooted. These sediments are relatively low in total phosphate but have the highest pH (8.1–8.3) in the moat samples—probably the result of inwash from the overlying mortared foundations. The interleaved organic lenses more probably resulted from intermittent inwash of detrital organic matter and *in situ* accumulations of organic matter. These basal deposits were formed under sub-aerial conditions that allowed biological weathering of the sediments by algae, higher plants and possibly soil fauna. The high levels of lead (280μg g^{-1}) are interesting and surely reflect the use of lead bonding in the masonry.

The rhythmic nature of the sedimentation implies a tidal influence, perhaps as much from rising ground water levels as from the Thames. This wetting and drying, which may have influenced magnetic susceptibility enhancement, would account for the iron replacement of plant material, secondary mineral formation and the poor pollen preservation in section B (see Chapter 3). Further up the sequence the lenses were more coarse, massive and contained more detrital material and fine charcoal. They also became more clay-rich (from 27.0 per cent to 32.4–46.7 per cent clay), with pyrite and gypsum. This implies greater inputs from the London Clay substrate exposed by the excavation of the moat and more continuously wet conditions—presumably as the new moat

became more permanently water-filled and in use. The last theory is supported by the rise in levels of phosphate-P (from 0.761 to 0.983–1.18mg g^{-1}).

It is particularly interesting that these sediments accumulated in what appeared to be a secondary cut through the backfill of the foundation trench. This suggests that the latter had already been filled in (either partly or wholly) before the timbers suffered their worst movements. The backfilling was presumably a deliberate act. We cannot be certain that this was a reaction to the structural problems, but this does seem to be the most likely context for such action. There would be little apparent logic in hiding the ashlar facing otherwise. The secondary cut was probably caused by the physical movement of the timbers through the relatively soft clayey fills, creating a void within them. This allowed the sedimentation to occur underneath oaks 2947 and 2948. Once again this supports the assertion that the upper surface at least of the masonry remained exposed, if not necessarily in use, for some time after 1240/1.

Further evidence for the sequence of events was found on the west side of the Victorian culvert. Three bands of clay and gravel (2843/6/7) 0.25m deep stretched between the two oak beams (2837 and 2845). The layers had been built up against the mortar and limestone infill (2959) of the eastern timberwork, sloping down to the west to abut the oak. They were overlain by a 0.1m-thick black humic silt (2842), which contained a single block of Purbeck ashlar. Layer 2842 was sealed by a 0.22m-thick mid- to dark-grey silt (2841) with a slight clay content and occasional (less than 2 per cent) black staining. An ashlar block was also recovered from this deposit. Both layers terminated against oak 2845. The area was then overlain by a 0.5m-thick dark-grey silty clay (2840). The extent of this is unclear, because it merged into layer 2855/8019 to the west. One of the beech poles (8000) and the two chase-tenoned oaks (8001 and 8002) lay within layer 2840. Thus it is clear that sediments had been building up in the base of the moat before the timbers suffered their final catastrophe.

A total of 32 fish bones were also recovered from context 2840, all of which belonged to one plaice/flounder recovered as a substantially intact skeleton. Body part representation confirms this. The clay layers were sealed by several very dark-grey silts (2838/9 and 2844). The latest of them (2844) overlay clay 2855 to the west. The sequence of deposits in the mid-13th-century moat will also be considered in Chapter 5 because of the relationship between the fills and the creation of Edward I's moat.

Other environmental evidence

Remains were very sparse in the water-lain sediments of Henry III's moat, in trenches 27 and 31, probably because silting was rapid. There were just a few examples of *Lymnaea peregra*, a snail of stagnant water, and a couple of seeds of *Ranunculus sceleratus* (celery-leaved crowfoot), a plant of nutrient-rich mud.

Practical constraints

Finally, the purely practical need for continuing landward access into the castle after 1241 needs to be considered. There was no apparent evidence for any attempt to rebuild a bridge on the starling positions marked out by the oak plates, but this does not preclude the possibility that some kind of structure was fashioned here. It is possible that a trestle structure was erected and completely removed subsequently. This, of course, is purely hypothetical, but presumably some kind of entrance was maintained in the inner curtain wall after the collapse, requiring the maintenance of access across the moat. Where else would this be if it was not achieved in some way over the damaged remains of the masonry and timberwork?

The only real option would be an entrance at the south-west corner, many years before Edward I's establishment of the Lion Tower complex. The piling of the London Clay here could perhaps have had a structural purpose, rising to form or support a bridge or causeway. Access could then have been contrived by a northward turn along what is now West Mint Street or perhaps by continuing eastwards in front of the inner curtain to the Bloody Tower gateway. This would, of course, bring the traveller into very close contact with the river Thames but by the 13th century the river may not have flowed hard against the masonry even at high tide. Dr Parnell's excavation in Water Lane against the inner curtain adjacent to the Salt Tower demonstrated that the river edge there had been reclaimed during the Roman period when thick layers of soil were dumped on the foreshore (Parnell 1983b, 98–9). Direct landward access to the Bloody Tower would have been feasible if the same reclamation extended between it and the Bell Tower.

Chapter 5: Period 2: The Late 13th Century (Edward I)

INTRODUCTION

It was inevitable that the works of Edward I should form a major focus of the archaeological and historical research. We were, after all, working on and within the very defences for which he had been responsible (Fig 57). A substantial amount of time and effort was therefore expended on gaining the maximum possible amount of information about the structures erected and the features dug at the King's behest. Specific attention was paid to the south-western and south-eastern corners of the defences, where the new moat had connected with the river Thames. The structural means by which this had been achieved in such a way that the moat waters could be controlled was of particular interest, both academically and within the context of the re-flooding feasibility study. Naturally enough, both the moat itself and the outer curtain wall that defined its inner edge were also the subject of considerable study. This chapter examines all these subjects in detail, starting with the moat itself.

THE CREATION OF EDWARD I'S MOAT AND THE OUTER CURTAIN WALL

Documentary evidence for Edward I's extension of the defences is abundant, although the sources covering the moat's actual creation are patchy. The main operation began in or by May 1275. This is shown by a Pipe Roll entry noting £90 19s 9d spent on wood and other materials to make various tools and pickaxes and on other implements for 'making the great ditch around the said Tower from the Thames towards the City to the Thames by St Katharine's hospital' (E 372/120, *rot comp* 2). The sum was expended *ad faciendum inde diversa utensilia tam ferra quam lignea et picosiis tam aliis diversis empcionibus necessariis emptis ad magnum fossatum faciendum circa castrum predicti Turris a Tamesia versus civitatem usque ad Tamisiam versus hospitalem beate Katerine*. The entry may also imply that the work was to progress clockwise around the castle. Further details concerning cost and operations also survive: the wages of the diggers and hodmen (*hottari*), for

Fig 57   A view of the west moat looking along the outer curtain wall, with the Beauchamp Tower on the inner curtain to the left and the river Thames in the background. Trench 27, covering Henry III's entrance, can be seen towards the bottom right-hand corner. Edward I's entrance causeway closes the west moat between the Byward and Middle Towers (to the left and right respectively). Bernard de Gomme's revetment wall, built around the outer edge of the moat in 1670–83, runs to the right of trench 27.

example, amounting to just over £2,484 (E 372/120, *rot comp* 1d–2. See also Colvin 1963, 716 and n 2). Large-scale work evidently continued until 1281, costing £4,150 in labour alone (E 372/121 *rot comp* 2d; E 372/123 *rot comp* 1; E 372/125 *rot comp* 2). After 1276, however, wage payments steadily decreased, suggesting that the bulk of the work had been achieved in the first twelve months. The operations were carried out under the direction of a Fleming, Master Walter, who was paid £1 per week for 19 weeks at the beginning of the project (E 372/120 *rot comp* 2). Presumably he was responsible for setting out the course of the moat, prescribing its width and depth, and devising means for controlling and exploiting the flow of water. The remainder of the work was probably supervised by Brother John of Acre, to whom payments continued to be made until 1293 (E 403/76 (Michaelmas 20 Edward I)).

The completed moat extended around the three landward sides of the castle only, the new curtain wall to the south being washed by the river. The inner edge was defined by the new outer curtain wall, the water lapping directly against the stonework, apparently without an intervening berm. The only indication today of the moat's original outer edge (at least as it existed by *c*1310) is the Postern Gate, the remains of which are displayed at the south exit of the A100 subway. This was necessarily positioned at, or overlooking, the north bank. The earliest additional evidence dates only from 1597, when Haiward and Gascoyne's survey (Fig 84) recorded a water-filled area as much as 50m across. This was surrounded by a broad, irregular and eroded bank. The width of the water-filled area, however, varied with the tides, until the creation of the near-vertical revetment in the 17th century (*see* Chapter 7).

The backfilling of Henry III's moat

The fills within the mid-13th-century moat have already been described in Chapter 4. Further consideration of the deposits is required here because of their interface with the new moat dug in the 1270s. The fills themselves are not described again, but the environmental evidence is presented fully here.

Pollen evidence

Section A commenced within the backfill of the Henry III moat identified in trench 27 (Figs 25, 58); the lowest 0.65m of the column sample lay within this sequence and two pollen zones could be identified in this. The first, comprising the lowest 0.4m (context 2840) is dominated by derived Pre-Quaternary spores (50 per cent) with small quantities of *Pediastrum* and Hystrichospheres. Spores of ferns are greater in this than the subsequent zone. Poaceae are dominant (50 per cent) with strong representation of cereal pollen (17 per cent) and oats (*Secale cereale*, 1–2 per cent). There are slightly higher numbers of *Sinapis* type (3 per cent), Chenopodiaceae (4 per cent) and *Plantago lanceolata* (4 per cent), *Polygonum aviculare* type and Lactuceae. Herbs of note include *Cannabis* type, *Linum usitatissimum* and *Centaurea cyanus*. Trees and shrubs comprise oak (*Quercus*, 16 per cent), alder (*Alnus*, 6 per cent) and hazel (*Corylus*) type (7 per cent), with sporadic occurrences of other taxa. Lindens (*Tilia*), beech (*Fagus*) and walnut (*Juglans*) are of note. Juniper (*Juniperus*) is present at the interface between the two zones. Marsh/aquatic plants (to 8 per cent) include Cyperaceae, *Potamogeton*, *Typha/Sparganium* type and occasional *Littorella*, *Myriopyllum* spp., *Lemna* and *Butomus*.

The upper 0.25m is delimited by a sharp expansion of *Pediastrum* (70 per cent at 55mm from the bottom of the zone). Meanwhile, derived palynomorphs and fern spores (*Pteridium* and *Dryopteris*) are reduced. Herbs remain broadly similar to the preceding zone, being dominated by Poaceae (wild and cereal types). Trees also remain the same with minor expansions of oak (to 19 per cent) but reduced alder and walnut.

Soil micromorphology

Sediments 2838–42 (trench 27) were deposited in Henry III's moat prior to the creation of Edward I's new moat. They consisted of massive yellowish brown silty clay (up to 62.3 per cent clay) with a crack microstructure (thin sections B lower, E, G and H). Fine lenses were also present throughout, and these can be calcitic. Secondary gypsum crystals were ubiquitous and pockets of fine sand (as seen in the London Clay) were also present. Organic matter levels were low, but increased slightly from 4.67 per cent to 5.62 per cent LOI further up the profile. Total phosphate shows a similar increase from 0.918/1.08 to 1.39mg g^{-1}. Molluscs occurred occasionally.

The high amounts of gypsum with sand pockets in these silty clays and clays probably derive directly from the London Clay (Bone 1998). On the other hand the basal fills (eg, 2842) were both finely bedded and massive, and calcareous with calcitic lenses and molluscs. By contrast the London Clay is poor in calcium carbonate with 10 per cent more clay and 10 per cent less silt. In addition, these basal deposits are more organic (compare 2.54–2.82 percent with a range of 4.67–5.62 per cent LOI, $n = 5$), contain more detrital organic matter and have a higher total phosphate content (compare 0.544–0.847mg g^{-1} with a range of 0.918–1.39 mg g^{-1}). The fine laminations are also indicative of gentle sedimentation in comparison to the redeposited London Clay of the Henry III coffer dam (Chapter 4) with its heterogeneous character of London Clay fragments that are more likely the result of dumping.

A moat sedimentary origin is also indicated by the increase in organic matter and total phosphate further up the profile, suggesting inputs of plant matter and cess during the backfilling of Henry III's moat. Meanwhile, the ubiquitous presence of gypsum and sulphate in these deposits is a close link with the London Clay. The low quantities of heavy metals demonstrate low levels of industrial contamination in the sediments. Secondary gypsum formation suggests that they were not continuously saturated.

Plant remains

The paucity of plant remains from the Edward I backfill of the Henry III moat in trench 27 would be entirely consistent with the rapid infilling of the earlier moat with clay dug out as part of the construction of the later moat. Higher numbers of shells of aquatic molluscs, particularly *Gyraulus laevis*, were, however, found in context 2844, the presumed top of the Edward I backfill. This deposit was perhaps sediment, which collected more slowly as the backfill settled.

The depth and character of the 13th-century excavation into the London Clay

Edward I's moat basically comprised a very wide ditch, cut deeply down into the London Clay. The latter provided a naturally impermeable seal to the bottom of the feature, which therefore retained water without the need for an engineered lining of clay or any other material. The clay itself was a potentially valuable resource and there is at least one specific reference to its sale for tiling. The Pipe Roll for the ninth year of Edward's reign saw Giles of Audenarde (Keeper of the Works) accounting for '14 pounds and 10 shillings income from the sale of earth from the moat of the said Tower for making tiles' (E372/125 *rot comp* 125). It is possible that this refers to brickearth rather than clay, but the point about the excavations also being a source of income is still well made.

The base of the moat was fairly flat, although minor undulations were noted in many trenches. It was also clear that the cut into the clay sloped downwards gradually from north to south, as the lawned surface of the moat does today. High values of 0.5m OD or more were recorded fairly consistently in the north moat (eg, 0.63m OD in trench 42). Much lower levels were found in the middle of the east and west moats, however, with values of 0m OD (trench 14, east moat; Fig 59) and c-0.35m OD (trench 27, west moat). The situation is more complicated at the south-eastern and south-western corners of the moat where it 'joined' the river Thames but, as already noted, the London Clay immediately to the south of Henry III's moat cut in trench 31 (northern extension) was found at −0.65m to −1.1m OD.

The London Clay tends to lie at higher levels than those recorded for the moat base around the outside of the castle, so it seems fairly clear that Edward I's engineers had excavated quite some way into the clay. This presumably reflected the obvious need to maintain a reasonably steady water level given the mainly tidal water regime within the ditch. The excavation must have removed a considerable amount of clay. Some of this may have been used in building works around the Tower, but one can imagine that there would still have been a need to dispose of quite large amounts. This probably explains the redeposited London Clay present in the upper fills of Henry III's moat. The latter, of course, had been dug to significantly greater depths than Edward I's replacement for it. Even with sedimentation during the intervening 35 years or so, the earlier moat must still have been an obvious feature and a tempting place for getting rid of some of the excess clay.

Evidence for the north edge of the moat

The evaluations did not provide any evidence for the form of the moat's outer edge because work was necessarily confined within the limits of the late 17th-century revetment wall. Boreholes were sunk in the north-west section of Tower Gardens behind the revetment in October–November 2000, however, providing useful archaeological information regarding the outer edge of the moat here. The natural/weathered London Clay base of the medieval moat was found sloping upwards in three separate borehole transects. These are shown in Figure 60.

As the sections demonstrate, undisturbed *in situ* London Clay was not found in every sample location, although either this, a weathered layer of the clay, or both was usually present. The weathered London Clay should still represent *in situ* material, and its upper surface is provisionally interpreted as the base of the moat cut. The most complete and readily interpretable exposure occurred in the western sample transect (BH4 and P107–9), where the surface of the weathered clay sloped gradually upwards from c1.5m OD at the south side of the gardens to 4.15m OD in the north. This broadly reflects the present slope of the garden surface, but some 6–7m below current levels. The lower level could still have been at or below the likely water level in the medieval moat, but the upper reaches of the sloping bank would certainly have been above the water.

The levels for the weathered and *in situ* London Clay in the central (P110–12) and eastern (P113–15 and BH5) transects were more difficult to interpret. The southern and central samples provided very similar results to those in the western group, but the northern boreholes (P112 and P115) showed a dramatic change. The weathered clay was found at a significantly greater depth in P115, while a 100mm-thick layer of clay at the very bottom of P112 was provisionally identified as London Clay. Such depths cannot be readily reconciled with the slope observed in P107-9. Presumably one or more major features (eg, ditches or pits) must have cut away the upper slope of the moat in these locations.

The considerable depth below ground of the weathered and *in situ* London Clay came as something of a surprise, particularly as Roman levels

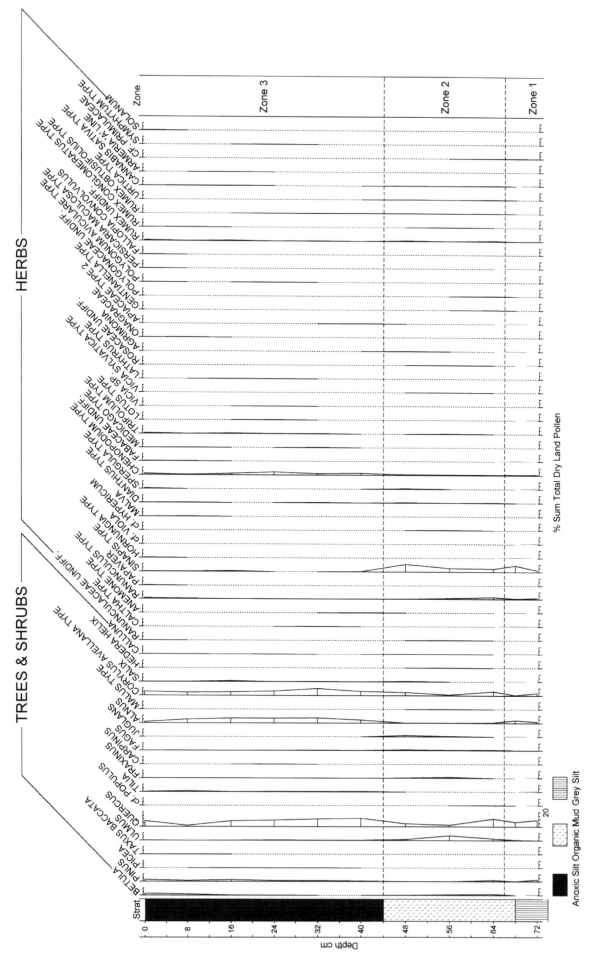

Fig 58   Pollen diagram, Section A, trench 27.

84

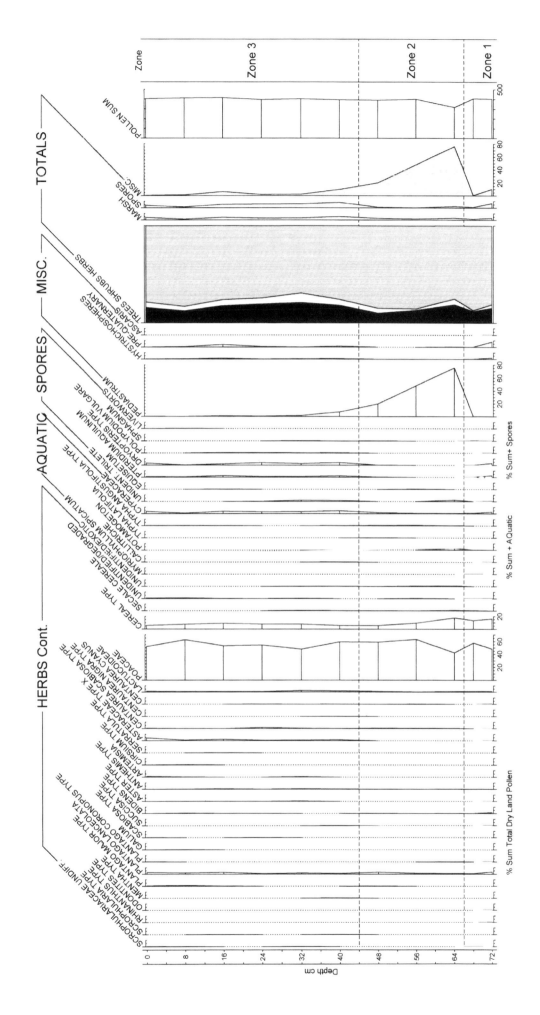

Fig 58 Pollen diagram, Section A, trench 27, continued.

85

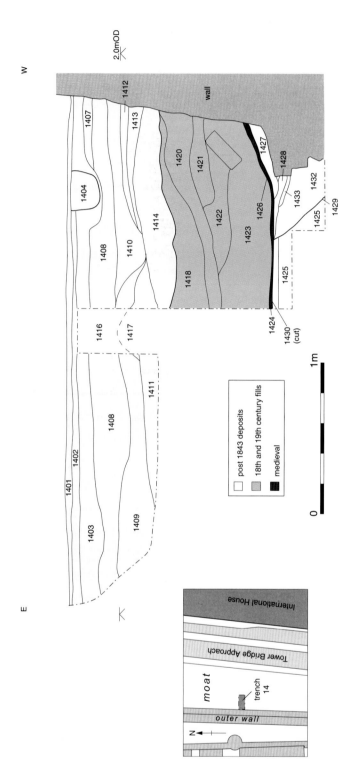

Fig 59   The southern section of trench 14, showing the moat fills in relation to the outer curtain wall and its foundations.

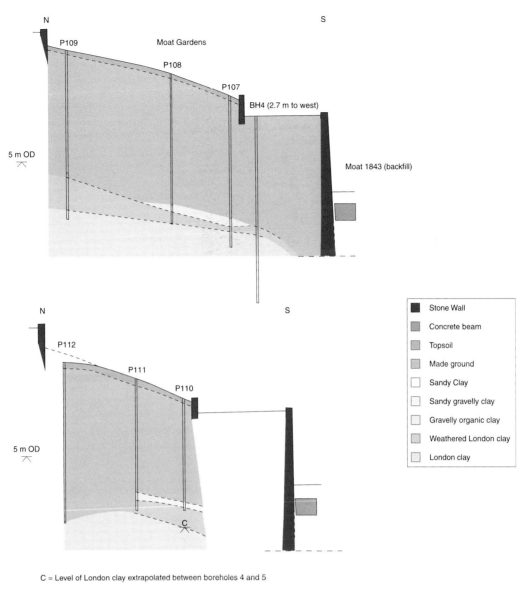

N   S

P109

Moat Gardens

P108

P107

BH4 (2.7 m to west)

5 m OD

Moat 1843 (backfill)

Stone Wall

Concrete beam

Topsoil

Made ground

Sandy Clay

Sandy gravelly clay

Gravelly organic clay

Weathered London clay

London clay

N   S

P112

P111

P110

5 m OD

C

C = Level of London clay extrapolated between boreholes 4 and 5

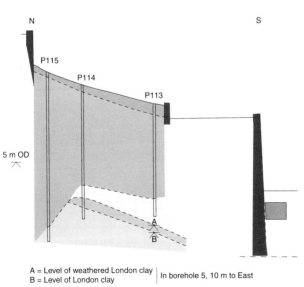

N   S

P115

P114

P113

5 m OD

A
B

A = Level of weathered London clay
B = Level of London clay | In borehole 5, 10 m to East

Fig 60   Reconstruction of the original profile of the north moat, taken from boreholes sunk in 2000.

around the city wall to the east are generally thought to lie at around 10m OD. Despite this, the ascription of weathered London Clay in the boreholes appeared clear enough, and there seems to be little reason to doubt that this is *in situ* material. The Postern Gate (built *c*1300) to the east of the boreholes survives at roughly the moat grass level (*c*3.5m OD), where it came to rest after a landslide in the mid-15th century (Parnell 1993, 42 and figs 28–9). Its original level at or towards the top of the slope would probably have been around 6m OD. Such a position is broadly in line with the data from P109. It has long been appreciated that the Tower of London sits within something of a 'bowl' in the natural geology (*see* BGS 1993), and this might also explain some of the disparities in level. It seems reasonable to assume that the investigations successfully located the base of the medieval moat and the extension of its sloping bank towards contemporary ground levels on Great Tower Hill to the north, although more data would be required before any degree of certainty could be attached to this interpretation.

The defences and the Thames foreshore

The pre-Edwardian foreshore levels in trench 31 have already been described (Chapter 4). Similar deposits were encountered between beech piles in trench 25 at the south-east corner of the moat (*see* below). Deep excavation was possible only in a very limited area of this trench, however, and it was thus difficult to obtain an adequate characterisation of the foreshore level. Greater success was achieved in the south moat, where most of the test pits (especially those against Edward I's outer curtain wall) encountered earlier foreshore deposits. For instance, layer 3632 was the earliest recorded context in test pit 36 at the junction of the outer curtain with the later Byward Postern. This layer of tenacious mid- to dark-grey silty clay (3632) extended across most of the base of the excavation and continued beneath it. It had been cut by and thus clearly pre-dated the outer curtain wall. The top of the layer sloped down from 0.4m OD on the west side of the pit to 0.06m OD on the east. These levels are notably higher than the values for the London Clay in the east and west moats noted above, reflecting the extent to which foreshore deposits (including material dumped from within the Tower) must have accumulated against the southern defences during the 13th century. Presumably the Edwardian engineers' decision to establish dams at the junctions of the east and west moats with the river largely represented a reinforcement and consolidation of such foreshore deposits.

Plant remains were sparse in the early foreshore deposits in trenches 37 and 39, which had been cut by the outer curtain and wharf walls respectively. All the samples contained charred glumes of spelt wheat (*Triticum spelta*). These had presumably been redeposited from Roman contexts.

The outer curtain wall

Edward I's outer curtain wall was examined at several points around its circuit including its southern side, which had been built out into the Thames foreshore. There were distinct differences in the construction there compared to that of the landward sides, and it is the latter which is described first here. A construction trench (1242, 1350, 1429 *see* Fig 59, and 2865) between 1.3m and 1.6m wide (measured from the base of the outer curtain) had been cut into the London Clay, probably after the moat had been dug out (though this could not be proved on purely archaeological grounds). In trench 27, cut 2865 also truncated the blue-grey gravel and clay (2825) that had been deposited against the beech piles (2772) along the eastern edge of the Henry III masonry structure. In most cases only the top of the foundations was exposed and no attempt could be made to excavate further into their trench for safety reasons. The greater area exposed in trench 27 (Fig 61), however, did allow an attempt to excavate into the foundations. These comprised Kentish ragstone rubble bonded with a mixture of sub-angular gravel and yellowish white sandy lime mortar (2864). A few pieces of Purbeck marble ashlar had also been incorporated in the foundations here. It is assumed that these derived from the failed Henry III masonry just to the west of the curtain. The foundation material was very heavily concreted and could be excavated to a depth of only 0.4m before it became impossible to remove by hand. The bottom of the foundations therefore had to be identified in four core drills. It lay at −3.05m OD in two of them and −3.73m OD in a third. The fourth core could not penetrate beyond −1.38m OD and had to be abandoned. This provided graphic testimony to the work of Edward I's engineers and builders. The cores did not provide any evidence for piling underneath the masonry foundations, but the narrowness of the cores means that this should not be taken as proof of the absence of such piling.

The top of the construction trench was filled with layers of mortar and yellowish brown sandy clays (1432/3, 2826/7 and 2860–3), containing roughly 40 per cent poorly sorted rounded gravel. In trench 27 these were sealed beneath a 0.15m-thick layer of tenacious reddish brown clay (2873). This was overlain in turn by a layer of fine light-yellow sand (2868) 0.12m thick and 1.2m wide forming a hard surface over the construction cut. Similar layers of clay, silt, sand and mortar overlay the foundations and the base of the wall in trenches 12, 13 and 14 (contexts 1236–8; 1335, 1340–5 and 1348; and 1427 respectively—*see* Fig 59). A fragment of a clump repair from a medieval shoe of turnshoe construction was found in layer 1342. These layers were thickest (0.2m–0.4m) against the face of the wall, sloping down before petering out 0.9m-1.4m from the wall. Mollusc shells were noted on the surface of these deposits in trenches 12 and 13. Dr Robinson believed that these were derived with the sand and silt content of the soils, and therefore they could not be

Fig 61 View of the outer curtain wall exposed down to foundation level at the east end of trench 27.

used as indicators of the contemporary environment during construction work. It is likely that these sloping layers had formed before water was allowed into the moat, and that they consisted of excess building materials dumped over the top of the foundations.

The wall above the foundations (2764 in trench 27—*see* Fig 61) was made up of roughly squared Kentish Rag blocks, with pieces of Bembridge limestone from the Isle of Wight and occasional pieces of flint. Stones varied in size from 0.16m by 0.12m to 0.5m by 0.25m and were bonded with a yellowish white lime mortar matrix. This appeared to be the same material as the earliest of the mortar layers (2863) over the foundations in the construction trench. The battered face of the wall sloped at a consistent angle of approximately 20° in all exposures to just above the current ground level. At this point the batter gives way to the near-vertical later 13th-century upper stage of the curtain wall (Parnell 1993, 43–6).

A quite different technique was apparent along the southern outer curtain. This had to be built into the relatively soft, unconsolidated silts of the foreshore edge. Therefore the wall was partially supported on oak piles with oak beams linking between the caps. The piles appeared to be quite widely spaced, with no more than two being found in any one test pit along the curtain. The timbers were generally in good condition, although the oak beams had rotted badly in places. The foundations themselves comprised compacted river gravel and stone rubble dug directly into the foreshore silts. The curtain rose near-vertically straight off the foundations. There

was no batter in the lower part of the wall, in contrast to the landward sides.

It is possible that the foundations here are of a slightly later period, because the southern outer curtain was comprehensively rebuilt in the 1320s and 1330s. A document of 1324–5, for instance, records the following works to the east of St Thomas's Tower:

Payment to master mason Walter of Canterbury ... for repairing the outer wall of the said Tower over the Thames, namely the Great Gate over the river down to the nearer gate towards the said hospital [ie, St Katherine's] that is to say, for taking down the same wall and building it anew thicker and higher of good limestone, to a length of 412 and a half feet (E 101 469/7 m5; translated by Jeremy Ashbee).

A document issued shortly afterwards in very similar terms took the rebuilding fully along to the Develin Tower at the south-east corner. An equivalent rebuild to the west of St Thomas's Tower had to wait until 1336, when Thomas de Dagworth and Simon of Dorset were paid for 'heightening, repairing, mending and crenellating a section of the outer wall between the gate of the Watergate and the common latrine next to the postern opposite the Mint gate' (E 101 470/1 m5; translated by Jeremy Ashbee). It is unfortunate that none of the references specifically describe any foundation works, but reconstruction on this scale might well have required them to be strengthened at least.

An interesting variation on the piling was found in test pit 36, against the junction of the curtain and the Byward Postern. Here the foreshore layer (3632) was sealed on the west side of the pit by a compact, mid-grey/brown layer of mixed clay and rubble (3614) up to 0.1m thick (though it may have continued beneath the limit of excavation). Three wood piles (3611–13) had been driven through this material. The piles were badly decomposed at the top, but appeared to be of beech, with a diameter of between 0.14m and 0.25m. One (3612) lay partly under the east wall of the Byward Postern, while only the north half of 3613 was within the excavation. Immediately to the north of the piles, layer 3614 was sealed by a layer of mortar and limestone blocks (3609). This rubbly deposit was hard and compact, measuring 0.95m (north–south) by 0.82m with a thickness ranging from 0.05m to 0.3m. It was difficult to be certain, but rubble layer 3609 and the below-ground portion (3608) of the outer curtain wall appeared to be contemporary. The stratigraphic relationships had been affected by the insertion of a brick culvert in the Victorian period, but the coarse rubble matrix of the wall/foundation seemed to be bonded with or possibly rise over 3609.

Layer 3609 was very similar to the rubble pile cap noted over beech piles in trench 31 (*see* below), and is interpreted in the same way here. It seems very likely that the piles in test pit 36 belonged to Edward I's reign as well. This is certainly so if they were beech—as discussed below this wood was rarely used for structural purposes after the 13th century. Although it was not realised at the time of excavation, test pit 36 seems to have provided the first solid evidence for the existence and location of a dam to contain the waters of the moat surrounding the half-moon Lion Tower. This dam would have run south from the position of the Byward Postern and would have been in operation until the wharf was extended toward St Thomas's Tower in the 14th century.

THE SOUTH-EASTERN (IRON GATE) CAUSEWAY

As noted already, the points where the moat joined the Thames were important for the successful management of water within the ditch. Not surprisingly, these locations saw some of the most extensive excavations carried out during 1995–7. In the case of the south-east corner, the masonry causeway between the Develin Tower on the outer curtain wall and the Iron Gate on the outer edge of the moat was known to be a medieval feature. The masonry had been cut down to below water level in the late 17th century (*see* Chapter 7). Excavation of a small trench (7) in 1995 established that the masonry did indeed still survive below ground, but the more extensive trench (25) dug in 1996 had greater success in establishing the origin and sequence of construction here (Figs 62–65). The most important evidence came from a 3.5m-long and 2m-wide sondage dug down

the north face of the masonry on the western side of a Victorian culvert (*see* Chapter 10).

Thirteen closely set beech piles (structure number 2637) were found at the bottom of this sondage. Several were directly overlain by a large baseplate (2636), also of beech, and at least one pile had a rebate cut in its top to receive the plate. Two pairs of narrow mortices had been cut into the upper surface of 2636 and one into each of the north and south sides. Both the large size (0.44m by 0.33m in cross-section) and the use of the double tenons suggest that the baseplate supported a very substantial structure. The western two upper mortices would have held a single, very substantial upright with its tenon secured by oak wedges (which survived *in situ*). This upright would have been braced by the angled timber rising from the pair of chase-mortices to the east. The brace could have been either internal or external to the main structure but the empty mortices in both the north and south faces of the baseplate show that the structure continued both north and south of this beam. A broad but shallow rebate at the top of the north side of the beam may have received a horizontal plank although the joint appears too shallow and isolated for a significant timber.

With the exception of the two wedges all six mortices were empty, implying that the structure was dismantled rather than being abandoned or collapsing. The absence of a timber extending from the mortice in the southern face is especially important, as the stone rubble base of the Iron Gate causeway had been built flush against the beam. This strongly suggests that the masonry represented a later structural phase succeeding the primary timberwork (*see* Chapter 6).

Dating the timbers: dendrochronology

Fifteen timbers comprising all 13 piles, the squared beam resting on them and a stray oak fragment were sampled for dendrochronology. All the samples except one of the piles were suitable for analysis, and all but one of these were successfully dated. The beech piles formed a very consistent group (Fig 66). The high degree of correlation suggests that they may have been derived from only a small number of trees. Each of these samples was complete to bark-edge and included a ring for 1276. The timber must, therefore, have been felled between summer 1276 and early 1277. The single oak sample did not include sapwood but the heartwood was complete to 1235. When allowance is made for missing heartwood and sapwood this sample may well be contemporary with the beech piles. The squared beech beam was also not complete to the bark-edge. Its ring sequence ended at 1266 and again there seems little reason to suppose it was not contemporary with the piles. Although not proven it seems likely that the beam is from a different tree or woodland group than the material used to make the piles.

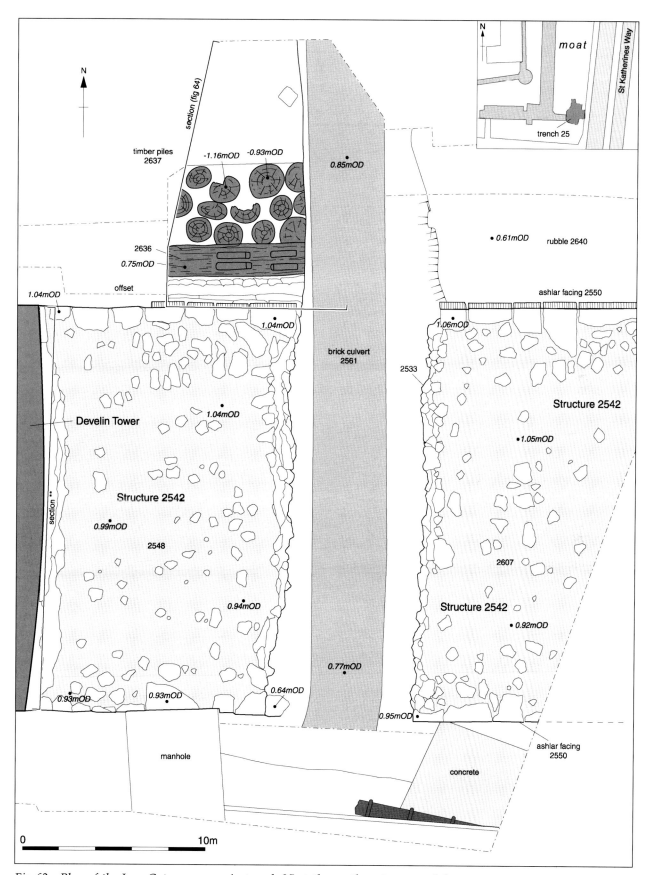

Fig 62   Plan of the Iron Gate causeway in trench 25 at the south-east corner of the moat.

Fig 63   The Iron Gate causeway as exposed in trench 25, seen here from Tower Bridge Approach.

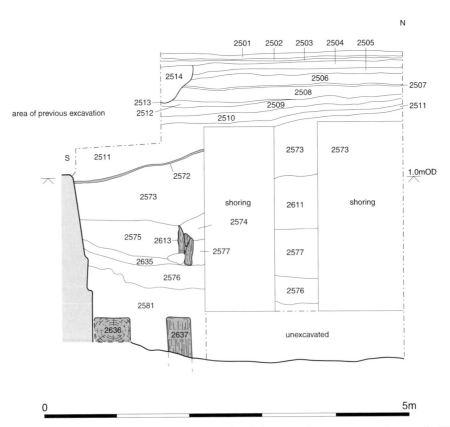

Fig 64   Western section through moat fills on the north side of the Iron Gate causeway in trench 25.

Fig 65   *The beech piles and beam found in the bottom of trench 25 at the south-east corner of the moat. The bark can be seen clearly on most of the piles, while the four empty mortices in the upper face of the beech are equally evident.*

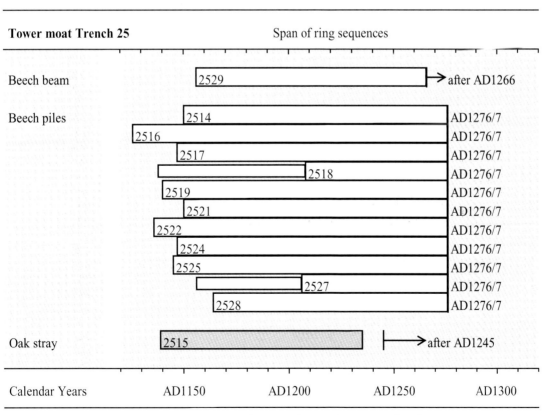

Fig 66   *Trench 25—dendrochronology bar diagram showing the dated position of each sample. White bars are beech, the grey bar is oak. Narrow bars represent counted but unmeasured rings. The interpretation for the oak sample based on the minimum estimated number of sapwood rings is also shown. For the beech samples, as in most cases the felling dates are derived from the survival of the bark edge.*

93

What function did the building serve?

An important source of information about the building and maintenance of the moat, at least as originally intended, lies in what we know of the water mills built by Edward I in association with his new works. The existence of mills is known from the Pipe Rolls and other sources. In 1278 660 beech piles were purchased for the construction of such a building on the east side of the Tower (E 372/121 *rot comp* 2d. See references to the *novum aliud molendinum versus Sanctam Katerinam*). Little more is known of the mill other than that it was for grinding corn and was almost certainly timber-framed. There is a reference for an income of 100 shillings from the mill at the Tower in the seventh year of Edward's reign (E 372/125 *rot comp* 125), but it does not specify which mill and, as we will see, there were several. This one was very short-lived, however, apparently being replaced by a masonry wall extending across the moat in 1292–3 (*see* Chapter 6).

The discovery of the beech piles in trench 25 and the dendrochronology results from them correspond remarkably with the Pipe Roll entry. The tree ring evidence strongly suggests that single trees could be divided into multiple piles, which adds considerably to our understanding of the reference. The moat mouth here would have been around 35m wide as dug in the 1270s, and this required closure. The size and spacing of the excavated piles, however, would mean that even 660 beeches would not be adequate to cross the space. If this figure is increased by a factor of between five and ten the task appears to be more realistic.

The beech beam, meanwhile, seems to be part of the mill structure itself. The oak wedges for the tenons perhaps suggest that the superstructure above the baseplate might have been of oak as well, but this cannot be proved. The wedges were a variation from the normal pegging of timber-framing and very probably reflected the unique strains and pressures of a mill with its rattling motion and its need for continual repair and adjustment. The rebating of some piles to receive the baseplate may also have been designed to prevent slippage.

THE SOUTH-WESTERN CAUSEWAY

Excavation at the south-west junction of the moat and the Thames centred on rather different initial priorities, though in many ways the results resembled those from trench 25. Trenches 30 and 31 lay on the south and north sides respectively of the great entrance causeway built by Edward I to stretch between his Byward Tower (at the corner of the outer curtain) and Middle Tower (Figs 67–77). The upper stages of the causeway are the product of at least one phase of rebuilding and much of the masonry above the moat lawn is of late post-medieval date (*see* Chapter 8). It was felt that original medieval work should survive below ground, and a major aim of these trenches was to establish whether this was the case. As so often happened throughout the excavations, the results far surpassed expectations.

Piled foundations

A Thames foreshore deposit of compact greenish brown silty clay (3147) was found across the bottom of trench 31. This layer was overlain by a grey silty clay (3138) with a 15 per cent limestone and gravel inclusion. This extended 3m north from the causeway and 0.8m into the northern extension where it partially covered clay 31222 (Chapter 4). Closely spaced timber piles (3146, 3154, 3176) had been driven through 3138 in a linear band from the Byward Tower westwards (Figs 67, 69). This band had evidently been continuous, but the insertion of a large brick-built culvert in 1843 had cut through the piles in the centre of the trench. Elsewhere they extended for *c*1m to the north of the causeway's face.

They were mostly beech (diameter up to 0.3m) with larger oak piles (diameter up to 0.64m) becoming more frequent towards the western edge of the trench. All the piles retained their bark. They lay at a level of −0.5m OD at the eastern end, rising to −0.3m at the western end of the excavation. Unlike the beech piles in trench 27, none of the tops appeared to have been chamfered and the pile-driving process probably caused most or all of the splits visible on several of them. Five piles were augered to establish their lengths. Three were *c*0.6m in length, the fourth was 0.95m long and the fifth 1.5m. All five augered piles were located towards the eastern end of the trench.

Wooden piles were also found on the south side of the causeway in the two small sondages that represented the only deep excavations possible here. A few beech piles (3068) were found to the west of the central arch in the causeway. These piles were at least 0.4m long and had been driven into a dark-grey clay foreshore layer (3069). Further beech piles (3064) were seen on the east side of the arch. They were 0.2m in diameter and had also been driven into Thames foreshore material (3063). The extremely restricted nature of the deeper excavations here made it physically impossible to take dendrochronology samples from either group of piles. Despite this it seems reasonable to conclude that they were contemporary with those on the north side of the causeway, as they had identical stratigraphic relationships with both the foreshore deposits and the original 13th-century masonry of the causeway.

The date of the northern piles: dendrochronology

Nineteen of the *in situ* piles found in trench 31 were sampled for dating (Figs 70, 71). Two had been felled in 1275/6 and the remainder in 1277/8, that is, one year after the material in trench 25. Three other beech timbers recovered from the backfill of the culvert put through the moat in the 19th century were also dated to 1277/8. These presumably came from the foundation raft; the culvert had been inserted so deeply into the moat (*see* Chapter 10) that the engineers would certainly have removed any piles in its way.

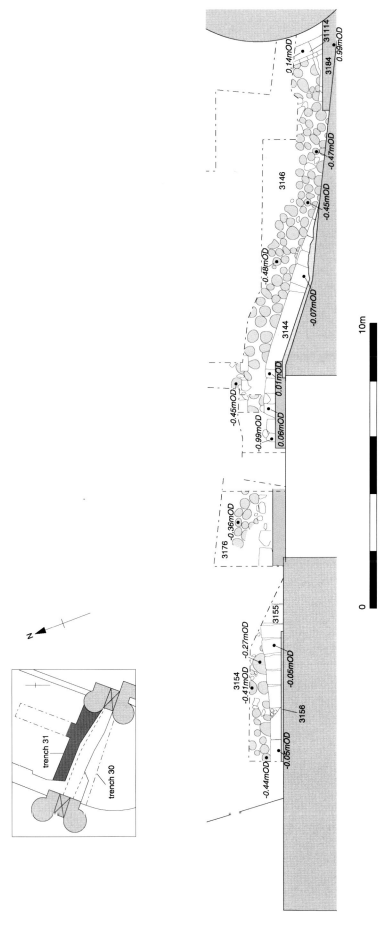

Fig 67 Plan of trench 31 on the north side of Edward I's western entrance causeway showing the late 13th-century beech piles and masonry.

Fig 68   Trench 31 and its extension on the north side of Edward I's south-western entrance causeway, seen from the top of the Byward Tower. The beech piles under the causeway are visible at bottom left, with the offset plinth over the piles. Note also the late 18th-century timbers in the centre of the main trench, the 19th-century brick culvert cutting that timberwork (immediately under the white pipes), and a further culvert at the south end of the extension.

The intercorrelation of this material is affected by the short overlaps between the groups of different date but the 1277/8 group is fairly internally coherent, suggesting a more restricted range of sources for the timbers than the 1240/1 material from either trench 27 or trench 31. The two samples from 1275/6 both derived from a much longer-lived tree. It is tempting to see these as part of a stockpile of older timber, but this cannot be proved. It is equally possible that they came from a recently dead tree within the stand being felled to provide the rest of the material.

The 13th-century masonry causeway: evidence from trench 31 (Figs 67, 72–4)

A 0.4m-thick mortar and Kentish Rag rubble pile cap (31115) overlay the piles at the far eastern end of trench 31. This provided the foundation for a single offset course of Purbeck marble (31114) at the base of the Byward Tower. The top of the offset lay at −0.14m OD. The wall (31101) of the tower's northern drum rose directly from the offset course with a 25° batter. The ashlar facing was partly concealed behind a thin tufa-like incrustation similar to deposits noted on other stretches of masonry that had been exposed to the tidal waters. This made it difficult to identify the stone type, but Dr Worssam believed that it too was likely to be Purbeck marble. The blocks measured from 0.5m by 0.24m to 0.6m by 0.22m. A mason's mark in the shape of a cross was identified on one of the ashlar blocks. A thin layer of white lime mortar (31113) overlay 31114 and butted against the battered face 31101. The deposit extended for only 0.4m and was 0.2m thick. It resembled the dumped mortar layers found against the outer curtain (*see* above).

Fig 69   Detail of the piles at the east end of trench 31. These piles are predominantly beech but a few oaks were used as well.

An east-west aligned wall (3184) also overlay the pile cap (31115). It was unclear whether the wall was keyed into the Byward Tower or simply butted against it. The lowest course appeared to be integral with the tower but the remainder of the wall seemed to butt against its battered face. Wall 3184 extended for 3m to the west of the Byward Tower and was constructed from eight courses of Purbeck marble to a height of 1.52m OD (Figs 72, 73). The characteristic small gastropods of this stone showed clearly in a number of places. The north face of the masonry comprised high-quality ashlar with very close jointing. The bonding matrix appeared to be lead. The bottom four courses seemed to terminate with a dressed western face, suggesting that the masonry returned to the south. A similar cross-shaped mason's mark to that seen on the Byward Tower was also found on wall 3184. This suggests that the two structures were broadly contemporary, despite the confused stratigraphic relationship between them.

A thin pile cap of grey lime mortar (3145/8 and 3153/8) with 20 per cent shell and crushed limestone inclusions covered the piles to the west of wall 3184. An offset of large roughly squared limestone blocks (3144, 3155 and 3180) had been built over the cap (Fig 67). The offset mostly consisted of a single course except for a small section to the east of the existing arch where two courses of smaller blocks were used. The offset course was not present immediately to the west of wall 3184, but entered the trench (as structure 3144) 7m west of the Byward Tower. It then ran west-north-west to east-south-east

to a point level with the eastern abutment of the existing archway position. The alignment then changed to east-west (structure 3180) across the face of the causeway's arch for 3.8m. The masonry appeared to be continuous in this stretch except where it had been cut away by the 1843 culvert. The offset then turned back slightly towards the causeway, running obliquely to it for 4m before returning east-west again (structure 3155) through to the western baulk.

The majority of the blocks were Reigate stone with occasional blocks of Purbeck limestone or marble. One block of calcareous tufa was also present. Dr Worssam identified this as a lithologically typical example, very porous with a pale yellowish grey colour (2.5Y 9/2). The stone formed at springs and was much used in Norman buildings in Kent. The Reigate blocks ranged in size from 0.45m by 0.3m to 0.68m by 0.3m. Cramp-holes were present on the northern faces of several blocks, suggesting that they were re-used. The holes tended to be very eroded (more so than had been noted on the Henry III masonry in trench 27). At least one of the Purbeck blocks was chamfered and may have derived from the structure that failed in 1240/1.

The dog-legged offset formed the foundation for the original construction of Edward I's causeway. It was overlain by a single 0.32m-deep course of chamfered Kentish Rag blocks (3156; Fig 67). This returned around the inner faces of the two abutments on either side of the central arch, proving that they were part of the original medieval structure

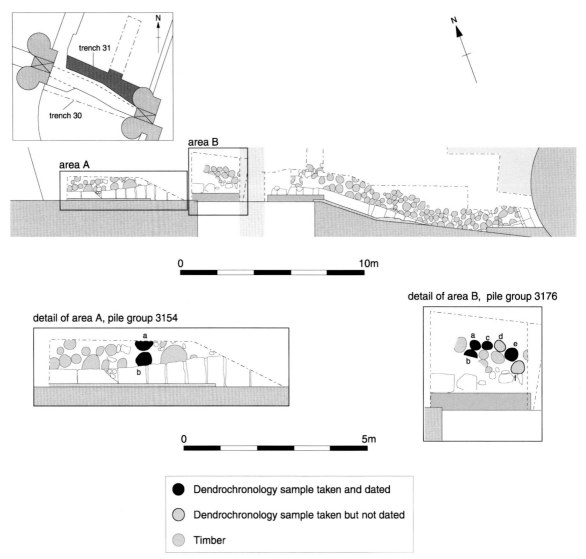

Fig 70   Plan showing the locations of dendrochronological samples taken in trench 31.

rather than a later reconstruction. The chamfer had been cut back to the wall face for 2.6m westwards from the western arch abutment during a later rebuild (Fig 74). The masonry above the chamfered course was constructed from ashlar blocks of Kentish Rag ranging in size from 0.2m by 0.21m to 0.65m by 0.31m. The facing (3157) was shown to be the original medieval work to a level of *c*2.4m OD (close to present ground level) to the west of the archway (Fig 72). Both abutments were also demonstrably original, showing that the 18th-century rebuild of the central arch had not totally destroyed the original construction. The ashlar also survived to the same level on the east side of the arch, but only for 3m. At this point the Reigate plinth, the chamfered course and the ragstone ashlar all passed behind a later phase of masonry facing (*see* Chapter 6). It was impossible to determine how far the original masonry continued back behind the later face.

The form of the 13th-century causeway on the Thames edge: evidence from trench 30

The abutments on either side of the central arch were also found to be original on the south side of the causeway (Fig 75). Here, the masonry to the west of the arch was largely faced with undressed, roughly squared limestone blocks (average measurement 0.6m by 0.4m by 0.3m). The western abutment itself, however, comprised blocks of Purbeck limestone ashlar (3014) measuring 0.7m by 0.4m. This abutment survived to a height of 2.5m OD. The eastern abutment, and indeed most of the original facing from there to the south drum of the Byward Tower, was also Purbeck ashlar. This is a pale grey to yellowish grey (10YR 8/2–3) crystalline shelly limestone. The curved shell fragments may be packed together in drifts, giving rise to the quarryman's name 'featherbed stone'. One particular block just to the west of the arch showed a transition downwards

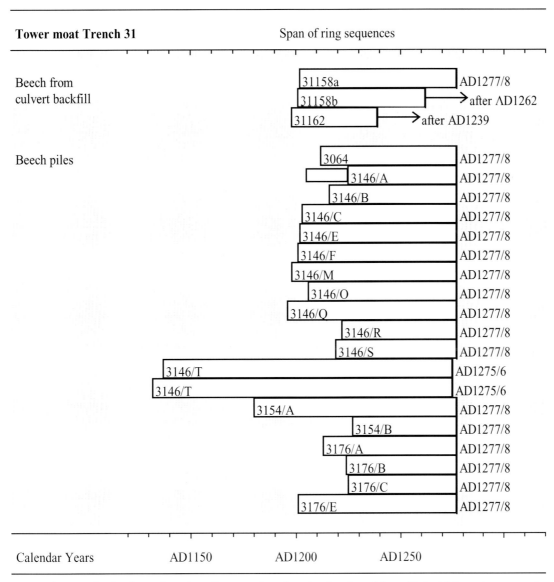

Tower moat Trench 31   Span of ring sequences

Beech from
culvert backfill
31158a — AD1277/8
31158b — after AD1262
31162 — after AD1239

Beech piles
3064 — AD1277/8
3146/A — AD1277/8
3146/B — AD1277/8
3146/C — AD1277/8
3146/E — AD1277/8
3146/F — AD1277/8
3146/M — AD1277/8
3146/O — AD1277/8
3146/Q — AD1277/8
3146/R — AD1277/8
3146/S — AD1277/8
3146/T — AD1275/6
3146/T — AD1275/6
3154/A — AD1277/8
3154/B — AD1277/8
3176/A — AD1277/8
3176/B — AD1277/8
3176/C — AD1277/8
3176/E — AD1277/8

Calendar Years   AD1150   AD1200   AD1250

Fig 71   Trench 31—dendrochronology bar diagram showing the dated position of late 13th-century samples. All the bars are beech. Narrow bars represent counted but unmeasured rings.

from crystalline shelly limestone in its top half to a limestone packed with small unbroken gastropods in its bottom half. The latter might thus almost be described as Purbeck marble. The true Purbeck marble occurs at a higher level in the Purbeck group than the Building Stones and the Broken Shell Limestone quarried for construction (Melville and Freshney 1982). Both the limestone and the marble would have been quarried on the Isle of Purbeck (Dorset) in medieval times and exported from Poole harbour to London.

The abutments and original facing appeared to be contemporary with a stretch of masonry (3052) returning south 2.5m to the east of the eastern abutment. Like the causeway itself this sat directly on the beech piles (3064). Structure 3052 (Fig 76) consisted of large roughly squared limestone foundation blocks (3061, 3062), which measured 0.5m×0.8m. The blocks were bonded with the

causeway masonry and ran south from it for 2m, continuing beyond the southern edge of the excavation. The structure above the foundations was built of Purbeck limestone ashlar measuring 0.3m by 0.5m. A fine lime-based mortar bonded many of the blocks, while lead yotting also survived in some areas. Both the east face of 3052 and the lower part of the causeway to the east of it (3026) were battered at an angle of c30° to a level of 1.6m OD. The causeway itself changed angle with a slight turn to the east 2.5m from structure 3052.

The east face (3053) of 3052 was eight courses high. These had been partially dismantled leaving only two blocks in each of the upper two courses. Three blocks survived in the next course down, while the next four all had five or six blocks. The lowest course continued into the south section. Five iron cramps (3055–3059) for joining the blocks were visible on the westernmost stones where the top faces of the blocks

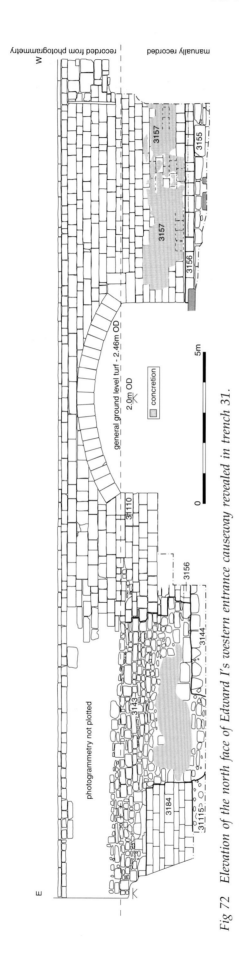

Fig 72 Elevation of the north face of Edward I's western entrance causeway revealed in trench 31.

were exposed, proving that the masonry had originally extended further to the south for its full height. Masonry 3052 was 2.4m wide with a core of irregular flint nodules and limestone bedded in a lime-based mortar. Most of the wall has been demolished to a level of 1.7m OD but it is visible to a height of 3.75m OD on the south face of the causeway. The west face (3051) of the buttress comprised roughly squared, undressed limestone blocks (measuring 0.15m by 0.25m on average) with a coarse lime-based mortar and was exposed to a depth of 0.15m OD. This masonry was much rougher than the east face but was very similar to face 3025 of wall 3017 to the west (*see* Chapter 6).

Historical considerations relating to Edward I's causeway

It is extremely difficult to determine the function of structure 3052, given the limitations imposed on the excavations by the post-medieval timberwork found in the trench (Chapter 3). Neither was a southern extension of the trench allowable because of constricted space on the Bowling Green. We are therefore left to speculate on what structure 3052 was and how it functioned. Three things are clear. Firstly, the masonry had extended further to the south than the fragment revealed in the excavation. Secondly, the east face (3053) was bonded in with the eastern part of the causeway and so the two were clearly part of the same build. Finally, the east and west faces (3053 and 3051 respectively) were of very different character in terms of materials and finish. This suggests that they were built at two different times. The evident contemporaneity of 3053 and 3026 (the eastern part of the causeway) strongly suggests that the crudely built west face was the later of the two.

Several implications flow from this conclusion. If face 3051 was a secondary construction, what did it replace? Had a fine ashlar face equivalent to 3053 been replaced at some time after the 1270s? This is not impossible but seems unlikely, unless there had been a major collapse of structure 3052. The remainder of the masonry (including the rubble core) was in good condition, however, and this perhaps militates against an explanation based on a catastrophic event like that which faced Henry III's builders. In fact it is clear that not only the faces of structure 3052 but also the face of the causeway itself to the east and west of it are of different character. Similar stones were used on either side, but the exceptional quality of the ashlar work on causeway face 3026 is not replicated from the west of 3052 to the eastern abutment of the central arch. Indeed the masonry here is mostly rubble and barely coursed up to approximately 2m OD. The masonry changes to reasonable quality limestone ashlar above this, but it is still not as fine as 3026.

There is a possibility that the causeway originally terminated at the eastern face of 3052, which would therefore have functioned as a revetment or

Fig 73   Purbeck Marble ashlar 3184, adjacent to the Byward Tower in trench 31. The stone may have been re-used from the Henry III masonry. Note the granite foundation pads for the ramp that provided access into the newly-backfilled moat in 1845.

abutment in the foreshore edge foreshadowing the reclamation of the Thames edge when the wharf was built during the 14th century. During the excavation there were suggestions that this earlier phase might even relate to Henry III's moat rather than Edward I's. This could not be tested adequately because of the restricted nature of the excavations, and especially because it was not possible to examine the junction of causeway masonry 3026 with the base of the Byward Tower's southern drum. It must be admitted that the theory of an early design is highly speculative at the moment, irrespective of who might have been responsible for it. It is worth remembering, however, that there was some evidence for changing designs on the north side of the causeway as well. The evident southern return of Purbeck marble wall 3184 was clearly at odds with the idea of a continuous causeway, for instance, though it might have acted as part of a drawbridge arrangement. Perhaps this was also related to an earlier design. Presumably this was soon changed to make the causeway an integral part of the defence-in-depth formed by successive Lion, Middle and Byward Towers, with drawbridges built into the linking causeways.

It is somewhat easier to relate the timber piles found in trenches 30 and 31 to documentary evidence. In 1276, 600 beeches were ordered to be felled in the King's park of Langley 'for piles to be placed under the mill to the west of the Tower'

(C 47/3/47. See reference to *DC fagis in parco Dm Regis apud Langleye prosternendis et pilos ad ponendum subtus molendinum ex parte occidentali Turris*). This western mill was repaired in 1292, but did not occur again in the sources and had vanished by 1335. The documents fail to pinpoint the exact position of the mill, but their evidence can be supplemented by practical considerations and, of course, the archaeological evidence. Given its rise and fall, the mills cannot have been run directly by the river, and so can only have operated by the tide, using the head of water backed up into the moat. As such they would have best been placed at the southern extremities of the moat, standing on or beside dams to retain the water. In the case of the western mill, the obvious position would have been beside the south-western causeway. Alternatively, although perhaps less probably, it may have stood to the south east, on a dam between the Byward Tower and the spur of wharf that already extended along the river's edge to that point (see the evidence for beech piles in test pit 36, above). In either case the documentary references coincide reasonably closely with the tree ring dates for the piles in trench 31. Perhaps the order was not carried out in full straight away, but over two seasons of felling.

It is worth noting here that Haiward and Gascoyne's 1597 survey shows three central arches in the south-western causeway. The single-span replacement built in the late 18th century (*see*

Fig 74 The offset plinth of Edward I's entrance causeway, founded on beech piles, to the west of the central archway. The masonry here is original medieval work in Kentish Rag. The left end of the chamfered bottom course (3156) has been crudely cut back, probably in the late 18th century.

Chapter 8) largely destroyed the evidence for the earlier formation. The insertion of a brick culvert through the arch in 1843 (*see* Chapter 10) probably removed any remaining evidence. At least we now know that the abutments of the arch below its springing are the original medieval work. Both the pile raft and the offset masonry foundation course appeared to be continuous across the archway, though this could not be used to prove whether there had been three arches originally or not.

On the face of it, to burden the castle's defended approaches with mills might seem curious. In an age when windmills were in their infancy, however, a potential power source on this scale was not to be wasted. A similar arrangement existed at Leeds Castle, where the ruins of a magnificent stone-built mill survive adjacent to the main entrance.

AN ISOLATED FRAGMENT OF THE BYWARD OR MIDDLE TOWER

A number of large blocks of stone were found in a layer (3060) close to the Byward Tower during the excavation of trench 30. The stones had clearly been dumped during the post-medieval period, but unfortunately there were no finds from layer 3060 to provide a more accurate date. Most of the stones were plain, but one (Fig 77) represents a near-complete capital from an engaged polygonal colonette. It is integral with its rear block, which contains joints to the voussoirs of arches springing to either side. Though the moulding has suffered extensive damage, its profile does survive in sufficiently good state for the complete moulding to be reconstructed with confidence.

The capital can be identified and dated securely by comparison with surviving examples elsewhere in

Fig 75   View of the central area in trench 30. The abutment under the west side of the central arch is original late 13th-century masonry. The block of masonry extending southwards from the face of the causeway just to the west of the abutment is a later medieval addition. The arch itself was rebuilt in the late 18th century.

the Tower of London. Its type is approximately diagnostic of date, conforming to the pattern sometimes called 'three-unit scroll' (Morris 1979, fig 16T). In this instance, the central element of the profile is not a scroll moulding but a keel, a common variant of particular currency in the west of England but by no means unusual elsewhere. Though the polygonal shape is less common than a round capital (mounted on a columnar shaft), this form has certain affinities with royal works in other places. These include Westminster Abbey and, even more closely, the chapel within the *Gloriette* in Leeds Castle, Kent, likely to date to the late-1280s (Colvin 1963, 695). Polygonal capitals and shafts can be seen, for example, in the basement of Little Wenham Hall, Suffolk, provisionally ascribed to the 1290s (Goodall 2000). Similar colonette capitals (also polygonal) can be seen elsewhere in the Tower, in the angle turrets of St Thomas's Tower, built as a water-gate between 1275 and 1281.

The function of the excavated fragment is confirmed by the survival on either side of the capital of the springings for flanking arches. These are set not in the same plane but at an angle of approximately 135°. Clearly they defined the inner faces of an octagonal or half-octagonal room. The Byward and Middle Towers are both (like St Thomas's Tower) works of the late 1270s and both contain octagonal rooms on their ground floors, with arched embrasures for arrow-loops. These are articulated by

polygonal shafts and capitals supporting the simple chamfered ribs of the stone vaults. There seems little doubt that the fragment originates in one of these two towers.

Mortar is present on more than one of the beds, which, with the additional evidence for finishing and breakage on the visible moulded surfaces, strongly suggests that the capital was installed as intended within the building, rather than being merely a reject from the masons' workshop. Both the Byward and Middle Towers have been subjected to heavy restorations, the latter particularly so in the early 18th century, when all of its windows or loops were replaced, most of them with large round-headed windows. Some on the ground floor were fronted externally with entirely unconvincing cosmetic arrow-loops, set in the new Portland facing (*see* PRO WO 51/100, /102, /103, /104). In the ground-floor room of the southern drum of the Middle Tower, works included the widening and heightening of the west-facing embrasure, creating clearance for a new round window-head. This inevitably involved the destruction of the medieval arch over the embrasure and, since the capitals are integral with the springing for this arch, almost certainly the removal of the capital itself. It is suggested that the fragment was removed from the building and jettisoned into the moat at the time of these works. Unfortunately, the accounts for the renovations of 1717–19 are not sufficiently detailed to identify this

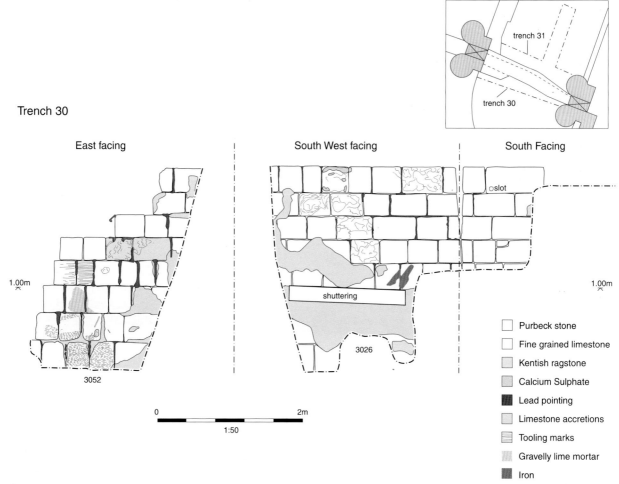

Trench 30

East facing · South West facing · South Facing

trench 31

trench 30

1.00m

shuttering

3026

1.00m

3052

0   2m

1:50

☐ Purbeck stone

☐ Fine grained limestone

☐ Kentish ragstone

☐ Calcium Sulphate

■ Lead pointing

☐ Limestone accretions

▤ Tooling marks

▨ Gravelly lime mortar

■ Iron

Fig 76   Elevations of masonry feature 3052 and causeway face 3026 immediately to the east of it in trench 30.

operation specifically in the documentary record, but‘ in view of the appearance of the window created, there is every likelihood that the alteration was made at this time.

The Byward and Middle Towers were constructed as part of a new and complex entrance into the fortress between 1275 and 1281. The Pipe Roll for 1275–6 mentions works to 'a certain barbican which has been built there on the river Thames', almost certainly the Lion Tower (PRO E372/120 *rot comp* 22). The construction of this building assumes that the designs for the other elements of the entrance (the causeways and the Byward and Middle Towers) were already finalised. Works to the towers were probably under way or even fairly advanced in the following year, when the Pipe Rolls mention 'Spanish iron for the catches, hinges and sliding bars to the new gates ... facing the city and wickets to the same' (PRO E372/121 *rot comp* 22). The first firm references to either of these towers occurs in 1278–9, in which it appears that the Middle Tower was known as 'the outer gate towards the town, which John le Picard guards'. The Byward was referred to as the tower with 'two small turrets' standing between the outer gate and the mill (itself probably standing due south of the Byward Tower on the spur

of the wharf; PRO E372/123 *rot comp* 20; E101 467/7 no 4: this location for the mill was first suggested by Beric Morley).

Unfortunately, as with all the accounts for Edward I's works at the Tower, there is no detailed evidence identifying master masons behind individual works, though the authors or directors of the Tower's works in general are known. Two figures are particularly mentioned in connection with Edward I's enlargement of the Tower: Brother John of the Order of Saint Thomas of Acre, and Master Robert of Beverley (eg, *Calendar of the Close Rolls, 1272–1279* (London 1900), 444. In this instance it is fairly certain that these two were responsible for design and execution rather than administration of the works: a third individual, Giles of Audenarde, was consistently named throughout the documents as 'keeper of the works' and it was in his name that accounts were rendered to the Exchequer). Brother John is the less well known from documentary sources, though his evident membership of a military order raises the suggestion that he may have been involved in the 'military' design of the new works at the Tower, several of whose features are innovative in the context of England. Master Robert of Beverley, on the other hand, is known to have been supervising

Fig 77   A colonette capital from layer 3060, trench 30. This must have come from the interior of either the Byward Tower or the Middle Tower.

works at Westminster Abbey from summer 1260 until November 1271, when Henry III appointed him viewer of the works at the Tower, Windsor and many other places (Colvin 1963, 108–9; 144). His name may less suggest a Yorkshireman than a product of the masons' workshop at Beverley Minster, during the construction of the chancel and transepts between *c*1220 and *c*1260. Robert, then, was an experienced master mason with an impressive portfolio of work on projects of the largest scale and highest quality.

THE USE OF BEECH IN THE TOWER MOAT

At this point it is worth pausing for an extensive consideration of the use of beech timbers in the Tower moat during the successive reigns of Henry III and Edward I. Today beech is widely regarded as being a very poor timber for outdoor use because it is not resistant to the weather and is prone to insect attack (for example Edlin 1971, 184). Certainly, when beech is excavated on wetland archaeological sites it is typically waterlogged and soft. This contrasts with the heartwood of oak, which remains extremely tough, and with elm, which appears not to become saturated. Beech was, however, the dominant species of timber used in the construction of buildings associated with the 13th-century moats at the Tower. It was used for piling in trenches 25, 27, 30, 31 and 36, possibly as scaffolding in trench 27 and as the baseplate for the probable mill of 1276 in trench 25. These trenches provide one of the largest excavated groups of beech from medieval Britain.

Many entries in medieval documents relating to piling make specific requests for elm and sometimes alder or beech (Salzman 1997, 84–5). Elm and alder are recognised today as the two specialist underwater timbers and elm piles were found under the Tower wharf's 13th/14th-century riverside wall during trial excavations in the 1920s (information from English Heritage archive drawings). Elm piles were also used in the foundations of the 14th-century Jewel Tower at Westminster Palace (Taylor 1996, 23). The reputation of beech as 'lasting excellently' under water was still believable in the early 20th century but is not recognised today. The frequent choice of beech for piling, now known from several London sites, indicates that it was considered a good underwater timber in the medieval period.

The use of beech will partly have been prompted by the relative cheapness of large straight-grown timber and its availability close to London. The beech piles of trench 25 are believed to be those requested to be cut from 'the King's park at Langley' (Impey and Keevill 1997, 22). The selection of this timber for such an important structural element as the underwater baseplate for the mill of 1276 in trench 25 cannot easily be explained as simply for cheapness and ease. The use of beech, both as piles and as a baseplate below the water level (with oak uprights rising from it), was also noted in late 12th/13th-century contexts in London at excavations at the Thames Exchange (Milne 1992, 59–60). Its use for what may be scaffolding in trench 27 would be more surprising, but for short-term work and with its feet in water this may have been a reasonable choice.

There is no evidence from the Tower moat that the medieval selection of this timber was unwise in any of its applications and none of the timbers had failed. It should, however, be considered inferior to elm and oak heartwood in that it does over centuries eventually become waterlogged, but in this aspect it is like another underwater specialist, alder.

The dendrochronology of beech

Since its beginnings in the 1970s modern dendrochronology in Britain has been focused on oak. Not long after this, medieval elms were examined (*see* Brett 1978) but with little success. Most other studies of elms have also failed to give useful interpretative information (eg, Tyers forthcoming), although a number of samples from Droitwich were successfully dated by direct reference to the oak chronology from the same structure (Groves and Hillam 1997). Softwoods and beech were the subject of independent attempts, beginning in the 1990s, to cross-match and identify absolute dates for these timbers. Softwoods were usually revealed in post-medieval contexts and both biogeographical and documentary evidence points to their non-local origins. Beech meanwhile is strongly represented in London sites of the 11th to 13th centuries but rarely thereafter. The beech from the Tower moat is one of the larger groups from London and comes from the later period of its use. The Tower data further strengthens the sequence—particularly for the 13th century, which had hitherto been fairly weak—and the data independently matches both oak and beech sequences (Table 2). This helps to confirm the reliability of the dates and provides evidence for the coherence of the beech data. Unfortunately, one side effect of this is that it is still not possible to identify when 'same trees' are present in a group such as this and when the timbers are just very similar. Comparative studies of modern beech are required to resolve this.

The Tower beeches again confirm the advantage to dendrochronologists of beech over oak: because there is no definable heartwood/sapwood differentiation the timbers tend to survive to bark-edge or not at all. Thus for most beech assemblages, felling dates are both forthcoming and well replicated. In contrast, oaks frequently survive only to the heartwood/sapwood transition and date-ranges for felling are commonly the best results that can be produced.

THE LION TOWER

The development of the Lion Tower Menagerie (based on research by Dr G Parnell)

As we have already seen, Edward I's expansion of the castle and its defences involved the construction of a new entrance into the south-west corner of the Outer Ward at the Byward Tower, the moat being crossed by a bridged causeway. The west end of the causeway was defended by the Middle Tower, which in turn was protected by a massive semicircular barbican outwork known as the Lion Tower (Figs 78, 79). The moat was taken around this and a second causeway bridged the north arm to provide access from Tower Hill. This second causeway was guarded by a gate tower (the Lion Gate). These arrangements survived unaltered into the early post-medieval period, as shown on Haiward and Gascoyne's survey of 1597.

There is much that is obscure about the early history of the Royal Menagerie at the Tower of London, not least the date and circumstances concerning the transfer of the animals into Edward I's great barbican at the western entrance. A reference to the making of a lock for the gate towards the lions and leopards in 1335 and another to the 'Lion Turret' in 1338 suggest, from their context, that the Menagerie was already established there by the reign of Edward III. This lends some credibility to John Stow's statement that the beasts had been kept in the barbican since Edward I's time. The precise name 'Lion Tower' is first recorded in a report on the condition of the castle prepared in 1531–2. The barbican is shown on some early depictions of London, such as Wyngaerde's panorama of 1544, but the earliest detailed cartographic evidence is Haiward and Gascoyne's survey of 1597. This shows the barbican surrounded by a water-filled moat with a building on the south-east corner which, from later documentary accounts, is known to have formed the official residence of the Menagerie Keeper.

John Stow, writing in 1598, makes it clear that the beasts were kept in the Lion Tower. Paul Hentzner, who visited the Tower in the same year, refers to the animals being kept in a small house near to the entrance of the fortress 'fitted up for the purpose with wooden lattices at the Queen's expense'. These were probably the structures that were extensively refurbished in 1604–6 with, among other things, new floors and trap doors operated by pulleys. The cages were evidently situated against the outer wall of the barbican beneath tiled roofs; they were two-storeyed with internal stairs to allow the lions to climb up and down. A new exercise yard was created in the northern extension of the moat to the west by the building of a brick wall to hold back the waters of the Thames. Within the yard a great stone cistern was erected 'for the Lyons to drincke and washe themselfes in'. Access into the yard was provided by two passageways cut through the 'thicke round wall' of the barbican. These were controlled by sliding doors operated by pulleys, with a great viewing platform overhead for 'the Kinges Ma[tie] to stande on'. The structure was replaced by a new one in 1622–3 described as 92 feet long and 10 feet wide.

Excavations on the Lion Tower site, 1996–9

Examination of the Lion Tower and its immediate surroundings was not a major priority of the 1995–7

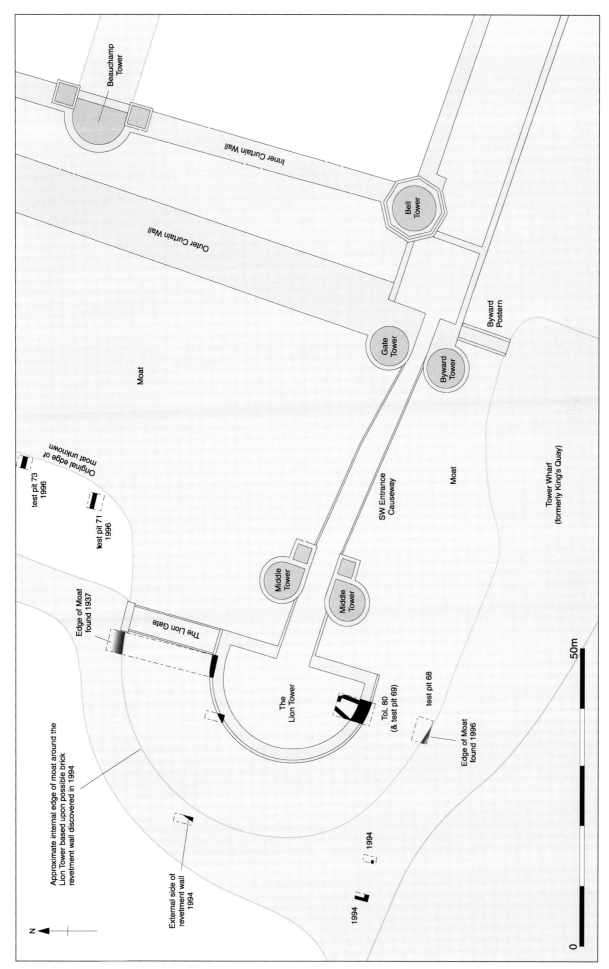

Fig 78 Reconstruction plan of the Lion Tower area in the mediæval period, using the evidence of archaeological observations from the 1930s and the 1990s.

Fig 79   A model showing how the Lion Tower area might have looked in the late 13th or early 14th century.

evaluations, although three test pits were excavated on its site in 1996. Subsequently a small area excavation was carried out in 1999. This was intended to do little more than confirm the position of the tower itself and, if possible, expose the top of one animal cage in plan. The excavation was carried out in association with a television production for BBC2's *Timewatch* series.

The medieval masonry was exposed successfully in each of the three test pits dug in 1996, despite the presence of densely packed modern services. Test pit 68 was excavated on the historically documented line of the revetment wall on the south side of the Lion Tower moat, immediately in front (east) of Salvin's pumphouse (now the Tower Shop). This located the medieval Reigate stone masonry surviving to 3.45m OD, capped by five courses of brickwork providing a further 0.5m of masonry (ie, to 3.95m OD). Test pit 69 was dug 8m to the north of the revetment and exposed the face of the Lion Tower itself. This survived to a height of 3.96m OD, with the top five courses again in brick. The latter was probably original 13th-century work. The outer wall of the Lion Tower was also found in pit 70, immediately to the north of the pumphouse's north-west corner. The top of the masonry survived at approximately 3.84m above OD.

The 1999 trench involved the re-excavation of test pit 69 and its extension northwards. The full dimensions were 6m by 4m (Figs 80, 81). A Victorian culvert ran in front of the south face of the barbican and restricted the extent to which the face could be investigated. Nevertheless it was po ssible to

establish that it comprised a patchwork of well-hewn Kentish ragstone blocks and red unfrogged bricks (9). (The context numbers in this description are from the 1999 excavations.) Two courses of stone and seven of brick were visible to a depth of 0.55m from the top of the wall. The bricks were bonded with a light-grey sandy mortar. No bonding material was visible between the masonry blocks. As before a further five courses of red and yellow unfrogged bricks (29) were found to a level of 4.08m OD. The bricks measured 260mm by 110mm by 70mm and were bonded with a yellow-brown sandy mortar. The inner face of the wall (23) was also revealed. It comprised roughly hewn limestone blocks of varying dimensions, bonded with hard grey mortar. Excavation down the face of the wall exposed four regular courses 0.63m deep in total. An original embrasure was identified between the two faces, although it had been much altered in the post-medieval period. The evidence for this and the remaining stratigraphy in the trench is considered in Chapter 8.

THE EAST MOAT TURRETS

Three turrets once jutted out from the outer curtain wall into the east moat. Only the southern of the three is still visible above ground. It has been suggested that the other two were slighted when the moat was drained and infilled in 1843 (Parnell 1993, 37). The south turret alone, however, is shown on the Haiward and Gascoyne and Holcroft Blood perspective plans of 1597 (Fig 84) and 1688 (Fig 115)

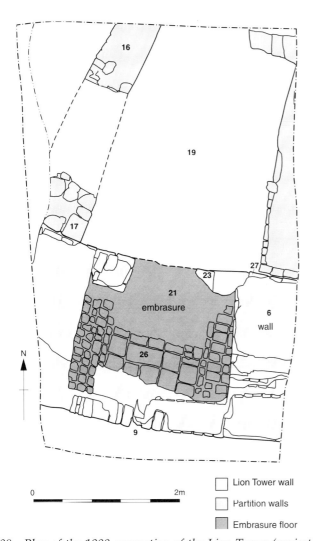

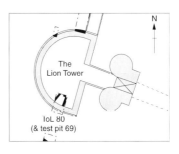

Fig 80   Plan of the 1999 excavation of the Lion Tower (project code ToL 80).

respectively. The Board of Ordnance survey of 1681–2 also shows one turret only, but with three thickenings of the outer wall face between it and the Brass Mount. A plan of 1726 (PRO Works 31/27) shows the three foundations, but again only the south turret stood above this level.

An early 19th-century illustration (*see* Fig 146) and especially a watercolour painted in 1826 by J Tugman (*see* Fig 147) may reconcile this discrepancy. They show the southern turret largely as it survives today but, crucially, part of the battered foundation was exposed above the moat waters. Indeed, the batter continued up to join directly onto the vertical face of the turret in a way that does not happen today. The middle and northern turrets are also visible on the Tugman painting, but here the battered face is taken continuously back to conjoin the outer curtain slightly above halfway between the water line and the parapet. There appears to be a door through the curtain onto the top of the northern 'turret'. There is an arrow-loop in this position now, so such a doorway might be plausible. There are many other points of detail which seem to be accurate from the artist's viewpoint, and so Tugman's depiction can

probably be taken as a reasonably accurate record of the early 19th-century scene along the eastern defences. Presumably, therefore, the middle and northern features were omitted from earlier surveys because they did not reach fully to the parapet. They evidently did rise above water level, and must have been reduced to their current level in the way suggested by Dr Parnell.

Archaeological evidence for the turrets (Figs 82, 83)

Peter Curnow in 1959–60 and Geoffrey Parnell in 1981 had already carried out excavations on the three turrets (or their remains) in the east moat. The three below-ground foundations had also shown up very clearly on the resistivity and radar surveys carried out early in 1996. The 1981 excavation had been very limited in extent, however, while the records of the 1959–60 excavation were frustratingly silent where moat fills were concerned. Much of the archaeological context for the structures was thus missing. Curnow's trench against the standing southern turret was therefore re-excavated in 1997 (trench 83). This involved little more than the

Fig 81   View of the 1999 excavation of the Lion Tower, seen from the top of the Middle Tower.

removal of his backfill and recording of the exposed sections, though a small amount of new excavation was carried out in the bottom of the trench to examine the relationship between the turret foundations and the moat itself. The moat fills are considered in subsequent chapters.

Natural London Clay (8403) was found at the bottom of trench 83 towards its eastern end at −0.7m OD (Fig 83). This was significantly deeper than the level recorded in trench 14 to the south (*see* above), perhaps because of the localised effect of the masonry. Equally, though, this exposure of the clay was close to the centre of the ditch rather than at its inner edge as was the case in trench 14. The clay was cut by the construction trench (8401) for a large masonry foundation (8313). The cut was seen only within the confines of a narrow hand-dug slot along the north side of the masonry. It appeared to be 0.32m wide, sloping down for 0.2m at 45° and then

vertically for a further 0.2m to a flat bottom at −1.08m OD. The primary fill of the construction trench was a 100mm-thick compact brown silty clay (8402) containing 15 per cent mortar and gravel. This formed the base for the masonry foundation.

The earliest part of the masonry structure consisted of a yellowish white mortar core (8382) measuring at least 1.7m by 1.65m. Only the upper surface and part of the north face were seen, but there was no evidence for substantial quantities of stone rubble in the core. The exposed north side of the core was faced with roughly squared Kentish Rag blocks (8383). Typical blocks measured 0.2m by 0.15m by 0.17m bonded by a hard yellowish white lime mortar. A single vertically set chamfered block (evidently re-used) was noted at the eastern edge of the foundation. This was identified as Purbeck limestone, a medium-grey crystalline limestone, packed with thin black arcuate shell fragments and

110

Fig 82   The battered foundations of a medieval turret against the outer curtain wall in the east moat, exposed in trench 83. The turret itself can be seen, with Victorian re-facing in the lower levels. The rest of the superstructure appears to be original, with the exception of the arrow loops. The Constable Tower, on the inner curtain wall (upper left), and the Waterloo Barracks (upper right) rise above the outer curtain in the background.

ostracods. Masonry 8383 was 0.8m deep, with the top lying at −0.29m OD. At least six courses of masonry were exposed, but the faced blocks were covered with lime mortar, making an accurate figure impossible to determine. The structure had been truncated by the 1843 culvert 11.6m out from the outer curtain wall.

The mortar core was overlain by two courses of Kentish Rag ashlar blocks (8379) in hard yellowish brown lime mortar. The east side of 8379 formed a pronounced step, faced with ashlar, rising directly from 8382/3. The blocks were all 0.65m in length. The lower and upper courses were 0.22m and 0.27m deep respectively, with the top course lying at 0.25m OD. The north face of the structure was made up of roughly squared and faced Kentish Rag (8381). The blocks varied in dimensions from 0.16m by 0.16m to 0.28m by 0.16m, with nine or ten courses bonded with a white lime mortar. The wall face was covered in the same accreted lime seen elsewhere in the moat excavations. The eastern end of each course was set

back from the underlying one, forming a series of steps. These were capped with wedge-shaped limestone creating a 30° battered face (8384).

The lowest nine courses of 8384 were made of Pond Freestone from the Portland Limestone Formation of the Isle of Purbeck. The upper two courses were absent or badly eroded, but several of the surviving pieces were identified as Bembridge limestone. Shelly Purbeck stone and Kentish Rag had also been used here. The top of the structure was a horizontal platform of ragstone rubble and mortar (8380) at 2.39m OD, 0.45m below the existing ground surface. This represented a demolition horizon (8386), and it is clear that the battered face originally rose much higher than this as shown by Tugman's painting, described above. The east face of the surviving buttress on the outer curtain wall has been substantially rebuilt or refaced to a height of 2.2m above ground level. The masonry appears to be original above this rebuild. The interface between the original and new builds probably marks the point at

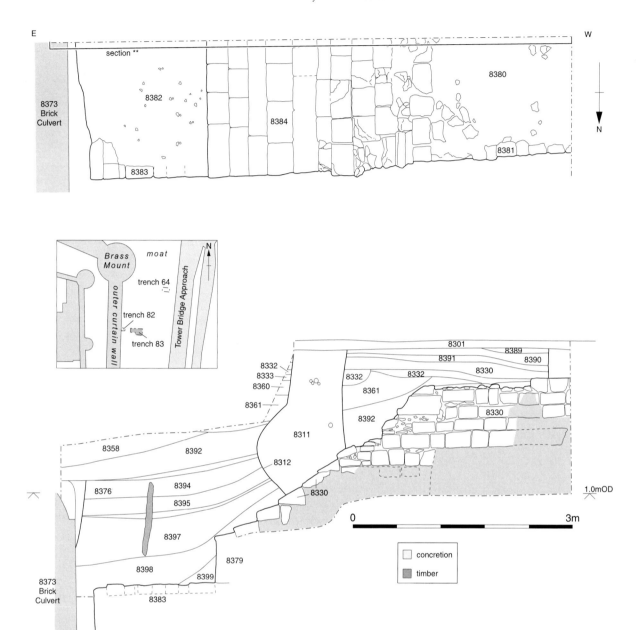

Fig 83   Plan and composite profile/section of the turret foundation excavated in trench 83 (east moat).

which the battered face would have joined the vertical turret wall. The rebuilding is most likely to have occurred during or very soon after the draining and infilling of the moat in the 1840s.

A number of loose worked stone blocks were recovered from the backfill of Peter Curnow's excavation. These were identified as Bembridge limestone (stones 51–3, 55–7 and 61), Reigate (stones 54 and 59) and Pond Freestone (stones 60 and 63). A further block (stone 62) was of uncertain identification but was also probably Pond Freestone.

Interpretation

The foundation (8313) below the battered Pond Freestone facing of the southern turret had also been seen in Curnow's 1959–60 excavations. Then, however, it had been described as a mortar and rubble raft. A similar feature was noted to the east of the middle turret. It can now be seen as part of a continuous foundation sunk to considerable depths in the moat. The foundation had been truncated by the 1843 culvert in the centre of the moat, so that unfortunately we cannot determine how much further it would have continued to the east. It seems unlikely that it would have been taken across the full width of the moat, not least because the same type of foundation appears to have been provided for the central turret (and perhaps for the northern one as well). That much is implicit from the record of an equivalent mortar and rubble 'raft' against the middle turret.

Straight joints were noted between each of the turrets and the battered lower portion of the outer curtain wall in the earlier excavations (Chapter 2). This seems to show that they had been built after the original part of the outer curtain had been completed, though Parnell believes that 'there is no reason to suppose that they are secondary' (1993, 37–8). He cites the use of Bembridge limestone in the battered face as supporting evidence for this. Dr Worssam's analysis of the masonry here confirms that some Bembridge stone was used, but that the Pond Freestone was more significant. Despite this it seems quite probable that there was no significant time lapse between the two constructions.

The function of the turrets remains something of a puzzle. They face outwards towards the extra-mural suburbs of the city, specifically onto the precinct of the Hospital of St Katherine. The latter may have felt aggrieved about losing tranches of its land to the growing Tower defences during the 13th century but can scarcely have posed a threat to the castle. The east side of Edward I's extended castle also seems to have been less heavily (or at least less ostentatiously) defended than the west. This imbalance becomes less apparent if one accepts Dr Parnell's suggestion (ibid) that they may have been 'intended to accommodate stone-throwing devices'.

Chapter 6:   Period 3: Later Medieval and Early Post-Medieval Activity in the Moat

INTRODUCTION

The development of the wharf during the middle and later decades of the 14th century represented the last major extension to or alteration of the Tower's defences until the late 17th century (compare Fig 84 with Figs 114–115). The wharf was created by reclaiming land from the north bank of the river Thames, thus finally closing off the defensive walls from the river water. There were some other new constructions, while many existing elements of the defences (including parts of the outer curtain wall) underwent significant modification. Once again these were obvious targets for archaeological and historical evaluation and research, usually in tandem with our aims to get back to the earliest phase in the history of each major structure.

THE CRADLE TOWER

This fine building on the outer curtain wall is the main survival at the Tower from Edward III's reign (1327–77). The Cradle Tower represented a private water-gate for the king giving direct access via Water Lane into the royal accommodation in the south-east quadrant of the Inner Ward. At least one document (E 101 471/2 m9) specifically refers to it as the 'King's Postern', establishing its significance as part of the royal palace. The new tower was built between 1348 and 1355, when the wharf only extended as far eastwards as St Thomas's Tower. It projects forwards from the curtain, and contains a central entrance archway protected by a portcullis.

Given that the tower was designed to provide a royal entrance to the castle from the river, it seemed

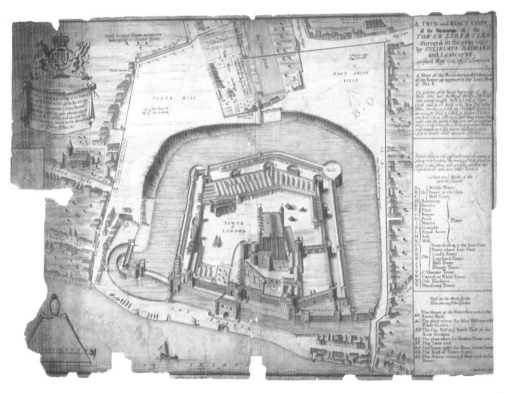

Fig 84   *A True and Exact Draught of the Tower Liberties, Surveyd in the Year 1597 by Gulielmus Haiward and J. Gascoyne, commissioned by the Lieutenant of the Tower, Sir John Peyton, and represented here in an 18th-century copy; the original is lost. The survey (see Keay 2001) is an essential source of information about the late Tudor Tower and Liberties, but is reproduced here for its depiction of the moat, which then retained its medieval form intact. Note the extension of the ditch around the semicircular Lion Tower (lower left), the battlemented Develin Tower causeway (demolished 1680), protected by the landward 'Tower above the Iron Gate', and the irregular un-revetted outer edge to the moat. The 'Cittie ditch'—shown here more schematically than accurately—had by then been cut off from the moat, which it had once joined.*

115

reasonable to expect some evidence for a landing stage associated with it. There was no evidence for what this might be, but some combination of a timber jetty with a hard-standing upon which vessels could be beached was anticipated. A similar contrivance was achieved using timber and chalk in the St Thomas's Tower basin and entrance in the 17th century (Parnell 1993, 62, fig 42; *also see* Chapter 2). Test pit 56 was therefore excavated against the south face of the tower in 1996 to determine whether there was any evidence for a landing area (Fig 85).

The excavation revealed an offset chalk plinth or raft (5625) apparently supporting foundations of compacted gravel and rubble (5609, 0.48m thick, over 5620, 0.25m thick). Certainly there was no visible evidence for the foundations cutting into the chalk, and the rubble had a noticeably irregular edge. The south edge of the chalk plinth lay beyond the edge of the excavation, but it must have been at least 0.6m wide. Two stakeholes (5616 and 5618) were found in the chalk surface at the base of the trench, with fragments of the timbers surviving *in situ*. They were probably contemporary with 5625. The masonry of the tower (5621–3) started at 0.2m OD (ie, c1.5m below grass level) and was offset by up to 1.2m over the rubble foundation. There was a chamfered offset course (5622) at 1.32m OD. It is possible that the chalk raft and associated stakes represented a landing stage, but the evidence is not entirely convincing and more extensive excavation would be necessary to confirm such an interpretation.

THE WHARF AND SOUTH MOAT

The construction of the wharf during the 14th century finally created a moat that fully enclosed the castle and separated the Thames from the curtain walls. Fourteen test pits were excavated against the wharf wall (ie, the wall running along the south side of the moat towards the Thames) in 1996 (Fig 86). Some of these were largely dedicated to the examination of later features such as the Victorian penstock in pit 34, but many also encountered evidence for the original construction work. They showed that the oak piles had been driven into the accumulated Thames foreshore silts to consolidate them before any further construction work occurred (Figs 87–8). This was essentially the same technique as had been used under the outer curtain wall along the river frontage in the 1270s and 1280s. The 14th-century piles were typically 0.5m in diameter and appeared to be fairly regularly if rather widely spaced. Only one pile was revealed in most of the 2m-wide test pits, but in one case (pit 48) two were located 1.6m apart. The remaining piles would broadly fit into a similar spacing. This accords well with the evidence from Curnow's excavations around St Thomas's Tower (Chapter 2).

In every pit where they were found the piles supported horizontal oak beams. These had presumably been part of a continuous sill underlying and supporting the masonry wall. The beams found during 1996 had obviously been laid between the piles, but it was not clear whether they were jointed

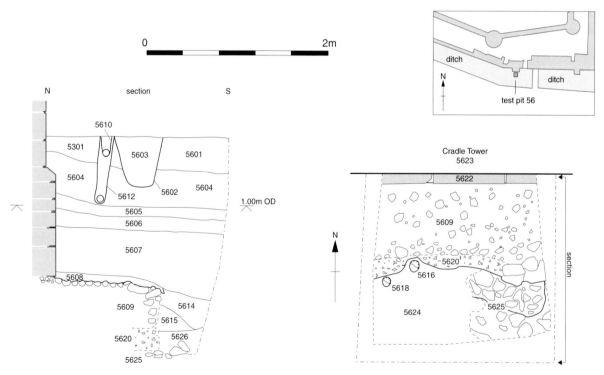

Fig 85 Section and plan of test pit 56 at the south-west corner of the Cradle Tower.

Fig 86 The Cradle Tower, front right, with a test pit being excavated against its south-west corner. St Thomas's Tower is in the background, and the wharf runs along the left-hand side of the photograph.

onto them. The sequential positioning of the wharf masonry, the sill and the piles meant that evidence for such joinery was always hidden from view, but it seems reasonable to assume that the beams were fixed onto the vertical timbers in some way. The timbers survived in good condition in most pits, but in a few cases either the pile or the beam—or sometimes both—had decayed. In a few extreme cases this left a void where the wood had rotted away. In one case (test pit 53) a raft of mortared limestone rubble was found beneath the timbers. It was impossible to determine whether this was earlier than or contemporary with the piles and beams, but

it seems most likely that they were set in at about the same time. Curnow, in the late 1950s, recorded similar rubble at the bottom of the wharf, with further horizontal beams and vertical piles linking back under the core of the wharf (Chapter 2).

In general the tops of the timber foundations were found at around 0.4m to 1m OD, but there was one major exception to this—test pit 39, located against the wharf wall just to the west of St Thomas's Tower, where the excavations reached −0.64m OD before foreshore levels were encountered. The wharf wall itself was offset by *c*0.58m at −0.17m OD and no timberwork was noted in the pit. This was located

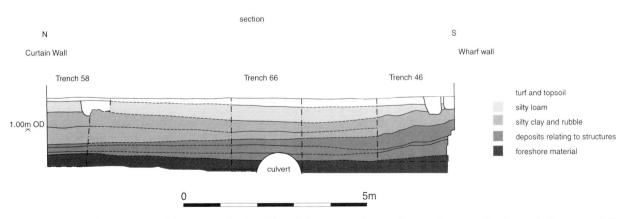

Fig 87 Section (reconstructed from test pits 58, 66 and 46) across the south moat between St Thomas's Tower and the East Drawbridge.

Fig 88   Test pit 45 against the wharf wall. An oak foundation beam is visible at the base of the wall. Note the stone masonry below turf level, with the brick re-build above.

very close to where the fine ashlar masonry inspection chamber over a deeply set culvert was found in 1959 (Chapter 2). No sign of such a culvert was found within the 1996 excavation, but it could either have lain still deeper or have been removed during a rebuild of the wharf wall at some undocumented point. In either circumstance the culvert and chamber seem most likely to provide the appropriate context for the exceptional depth of excavation required in test pit 39.

The timber foundations therefore seem to have provided a laced platform upon which the wharf itself (and its facing walls) could be built. The wall on the moat side of the wharf has been rebuilt on several occasions since the 14th century, resulting in much of the original work being obscured or removed (especially in the predominantly brick wall above the current moat grass level). The lower parts of the wall revealed in the test pits mostly appeared to be the original build, however, and consisted entirely of stonework. This was poorly coursed if at all. Some stretches of the medieval masonry display severe bulging, especially at the extreme east end where the distortion appears to have been caused by root growth from plane trees on the wharf behind the wall.

THE IRON GATE CAUSEWAY

The timber mill and dam at the south-east corner of Edward I's moat were replaced by a stone causeway during the 14th century (Fig 89). The survival of the masonry below ground was proved by the excavation of trench 7 in 1995, but this did little more than locate its north edge. The much larger trench (25) excavated in 1996 provided far more detail about its construction and development. The top of the structure (2542) was fully exposed for a maximum length of approximately 10m eastward from the Develin Tower (Figs 62–3). It was impossible to expose any of the south face because of a succession of Victorian and modern features running through, alongside and against it, but the north side was investigated to its full depth in the sondage already described in Chapter 5. The causeway was 5.3–5.4m wide at a level of c1m OD, where it had been truncated by demolition in the late 17th century (Chapter 7). The following paragraph largely relates the results from the northern sondage (Figs 64, 65, 90).

Six irregular courses of Kentish Rag rubble bonded with yellow-white lime mortar formed the base (2580) of the causeway, resting on the late 13th-century beech piles (2637) and against the south face of beam 2636 (Chapter 5). The stones measured between 0.1m to 0.45m in length and 0.06m to 0.15m in height. A 0.15m-deep offset was present above the fourth course, with a further 0.1m offset above the top one. Three courses of fine ashlar (2550) completed the masonry, in beds of 0.32m, 0.36m and 0.42m thickness from top to bottom. These courses were battered, the lower ones being vertically faced. The top course on the south side was clearly battered

Fig 89   A different view of the model shown on Figure 79, showing the Iron Gate causeway as it may have looked in the later medieval period.

as well and it is likely that this would have continued down at least the upper face there. The blocks on the north side were 0.4m to 0.9m long and 0.2m to 0.4m thick where visible. The rear (internal) faces of the top course were visible due to the late 17th-century truncation, and the stones were very irregular. This was confirmed when numerous blocks from the structure were recovered from the backfill of the 1843 culvert (*see* Chapter 10).

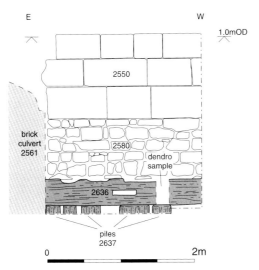

Fig 90   Partial elevation of the north side of the Iron Gate causeway as exposed in Trench 25.

The ashlar was bonded with yellowish white lime mortar, indistinguishable visually from the matrix in the lower seven courses. The causeway core (2548 and 2607), meanwhile, was formed of Kentish Rag rubble pieces up to 0.35m across bonded with the same material. The rubble showed no sign of coursing where it was exposed by the culvert trench, but seemed to have been poured in. There was no evidence for a break in the core between the lower freestone courses and the ashlar above. The two are therefore believed to represent a single build.

The finish of the Kentish Rag was of very high quality, with fine tooling and jointing to the battered north face. The batters mean that the faces were formed in 'skew ashlar', with the top and bottom of the stones parallel but with the outer face sloping. Bernard Worssam pointed out that this method (spelt 'scuassheler') is mentioned in the accounts for the repair of Rochester Castle from 1367 to 1369 (Larking 1859; Worssam and Tatton-Brown 1994, 107). He also noted that the large slab size was consistent with sources available from about 1380 (eg, the West Gate at Canterbury) to the early 16th century (eg, St John's Priory gatehouse, Clerkenwell; Worssam and Tatton-Brown 1994). The timber mills and dam at the south-east corner of the moat had been replaced by a stone wall in 1292 (E 403/79. Note payment of £161 11s 2½d to Brother John of Acre *assignato ultra operaciones muri construendi apud Turrim loco molendinorum versus domum Sancte Katerine*). This wall carried a roadway across the moat to the Develin Tower (or a preceding structure on the site) by 1323, when the 'postern of St Katherine's' was mentioned (E 469/7. See payment of 7s 6d on 17 July 1323/4 to three carpenters for six days' work *operantibus super quedam ponte versus Thamsis sub posterna propinquiora domum Sancte Katerine... per preceptum Regis*). Reference is made in 1373 to a 'bridge between the Tower and the Hospital of St Katherine' (*Calendar of Plea and Memoranda Rolls of the City of London*: 1364–81, 156). In 1384–8 the outer landward defences at this point were again rebuilt (E 101/473/2 m 5. See references to masons working Reigate stone *pro quibusdam novis muris lapideis vocatis Wardewalles inde faciendis extra portam extendentibus se versus hospitalem sancti Katerine*). Very probably the causeway itself was also remodelled at this time, as is suggested by the dressing, style and materials of the stonework excavated in 1996.

Dr Worssam identified a stone from the rubble core as a pale grey finely glauconitic crystalline limestone typical of Kentish Rag from the Maidstone area. The ashlar was harder to place. It had a dark-grey colour (10YR 6/1) common in Kentish Rag and a crystalline calcite cement. Nevertheless it could be better described as a sandy limestone containing abundant well-rounded quartz grains (0.1–0.2mm diameter) and similarly sized but sparsely scattered glauconite. One block included a number of small fossils including ostreid fragments and a ribbed shell, possibly a rhynchonellid. Another block displayed the concave cast of a bivalve 30–40mm in diameter on its top surface. Such fossils would not be expected in ragstone from the Maidstone area and, taken with the fineness of grain, might indicate an origin in east Kent. Dr Worssam regarded the causeway ashlar as an east Kent variety of ragstone from a bed not hitherto recognised as an ashlar source.

THE BYWARD POSTERN

The probable late 13th-century foundation (3609) underlying the Byward Postern was overlain by two courses of four bricks each (3635), which also abutted the outer curtain wall foundations (3608). The bricks filled the north end of a 0.18m-high void under the base of the Byward Postern wall (3633) where a timber had evidently rotted away completely. The void continued back for 0.3m under the masonry face (Fig 91). It was notable that the bricks did not extend beyond the southern limit of 3609 and that there was no underpinning of the void beneath wall 3633 where the badly decayed beech piles were found. A mixed silty clay and rubble layer (3625) up to 0.42m thick butted against but did not enter this void and probably abutted the brick underpinning as well, though a large Victorian intrusive feature made it impossible to be certain of this. A single small sherd of pottery dating to the 15th/16th century was recovered from the rubble layer. Presumably the latter formed while the timber still

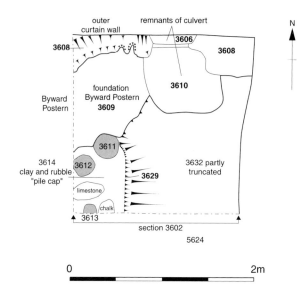

Fig 91   Plan of test pit 36 at the Byward Postern.

presented a reasonably solid edge, so one can tentatively suggest a late medieval date for the timber itself.

Parnell (1993, 47) states that the postern had its origin in Edward I's extension of the castle's defences (Chapter 5) but was then remodelled and rebuilt during the middle decades of the 14th century. Henry VIII remodelled the building again in the 16th century. The decayed timber could therefore belong plausibly with the 14th-century works, while the brick underpinning might well belong to Henry VIII's work. Further archaeological work planned for the Byward Postern will allow more detailed exploration of its origins and development.

ALTERATIONS TO THE SOUTH-WEST CAUSEWAY

Both faces of the causeway between the Middle and Byward Towers display plentiful evidence of rebuilding, both in the above-grass levels and—more importantly—in the portions revealed by excavation during 1996. It is difficult to date these rebuilds on the basis of the masonry alone, although the late 18th-century work described in Chapter 8 is clearly definable. The excavations showed that the east end of the north face had been rebuilt from the plinth level upwards before the late 18th-century changes occurred. The original Kentish Rag ashlar facing (31110) was truncated by the construction cut (31118) for a partial rebuild or refacing of the causeway. The cut partially removed some of the pile cap (31115), providing a solid platform to construct a very roughly coursed wall (3143) between the original facing and Purbeck marble structure 3184 at the eastern end of the trench (Figs 72, 92). The existing foundation (3144) and ashlar facing clearly continued behind the rebuild. The latter was constructed of roughly hewn Kentish Rag with occasional

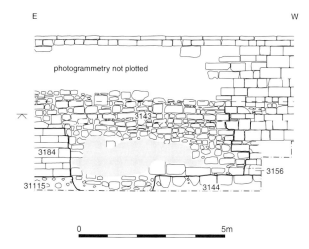

E   W

photogrammetry not plotted

3143

3184

3156

31115   3144

0   5m

Fig 92 Later medieval masonry infill 3143 on the north side of the south-western causeway.

re-used dressed stones. It filled an area 6m wide to a level of 2m OD and then extended a further 4m to the east to butt the Byward Tower to a level of 4.5m OD. A cross-shaped mason's mark similar to those seen on wall 3184 and on the Byward Tower was also evident in the rebuild.

Pottery from soil layers associated with cut 31118 (eg, 3137 and 3136) suggests that the reconstruction had occurred by the 15th century or perhaps even before this (the dating evidence is considered more fully below). The purpose of the new masonry is, to say the least, unclear. It may be infilling an arch or drawbridge position associated with the Purbeck marble structure 3184, although no such feature is known here in the medieval period. This, however, may simply be an accident of the historical record and the perspective of early depictions of the castle, which invariably show views of the castle from the south (ie, with the Thames in the foreground). No late medieval documentation for the rebuilding has been found to date, but this may be remedied by further research.

There was evidence for alterations on the south side of the causeway as well, although there was no dating evidence available here and it is therefore impossible to tell whether it was contemporary with masonry 3143. A stone wall (3025) had been built at right angles to the causeway 2.3m west of the central archway. The relationship between the two structures was not clear because of the late 18th-century rebuilding works, but there was little doubt that the north–south wall was an addition to the late 13th-century structure. This was nowhere better demonstrated than at the base of 3025, which rested on timber piles (3068) whose tops lay some 0.2m above the original beech piling (Fig 132). The gap between the base of the masonry and the original piles was filled with silty clay, apparently waterlain (as one would expect in the moat).

Wall 3025 extended 2.4m southwards to the edge of excavation; it may have continued beyond this,

although there was little sign of it in the geophysical or radar surveys. This, however, may be no more than a symptom of the signal response problems noted in Chapter 3. Only the east face and core (3017) of the wall were exposed, with a combined width of 2m. The east face consisted of roughly squared limestone blocks (average measurement 0.6m by 0.4m by 0.3m), while the core comprised flint and limestone rubble bedded in a lime-based mortar. The wall appeared to have been demolished down to approximately 1.80m OD, giving a standing height of 2.6m.

THE MOAT AND ITS FILLS

While there was relatively little building activity associated with the moat in the 16th century, strenuous efforts were made by the authorities to cope with the worsening problem of its maintenance and degradation. The sources for the second half of the century are particularly graphic. A Court Leet of the Tower taken *c*1564–70 states that 'the Tower ditch as well towards London as in other places of the Tower' was 'overgrown with weeds and reeds' and 'needful to be repaired'. The longstanding problems caused by the city ditch were still an issue, since the Chamber of London was indicted 'for a sluice coming out of London ditch into the Tower ditch', which sluice the Chamber were to amend 'upon pain of forfeiture of ten pounds'. The water in the moat was also being polluted by the tanners 'that wash their skins in the Tower ditch within the liberties of the said Tower'. The Leet jury complained that 'the filth thereof is a destruction to the fish within the said Tower' and the tanners were warned to avoid causing further annoyance, subject to a fine of £5.

To industrial pollution was added the problem of domestic waste, either carried down and dumped by the Tower Liberty inhabitants, or discharged directly from the houses that were by now encroaching on the moat's edge. The inhabitants of the Bulwark 'or else within the Liberties of the said Tower' were presented for 'casting their rubbish into Tower ditch or on the Tower Hill'. They were ordered to 'cause the same to be conveyed before the feast of St James next ensuing upon pain of forfeiting for everyone so casting—5s' (BL Add MS 14044, fols 38–43). Frequent references were made to 'noisome gutters' or 'sinks' overflowing into the moat (BL Lansd MS 14044, fol 40). Concern was also expressed about (for example) Robert Heming, bailiff of St Katharine's, having allowed his livestock to graze or feed upon Tower Hill near the Postern, which was said to be 'hurtful to the Tower ditch and also noisome to the Queen's subjects' (BL Lansd MS 14044, fol 42).

Proposals for improvement

An order by the Privy Council in 1590 gave rise to the first of a series of reports into the condition of the Tower moat and recommendations as to what should be done (BL Lansd MS 65, no. 13. 'A special note of such remembrances as are to be examined by the Commissioners appointed for the view of the state of the Tower as it is at this present', dated 23 June 1590). The main problem was the deliberate encroachment on the moat of houses and gardens and the silting, filling and pollution of its remaining water. The 1590 report led the Council to order the Lieutenant of the Tower to evict the inhabitants of 'those dwellings situated on the Moat and Wharf', by force if necessary. He was also to warn 'divers persons determined to erect new buildings upon the Tower Wharf and Ditch and places near adjoining' not to do so (*Acts of PC* 1590–91, 58–9). Haiward and Gascoyne's *True and Exact Draught* of 1597 (Fig 84), which shows the moat edges free of buildings except for a huddle of shacks to the north of the western entrance, suggests that the Lieutenant had some success in doing so.

Nevertheless, the problem soon recurred, not least because of the influence of a succession of Gentleman Porters (Tower officials with considerable independence), who traditionally claimed rent from any occupants of Tower Hill. A new initiative was taken in 1608 by the energetic Lieutenant William Waad (in office 1605–13). He formally complained about the Porters' activities and set up a commission to examine the state of the moat. Little, however, was achieved: a report presented to the Privy Council in 1620 reiterated the old problems with a vengeance (*Acts of PC* 1619–21, 236–8).

An interesting project submitted by the King's engineer, Gavin Smith, was also ignored. Smith's idea was to free the Tower 'from the annoyance of the filth and soil issuing which have passage and recourse by the postern via the Tower ditch'. This was to be achieved 'by erecting on the land side of the Tower ditch towards the hill within the ancient ground of the said ditch, a channel of brick and stone answerable to that provided for the city ditch [BL Add MS 12503 fols 210–18] intended to empty directly into the Thames at or near to the Iron Gate'. By this means, Smith claimed, the 'water of the ditch will be sweet and clear, fit for the use of all the inhabitants thereabout that shall have need thereof, and fit for the breeding and increase of fishes and pleasing in itself'. Nothing was done, of course, but Smith's feeling that the moat could be rendered 'pleasing in itself' is of interest as an early instance of the moat being regarded as a visual asset rather than simply as a line of defence.

The 1620 report did lead, however, to the drawing up of one of the most detailed studies of the moat's condition ever made, presented to the Council in 1623 (SP 14/156, no. 13). Some of this is worth quoting. The moat was 'much overgrown and filled up with earth of purpose for gardens'. 'Round about the counterscarp and within the moat are placed many houses, sheds, timber yards, coal yards, wheelers yards and such like'. The ditch had formerly been 10 rods and 8ft (163ft/49.68m) wide from the entrance bridge to the Brass Mount, beyond which, as far as the Iron Gate, it was 9 rods (139ft/42.36m) across. Estimates were given as to how much infill there was and the cost of its removal, while attention was called to the defensive weaknesses in the Iron Gate area caused by drastic narrowing of the moat and the encroachment of houses. The principal recommendation anticipated the activities of the 1670s (Chapter 7) by suggesting that 'a brick wall should be made upon the base of the counterscarp of the moat being 16ft high and 5 and 8ft thick below'. The aim was to prevent 'the inconveniences of encroachments upon the moat with gardens and dwelling gardens and dwelling houses, the washing of earth into the said moat upon great and sudden rains, the ebbing and flowing of the moat against the counterscarp' and the 'climbing of men and boys up and down [the counterscarp] which filleth up the moat with earth'. The total cost was estimated at £2,378.

Later medieval and early post-medieval moat fills

Silty clay layers were found in the lower levels of most excavations, usually being absent only if a late feature such as a Victorian culvert had disrupted or removed earlier stratigraphy. Fortunately this was relatively rare, and even where intrusive later features did exist small pockets of *in situ* fills frequently survived. These were usually too restricted in extent to have much interpretative value, however, and the best data qualitatively undoubtedly came from the larger excavations. Trenches 27 and 31 were particularly valuable from this point of view, not least because the bulk of the earlier finds and the most important environmental data came from there. Some of the fills were not only very thick but also laminated, and appeared to have accumulated over long periods of time. The evidence for the water environment in the moat from the 1280s to 1840s is considered in Chapter 9. It is worth stating, however, that most and perhaps all of the deposits described below probably formed at least partly through siltation in an aquatic environment. Doubtless there were other inputs as well, such as deliberately dumped soil and cess.

The sequence of deposits in trench 31 was effectively divided into two separate groups by the Victorian culvert. The earliest moat deposit to the east of this was tenacious blue-grey clay 3137. This extended for c10m and varied in thickness from 30mm to 0.4m. It was overlain by greenish brown clay 3136 containing patches of silt and occasional shells. Fragments of a wicker fish trap or basket were found in this layer. They were too small for detailed analysis but appeared to be of the same construction as the nearly complete example found in trench 27 (*see* below). Layer 3136 extended for 12m east–west with an average thickness of 0.22m. At the eastern end of the trench it extended over the pile cap (31115) and butted against the foundations of the Byward Tower, where it banked upwards to a thickness of 0.6m. On the west side of the culvert a

sf 148

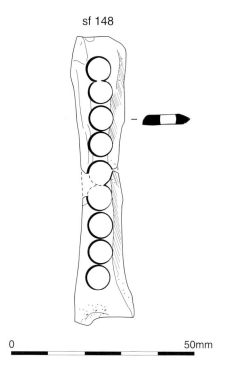

0   50mm

Fig 93   Bone blanks that have had circular pieces cut out for the manufacture of buttons. SF 148, context 3141.

layer of tenacious blue-grey silt clay (3152), which appeared to be identical to 3137, overlay the pile cap (3153/8) and butted against the causeway's foundations. Layer 3152 was 0.25m thick and extended for 4.6m from the western limit of excavation. It was overlain by a greenish brown clayey silt (3141) with a 15 per cent inclusion of organic matter. This was 0.54m thick and also extended for 4.6m. The top of the deposit lay at 0.48m OD.

The London ware sherds from context 3137 appear to provide a good 13th- to 14th-century end-date for the contexts below. Some caution is needed, however, as the pottery from the equivalent layer 3152 is of slightly later date (14th–15th century). The contexts need not be absolutely identical, but they seemed similar enough to be viewed as a single deposit group, at least. The dating of the contexts above them is also slightly different, with 3136 and 3141 having 15th-century and 16th- and 18th-century pottery respectively. The low quantities of pottery in

these levels suggest that the moat was well maintained at this period.

Clayey silt 3141 also contained two waste fragments of bone (SF 148) and a copper alloy strap fitting (SF 149). The bone waste fragments were flat sheets cut from cattle long bones and drilled with holes 12–13mm in diameter to produce blanks for buttons (Fig 93). Similar button production waste has been recovered from many medieval sites (MacGregor 1985, 101–2). The sheet metal strap fitting was found attached to a section of leather; it was a rectangular plate with a rivet through each corner for attachment (Fig 94). It had been incised with lettering set against a background of rocker-arm decoration. The four letters (D, O, E and N) are identical in style to stamped lettering found on leather girdles from London dating to the late 14th century (Egan and Pritchard 1991, 45–6). The leather had been cut from a 15mm-wide strap of cattlehide before being discarded. This must therefore have occurred at some point after the 14th century. The stratigraphic position of layer 3141 and other dating evidence for the sequence of deposits here suggests that the 18th-century pottery in this context is likely to be intrusive.

Trench 27 and the fish trap (Figs 95–101)

The primary fill of the Edward I moat (8094) was a waterlogged tenacious mid-grey to green silty clay (2854). The deposit had a slight dark-grey mottling and contained occasional small rounded gravel. The deposit extended 15.4m in section (all extents in this description are east–west unless otherwise stated), terminating 3.4m from the revetment wall. It varied in depth from 0.3m in the centre of the trench to 0.7m at the western end. The nature of the deposit enabled a high density of pottery to be recovered as well as pieces of preserved leather (SFs160 and 167, below). The most significant find was an almost intact wicker fish trap (SF166) containing fish bone, described below.

A series of fills formed three distinctive horizons above the primary fill. The first band extended for 18m and varied in depth up to a maximum of 0.4m. It comprised three layers of tenacious dark-grey/green silts (2852–3 and 2937). All the deposits contained very small amounts (less than 1 per cent) of rounded gravel and organic matter. The layers ran

sf 149

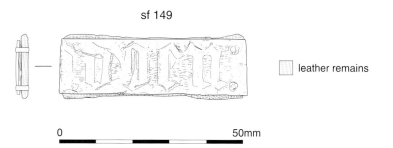

▨ leather remains

0   50mm

Fig 94   Copper alloy strap fitting rivetted onto leather strip. The letters D O E N have been incised into the surface, which is also treated with rocker-arm lines. SF 149, context 3141.

horizontally except at the eastern end, where they formed a slight dip. The second band had formed within this hollow and consisted of three fine black silty clay lenses (2835 and 8026/7) totalling 5m in length. Each of the lenses was no more than 50mm thick, the overall depth of the group being 0.12m. These contexts were overlain by the third band, which extended for 17m west from the 1840s culvert and was up to 0.42m deep. It completely sealed the black clay band and partially covered the more extensive green silts of the first group. Similarly, it was also formed of three individual deposits (2833/4 and 2857). All were tenacious dark-grey silts. The third deposit in this horizon (2833) was truncated by a shallow concave cut (8030), 1.5m wide and 0.4m deep. It was filled by compact dark-brown silty clay 8031.

These fills produced a relatively high quantity of 13th-century and later medieval pottery. Several contexts contained later material as well, which causes some difficulties for the stratigraphic interpretation. Context 2854, for instance, is mixed in character, containing a range of material from Romano-British pottery through medieval sherds to a 17th-century earthenware money box. This layer was quite thick (but variable) and also contained the fish trap. There is little doubt that this silt accumulated over a considerable period of time.

The fish or eel trap (SF 166) was discovered when fragments of wickerwork were noticed protruding from the edge of a section towards the revetment wall end of trench 27. Further investigation rapidly established the nature of the find and it was immediately obvious that this would be the most spectacular individual artefact from the excavations. It is worth dwelling on how the trap was excavated—both on and off site—before it is described more fully.

The wickerwork was in exceptionally good condition, having been preserved by the waterlogged moat clays and silts (Fig 95). The very act of exposing the piece immediately made it vulnerable to rapid deterioration. The unseasonably warm and sunny weather at the time of discovery (April 1997) scarcely helped in this respect. The trap was therefore exposed, cleaned, recorded *in situ* and lifted out of the moat on a supported block of the underlying silty clay within the space of 24 hours (Fig 96), being kept damp with water sprays throughout this time. It was then stored in a cool, dark and damp basement under Tower Bridge Approach while further excavation and recording took place.

Before this could happen, the upper face of the wickerwork was encased in quick-drying plaster of Paris. This was needed to protect the piece while it was turned over so that the bed of silty clay on which it rested could be removed to reveal the bottom of the trap. Fish bones were recovered while the clay was being excavated, so all the soil was retained for careful sieving. The initial lifting and subsequent turning were nerve-wracking processes in their own right, having to be carried out by hand

Fig 95   The fish trap in situ in trench 27. The intricate interweaving of the warps (longitudinal pieces) and wefts (the woven 'hoops' that encircle the body) is clearly visible, along with the flint weights at the selvage (open end) of the trap.

Fig 96   The hard physical task of manually lifting the fish trap out of trench 27, supported on its bed of clay.

because of the fragility of the wicker. Taking the clay away from the outside was by no means the end of the problem, however. After all, we were dealing with a three-dimensional artefact, albeit one that had been partially flattened during its long years of burial in the heavy moat fills (Fig 97).

Once the outer clays had been removed the trap could be taken to English Heritage's conservation laboratory for further work, but debate now turned to the removal of the silty clay from the interior of the piece. This was complete apart from limited areas of damage that had occurred during the centuries of its burial. The opportunities for extracting the fill from inside the wickerwork without further damage to it therefore seemed to be limited. Immediately before it was taken to the laboratory, however, the trap was passed through a body scanner at the Royal Brompton Hospital. This gave us a remarkable series of virtual 3-D images, demonstrating that the interior of the artefact was more complicated than expected (Fig 98). There were three interwoven baskets—not two, as the exterior had led us to believe. Ronnie Gibbs, therefore, a conservator from HRP's Textile Conservation Studio, spent many weeks painstakingly excavating and gently washing the soils out from the inside of the trap (Fig 99). Once again he retained fish bones and all of the soil for subsequent sifting and analysis. Finally the piece was clean and could be soaked in polyethylene glycol (PEG) before being freeze-dried. It was eventually ready to be put on display back at the Tower of London in the spring of 2000.

The fish trap was a complex piece of basketry (Fig 100) made of willow or poplar stems (the two species are indistinguishable for identification purposes) no more than one year old. It was recorded both in the ground and subsequently using the techniques and forms described by Adovasio (1977, 21–2). The surviving elements measured approximately 1.04m long, a maximum of 0.32m wide at the selvage (mouth end) and 0.1m high (again at the selvage). The stems were mostly from 5.4mm to 7.8mm in diameter, though a few were outside this range. Unfortunately the starting point was not present, having perhaps been removed unnoticed during an earlier stage of excavation (though the breaks in the warps did not appear fresh), but only a very small amount can have been lost. The trap was otherwise intact apart from small areas of ancient damage on the upper surface, including a small area where the basketry was entirely absent. This was crucial to the cleaning of the interior, which probably would have been impossible without this small open area.

The three conical baskets (or chairs) all appeared to employ an open plain weave with the wefts (horizontally or cross-woven stems) being quite widely spaced around the tightly spaced warps (vertical or long stems). The intervals between wefts varied from about 45mm to 70mm, with the wefts comprising one rigid member (eg, a continuous stem around the outside of the basket) and three active ones (stems weaving round the rigid member and through the warps). The outer two baskets had been spliced together about three-quarters of the way

Fig 97   The Chief Yeoman Warder, Tom Sharp, inspecting the fish trap during excavation.

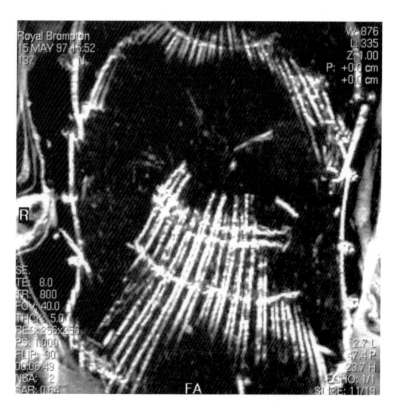

Fig 98a   MNI scan of the fish trap. The scan provided detailed three-dimensional information on the trap's interior structure. This was of vital importance when the clay filling was being removed from the inside of the wickerwork.

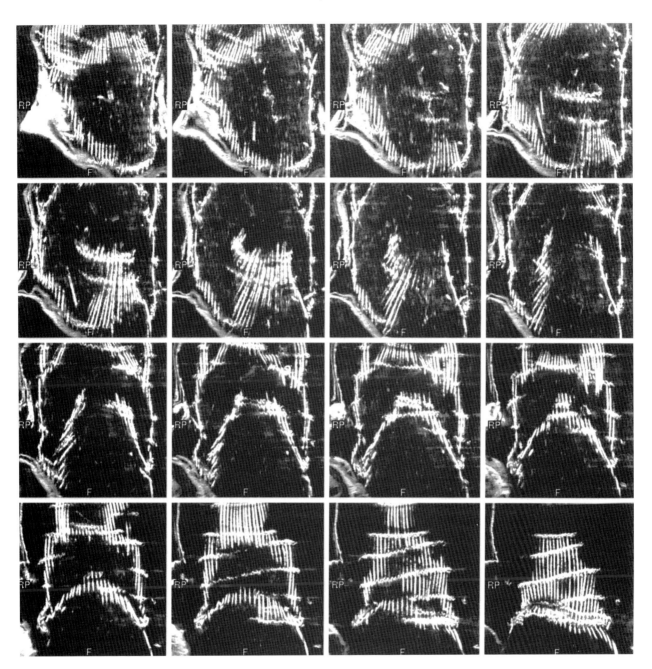

Fig 98b   MNI scan of the fish trap.

along from the starting point. The selvage of the second basket had been formed by bending back the warps. These were secured with an independent single weft spanning either single or double warps. The 3-D scan showed that the warps of the second basket continued into the interior of the first and formed a cone within it. The wefts continued down to an open starting point. This shows that the two baskets must have been made independently of each other before being spliced together.

It is likely that weaving had started around a post or similar cylinder, which, in the case of the outer basket, could then be used as a removable bung. Warps had then been introduced (splayed) into the

weave at intervals to increase the width of the outer basket at least. These introduced warps can be seen quite clearly on the drawing (Fig 100). The wefts, meanwhile, were woven in what appeared to be a continuous spiral usually with three warps being engaged at a time across 21mm–24mm. The first spiral had been tied off and a new one started just before the second basket was splayed into the first. Again, these points can be seen very clearly on the drawing. The splaying is most evident on the upper face while the weft alteration can be seen on the underside.

The third (inner) basket appeared to be removable rather than spliced in with the other two. The warps

Fig 99 The fish trap during cleaning and conservation. At this stage all of the fine clay has been removed from the interior of the trap.

were more widely spaced at least at the selvage, and the 3-D scans suggested that they continued to be more open as the basket tapered from its starting point. This was open and could be seen very clearly on the scans, with a double weft visible just above it. There were several more single wefts between here and the selvage. The latter had been badly damaged on its upper surface during its long rest in the moat fills, but the underside survived intact. This showed that the selvage had been formed by bending the warps back around a single stem of somewhat larger diameter than all the others. A double weft apparently of three active members only (ie with no rigid stem) was then used to bind in the bent-back warps.

The trap was clearly *in situ*, in the location where it had last been placed. Flint nodule weights had been attached to either side of the selvage by wrapping a stem around the nodule. The stems had then been woven round the warps of the removable basket in one case, and the outer basket in the other. A similar method of attaching flint weights was also evident in the much more fragmentary remains of the fish trap recovered from trench 31. A small wood peg had also been used to hold the trap in position; it seems likely that there would have been pegs to either side of the selvage originally, but the second one was not present. The weights and peg held the bottom of the trap in the clay at *c*-0.06m OD, approximately 0.65m above the level set by Edward I here. The location thus provided an important indicator of the

contemporary base of the moat at this point. Pottery from the soils around the trap suggests that it was in use during the late medieval or early post-medieval period, but a more precise date could not be ascertained. Unfortunately, the morphology of the basketwork is of little use for dating it, as fish traps vary little in shape through time (J Watson 1992, 115).

Medieval (and indeed earlier) fish traps fell into two basic categories. The first was as much structural as artefactual and was usually used in a fixed position across rivers. A series of stakes driven into the river-bed supported hurdle or wattle work arranged in a V-shape. Fish would thus be channelled into a narrow opening where a basket might be set. Anglo-Saxon examples have been found on the river Trent in Nottinghamshire and examples of a similar or later date are now well known on the tidal Thames through London because of the work of the Thames Archaeological Survey during the late 1990s. An alternative means of achieving the same end would be to set a long rank of traps across the river channel. This method—still in use on the Severn estuary and elsewhere in the later 20th century—might also involve stacking the traps vertically along the rank to create a formidable barrier for the fish. The baskets could be very large indeed, with the Severn examples (known as putts) being as much as 3.66m (12ft) long and 1.83m (6ft) wide at the mouth (Jenkins 1974, 31–66). They were usually held within a frame of timbers, including

128

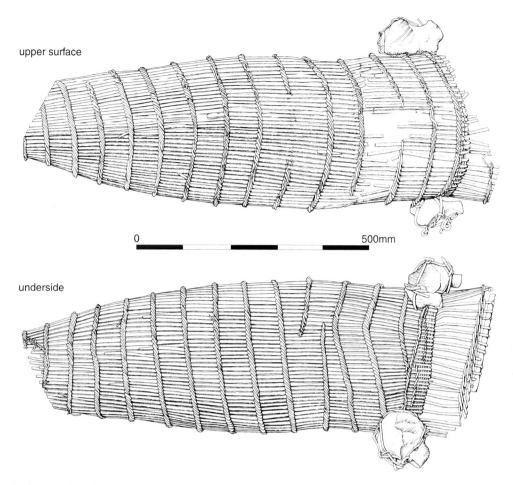

upper surface

0   500mm

underside

Fig 100   The late medieval fish trap found in trench 27: top and bottom views.

stakes driven into the river-bed, so structural remains of early traps that used this method might survive in the right circumstances (eg, waterlogging). The closely woven end basket (chair) from a trap of this kind dating to the 10th/11th century has been excavated in the Burghfield area of Berkshire (J Watson 1992, 115 and fig 43).

The other kind of trap was essentially a scaled-down portable version of the putt; the Tower moat example falls into this category (Fig 101). Technically this type is an eel trap and would be bated to attract the eels, but doubtless it would catch fish as well (as the bones from the moat trap show). Similar pieces are still in use today, though usually in wire. Those from eastern England (eg, Lincolnshire, the Fens, etc) tend to be closely woven, but western examples (especially from the Severn) usually employ a more open weave akin to the moat trap (*see* Wright 1959, figs 11, 12; Jenkins 1974, 277–83). The baskets, which came in a variety of sizes, and their component parts had names that varied from region to region (ibid). Jenkins' example B on page 277 is virtually identical in form and of roughly the same size as SF 166. The eel (or fish) would swim into and through the succession of baskets and thus became trapped inside them because it could not force its way back

out of the narrow holes at the end of the cones. The trap could work equally well on both the ebb and flow tides, with the selvage pointing up or downstream accordingly. It could be used in many circumstances, for example, on rivers or mill races. Jenkins (1974, 282) points out that eel traps are illustrated in the 14th-century Luttrell Psalter and the 16th-century Peniarth manuscript. Bond provides a typically thorough examination of medieval monastic fisheries with several references to eels (Bond 1988, especially 92).

Water flow may not have been a major factor in the Tower moat, which was truly tidal only during the 13th and first half of the 14th centuries. Thereafter the development of the wharf may have significantly reduced the tidal influence. The trap was found some 75m back (north) from the south-west entrance causeway and thus a significant distance away from the tidal inflow even when this was evident. Having said that, the selvage was pointing roughly towards the entrance. It is hard to see why the trap was not recovered: it was intact and obviously still in working order. Perhaps it had been placed illicitly—its position towards the outer edge of the moat might support this—which would make its loss understandable.

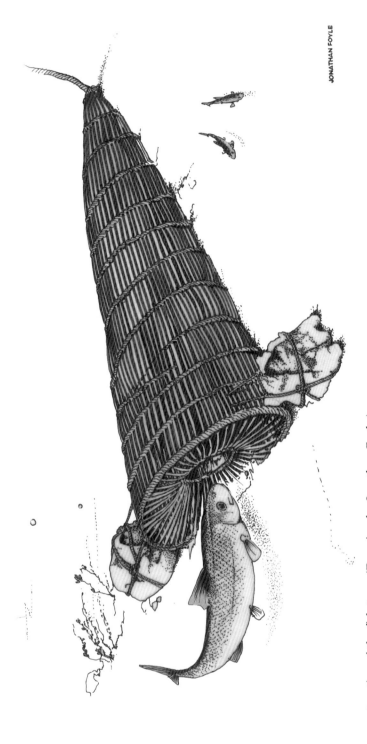

JONATHAN FOYLE

Fig 101   A reconstruction of the fish trap. (Drawing by Jonathan Foyle.)

A total of 177 fragments of fish bone associated with the trap were identifiable to species or family (Table 3). The majority came from inside the trap, although a few (23) came from the silt immediately below it. Most of the bones belonged to indeterminate cyprinid and chub; most of the former probably also belong to chub, although tench were present in small numbers. Several flounder bones were also present; it is the only flatfish to penetrate into estuaries and able to live in fresh water for short periods (Wheeler 1969). Body part representation indicates that a minimum of one eel, one tench, six chub and two flounder were originally present in the trap (Tables 3–4).

The types of fish present in the trap are not surprising given the location of the Tower of London. The Thames is tidal today as far west as Teddington Lock and although cyprinids are principally freshwater fish both chub and tench can occur in brackish water (Wheeler 1969, 208; 1979, 185). Flounder is known to have been present in the Thames in considerable numbers during post-medieval times. In 1758 Robert Binnell wrote 'there is no River in all Europe, that is a better, or a more speedy Breeder, and Nourisher of its Fish (particularly the

Flounder) than is the Thames' (Wheeler 1979, 79). Eels also spend part of their life-cycle in fresh water before migrating to marine spawning grounds. Fresh marine fish would have been available to people living in inland areas such as London at this time but only as a luxury item. Fish caught locally would therefore have made a welcome addition to the diet.

Other finds evidence

Metal

Four metal objects were recovered from test pit 39: a coin (SF58), a hook (SF59), a loop (SF66) and a pin (SF60). They all came from conglomerated layer 3912 at the base of the pit overlying Thames foreshore layer 3916. The layer was interpreted as possible workshop residue. The coin was a silver groat (fourpence) of Henry VI (Annulet issue, 1422–7, Calais mint). These remained in currency until the 1460s, a few surviving even later. This piece is relatively unworn and a deposit date in the 1430s to 1450s can be suggested. The hook was small and decorative, with a perforated loop at one end for

Table 3   Fish bones from the late medieval fish trap: species and anatomical representation

	Eel	Chub	Tench	Cyprinid	Flounder	Flatfish	Total
Vomer	1				1		2
Frontal		1		1			2
Bassiocipital		2		1			3
Parasphenoid				3			3
Articular					2		2
Dentary	1	2			2		5
Maxilla		2			2		4
Quadrate		1			2		3
Brangiostegal ray		1		5			6
Ceratohyale					2		2
Hyomandibular	1	1		5	2		9
Interopercular		1		2	1		4
Opercular		4		4	3		11
Preoperculum		1		1	2		4
Suboperculum		6	1	1	1		9
Urohyal		2			1		3
Lower pharyngeal		3		1			4
Basiptergium		2					2
Cleithrum		8			2		10
Supracleithrum		1					1
Pterygiophore					1		1
AAV		2		1			3
PAV	2	8		20		7	37
CV	1	11	2	14	9	12	49
Total	5	59	3	59	32	19	177

AAV = anterior abdominal vertebra.
PAV = posterior abdominal vertebra.
CV = caudal vertebra.

Table 4 Fish bones from inside the late medieval fish trap: minimum number of individuals (MNI)

	Chub		Flounder	
	Left	Right	Left	Right
Frontal		1		
Articular			1	1
Dentary	2		1	1
Maxilla		2		2
Quadrate		1		
Hyomandibular	1		1	1
Interopercular	1			
Opercular	1	3	2	1
Preoperculum	1		1	1
Suboperculum	2	3		
Basipterygium	1			
Cleithrum	6	2		1
Supracleithrum	1			
MNI	6		2	

attachment. It may have formed part of a clasp to secure a book or small casket. The loop may have been the end from an ear scoop or toothpick. This type of object was cheap and easy to make in the medieval period. They are known from the 13th century but are more common from the middle of the 15th (Egan and Pritchard 1991, fig 251, No.1766).

Leather

A complete front latchet-fastening shoe (SF110; Fig 102) of turnshoe construction (Fig 104, 1) was found at the interface between the medieval moat fills and the Thames foreshore (context 4500). The calfskin shoe has a long, outward-pointing toe stuffed with moss. Shoes of this general style have been found previously in the City of London in late 14th-century contexts (Grew and de Neergaard 1988, 33, figs 46 and 69, fig 103).

The forepart of a turnshoe sole (SF163) was found in redeposited clay (context 2855), which probably formed during the 13th/14th centuries. The sole could be contemporary with this, though a later date might be more appropriate. A large clump sole repair piece (SF76) and a semi-circular fragment, possibly from a heavy mitten (SF160; Fig 103), of cattlehide were found in the overlying deposit (2854). This probably accumulated during the later medieval period into the early post-medieval era. The shape of the fragment (SF 160; Fig 103) is reminiscent of a sole or an insole from a broad-toed shoe of a type popular in the reign of Henry VIII and found in later deposits. The position of the seam and the presence of a second line of stitching close by, however, preclude this identification. The shape and seaming is compatible with that of a leather mitten.

A small number of these have been found in London. One has been recovered from an early 16th-century context at Abbots Lane, with another at Queenhithe (Geoff Egan pers comm). It is possible, but not certain, that this is a fragment from another heavy leather mitten, in this case worn flesh side outward. The additional stitching suggests it had been lined.

Two repaired shoes of turnshoe construction and two separate clump sole repairs (SFs167, 169.2), along with a layer from a patten sole (SF87), were found in late medieval/early post-medieval moat silts (context 2852, 2853). The shoes (SFs159, 169.1) had clump sole repairs sewn on to wide rands rather than directly to the soles themselves (Fig 104, 2). These shoes lacked other diagnostic features but their use of wide rands to attach sole repairs suggests a 15th-century date. One (SF169.1; Fig 105) had the remains of its calfskin upper present; this had been deliberately cut away above the lasting margin, suggesting it to be cobbling waste. A fragment from a turnshoe vamp that laced over the instep was also found (context 3136).

The single layer from a patten or sandal with a multiple-layered leather sole (SF87; Fig 106, 4) with a long pointed toe (poulaine) and a narrow waist is of a style popular during the late 1450s and 1460s. Pattens are commonly found in 15th-century deposits in the City of London (Grew and de Neergaard 1988, 101). This style is shown being worn with hose rather than as a true overshoe in contemporary illustrations (ibid, 91). An 18th/19th-century D-shaped heel lift from a welted shoe (SF69) was found in the same deposit and indicates some later contamination.

A sole of turnshoe construction (context 3151 Fig 106, 5) and an insole of welted construction (SF57 Fig 106, 6) each come from shoes which, though made using different constructions, share the same broad, blunt toe style popular at the beginning of the 16th century. They were made at a time when the turnshoe method of construction (and its derivative the turn-welt construction) were being replaced by the welted construction (Fig 104). The length of time taken for the welted construction to have been generally adopted by shoemakers in the country is uncertain, but those working in the capital were perhaps more likely to have taken up the new method quickly. Shoes of both constructions were recovered from the *Mary Rose* (sunk in 1545). The insole was found in a thick late medieval moat silt (context 2849), while the sole was found in a slightly later (17th century) layer.

A near-complete shoe (SF182; Fig 107) of welted construction was clearly residual in an early 19th-century layer (3128). The extended front seam of the quarters was seamed to the vamp throat. This style of shoe has been found at Jenning's Yard, Windsor (Mould 1993, fig 31, 8 and fig 32, 9). The two examples there were dated by comparison with others from Holland (ibid, 65) to the middle or later 16th century. Characteristics of this shoe—a straight

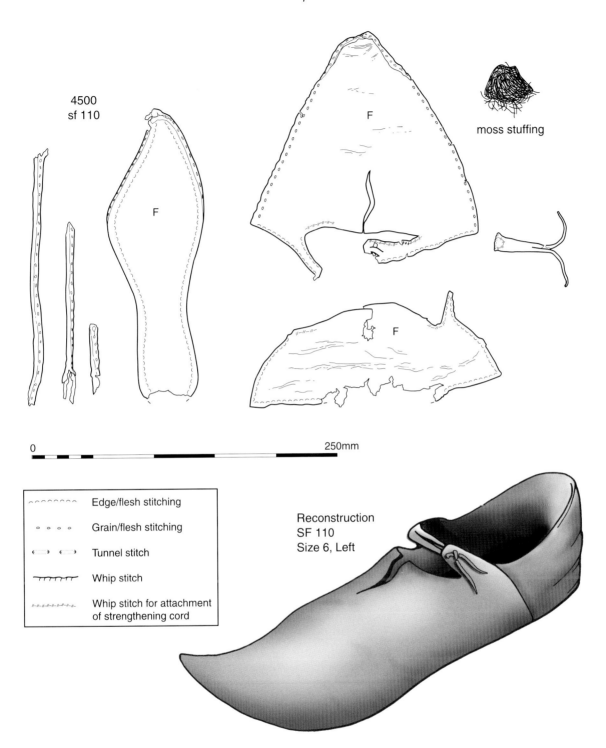

4500
sf 110

F

F

moss stuffing

F

0   250mm

~~	Edge/flesh stitching
o o o o	Grain/flesh stitching
←▭→ ←▭→	Tunnel stitch
ΤΤΤΤΤΤ	Whip stitch
‖–‖–‖–‖–‖–‖–	Whip stitch for attachment of strengthening cord

Reconstruction
SF 110
Size 6, Left

Fig 102   Front latchet fastening shoe of turnshoe construction for left foot comprising sole, rand, vamp, one-piece quarters and fastening latchet. Sole complete, but worn away at exterior seat, with outward curving, pointed toe, medium tread, waist and seat with edge/flesh seam around the perimeter. Three pieces of triangular-sectioned rand. Vamp with extended toe with moss stuffing. Plain throat with central sinuous cut running toward toe to relieve pressure across the instep. Butted edge/flesh side seams, the right extending to join the separate latchet with bifurcated lace fastening, the left extending into a small integral latchet with paired slits through which the bifurcated lace passes before being tied over the instep. One-piece quarters, worn away at the heel, with plain cut top edge raised at centre back and peaked on left side. Whip stitching to hold strengthening cord is present on interior at throat, junctions of front seams and latchet. Leather worn calfskin. Sole length 240mm, width tread 79mm, waist 40mm. Height at centre back c75mm. Adult size 4, size 6 with 10% allowance for shrinkage. SF 110, context 4500.

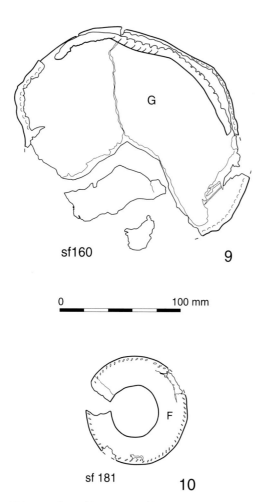

sf160 9

0 ————— 100 mm

sf 181 10

Fig 103   Leather objects. Possible mitten fragment, worn on the flesh side, with edge/flesh seam around the surviving edge. A line of widely-spaced whip stitching roughly follows the curved edge on the grain side, not visible on the flesh side. Wear suggests it was flesh side outermost in use. Leather cattlehide. Width 180mm. SF 160, context 2854. Circular facing with large central hole and grain/flesh seam running around the outer edge. Leather sheep/goatskin. Diameter 82mm. SF 181, context 3128.

sole and a single lift at the heel—suggest that it belongs to the later part of the century. The shoe laced over the instep through three pairs of fastening holes, two in the vamp and another in the extensions of the quarters. Unusually the laces partly survive, showing the method of cross-lacing used. A washer-like object (SF181; Fig 103) with a central hole was found in the same context; a line of grain/flesh stitching runs around the outer edge suggesting it to be a circular facing.

Environmental evidence

Plant remains

A seed of wall lettuce (*Mycelis muralis*) in context 2854 (trench 27) suggested that this plant had

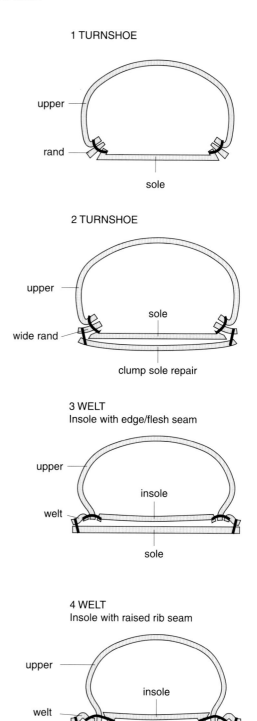

Fig 104   Shoe constructions found.

become established on shady parts of the outer curtain wall or some other stone building. There is little or no evidence for the general dumping of refuse into the moat during its early years, although a frond fragment of bracken (*Pteridium aquilinum*) in context 31177 (trench 31) probably represented material originally imported for animal bedding.

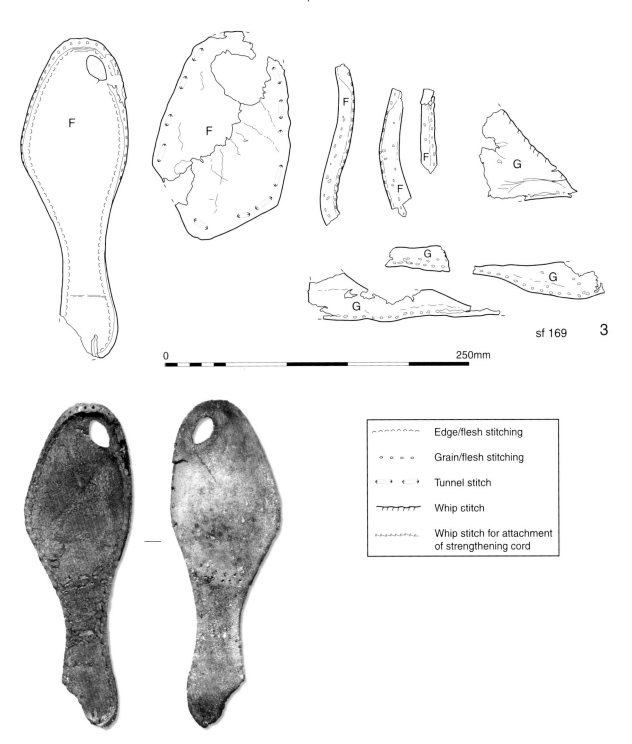

Edge/flesh stitching

Grain/flesh stitching

Tunnel stitch

Whip ctitch

Whip stitch for attachment of strengthening cord

Fig 105   Remains of shoe of turnshoe construction for left foot, comprising sole, clump repair, rand, heel stiffener and upper fragments. Sole with an oval hole worn through at toe and worn along outer edge of the seat. Oval toe, petal-shaped tread, medium waist and seat. Edge/flesh seam around edge and worn tunnel stitching on grain side across waist to attach clump repairs to forepart and seat. Torn remains of forepart clump sole repair with worn tunnel stitching on flesh side around the surviving edge. Three fragments of wide rand with matching grain-flesh seam and line of tunnel stitching to attach the forepart clump. Three fragments of upper deliberately cut and torn away above the lasting margin. Right side of heel stiffener with whip stitching to attach to interior of quarters and lower edge incorporated into the lasting margin, top edge and left side torn away. Leather upper worn calfskin, heel stiffener worn possibly sheep/goatskin. Sole length 256mm, width at tread 88mm, at waist 34mm, at seat 48mm. Rand width 10–12mm. Adult size 5, adult size 8 with 10% allowance for shrinkage. SF 169.1, context 2852.

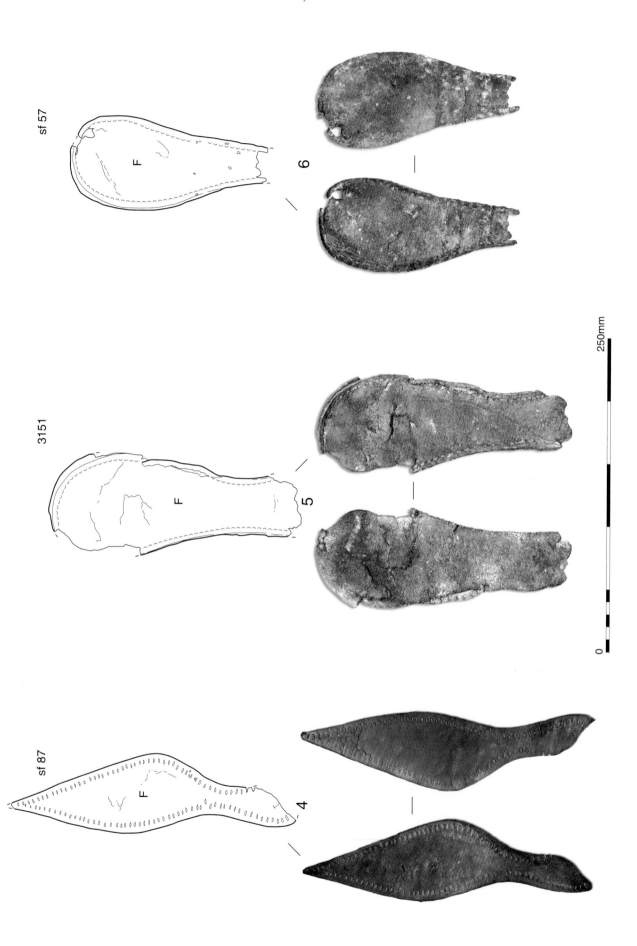

sf 57

3151

sf 87

250mm

0

Human sewage does appear to have been discharged into the moat from an early stage. Most of the seeds in context 1424 (an early *in situ* layer in trench 14) were from food plants likely to have passed through the digestive tract. Black mustard (*Brassica nigra*), plum (*Prunus domestica*), grape (*Vitis vinifera*), sweet cherry (*P. avium*), raspberry (*Rubus idaeus*), apple (*Malus* sp.), wild or alpine strawberry (*Fragaria vesca*), fig (*Ficus carica*) and pepper (*Piper* cf. *nigrum*) were all present. Cereal bran, apple core (endocarp) fragments and a hazelnut shell fragment (*Corylus avellana*) were also found.

The remains suggest a diet rich in fruit and flavourings. Figs with robust seeds belong to the Smyrna varieties and would have been imported dried from the Mediterranean region because they do not fruit in northern Europe. It is also possible that the grape pip was from imported dried fruit. Of particular interest is the pepper seed (*Piper* cf. *nigrum*), a tropical import perhaps from India. There are medieval documentary references to pepper and it has been found in 13th-century deposits in Germany, but the only other medieval British example is from a 15th-century context at Worcester (Greig 1995, 227–8). The Tower of London, however, is just the sort of high-status site where medieval consumption of pepper might be expected. It seems highly likely that a garderobe chute discharged into the moat near trench 14; the only one known at the moment is on the south side of the Brass Mount, perhaps too far distant at 80m away from the trench.

There continued to be little evidence for the dumping of refuse in the moat in later medieval contexts. Cereal bran and a couple of seeds of wild or alpine strawberry (*Fragaria vesca*) in context 2836 (trench 27) were probably derived from sewage.

Pollen

In Section A (2703; Fig 58), only the central 0.18m of the column sample (contexts 2834–6 and 2854) appeared to belong to the later medieval and early post-medieval periods. *Pediastrum* declines dramatically to 10 per cent, with increases in spores of fern (*Pteridium aquilinum* 10 per cent and *Dryopteris* type 8 per cent) and pre-Quaternary palynomorphs (c20 per cent). Herbs remain similar to the preceding zones. Oak (*Quercus*) remains at 15 per cent, with some

increase of alder (*Alnus*) and hazel (*Corylus*). A single grain of spruce (*Picea*) was noted.

In Section C (3113; Fig 108), the lowest 100mm of the column sample lay within context 3137, which is dated to the late 13th–14th centuries. This deposit is dominated by herbs (80–85 per cent) with Poaceae being most important (to 78 per cent). Cereal (18 per cent with oats, *Secale cereale*) and *Sinapis* types are also important (9 per cent). Trees include oak (*Quercus*, 11 per cent) with small numbers of other taxa such as poplar (*Populus*), linden (*Tilia*) and walnut (*Juglans*). The absence of *Pediastrum* in this zone is significant. Values of Hystrichospheres (less than 5 per cent) and pre-Quaternary pollen/palynomorphs (8 per cent) are greatest in this zone, though still small. The middle 0.3m (context 3136) is probably to be dated no later than the 15th century, and is characterised by high values of *Pediastrum* (80 per cent). Herbs remain largely the same but with some reduction in cereal pollen values. Poaceae and *Sinapis* still dominate but a very diverse range of other herbs is present. Trees see increases in ash (*Fraxinus*), beech (*Fagus*) and walnut. Shrubs comprise hazel (*Corylus* type, 6 per cent), *Prunus/Malus* type, *Salix*, *Hedera* and *Calluna*. There are few marsh/aquatic types, but *Potamogeton*, *Typha angustifolia/Sparganium* type, *Typha latifolia* and Cyperaceae are present.

Discussion of the pollen evidence

The constant record of oak with hazel pollen is typical of the Roman and post-Roman period, suggesting that woodland (probably managed) remained in the region after extensive late Bronze Age clearance (especially the now widely evidenced *Tilia* woodland of southern and eastern England). These taxa being anemophilous may be dispersed over wide areas. This similarly applies to birch (*Betula*), pine (*Pinus*) and possibly hornbeam (*Carpinus*), poplar (*Populus*) and alder (*Alnus*), all of which are wind pollinated. The small values for these trees suggest at the most only occasional local presence or derivation from the wider region. Airborne or fluvial transport may be the principal transport mechanisms. For London this constant historical record of oak and hazel is also clear in the more continuous pollen records obtained from the Thames floodplain

---

Fig 106   Layer of multiple-layered bottom unit of patten for left foot with long, pointed toe, medium tread, narrow waist and medium/narrow seat. Seat worn away along outer edge. Line of large, horizontal, oval-shaped holes for stitching or thonging around the perimeter. Cattlehide. Length 235mm, width tread 61mm, waist 25mm. SF 87, context 2853. Turnshoe sole for right foot, worn away along left side of toe and tread and around the seat. Broad, round toe, wide tread tapering to a medium waist and seat. Edge/flesh seam around the perimeter. Worn cattlehide. Length 207+mm, width tread 80mm, waist 44mm, seat 47mm. Context 3151. Welted insole for right foot, worn at the toe and across the seat, with broad round toe, tapering to a medium tread and narrow seat, no distinct waist. Edge/flesh seam around the perimeter. Worn stitching from attachment of clump repair pieces to tread and seat. Worn cattlehide. Length 162+mm, width tread 72mm, seat 32mm. SF 57, context 2849.

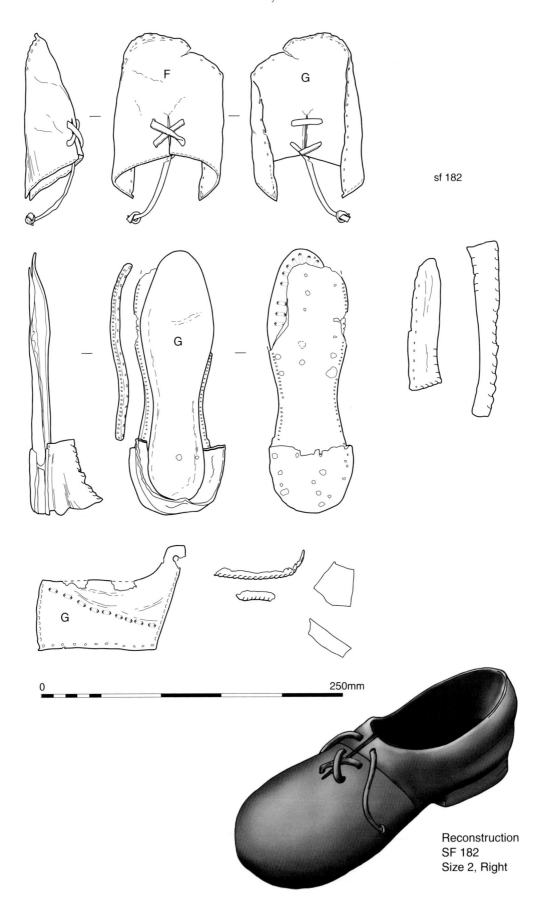

sf 182

0   250mm

Reconstruction
SF 182
Size 2, Right

peats and minerogenic sediments (Scaife in Sidell *et al* forthcoming).

The sporadic occurrence of a number of other trees and shrubs is more interesting, possibly relating to growth adjacent to or in the neighbourhood of the moat. These taxa include lime/linden (*Tilia*), elm (*Ulmus*), beech (*Fagus*), ash (*Fraxinus*) and yew (*Taxus*). Other trees and shrubs of interest are walnut, spruce (*Picea*) and juniper (*Juniperus*). Walnut is generally regarded as a Roman introduction into western Europe. There are occasional records in pre-Roman sediments (Long *et al* 1999; Scaife in Sidell *et al* forthcoming), but in London it has usually been recorded in Roman and post-Roman sites. The former include the Temple of Mithras (Scaife 1982b) and Number One Poultry (Scaife in Sidell *et al* forthcoming). Post-Roman examples include Saxon deposits at Cromwell Green (Greig 1992), Tudor sediments at Broad Sanctuary, Westminster (Scaife 1982a), the most recent levels of Hampstead Heath (Greig 1992) and the upper levels of Storey's Gate and St Stephen's East along the Jubilee Line (Scaife in Sidell *et al* forthcoming). Therefore the records from the Tower moat are not unexpected but provide useful additional information on the continuance of this exotic introduction. Here walnut pollen is more abundant in medieval deposits and only sporadic in post-medieval contexts. Overall, this suggests that once introduced into London by the Romans, it continued to grow or be grown locally for its nuts (*Juglans regia* L. have been found in London sites) or as an ornamental tree.

Spruce has been found in the post-medieval zones of sections A and C. It has previously been found at other sites such as Palace Chambers South and St Stephen's East (Jubilee Line site; Scaife in Sidell *et al* forthcoming). Post-medieval occurrences are relatively commonplace in pollen spectra and as with walnut, spruce is most likely to be from the planting of exotic trees in parks and gardens (not being a native taxon in this interglacial period). Alternatively its pollen may have derived from fluvial/marine transport via the Thames. Spruce has been noted in marine sediments on the south coast at Lottbridge Drove, Sussex (Jennings and Smythe 1982, 16) and Poole Harbour, Dorset (Scaife in Long *et al* 1999), indicating possible long-distance marine transport. Dyakowska (1947) and Stanley (1969) demonstrated

the potential for marine-borne pollen being carried up the Thames.

The presence of lime/lindens, yew and elm may also be significant. Both the lindens and elm pollen appeared morphologically different to the more common prehistoric occurrence of *Tilia cordata* and *Ulmus glabra*. In many cases the lindens had similar morphological characteristics to *Tilia platyphyllos/Tilia europaea*, while the elm had substantially more pronounced rugulations and larger size. Both are considered as being 'exotic' introductions and work is in progress to characterise their species and geographical source. It is suggested that these were trees planted within the grounds of the Tower of London or in adjacent parks and gardens. Beech and ash pollen are always poorly represented in pollen spectra and even small numbers of these taxa as found here imply local growth. The sporadic/occasional presence of juniper is more enigmatic. It is unlikely that this is natural growth and pollen may come from planted shrubs or from juniper berries used in brewing (gin?).

The dominance and diversity of herbs in all of the profiles is typical of Roman to medieval and later pollen sequences from areas of occupation. Local vegetation communities and inputs from domestic refuse tend to have a swamping/masking effect on the more regional pollen/vegetation component in the pollen spectra. Inputs of secondary pollen form a substantial part of the herb assemblages while there is also a strong local representation of plants growing in the moat and its immediate vicinity. The substantial quantities of cereal pollen are diagnostic of urban pollen assemblages, especially where there is cess/ordure present in the sediments. Cereal pollen and associated weeds of arable and disturbed ground remain in the heads of cereals (Robinson and Hubbard 1977) and may be liberated during crop processing or become incorporated into food (bread, porridge). Once ingested this easily survives in and passes through the gut (Scaife 1986, 1995b) and ultimately finds it way into cess pits or, as here, into the moat. Medieval cereal pollen (to 20 per cent) comprises *Triticum* type (broadly wheat and barley) and oats. Weeds such as charlock (*Sinapis* type), spurrey (*Spergula*), black bindweed (*Polygonum* spp) and blue cornflower (*Centaurea cyanus*) may be from these sources. It was expected

---

Fig 107   Front-lacing shoe of welted construction, made straight but worn on right foot comprising sole, middle packing, insole, welt, vamp, two-part quarters, heel stiffener and lining. Worn sole with closely-spaced, grain/flesh seam around perimeter, nails present at the tread. Middle packing between sole and insole. Insole with oval toe, medium tread, waist and seat and raised rib seam around the perimeter. Single D-shaped lift at the seat secured by wooden pegs and nails, the lift is cut in two pieces and may have been added as a clump repair. Narrow welt present. Vamp with rounded toe, high throat with fine, butted edge/flesh seam to join to the extended front seams of the two-piece quarters, left side quarters present. Opening at centre front with two pairs of lace holes in the vamp and one pair in the quarters with lace with knotted end present. Heel stiffener and two internal linings whip stitched to interior and incorporated into the lasting margin. Upper of calfskin flesh side outward. Insole length 205mm, width tread 60mm, waist 37mm, seat 42mm. Height at centre back 49mm. Child size 12, Adult size 2 with 10% allowance for shrinkage. SF 182, context 3128.

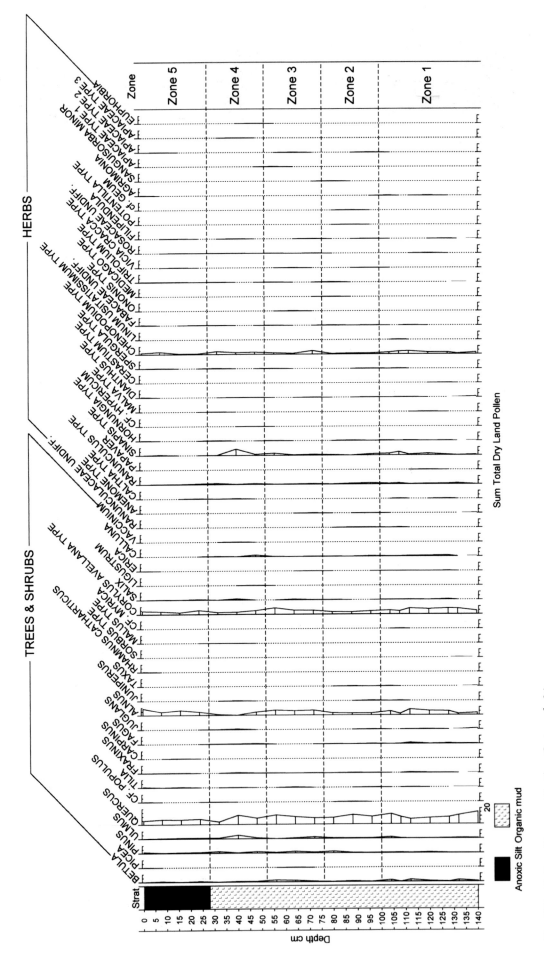

Fig 108   Pollen diagram, Section C, trench 31.

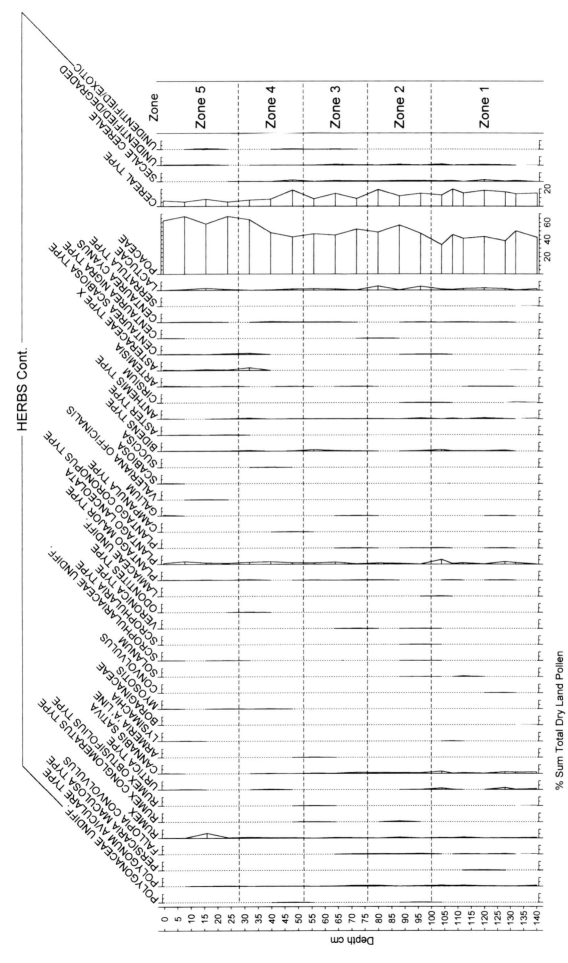

Fig 108 Pollen diagram, Section C, trench 31, continued.

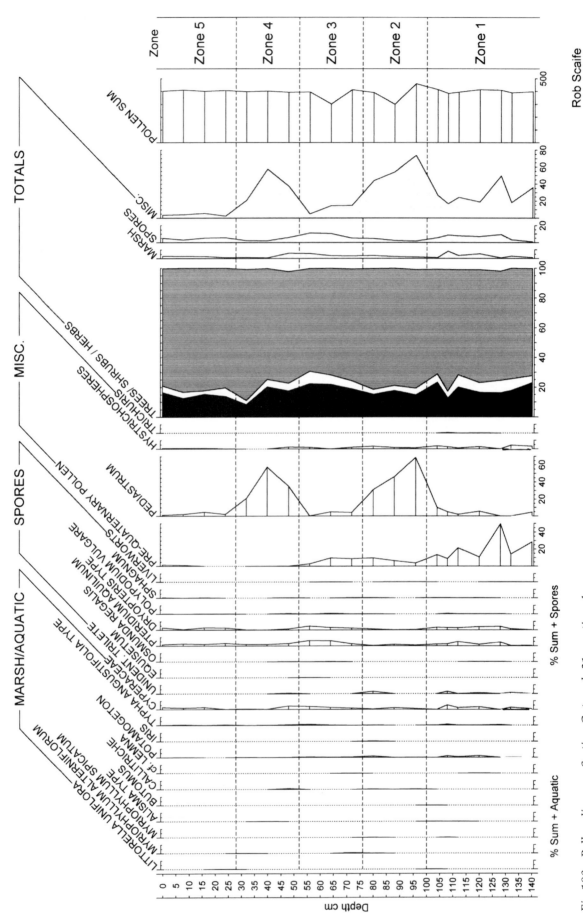

Fig 108 Pollen diagram, Section C, trench 31, continued.

that some pollen of exotic/culinary herbs and spices would also be found (*see* Plant Remains, above) but surprisingly they were absent. Apart from cereals the only cultivated crops were *Cannabis* type (hemp and hop) and flax (probably *Linum usitatissimum*). In the medieval period both types were used for fibre.

The diversity of herbs reflects the diversity of human habitats. Non-cereal Poaceae (wild grasses) form the most important pollen group in all the sections examined. As with cereal pollen, such high values are diagnostic of urban pollen assemblages (Greig 1981, 1982; Scaife 1982a, 1999). It is difficult to define the source of these grasses but a mixture is most plausible, including the moat edge, adjacent grassland or pasture, thatching waste, animal faeces and offal waste (animals fed on hay). These may have been disposed of in the moat and river/stream courses flowing into the moat. It is not possible to delimit specifically the sources of many of the pollen types. For example, the Ericaceae (*Calluna, Erica* and *Vaccinium*) are represented and while these are clearly heathland/acid soil shrubs, there is the strong possibility that pollen comes from their use in domestic situations (eg, floor coverings). *Sanguisorba minor* is another case in question: the single example of this could be from either calcareous (short) pasture or culinary use.

Chapter 7:   Period 4: The Later 17th Century

BERNARD DE GOMME AND THE REVETMENT WALL

The medieval defences of the Tower had become obsolete by the middle of the 17th century, overtaken by developments in military hardware (especially artillery) and strategic thinking (Fig 109). The curtains would be vulnerable to bombardment, while the moat would have been ineffective even without the encroachments that had steadily taken place on virtually all sides. Sir Bernard de Gomme, the Board of Ordnance Chief Engineer, was asked to report on the defences and his proposal to strengthen the outer edge of the moat by building a near-vertical revetment wall was enacted (Fig 110; *see also* Figs 114, 115). The moat was narrowed by more than 5m in the process, but this was seen as a necessary sacrifice. The Board of Ordnance accounts provide a running commentary from the late 1660s into the mid-1680s, with details of time, manpower, materials and cost. As early as April 1667 de Gomme was employed on survey work preparatory to widening and deepening the moat (WO 51/9, fol 22; Parnell

1983c, 339). Between July 1670 and December 1672 the revetment wall to the north and west sides of the moat was completed at a cost of over £1,500 (WO 51/12, fols 146–8, 157; WO 51/13, fols 37, 46, 55, 79, 100; WO 51/14, fol 55; WO 51/17, fol 4). The eastern revetment 'beginning where the brickwall was left off near Little Tower Hill to the Iron Gate' was not completed until 1683, at a cost of £1,330 10s (WO 47/13, fol 21; WO 51/27, fols 98, 177).

The documents show that the first operation involved the excavation of a wide and deep foundation trench into the accumulated fills around the outer edge of the moat. Shoring seems to have been used to maintain the sides of the trench before the foundations were laid in, and regular baling out was required. Some of the accounts refer to the construction of temporary dams as well. Even so there were a number of collapses of the trench sides and several entries in the accounts refer to cleaning out after such episodes. In some cases the fill from the trench seems to have been dumped to one side, but there are also references to the earth being carried away. The wall was then built up within this foundation

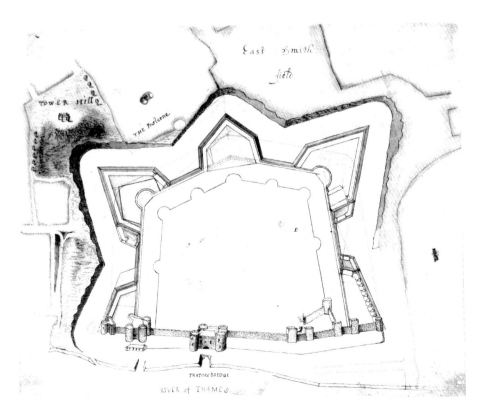

Fig 109   A scheme for the refortification of the Tower and a realignment of the moat, prepared by the Chief Ordnance Engineer, Sir Bernard de Gomme, in 1666. The medieval ramparts on the landward side would have been reinforced with massive ravelins to allow flanking fire along every exposed wall face, bringing the defences up to a contemporary European standard. This was not carried out. The scheme was reduced to a simple revetment of the outer edge.

145

Fig 110   View of the revetment wall in the west moat (trench 27).

trench, with buttresses on both front and rear faces. Presumably the area behind the wall was infilled.

Most of the western and roughly half of the north-eastern revetment survive from this work—in a few places the survival appears to be complete to the coping. The wall face is battered and integral buttresses respect this. There are obvious (and in places extensive) repairs to the masonry. Part of the east revetment may also be preserved within the sub-structure of Tower Bridge Approach (Chapter 10). The revetment was examined at many locations around the moat during 1995–7, usually with small test pits, although a longer length was exposed at the west end of trench 27.

A possible early construction phase

Test pits 15, 16 and trench 27 showed that the western arm of de Gomme's revetment sprang directly off a stone wall (Figs 111, 112). This appeared to represent a hitherto unsuspected earlier constructional phase providing a ready-made foundation and alignment for de Gomme on the west side of the moat. The southern and northern extent of the earlier structure is unknown and modern

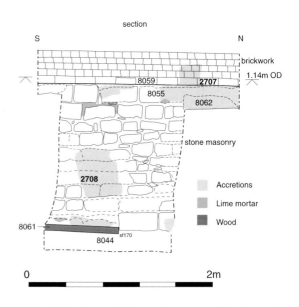

Fig 111   Elevation of the revetment wall in trench 27, showing the stonework of the lower courses and the brickwork above.

Fig 112   View of the stone base of the revetment wall at the west end of trench 27.

concrete (Chapter 10) has precluded any attempt to determine whether it continues around the north-west moat towards the Postern. This might be implied, however, by a reference in the works accounts for the early 1670s distinguishing between rebuilding the revetment from the Lion Tower area as far as the Postern and making a new wall from there onwards. A report of 1623 had recommended the construction of a brick revetment and the west moat masonry might be related to this. Alternatively, it could be an early stage of de Gomme's work.

The stone wall (contexts 1521, 1628 and 8055) was constructed from roughly squared Kentish Rag blocks. Seven courses were present in pits 15 and 16, with the base founded in the London Clay at approximately 0m OD; the upper surface lay at 1.12m OD. Ten courses were noted in the exposure at the west end of trench 27, however, based at −0.5m

OD and topping out at 1.08m OD. The blocks were irregular in size (0.1m by 0.2m average), with larger well-dressed blocks (0.2m by 0.5m) in the bottom course. The mortar was a coarse lime-based matrix applied liberally. The masonry was battered in each of the three exposures. A concretion was found on the wall-face in trench 27. Similar deposits on masonry of Edward I's outer curtain wall and other structures appear to result from water drawing calcitic material from the stone and/or the mortar bonding.

It was difficult to determine how the stone wall functioned—whether it was a foundation or upstanding masonry (in whole or in part). No foundation trench could be recognised in test pits 15 and 16, in the former case because the danger-ously unstable sides of the pit prevented detailed recording. Evidence for a foundation level may have

147

gone unrecognised in test pit 16 because of the shoring that masked the sections and the inflow of water that hampered excavation and recording, but no cut was noted when the sections were first exposed.

A feature (8078, fills 8071 and 8072) running parallel to the stone wall in trench 27 may be a foundation trench. The cut started at a level only just below the top of the masonry. The presence of later post-medieval timberwork both on the outer edge of the cut and driven through its fills close in against the wall obscured potentially crucial areas of stratigraphy so that the interpretation of 8078 must therefore remain provisional. Two sherds of early post-medieval pottery were recovered from a layer (8050) cut by 8078. If the provenance of the finds is secure (they could represent contamination) one would have to accept that the stone wall was built either within a period of about 20 years before, or as part of, de Gomme's work on the revetment. The layers succeeding the infill of 8078 contained finds dating to the mid-17th century or later.

De Gomme's foundations (Fig 113)

A construction trench for de Gomme's wall was clearly visible in test pits 21 and 22 (contexts 2126 and 2221). The trench had been cut from a level of *c*1.45m OD, though identification of the level in

test pit 22 was complicated by the presence of a later cut, 2222. This had truncated the upper part of 2221 and obscured some of the stratigraphy. The edge of 2126/2221 was near-vertical. It cut through early post-medieval and medieval deposits into the London Clay, bottoming out at 0.28m OD and −0.2m OD in pits 21 and 22 respectively. The battered brick foundations rose from there. A mixture of clay and mortar had been used to fill the remainder of the construction trench. The masonry topped out at 1.3–1.32m, where four consecutive offset courses continued to a height of 1.5–1.54m. The wall then continued with a slightly more pronounced batter than the foundations. The brickwork appeared to be English Bond throughout.

There was no evidence in test pits 21 or 22 for the timberwork (piles and/or more temporary support works) described in the works accounts, despite the perfect conditions for preservation of organic artefacts. Leather objects were recovered from layers 2123 and 2220, for instance, each of which was cut by the foundations. It is possible that timber formwork would have been removed for re-use elsewhere in the foundations, though the absence of piles is more difficult to explain. In trench 27, meanwhile, a timber post (8082) was found driven into the upper clay backfill of the foundation trench. The post stood proud of the fill by 0.5m to 1.1m OD and lay at the outer edge of the cut, 1.8m from the wall. The timber

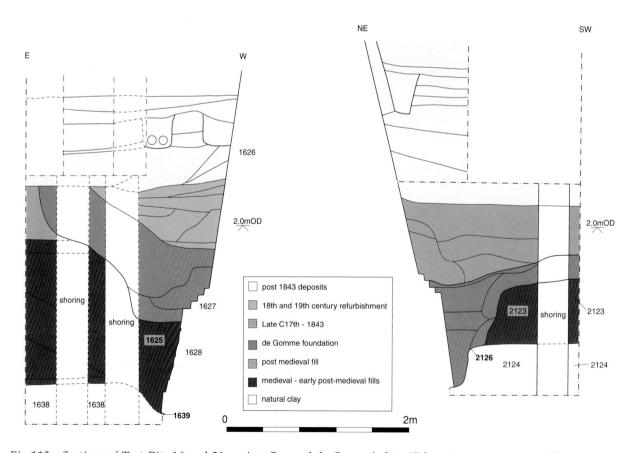

Fig 113   Sections of Test Pits 16 and 21 against Bernard de Gomme's late 17th-century revetment wall.

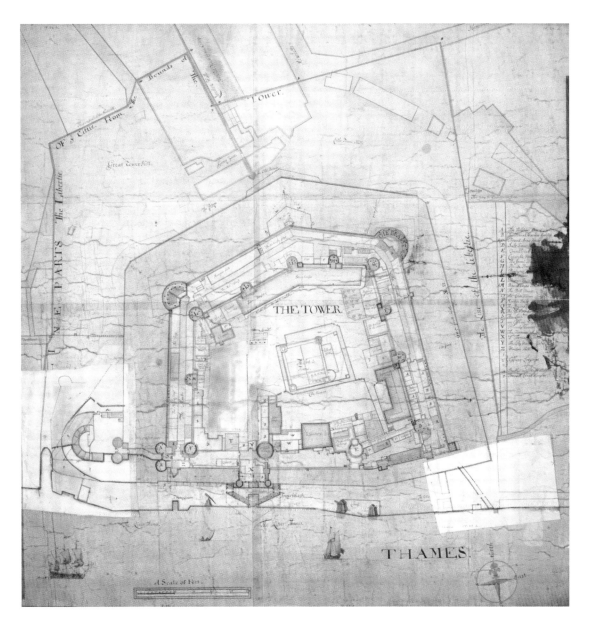

Fig 114   Plan of the Tower prepared by the Board of Ordnance in 1681–2. This is the earliest accurate land survey of the castle, and it shows the boundaries of the Tower Liberties with great precision. The plan is also valuable for certain details such as the new revetment wall, and the extent to which the moat around the Lion Tower had been backfilled to the north of the Middle Tower, with buildings erected on the newly reclaimed ground.

had been sawn to a roughly square section of *c*0.2m scantling. A north–south timber beam (8056) abutted the upright's western face. The beam was also roughly squared, being 0.3m thick and 0.2m deep. It was at least 3m long but extended beyond the limit of excavation to the south. These timbers could conceivably have been part of the late 17th-century formwork, but their stratigraphic position would suggest a later date. The limited finds evidence available might place this in the 18th century, in which case the timbers could have been associated with an episode of repair.

The four consecutive offset brick courses were found again in the west moat, rising there from the stone foundations already described but at a slightly lower level than in pits 21 and 22. This reflects little more than the level at which the stone wall terminated. A distinct cut (1625) was found in test pit 16 and was interpreted as the foundation trench for de Gomme's work. This would imply a construction level of *c*2.4m OD, but this cannot be supported on the basis of trench 27, where the more extensive excavation provides much more reliable evidence. There was no obvious construction trench here, unless context 8079 is the fill of such a feature. It seems more likely that the brick wall (1626, 8054) was built directly off the existing stone masonry (eg, *c*1.1m OD). Cut 1625 could relate to subsequent

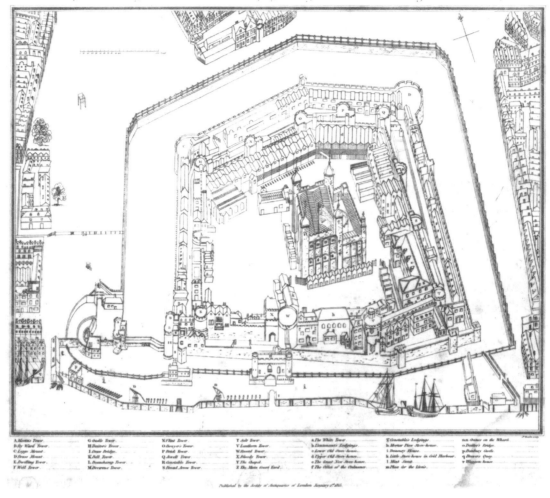

PL. XXXIX.

PLAN OF THE TOWER OF LONDON,

from a Drawing made between 1681 and 1689 by Order of L.ᵈ Dartmouth, Ma.ʳ Gen.ˡ of the Ordnance

Fig 115 *'Draught of the Tower raised in perspective' by the Ordnance engineer Holcroft Blood, dated to 1688 and here in a copy dated 1815. This is effectively an extruded version of the Ordnance plan of 1681–2 (Fig 114).*

repair or refacing of the brickwork, as suggested for timbers 8056 and 8082 in trench 27.

Early clay pipes were generally very rare in the excavations (*see* below and Appendix 2). Some late 17th-century pipes were recovered from backfill layers in the construction trench for the new revetment wall—these pipes, though not numerous, do provide excellent archaeological corroboration for the historically attested date of the wall and, at the same time, the history is an equally valuable independent check on the dating of the pipes. For example, a bowl from layer 2226, the top fill of the construction trench in test pit 22, is a tall version of the Type 18 pipe that was dated to 1670–1700 before its context was known. The moat find confirms that this style was in production by the 1670s. This taller variant of the basic Type 18 repeatedly occurs as a distinct type in assemblages from London and should now be added to the Typology as a discrete form.

THE DEMOLITION OF THE IRON GATE CAUSEWAY AND REFACING OF THE DEVELIN TOWER

The building of the revetment was accompanied by attempts to improve the management of the moat water. This included demolition of the Iron Gate causeway to improve the circulation of water and rebuilding (or at least refacing) the Develin Tower. On 13 February 1680 a contract was signed for the removal of the 'passage' between the 'Divills Tower' and the Irongate so that the water of the Ditch may run round' (WO 51/22, fols 113–16). Evidently the causeway had been too successful as a dam, despite the existence of a sluice specifically referred to in the demolition order. There was plenty of evidence for the demolition in trench 25. As already described in Chapter 6, only three courses of ashlar survived. A thick layer of rubble on the north side of the structure incorporated several ashlar blocks that clearly derived from higher levels of the super-structure. One piece appeared to be a coping stone—the demolition order also referred to 'taking away the Two side walls on both sides of ye passage as low as ye ground of ye said passage' (ibid) and the coping probably derived from one of these.

Two layers of clay silts (2581 and 2576) overlay the late 13th-century beech timbers in the northern sondage (Fig 64). The remains of a damaged timber structure (2613) separated the deposits above this. Five vertical planks or stakes survived in the western section of the sondage; a further five within the excavation showed that the structure ran north-eastwards (Fig 116). A 0.2m-square post was found on the line of the structure near the eastern limit of the sondage. The planks tapered to points. The surviving timbers were up to 0.4m long and 0.25m wide. Their tops had been broken or cut off at 0.3–0.45m OD. Silty clay 2635 and limestone rubble (2575) over 0.5m thick butted against and partly overlay the timber structure, extending south to the north face of the causeway. Layers of silty clay (2577, 2611 and 2574) ran north from the timbers. Context 2574 contained pieces of wood similar to those in structure 2613, and one small 17th/18th-century pot

sherd, while layers 2611 and 2635 contained 18th-century pottery. Given this dating evidence, it seems most likely that the timbers were part of the enabling works for the demolition contract. The planks and stakes probably acted as shoring to support the edge of a trench dug into the moat fills.

The contract centred on the removal of the carriageway itself. The surface of the causeway exposed by the excavations (2548) was fairly even (at c1m OD), in contrast to the random rubble core exposed where the Victorian culvert had cut through the medieval structure. It clearly did not represent the original carriageway and a further 0.53m of the latter's core (2579) survived against the Develin Tower, sloping out c0.3m with the ashlar facing still *in situ*. This corework argues for a substantially higher original surface level. The order also provided for topping off the demolished causeway, presumably to avoid further degradation of the structure from water penetration, and this is probably the level exposed by the excavation. The arch at high level within the existing east face of the tower does not provide a credible level for the medieval carriageway, not least because it is part of 19th-century refacing (*see* Chapter 10).

The ceramics support the dating of the causeway's reduction, with a preponderance of potentially 17th-century types such as English tin-glazed ware. The lowest levels in the succeeding sequence, both of which immediately post-date the destruction (2606, a thin lens directly overlying the causeway, and 2635, just to the north), contained just one sherd each, of Midland Purple and post-medieval black-glazed ware respectively.

Three courses of Kentish Rag ashlar (2647) rose 0.9m above the medieval corework on the tower's east face. The top of this work lay just below the existing surface level within the moat and the masonry above this was of a different (19th-century) build. The three courses were not regular across the width of the Develin Tower, with a discontinuity apparent on the east face between 0.9m and 1.55m north of the south-east corner (Fig 117). Several of the ashlar blocks had mason's marks and many had characteristic 17th-century horizontal drafting (marks made by the mason's chisel). Each course had a central band of close parallel grooves within a wide, smooth border. The batter of the causeway continued up for three courses on the south face and up the north face to above ground level. The tower rises vertically thereafter.

Finds corroded onto the demolition surface

Soon after the masonry had been reduced to below the water level finds began to accumulate on and become corroded onto its truncated surface. Most of the 25 metal objects from this trench were found here (Fig 118). The assemblage comprised four coins (SFs4, 9, 10 and 11), three lead (SFs19, 20 and 21) and one copper alloy (SF8) discs, eight sewing pins (SFs17, 23 and six unnumbered), three buttons (SFs7,

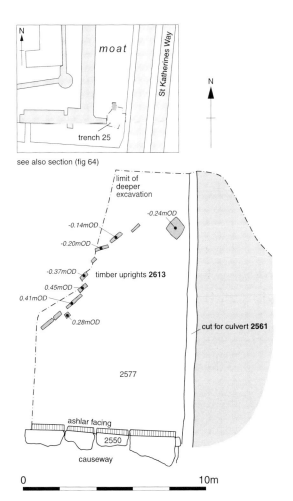

Fig 116 Plan of the 'coffer dam' revealed to the north of the Iron Gate causeway in trench 25.

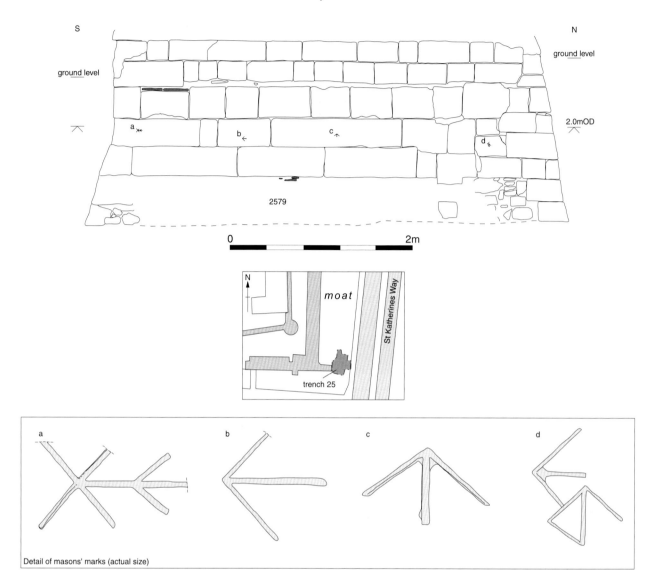

Fig 117 Elevation of the base of the Develin Tower as exposed in trench 25 at the south-east corner of the moat, with details of masons' marks.

15 and 17), a lead shot (SF5, 16mm diameter) and a larger iron shot (SF6). Some of the finds are of 18th- and 19th-century date and would normally be considered in Chapter 8, but their true significance rests here.

The three lead discs are all very damaged, but SFs19 and 21 are of 17th-century date. The pins are all fine 'sewing pins' with wire wound heads. The earliest examples of such pins come from 13th- and 14th-century contexts at sites such as Winchester (Biddle and Barclay 1990) and Southampton (Harvey 1975). They are more commonly seen in later contexts, however, with many hundreds or thousands coming from 17th- and 18th-century urban deposits. The three buttons are all post-medieval in date. One (SF15) is identical in form to a button (SF12) from context 2546 and is of 18th/19th-century date (Biddle and Cook 1990, 573, fig 155, no. 1726). The others are not diagnostic. The lead shot would

have been suitable for firing from a musket. The larger iron shot has a diameter of 1.5in (38.1mm) and weighs a little over 8oz (226.8g). This could be from a breach-loading gun of the 16th century or from case or grape shot of the 19th century (I Scott pers comm). The four coins are all very worn but are probably 19th century in date. The faint image of George III is visible on the X-ray of SF9.

It seems clear that the purpose of the demolition—to allow free flow of water around the south-east corner of the moat—was successfully achieved. Soon afterwards the metal finds described above began to accumulate on, and then become corroded onto, the residual surface of the structure. The corrosion was well beyond that expected even in the damp soil conditions within the backfilled moat, and can be explained easily enough by the constant presence of moat water over the causeway. The date-range of the finds is more puzzling, however,

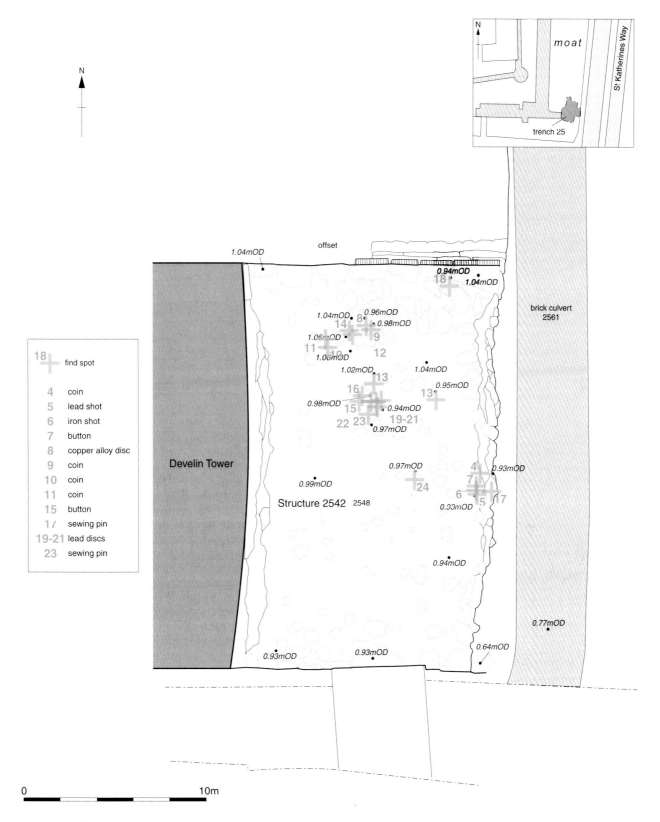

Fig 118 Plan of metal finds corroded onto the surface of the demolished Iron Gate causeway.

with finds of 17th- to 19th-century date being present. The method of deposition could have been a combination of accidental loss and 'wishing well' practice (there seem to be too many finds for casual loss to be the sole factor). One would expect the demolition surface to become buried by soil layers forming under normal waterlain siltation processes, however, and these should have provided a closer

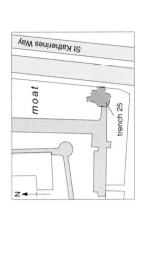

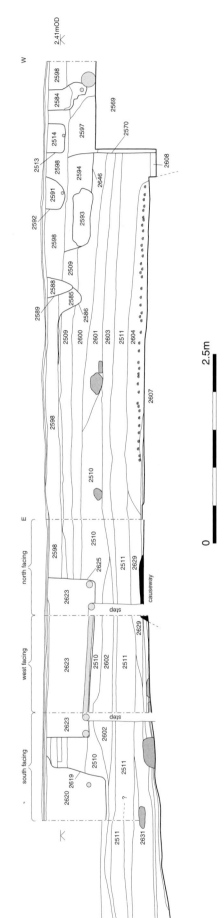

Fig 119   Composite eastern section of trench 25, showing post-1680 fills over the top of the demolished causeway surface.

date-range. Indeed, *in situ* waterlain deposits were found on the east side of the trench (Fig 119 and *see* below), but not on the west side. As will be described in Chapters 8–10, periodic—and often major—attempts were made to clean the moat, usually by dredging it. Presumably this led to the occasional re-exposure of the causeway to the moat water, and hence to further accumulations of finds on its surface.

Soil micromorphology

Sediments appear to have accumulated over the Iron Gate causeway soon after its demolition in 1680. Samples were taken for detailed soil analysis (context 2604, Fig 119). The deposit was a humic (9.43 per cent LOI), calcareous (11.3 per cent carbonate) brown silty clay. It had a massive and crack microstructure, with mollusc shells and high amounts of detrital organic matter, charcoal and anthropogenic inclusions (thin section M). The latter included sand-size quartz, chalk, mortar, red slag and black metallic cinder. The sample also recorded the highest magnetic susceptibility in the moat ($83.9 \times 10^{-8} \mathrm{m}^3 \mathrm{kg}^{-1}$). Probably coprolitic stained bone is present. Secondary gypsum and pyrite characterised the deposit, which also featured a very high total phosphate (2.35 mg g^{-1}) content and high levels of lead, zinc and copper.

The post-1680 sediment was much darker and 'dirtier' than medieval deposit 2576 (Chapter 9). It reflects deposition after the razing of the causeway, at a time when earlier London Clay-rich moat sediments were redeposited after a scouring out of the moat. The relatively high amounts of organic matter, phosphate and heavy metals, alongside anthropogenic materials such as charcoal and slag/cinders, resulted from increased amounts of urban and industrial contaminants reaching the moat.

WAS THE MOAT SCOURED EXTENSIVELY IN THE LATE 17TH CENTURY?

Later attempts to clean the moat are well documented historically, as well as being recognisable in the archaeological record. What of earlier attempts to keep it clean? Edward II's reign (1307–27) opened with an operation which was to dominate the history of the moat until 1843—an attempt to cleanse and dredge it. This had been necessary as early as 1293 (E 403/76 (Michaelmas 20 Edward I)), but was required again in 1308 (E 101/468/21 fols 91v, 94v). The main problem then, as later, was probably tidal silting, exacerbated by the dumping of refuse and sewage from the castle itself and no doubt from its

outer edges as well. Worse problems were caused by discharge from the city ditch, then still at least seasonally water-filled and linked to the north edge of the moat. In March 1353 a writ was issued to the Mayor and Sheriffs 'bidding them remove the filth which had accumulated in the Tower ditch owing to the City's ditch in the vicinity not having been kept clean, contrary to former repeated orders' (*Cal Letter-Books of the City of London:* Book G (Edward III), 27). Two years later more work was done to clean out the ditch. As we have already seen in Chapter 6, records for the next few centuries show that these problems did not go away.

It is more difficult to recognise archaeologically the physical response to the regular demands for cleaning. The level at which the fish trap was found demonstrates clearly enough that some silts resisted all attempts at dredging, and the process can rarely if ever have been totally successful. Even with modern pumps and earth-moving machinery in support the task of excavating the moat fills was an arduous and occasionally soul-destroying task for the archaeological team. It must have seemed far worse for generations of earlier labourers (the scavelmen and others of the historical record) working in much more difficult circumstances. Nevertheless some success was achieved, as the lack of clearly definable 16th- and 17th-century fills shows.

The lack of early clay pipes seems crucial, with the vast majority of the pipes recovered from the excavations dating from the late 17th to the mid-19th centuries. The castle, with its royal and military functions, would seem to be the classic location for early tobacco and therefore pipe use (and loss), so the low numbers of pre-1670 pipes must be significant. It suggests that clearance works were fairly effective up to, or at, this date, removing the majority of the early post-medieval deposits. For instance, the construction level of 1.1m OD for the revetment wall in trench 27 may represent roughly the level to which the moat had become silted up (at least on its outer edge). Alternatively it may be that the moat was scoured down to this level as part of the construction works. After all, de Gomme had been involved in 1667 on planning for the widening and deepening of the moat.

OTHER FINDS

A small number of components of 17th-century shoes were found, though not in contemporary contexts. A vamp (SF226) came from an 18th-century layer (context 31133) in trench 31. An insole (SF229) with an extended square toe of a style popular during the middle of the century was unstratified.

Chapter 8: Period 5: The Moat and Associated Works during the 18th and early 19th Centuries

INTRODUCTION

In many ways the later post-medieval period was one of the busiest for the moat and its associated buildings. Many of the major defensive structures continued to be the subjects of significant alterations during this period. In some cases (particularly that of the Lion Tower and its surroundings) this called into question the extent to which they could still be regarded as even remotely defensive. Meanwhile, the Tower authorities struggled (and arguably failed) to keep up an adequate maintenance regime in the moat throughout the 18th and early 19th centuries. What had once been a fundamental part of the ring of defences gradually declined in importance. There is plentiful evidence for this both in the historical record and among the archaeological remains. In the latter instance, this is the dominant period for all categories of finds and the animal bone. This chapter thus contains more of such evidence than most of the others.

CHANGES AROUND THE LION TOWER

The later history of the Lion Tower
by Dr G Parnell

By 1726 a number of buildings had been constructed in the exercise yard (Figs 120, 121), but the arrangement within the barbican itself appears to have altered little. At some stage after the middle of the 18th century, and before a drawing of the interior of the Lion Tower was executed in 1779, the longstanding arrangement in the barbican was renewed. The 1779 illustration shows two-tier cages set within a substantial brick arcading that rises as high as the wall walk of the Lion Tower. The brickwork is surmounted by a corbelled timber structure, probably the eaves of a roof.

In 1806 it was reported that the cages in the Lion Tower were divided into three levels. It is possible that the extra storey was formed in 1802, when the wooden fronts to the cages were replaced by stone and iron devices, or in 1810 when 'moving dens in each of the apartments' were introduced (Fig 122). In any event there is no evidence for further alteration to the Lion Tower until the last of the animals were removed in 1835.

The cages, together with the fixtures and fittings of the Menagerie, were sold by public auction on 22 October 1835. The Lion House, the official residence of the Menagerie Keeper, was not demolished until September 1853 following the death of the last Keeper who, by way of letter patent, was entitled

to the house for life. The Lion Tower and the rest of the Menagerie buildings had probably been removed a little earlier following proposals put forward by the Royal Engineers in a report produced in 1845.

Archaeological evidence

The test pits excavated in the Lion Tower area during 1996 produced very limited information regarding its post-medieval development. The excavations had to be strictly limited in area, and all the pits had to be kept to quite shallow depths (typically less than 1m maximum). Thus the work was largely, if not wholly, confined within the demolition and fill layers deriving from the decision to clear the whole area of buildings after 1853. Fortunately, the somewhat larger but still limited excavation in 1999 (Chapter 5) was more successful in examining the accommodation provided for the lions inside the great medieval barbican (Fig 123; *see also* Fig 80).

Two walls (5 and 16) abutted the inner face of the Lion Tower and ran away from it at an approximately perpendicular angle. The walls were 0.6m wide and 2.8m long. They were not parallel, but tapered towards each other slightly to the north from 2.4m apart to 2m. The eastern wall (5) was identified at a level of 4.29m OD and comprised six courses of red and yellow unfrogged bricks to a depth of 0.5m. A possible buttress or jamb (36) measuring 0.51m by 0.4m was identified 1.2m from the inner face of the tower along wall 5. This consisted of three courses of red and yellow bricks and appeared to have been heavily robbed. The western wall (16) was identified at 4.07m OD and consisted of unfrogged red bricks over a limestone rubble foundation (17). Both walls were bonded with a yellow sandy mortar. A construction cut (31) filled with sandy loam (32) was identified for wall 16. The cut was excavated to a depth of 0.4m but not bottomed. No construction cut was identified for wall 5.

Three courses of irregular roughly hewn limestone blocks (37) were identified in the north-east corner of the trench. The structure appeared to cross between the ends of walls 5 and 16. It had been partially robbed (38, 39) and had suffered from root disturbance. The partition walls (5 and 16) represented the separation of the Lion Tower into individual cells/cages. Structure 37 is thus interpreted as the end wall of the cage defined by 5 and 16. Its internal area was therefore c6m².

A series of make-up layers and floors was found within the cage and the medieval embrasure in

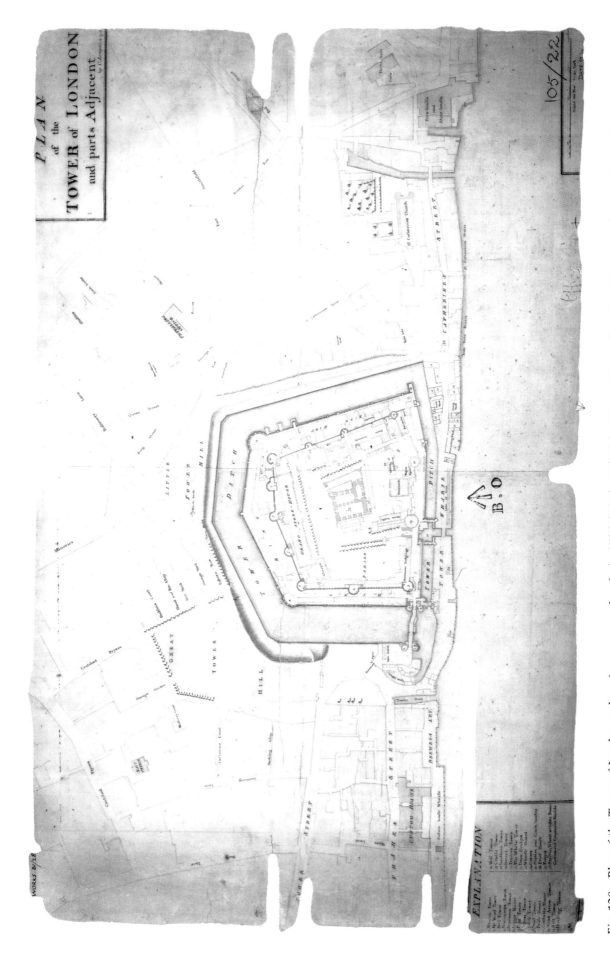

Fig 120   Plan of the Tower of London and environs prepared early in 1726 (Works 31/28) by Clement Lemprière, draughtsman to the Board of Ordnance. The southern arm of the Lion Tower moat was then still filled with water, but a second map by Lemprière (Works 31/36, Fig 135) shows that it had been filled in soon afterwards.

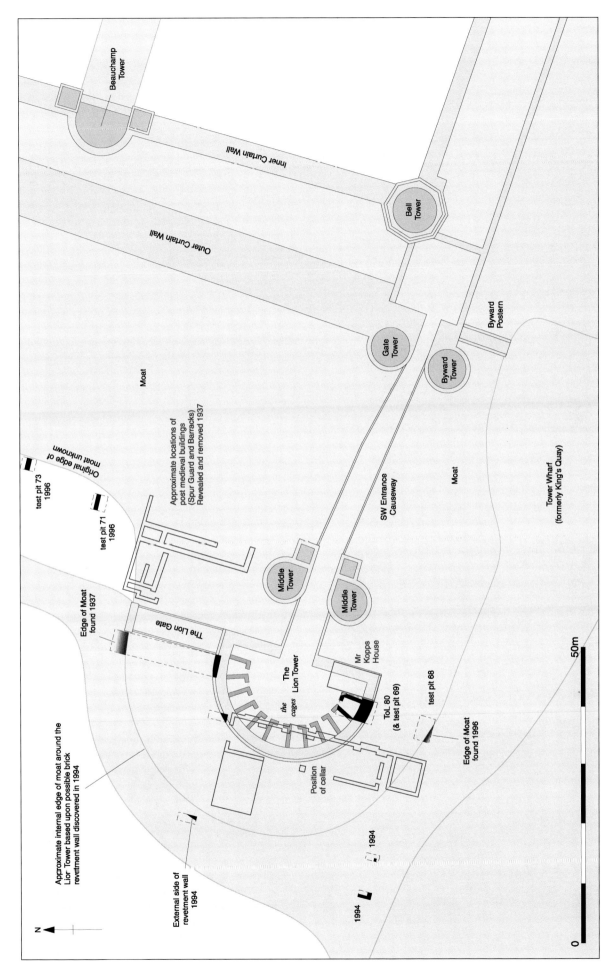

Fig 121 *Plan showing archaeological evidence for post-medieval buildings to the north of the Middle Tower, excavated in 1937, and for the Lion Tower cages.*

Beauchamp Tower

Inner Curtain Wall

Outer Curtain Wall

Bell Tower

Moat

Gate Tower

Byward Tower

Byward Postern

Approximate locations of post medieval buildings (Spur Guard and Barracks) Revealed and removed 1937

Original edge of moat unknown

test pit 73 1996

test pit 71 1996

SW Entrance Causeway

Moat

Tower Wharf (formerly King's Quay)

Edge of Moat found 1937

The Lion Gate

Middle Tower

Middle Tower

Approximate internal edge of moat around the Lion Tower based upon possible brick revetment wall discovered in 1994

the cages

The Lion Tower

Mr Kopps House

ToL 80 (& test pit 69)

test pit 68

Edge of Moat found 1996

External side of revetment wall 1994

Position of cellar

1994

1994

N

0   50m

Fig 122   *The two-storey lions' cages in the Lion Tower, illustrated in 1779.*

Fig 123   *Overhead view of the Lion Tower cage during the 1999 excavation, with a television camera crew recording the progress of work.*

the Lion Tower wall. These were all exposed in plan or in the sections of later features and could not be excavated because of the restricted aims of the project (ie, to prove the location of the tower and if possible define a whole cage). Clay and loam levelling deposits (28, 33–5) were the earliest deposits recorded. They were overlain by an ashy occupation layer (21). Sand and clay make-up layers (24, 25) under a brick and tile floor surface (26) were found within the embrasure. The floor measured 2.2m by 1.1m and consisted of roughly square floor tiles measuring 230mm by 250mm flanked by red and yellow half-brick sets measuring 120mm by 140mm. Two mortar floors (19 and 20) between the two partition walls (eg, within the body of the cage) may have been contemporary with floor 26.

Unfortunately, the limited excavations meant that no dating evidence was recovered from any of these contexts. The cage, its component structures and floors are therefore essentially undated, although it seems reasonable to suggest that they are of relatively late date. The end wall (37) can probably be associated with the new stone and iron fronts erected in 1802 (Parnell, above). The brick walls, and the brick and tile floor in the embrasure, might be of 18th-century date, but such a suggestion is only tentative.

ST THOMAS'S TOWER SLUICE

There had been an arched opening through the west side of St Thomas's Tower into the south-west moat close to the inner curtain wall at least during the post-medieval period. It cannot have been an original feature, however, as it cut across an Edward I arrow-loop embrasure. Anthony Salvin evidently blocked this arch when he had the west side of the tower refaced in 1864–6 (Parnell 1993, 101). Even so the opening is very clearly shown on numerous plans, elevations and other illustrations. On 16 October 1789 the Chief Royal Engineer suggested that the 'turning gate' in this position 'should be restored in order to scour the stretch of ditch between the Byward Tower and St Thomas's Tower' (PRO Works 14/1/2). One early 19th-century plan also shows a triangular projection in front of the opening in the south-west moat (Fig 124). A plan drawn up in 1914 to reflood the moat around the Lion Tower and up to St Thomas's Tower would have involved re-opening this sluice, but it is not clear whether those who devised the scheme actually knew of its existence. They may simply have intended to open a breach in the wall. It seems most unlikely that they would have been aware of the archaeological sensitivities of the area, even if they did know about the arch blocked by Salvin.

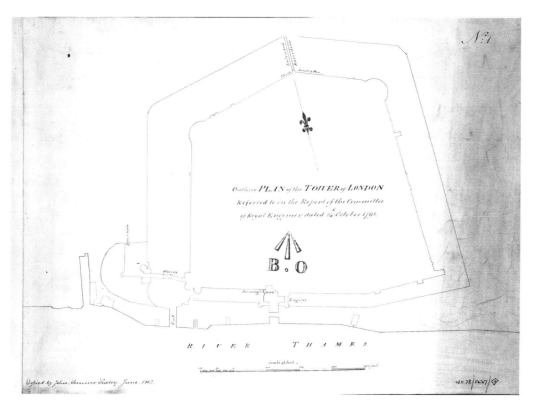

Fig 124   An early 19th-century copy (Works 78/1227) of a late 18th-century plan of St Thomas's Tower and the south moat, showing the opening (marked 'turning gate') in the west wall of the tower hard against the inner curtain wall. This is the location of the sluice base found in test pit 38. Note also the location of the 'intended batardeau' in the north moat, and the 'cut' through the wharf to the south west of the Byward Tower.

Test pit 38 was dug in the angle between Edward I's outer curtain wall and the west side of St Thomas's Tower. The pit was intended to investigate the foundations of both structures for engineering and conservation purposes, but this proved impossible because a substantial masonry (3831) and timber structure (3826) was found instead. This consisted of a strong platform or apron of planks on edge-plates with a second, triangular tier with mitred sill overlying the eastern end. All of the timbers were elm (and thus unsuitable for dendrochronology). The structure coincides with the position of the 'turning gate' and probably formed the apron to it.

The structure measured between 2.75m and 2.8m in length and was between 1.75m and 1.82m wide (Figs 125, 126). The foundations directly overlay the natural gravel of the Thames foreshore (3810) and comprised a single course of Portland limestone ashlar. Dr Worssam commented that the lithology of the stone provided a very close match to the paving (dated to 1788) in the nave of Canterbury Cathedral. Each block was 0.72m deep, standing to a level of c0.22m OD. One of the blocks was chamfered in the top right corner suggesting that some at least of the masonry had been re-used. The masonry butted against both the outer curtain wall and the western face of St Thomas's Tower.

The platform had a north–south transverse beam (38261) along its west edge. The east side of the beam had been rebated to receive nine east–west planks (which thus hid the rebate). These were of unknown thickness as they had been laid flush to each other with an additional plank on edge along the south edge to make an exact and watertight fit. They had been secured to the rebate in 38261 with two nails on each plank, and presumably had been similarly attached to another transverse beam at their eastern end, unseen beneath the triangular platform. Two longitudinal beams (38288 and 38262) formed the northern and southern edges of the platform respectively. Presumably these were tenoned into the western beam. The joints had been secured with pegs after the over-cut of the rebate had been filled with two small chocks (38263 and 38289). The beams formed three sides of a presumed box-frame, and the presence of a central bracing timber between 38288 and 38262 is suggested by the series of nails seen at the mid-point of the planks.

It is unclear how the upper triangular tier was secured to the lower deck but it had been built off a large transverse beam (38274) with a central horizontal timber tenoned and pegged into it. Two sill beams mitred at 112° from the end of this, and also tenoned into the main beam, completed the triangle (Fig 127). The sills were lapped over each other at the apex where the central beam also lapped over them. Finally, the three timbers were secured by two iron bolts. All four components had been rebated to receive triangular planking or blocks infilling the central spaces. The infilling had been nailed into position.

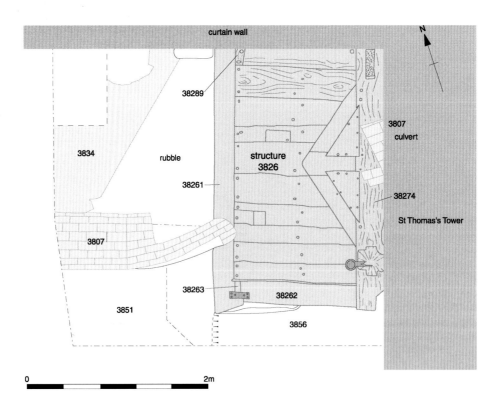

Fig 125   Plan of the elmwood sluice in test pit 38 against the north-west corner of St Thomas's Tower.

Fig 126   The wooden sluice foundation against St Thomas's Tower in test pit 38. The triangular spur in front of the masonry consists of at least four timbers. Elm was used throughout. The drain emerging through the wall is Victorian and was inserted as part of the backfilling process in 1843–5.

The main back-beam (38274) also bore the remnants of tenoned and squared posts, 0.3m thick in cross-section, at either end. Very little remained of the northern post, although the tenon did survive in the mortice with a wedge driven in to secure it. The base of the southern post was in better condition, however, and still bore part of its iron hinge. This had corroded, thus helping to preserve the timber to

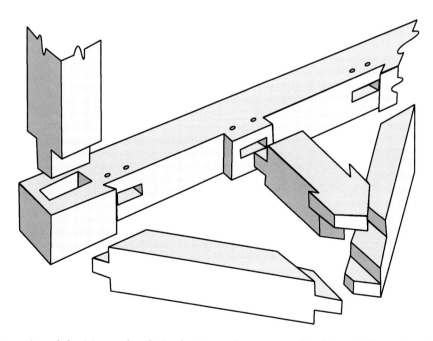

Fig 127   Reconstruction of the joinery details in the triangular spur on the sluice platform, based on analysis by Julian Munby.

163

0   5cm

Fig 128   Four soldiers' buttons, recovered from test pit 38.

its higher level. The irregularity of the remnant gateposts is due only to rotting at the level of waterlogged preservation. This shows that the gates were left to rot and were not dismantled.

The use of elm throughout this structure was a specific choice made because of the uniquely durable properties of this species in consistently wet conditions. It is a natural choice for lock-aprons. The only repairs required may be represented by the three anomalous blocks of elm, tightly fitted within the planking of the lower deck.

The structure was probably intended to control, and more particularly to retain, tidal water in the moat. The posts at either end of beam 38274 would have held the sluice gates which would have closed against the beams of the raised triangular platform. This would then have borne (and deflected) much of the water pressure. Presumably the front edges of the gates would have been mitred to ensure a tight fit and would have been pressed tighter together as the water pressure increased behind them. The closed gates would prevent the water draining from the moat at low tide and would be opened to top up the water level or to drain it during times of dredging or building within the moat. The detailed and intricately designed style of carpentry, in combination with the squared form of the bolts holding the three platform timbers together, suggests an 18th-century date. It has been postulated that early locks may have more acute angles of mitre sills; an 'early' example of 1710 on the river Tern had doors which closed at less than 90° (Harding and Newman 1997, 35). The sluice gates against St Thomas's Tower closed at 112° and so would be later if this formula is followed. The sluice position itself may be earlier.

Finds

One of the larger finds groups was recovered from test pit 38. This included a fragment of a post-medieval repaired welted sole (SF142) in silt 3857 around the sluice platform. Inorganic finds included a 19th-century coin (SF116) from silty clay 3845, but the bulk of the finds came from context 3802,

the primary fill of culvert 3834, probably inserted after 1843. The majority of these finds are considered in Chapter 10, but a few deserve mention here. A group of buttons (Fig 128), for instance, included one (SF127) with an embossed Tudor rose with a crown above and 'YORK' below. Another (SF131) is a button of the 1st Foot Grenadier Guards dating to *c*1820 and bearing the inscription 'HONI SOIT QUI MAL Y PENSE' (Major C P Bowes Crick pers comm). Finally, one of the two coins (SF129) was a silver sixpence of William IV with the reverse value in a wreath, dated 1835. The pottery from this pit was all of 19th-century date.

FURTHER ALTERATIONS TO THE SOUTH-WEST CAUSEWAY AND ASSOCIATED WORKS

Major building works during the late 18th century were concentrated at the western entrance. Clement Lemprière's drawings from the early years of the century show the Middle Tower and causeway substantially in a medieval form (although perhaps partly rebuilt after 1548), but both had been in poor condition for some time. Between 1717 and 1719 the tower was largely refaced in Portland stone, re-windowed and adorned with the arms of George I over the outer gate—leaving it much as it remains (Parnell 1993, 84). Later in the century the bridge and causeway across the moat were also remodelled. The work began with clearing access to the structure through the moat fill, a master scavelman being instructed in 1780 to 'clear way for the Masons to build a new bridge and entrance into the Tower', beginning work on 7 November (WO 51/286 no. 1822, 145r). The next stages involved remedial works to the stonework to be kept (WO 51/286 no. 1846, 164r ff) and 'taking down old stone walls between Martins Tower and the Warden Gates' (ie, the Middle and Byward Towers respectively). These were the parapets to the causeway shown by Sandby in 1747 (Fig 129). This was followed by the replacement of the three-arched passage under the causeway (best known from Haiward and Gascoyne's view, Fig 84, though the crowns of two

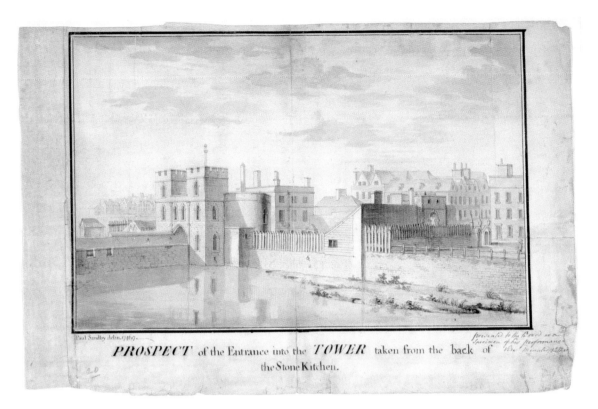

Fig 129 Watercolour by Paul Sandby (1731–1809) as an applicant for the post of draughtsman to the Board of Ordnance in 1747. The view shows the rear of the Middle Tower, as remodelled 1717–19, but still retaining a length of the medieval causeway parapet to the left of the gate. Note the huddle of buildings around and built into the Lion Tower (then still housing the Menagerie), the gateway and palisade area facing Tower Hill, and the mudbank and vegetation on the far side of the moat. The Stone Kitchen was a tavern, built along and across Mint Street and overlooking the outer curtain wall. It was demolished in 1846.

arches are perhaps just visible in Sandby's drawing as well) with the existing single span of Portland stone (WO 51/307 no. 8652, 56v ff). At the same time the causeway was substantially refaced, widened at the west end of its north side to accommodate the existing sentry box and repaved (WO 51/310 no. 1351, 60r).

Trench 31: timberwork and associated contexts

A line of mortared slabs and rounded limestone blocks (3175) overlay the dog-legged offset foundation (3180) of the medieval causeway in front of the central arch (Fig 130). There was some evidence for the trench that must have been cut into the moat fills to allow the construction of 3175, but this was confused by the 19th-century culverts. The slabs were covered with a 0.2m-thick deposit of degraded greyish white mortar (3174) with a 30 per cent inclusion of rounded pebbles and cobbles. This formed the bedding for a predominantly softwood timber structure which had been thrown across the central archway. The timberwork had been bisected by the main 1843 culvert and thus was not continuous. The two sections were numbered 3159

and 31167 to the west and east of the culvert respectively.

The two sections would originally have consisted of a single large timber baseplate *c*7m long and at least 0.35m wide. It had six mortice positions on its upper surface, two of which retained the truncated remains of timber uprights (Fig 131). The latter supported a tie-back beam which overlay the baseplate but was only partly revealed within the excavation. The remains of three timber planks extending southwards were nailed to the tie-back beam, but only the northern ends of these were revealed in section. They formed what appeared to be a timber floor surface at about 0.25m OD underneath the causeway's arch. A dark brown silty clay with a 70 per cent rubble and brick inclusion (31168) butted against the timberwork. The deposit appeared to be deliberately laid, possibly to secure the baseplate in place. The whole structure resembled the base of scaffolding.

The upper part of the causeway, including the central arch (from *c*2.2m OD), was rebuilt in regularly coursed Portland ashlar to a level of 4.5m OD (Fig 72). The blocks were of various sizes with an average dimension of 0.6m by 0.3m.

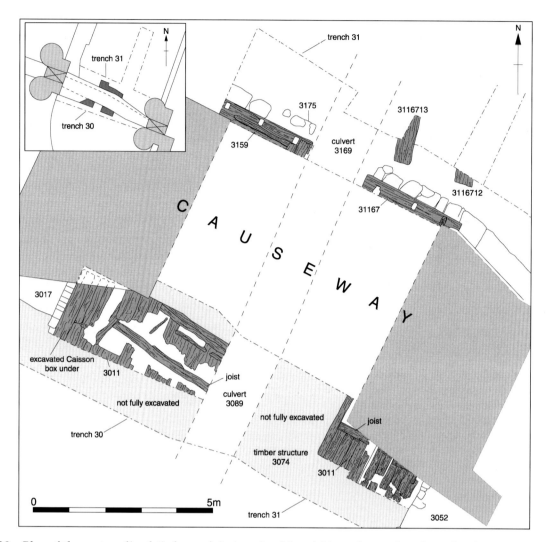

Fig 130 Plan of the post-medieval timberwork in trenches 30 and 31 on the south and north sides respectively of the rebuilt central arch through Edward I's western entrance causeway.

The reconstructed archway was 6.3m wide and sprang from the original medieval abutments in walls 3157 and 31110. The uppermost course of the rebuild contained a concentration of Purbeck limestone and Caen stone. The Portland and Caen ashlar survived in a reasonably good condition but the Purbeck limestone blocks were badly eroded. A single 70mm-thick course of Portland stone capped the causeway, forming the parapet at 4.6m OD.

Trench 30: timberwork and associated contexts

Timber structure 3074 (Fig 130) was 10.7m long (east–west) and 2.4m wide within the excavated area. It was wholly confined between the two medieval walls on either side of the central arch, although its southern edge lay beyond the limits of excavation. The structure comprised a network of wooden boxes that were built over the medieval beech piles (3068) and supported a joisted plank floor. The boxes varied in size from 0.8m by 0.9m to 1m by 1.4m and were made from a series of

horizontal and vertical planks nailed to a frame of cross-beams. The boxes were filled with several layers of rubble and grey clay (3013, 3066, 3067 and 3073). Only the south-western box was fully excavated (Figs 132, 133). This revealed that several of the vertical planks had been branded with the Board of Ordnance's broad arrow-mark. The infilled boxes had been covered with a platform of wooden planks (3011) laid transversely over east-west joists. The platform lay at 0.08–0.22m OD and may have connected with the planks noted in trench 31 under the north side of the arch. Unfortunately, the uppermost timbers were in very poor condition, evidently because they lay close to the limit of waterlogging in this part of the moat. This was an important consideration in the decision to close the excavation of trench 30 as rapidly as possible.

Structure 3074 was sealed by a compact deposit of mid-brown clay (3072) containing patches of decomposed wood (3018). A complete 18th-century London stoneware bottle stamped 'Geo Price, Fulham' was recovered from layer 3072. A 1m-thick deposit

Fig 131   Timberwork for the rebuilt central arch in trench 31. The softwood beam contains two empty sockets, but an oak upright survives at the left (east) end. The upper part of the post has rotted away. Note the spade sticking out of the section just above the beam and to the right of the post. This is not an excavator's accident! The spade is contemporary with the timbers, and was probably abandoned here when the shaft broke.

of dark brown silty clay (3060) was encountered towards the east end of the trench. This deposit contained several large blocks of Purbeck stone ashlar that had probably derived from the original causeway superstructure and been dumped when the upper part of the causeway was rebuilt.

The infilled boxes formed a caisson, providing a solid foundation for the planked platform. Caisson foundations were first used on an extensive scale in England from 1738 during the construction of London's Westminster Bridge over the Thames (Ruddock 1979, 3–19). The design process for this had begun four years earlier, so the example at the Tower of London was using a well-established construction method.

The caisson is interpreted as the base for a timber bridge. The superstructure would have risen from the platform and would probably have used the traditional trestle form. The construction of a new central arch in the causeway by definition involved breaching it, thus closing what was by this time the only landward entrance into the Tower of London. Clearly access still had to be maintained and the timberwork ran between the conveniently positioned medieval wing walls to stem the breach. The temporary arrangement would presumably have been at about the same level as the existing causeway carriage. The planking over the caisson boxes

would have lain far too deep for use as a crossing in its own right. Indeed it must have been under water for most (probably all) of the time.

No traces of the putative trestle bridge survived. This is not surprising—the timberwork would have been easy to dismantle and could doubtless have been used on building programmes elsewhere in the Tower or on another site entirely. The caisson, however, was a very solid structure dug and driven well into the depths of the wet moat. Any attempt to recover the timbers would have required a huge outlay of manpower and expense to drain this part of the moat, dig out the rubble infill and then remove the timbers. A pragmatic decision to leave the structure in place was perhaps to be expected of the Board of Ordnance.

THE NATURE OF THE MOAT IN THE POST-MEDIEVAL PERIOD

Apart from the loss of the Lion Tower ditch, 18th-century activity was mostly confined to maintaining the revetment and bridges, along with the continued struggle against silting and pollution. Maintenance work in or at the edges of the wet moat, however, was a complex operation, and some interesting detail survives as to how it was carried out. Between 1717 and 1723, for example, temporary earth dams had to

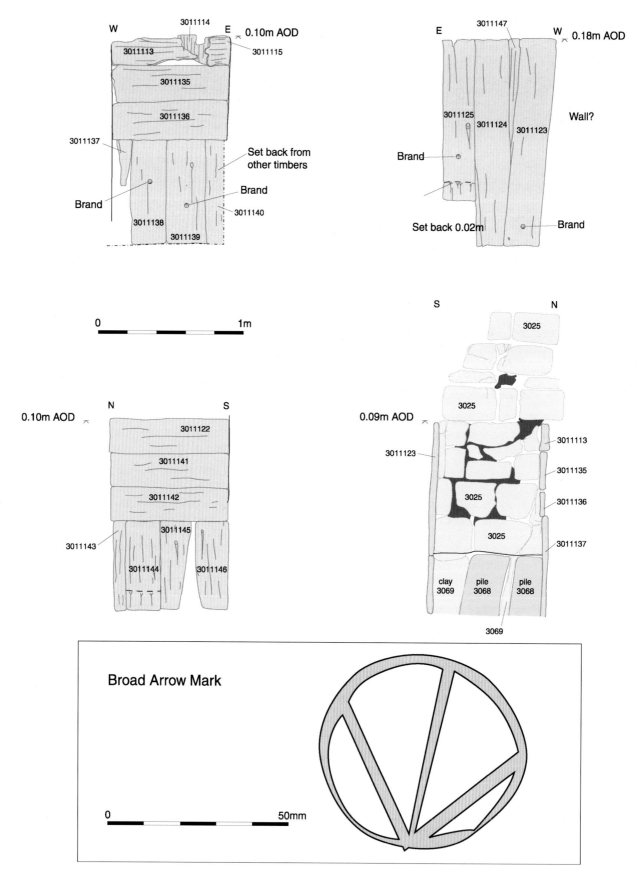

Fig 132 *Elevations of the caisson box in trench 30, with a detail of a Broad Arrow brand of the Board of Ordnance.*

168

Fig 133 View of the excavated caisson box in trench 30. Note the late 13th-century piles, mostly beech, exposed at the bottom of the box.

be laid across the south moat to repair the sluices at Traitors' Gate (*see above*) (WO 51/98, 96r ff, 26 June 1717; PRO WO 51/114, 117r–118r, 31 Dec 1722–29 Sept 1723: 143 days work). In 1743 (WO 51/153, no. 4826, 72r ff) and 1774 'dams were made from Earth and rubbish from Tower Hill... to keep out Water whilst the foundation of the new east draw-bridge was laying' (WO 51/266, no. 4186, 37r). Inter-mittent attempts were made to scour the moat, notably in 1737 (WO 51/139, no. 6766, 104v, 31 Dec 1737) and 1779 (WO 51/284 no. 6737, 141v), but on a small scale only. In 1787, however, a report detailing the condition of the moat and the depth of water (WO 78/2527) led to drastic action. It recommended that a canal 'be cut through the Tower Wharf a little to the east of the Traitor's Bridge'. This was carried out, after some dispute, in 1789 (Works 14/1/2—letter of Sir William Green, Chief Royal Engineer to the Master General of HM Ordnance, 16 Oct 1789; also see Works 31/1256—a plan showing the canal cut through Tower Wharf). The gap remained until 1802 (WO 78/1227—section and plan showing the Tower Wharf and the plan for closing it; Fig 124). The aim was presumably to enable the easy return of incoming silts to the river, but its effectiveness is doubtful.

Other activities included the sealing-off of the north-eastern and western arms of the moat by a dam or 'batardeau' across the north moat (the site of the 'intended Battardeau on the north side of the Tower Ditch' is indicated on the outline plan accompanying this retrospective report of the Royal Engineers of 14 October 1795, WO 78/1227, no.1). This was intended to retain water for the use of the Mint, at that stage still operating from within the Tower. The dam, complete with its sluices, is shown in several 19th-century views (*see* G B Campion's view of the Tower Ditch from the north west (Guildhall Art Gallery) made in about 1840, showing the late 18th-century 'batardeau'; Fig 144). The structure was presumably substantial, but it resisted several attempts to locate it through geophysical survey and trial excavation (trenches 4 and 81) during 1995–7.

Moat fills and the timber 'platform' in trench 27

A series of rubble and clay layers were found over the later medieval and early post-medieval fills in trench 27. The high levels of finds from these contexts (*see below*) and the rubble content showed that they incorporated significant amounts of dumped refuse, though they were probably still laid down in a broadly aquatic environment. The de Gomme revetment foundations and associated contexts at the west end of the trench were sealed by rubbly clays 2888–9, both datable to the 18th century. Two further dumped layers overlay these. One was a tenacious brown silty clay (2881), 0.5m thick and extending for 4m from the wall, while the other was a loose brown sandy silt (2955) 0.45m thick and continuing eastward for a further 5m.

The two were broadly contemporary (2881 also contained 18th-century pottery) and in the same horizon, but they were separated physically and stratigraphically by narrow linear feature 2887. This was aligned roughly north-east to south-west, with a flat base and near-vertical sides. The feature, 0.5m deep and between 0.8m and 2m wide, contained a timber structure (2830) of beams (2832) and planks (2831), the base lying at 1.06m OD (Figs 36 and 134).

The timbers were mostly Baltic softwoods, with an occasional piece of oak. The beams formed the foundation for the structure, with the planks forming a crude but fairly even surface. There was no sign of joints or bonds of any kind on the timbers. The structure sloped downwards by 0.3m to the north-east, describing a gentle arc lying obliquely to the long axis of the moat here. The base beams were crudely squared trunks, the largest measuring 0.24m by 0.26m by 2.28m. Several had 45° sawn ends. The planks rested directly on the beams and along the same alignment. They were up to 0.33m wide, 0.08m thick and 1.86m long. The structure rested on a thin (20–100mm) layer of blue-grey clay containing up to 20 per cent organic matter. The platform was covered by a 100mm-thick layer of whitish yellow sandy mortar (8013).

The structure may have functioned as a temporary platform during an attempt to dredge this part of the moat. Samples were taken from all the structural timbers as part of ongoing research into softwood chronologies by English Heritage and the dendro-chronology laboratory of the University of Sheffield. The softwoods could not be dated. Two of the oak samples were datable with regional reference sequences. Both were early/mid-16th century in date but had obviously been dumped into the moat well after this. A late 18th- or early 19th-century date for the structure seems reasonable on the basis of the finds dating from layers underlying the timbers. It may even be that the timbers were taken from the trestle bridge which had stood above the caisson on the south side of the western causeway in the 1780s.

Test pit 35: a timber platform and coffer dam

Test pit 35 was situated at the junction of the wharf wall and the curving revetment that had been built to close off the backfilled moat around the Lion Tower. A plan of 1726 prepared by Clement

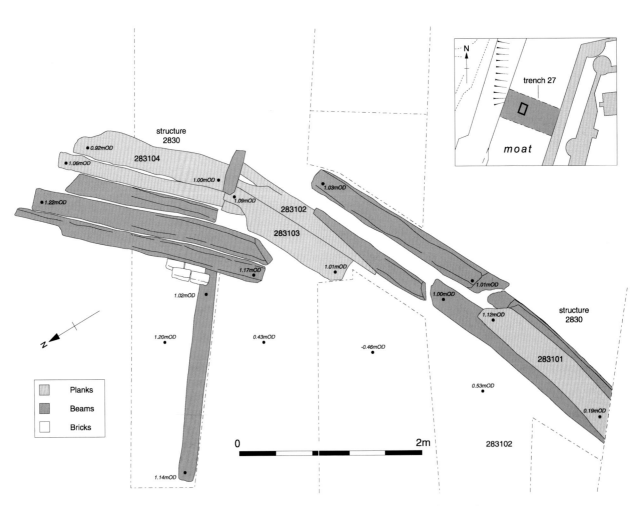

Fig 134 Plan of the softwood raft at the west end of trench 27 (see Fig 36 for location).

170

Lemprière (Fig 120) shows that by then the greater part of the Lion Tower moat to the west of the semi-circle had also been drained, partially filled and built over (Works 31/28). Another survey by Lemprière (Fig 135) shows that the remainder of the southern arm had been filled in by the end of the year and a new revetment wall created, on a line similar to the existing western boundary to the Bowling Green. This area had also been substantially built over by 1760 (Works 31/203).

Two timber structures were found in the pit (Fig 136): a timber platform (3514) and a coffer dam (3512). The platform consisted of a base beam supporting two horizontal planks butting against both the wharf wall and the revetment. The surface of the platform lay at a similar height (c0.29m OD) to the plank floor (3011) over the caisson in trench 30, 18m to the north-west of pit 35. The coffer dam ran along the eastern edge of the pit. It comprised four vertical planks (351201–351204) of varying width (0.15–0.24m). These had been laid horizontally, and continued for 0.7m from the wharf wall before passing beyond the north edge of the pit. Plank 351201 had been branded with the broad arrow of the Board of Ordnance in an identical manner to the examples from the caisson box in trench 30. The planks were held in place at the south end by a vertical stake (3518) at least 1.5m long. It seems likely that a further plank would have retained them to the north.

It is difficult to interpret the function of the timberwork in pit 35. The plank platform seemed to post-date both the wharf and revetment walls clearly enough, so it should be later than the 1720s. The remains of two welted shoes likely to date to the 18th century were found in a silt dump (context 3511) that appeared to post-date the timber structures. This broadly confirms the historically derived date but does not assist in defining the function of the timbers. It is conceivable that they were part of the wider campaign of reconstruction being carried out by the Board of Ordnance in the 1780s, centred on the south-western causeway (*see above*). It must be admitted though that there is a considerable distance between the causeway and pit 35—perhaps the timberwork in the latter should simply be seen as evidence for refurbishment of the wharf or (more probably) revetment walls.

Trench 31: moat fills

The area to the west of the central arch was covered by a 0.3m-thick layer of loose mortar (3173). It included both limestone (30 per cent) and shell (10 per cent) and became mixed with a 0.35m-thick blue-grey silty clay (3151) that continued to the western baulk. Layer 3151 was overlain by two lenses of sandy silt (3149 and 3150), both 80mm thick and extending for 2m at the western end of the trench. Layer 3149 was overlain by a 0.5m-thick clay deposit (3166) extending 9m from the western end of

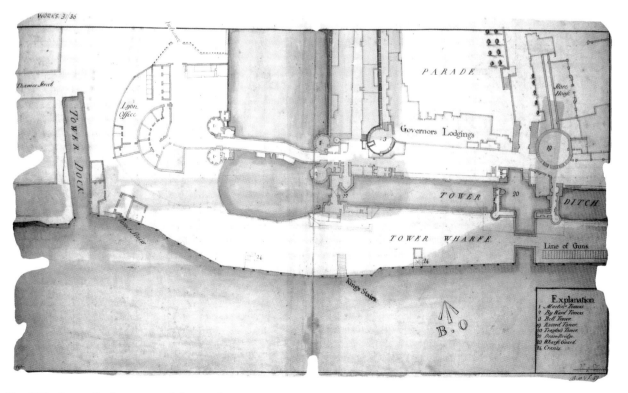

Fig 135 Lemprière's survey of the south-western entrance causeway in 1726 (Works 31/36 – the survey appears to bear an amended date of 1747 in a marginal alteration, but there are no very obvious changes to the drawing itself).

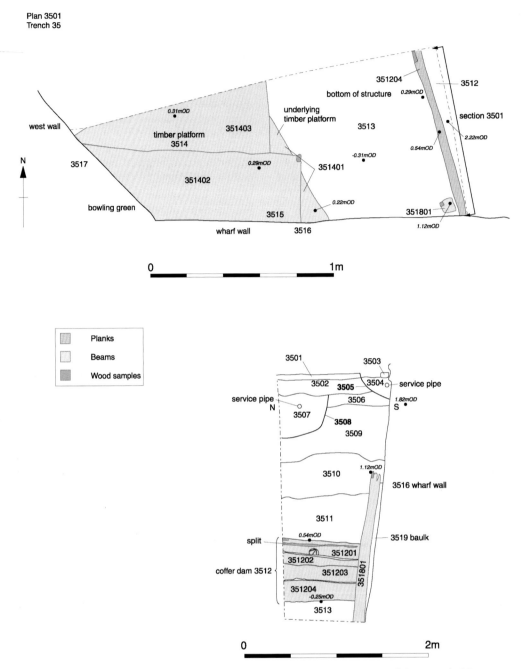

Plan 3501
Trench 35

Fig 136   Plan and section of post-medieval timber platform and shuttering exposed in test pit 35.

the trench and filling the western end of the trench to a level of *c*1m OD. Grey-brown silty clay 3133 extended eastward for 13m from the archway. Thickness varied from 0.11m at a level of *c*0.1m OD to 0.8m at a level of *c*0.9m OD. The equivalent deposit in the northern extension was numbered 31129. This contained a tankard (SF227) and an object (SF202). The tankard, which is complete, has a raised ridge running around the circumference at the base of the handle and another just above the base of the tankard. The object consisted of a tube and a second piece came from context 3128; one fits inside the other. One end had a T-shaped handle while the other had an L-shaped lever. The tubing has an

opening down one side and three internal compartments. It could be a measure for gunpowder.

A series of five deposits (3128–3132) filled both the northern extension and the area to the east of the causeway's arch to a level of *c*1m OD. Several of these contexts incorporated many artefacts, including large and/or substantially complete pieces; these clearly represented refuse disposal within the moat waters. A lead musket shot (SF199, diameter 17mm) and two buttons (SF205, bone, and SF206, copper alloy, damaged) were recovered from context 3129. A vessel (SF204) came from context 3130 while a further two vessels (SF211 and unnumbered) and a blade fragment were

172

recovered from context 3131. The vessels were all of sheet-metal in poor condition. SF204 had an ovoid flat bottom and straight sides. It appeared to have a flat lid with a strap handle. Three lengths of circular-sectioned rod were found with the vessel: two of them had looped ends and could have formed part of a handle. SF211 had a circular base and straight sides and, despite its very damaged and corroded condition, appeared to have the remains of a spout and a handle. It may have been a watering can. The second vessel was very fragmentary and the profile was incomplete. It would have had a diameter of approximately 220mm.

Clay 3128, which overlay the silts, contained the blade of a socketed spade (SF188; Fig 131). The handle had sheared off at the socket mouth, but it would have been held in place by two rivets (these survived). It is possible that the damage occurred at exactly the spot where the spade was found. The edge of the blade was very worn. Layer 3128 also contained four sheet-metal saucepans (SF180 and three unnumbered), two complete pewter tankards, a boat hook (SF177) and a long-handled bone toothbrush. Two of the saucepans had straight sides and tubular handles while the others had sloping sides and cast handles. They all comprised two sheets of metal soldered together with circular bases (diameter 178–217mm). The handles had been attached with a triangular plate riveted at each corner.

The tankards were identical in size. One had three raised ridges around the circumference just above the base and is identical to SF227 (layer 31129, above). The other had only two and is identical to a tankard from a 19th-century layer (31163, SF186) and another inscribed example (SF228, Fig 137 also from a 19th-century context, culvert fill 31135). Tankard 228 is inscribed with the words 'T Dobson, Stone Kitchen Tower'. A shield with the cross of St George and a crown with the letters W and R (William IV) on either side sit above the inscription. The initials D, E and S had been inscribed at the top of the handle. These tankards were clearly used in the Stone Kitchen Tavern which stood adjacent to the Bell Tower at the entrance to West Mint Street (Fig 138).

The socketed iron boat hook from layer 3128 still had its wooden pole (Fig 139). The total length of the hook (including the pole) was 2.93m. It had a long point for fending off other boats and a hook for grappling. The hook was attached to the pole by two nails. The form of the boat hook has changed little through time, and the only variation is in the size, which depends upon the type of boat it was being used on.

A pistol (SF251) was also found in culvert fill 31135. It was a complete military flintlock pistol with a 'Paget' stirrup ramrod. This type of ramrod was attached to the muzzle by means of a link (stirrup) so that there was no chance of the ramrod being accidentally dropped. This example is similar to the pistol first issued to the Light Dragoon regiments in 1759. The paget weapons were so successful that they continued in use until flintlocks finally disappeared from the Army (Rogers 1960, 146–7). Presumably the tankard and pistol were discarded into the culvert from within the castle after 1843 because they were no longer of any use.

Dating contexts: the pottery evidence

Two contexts in trench 12 produced two 19th-century or later sherds. The only pottery-producing context in trench 13 contained six sherds, including two from a large pedestal bowl, or *tazza*, in English tin-glazed ware. The latest piece is a fragment of a bowl in Staffordshire white salt-glazed stoneware, datable to the middle part of the 18th century. Trench 14 was the most productive, with six contexts producing 22 sherds. The earliest piece was a fragment of yellow-glazed Border ware chamber pot. This was the only pottery from context 1422 and so, although this find is 17th century in date, it is unsafe to use it to date the deposit. Contexts 1407, 1414 and 1423 may be dated to the 18th century on the basis of the ceramic vessels, and contexts 1409 and 1420 to the 19th century. One piece of note is a Chinese porcelain tea bowl with a factory mark on the base.

Later post-medieval pottery was also present in deposits post-dating the demolition of the Iron Gate causeway. Context 2511 produced mainly post-medieval redware and Border ware but also a sherd of Creamware. The contexts are somewhat mixed in nature, as shown by the presence of late medieval types including English sandy ware and a Spanish tin-glazed bowl. The pottery suggests that, if these fills were laid down during the post-Edwardian life-span of the moat, then the 18th century was a period when cleaning took place less regularly.

In trench 27 17th- and 18th-century types were the most common ceramics in the pre-1843 contexts. This may indicate that the moat was well maintained before that period and subsequently somewhat more neglected. This is confirmed by the presence of 17th-century pottery in some of the lowest levels in this phase. Context 8050 produced the base of a Staffordshire slipware plate, while 2852 contained 17th-century redwares and a sherd of North Italian marbled slipware. Context 2937, directly above 2852, produced exclusively late medieval types, including Coarse Border ware, Cheam whiteware and Langerwehe stoneware. This apparent reversal of strati-graphic position reflects the mixed nature of many moat deposits. One of the most productive contexts was 2822, which contained 56 sherds (2.295kg). The presence of Creamware, English porcelain and Staffordshire white salt-glazed stoneware indicates an 18th-century date and there are also late red earthenwares, Westerwald stoneware and Chinese porcelain. Context 2850, more or less in the middle of this sequence, was also very productive, with 98 sherds (5.884kg). Most of this was post-medieval redware and Border ware but English tin-glazed ware, Metropolitan slipware, Verwood-type ware, post-medieval black-glazed ware, London,

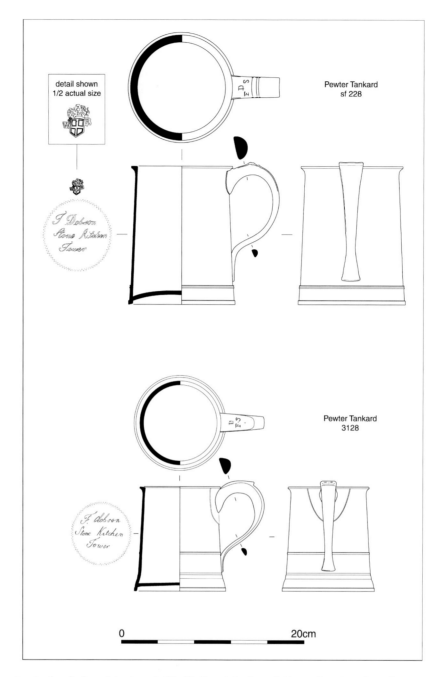

Fig 137   Two pewter tankards found in trench 31. Both retain inscriptions showing that they were used in the Stone Kitchen Tavern.

Nottingham and Frechen stonewares and Chinese porcelain were also represented. A date somewhere between contexts 2852 and 2822 is indicated and this confirms the validity of the phase and the date-range assigned to it.

In trench 30, layer 3012 contained a sherd of post-medieval black-glazed earthenware and a piece of Staffordshire slipware while 3072 produced a bottle marked 'Geo. Price Fulham' (Fig A1.8). These sherds may all be dated to the 18th century. The contexts overlay the timber platform and were most probably deposited between 1780 and the 1843 drainage programme.

Trench 31 contained probably the largest ceramic sub-group from the excavations, most of the sherds belonging to the life-span of the moat up to the 1840s. The date-range of the pottery is similarly broad, from 13th-century London ware to 19th-century transfer-printed ware. The lowest pottery-producing context in this group, 31133, contained a London ware sherd and some Coarse Border ware but also late 17th- or 18th-century types such as an English stoneware Bartmann jug and a complete post-medieval redware bowl. These contexts are strikingly different from the 13th/14th-century deposits lower down the sequence.

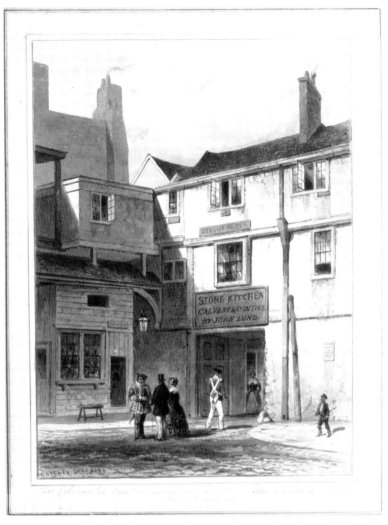

Fig 138 A watercolour of the Stone Kitchen Tavern by Thomas Hosmer Shepherd (1792–1864), with the rear of the Byward Tower to the left.

The subsequent context (3141) produced a high proportion of late medieval pottery, including Coarse Border ware, Saintonge whiteware, Low Countries redware and Siegburg stoneware, but also post-medieval redware and yellow Border ware.

Layer 3151, two contexts above 3141, contained London stoneware, Creamware, Pearlware, Chinese porcelain and garden pottery and must be dated to the 18th century. Layer 3132, four contexts above 31133, also produced English stoneware and Creamware but also refined earthenware. Context 3193, stratigraphically similar to 31133, contained a large quantity of post-medieval redware with Border ware, English tin-glazed ware, Creamware, Staffordshire white salt-glazed and Westerwald stoneware. An 18th-century date is again suggested. Context 3133, which lay above 3193, also contained much post-medieval redware and English tin-glazed ware, with English stoneware, Creamware, English porcelain and refined earthenware. The smattering of late medieval pottery must be regarded as residual, and ceramically there is a clear gap between these contexts and the underlying medieval material. The lack of obviously datable late medieval and early post-medieval deposits suggests that the moat was kept clean at least until the second half of the 17th century. In contrast, the 18th-century contexts were the most productive in trench 31 affirming the view that there was a point at which soil and waste dumping was carried out unchecked.

Other small finds

Trench 27 (west moat)

The majority of metal and other finds came from 18th-century contexts. Layer 2889 contained four bone objects, comprising two pinner's bones (SF/8 and SF198), a point and an antler fragment. The latter two items are not discussed further. Pinner's bones (Fig 140) were used in the production of pins up until the mechanisation of the process in the late 18th century. Before then it was customary to file the points by hand, using a bone holder to improve

preserved remains of
wooden shaft handle

0   200mm

Fig 139   A boathook found in front of the central arch in trench 31. The shaft is of wood and the hook of iron. The inset detail shows a drawing of the iron hook.

sf 70

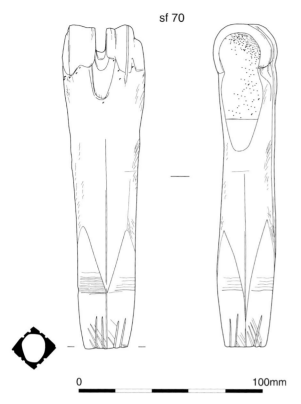

0   100mm

Fig 140   A pinner's bone (SF 70) found in layer 2852, trench 27.

the grip and stop the pins from bending. Pinner's bones were generally made from cattle metapodials squared off at one end to produce four flat facets in which two or three longitudinal grooves were cut with a saw. The pins were held in these grooves while the points were filed (MacGregor 1985, 171).

Two further pinner's bones (SF70 and unnumbered) were recovered from contexts 2852 (probably 17th-century) and 2849. In addition to the pinner's bone, context 2849 also contained a highly polished antler tine fragment (SF54) and a lead shot. The latter retained a casting ridge around the circumference and remains of the pontil, indicating that it was made in a two-part mould. It was 13mm in diameter and would have been suitable for firing from a musket.

Context 2822 contained a cannon ball and two copper alloy mounts. The cannon ball was 2¾ inches (c70mm) in diameter and weighed 2lb 5oz (1,069g); it was designed for use with a 16th/17th-century 'Falcon' gun. The two mounts were large and circular with a domed centre. One had a central perforation and two rivets for attachment; the upper face was decorated and originally would have been plated. The second (probably a boss) had three iron rivets for attachment and a central perforation. The centre was decorated with a finely incised Star of David. There were traces of fine incised decoration and cross-hatching in the form of flowing foliage around the outside. These pieces probably came from horse harnesses.

A further fragment of roughly worked bone was recovered from context 2833 (17th/18th-century). It was in the shape of a 'pistol grip' type handle and may be a discarded blank for an implement handle.

The south-western entrance causeway

The greatest quantity and range of small finds from any of the excavations were recovered from post-medieval contexts in trench 31 to the north of the causeway, with a much smaller number from trench 30 to the south, where, admittedly, excavation was less extensive. The quantity of finds is perhaps not unsurprising given that the causeway provided the only landward access to the castle in this period. Many of the finds were mundane (blades, buttons, buckles, pins, lead shot etc) and do not merit further consideration here (full descriptions are in the project archive). Some are useful for dating evidence, such as the George III trade token (SF119) dating layer 3173 to 1815, and the very worn 19th-century coin (SF178) from layer 3128. Others, however, were clearly residual, such as the brass 'Venus penny' from the Netherlands dating to c1490–1550 (Mitchiner 1988, 266–73), from layer 3133. The remaining finds are of greatest interest because of their historical context and have therefore been considered in the relevant text sections above. Other interesting finds of this period were residual in later contexts. Layer 3109, for instance, contained a token (SF79) among several other small finds. The token is a copper halfpenny token of Mail Coach type (Dalton and Hamer 1910–1918, 363) issued around 1797, but deposited here in a layer which clearly post-dated the infilling of the moat in 1843.

The only significant find from trench 30 was a jew's harp (SF98) from the 18th/19th-century context 3018. The harp had a diamond cross-section and a rebate for the iron tongue, a small fragment of which is still present between the jaws. Jew's harps have a long history, from the crusades to the modern day, and this example is a well-attested post-medieval type (Lawson 1990, 724, fig 2269).

Clay pipe

Clay pipes are particularly sensitive as dating indicators and can often provide a good framework for the phasing of post-medieval deposits. Pipes are also very fragile and rapidly become broken or battered in trampled or frequently disturbed layers. Their state of fragmentation and degree of residuality can therefore be used as indicators of the nature and depositional history of a deposit. In the particular case of the moat two unusual circumstances apply. First, the majority of the pipes were recovered from silting deposits. Many were clearly discarded into the moat in a complete or substantially complete state and the soft silts provided ideal conditions for their preservation. At the same time the moat was subject to repeated attempts to scour or clean it, resulting in the unusual truncation, mixing and redeposition of the deposits. Secondly, being an important royal and military site, the various building, demolition and cleaning activities at the Tower are exceptionally well documented. These two factors combine to provide well-preserved groups of pipes, many of which come from individual phases or deposits that can be securely linked with documented events.

In terms of the general distribution of pipes it is worth noting that trenches on the north and east sides of the moat, including the large area of trench 25, produced material that almost exclusively dated from c1670 to 1770. This also largely holds true of trench 27, where the majority of pipes dated to before 1800. In contrast, trenches 30 and 31 produced good groups of material running right up to the 1843–5 draining of the moat. Although the Stone Kitchen Tavern was situated just to the north of the main entrance, these pipes seem too far away to be directly associated with it (but see above for tankards). A more likely scenario is that the pipes were discarded by visitors entering the Tower as they crossed the moat in much the same way as a visitor might extinguish a cigarette before entering a building today. There may even have been regulations restricting the smoking of pipes within the Tower complex, parts of which would have contained explosives.

The deposits from the south side of the moat are more diverse. The pipes from this side include quite a number of earlier 17th-century pieces, especially from the western end. The excavated groups are not particularly large so it is hard to draw any firm conclusions. One possibility may be that the proximity of the river and the general fall of the moat to this side meant that artefacts of mixed date ended up in deeper water where they were more difficult to remove. Many of the cleaning projects relied on the scouring action of water to remove material from the main moat, material which would clearly have ended up on the southern side.

Supply sources

There is nothing to suggest that the pipes recovered from the Tower excavations are anything other than a normal cross-section of London products. Some of the marked pipes—for example, those produced by the Manby family—are more numerous than others but this is a natural reflection of the large-scale workshops that they operated. There is no evidence that pipes were being centrally ordered or specially supplied for use within the Tower complex. The percentage of imported pipes is extremely low (less than 1 per cent). There was one Hunt pipe, probably from the Bath area, one Birchall pipe from Chatham and an unusual imported European pipe. A small number of imported pipes are regularly found in London, where they probably represent a mixture of individual movements and small-scale trade. There

is no evidence of any substantial import trade to the capital.

Style and status

The style and status of the excavated pipes also appear to fit in with the general picture for London. There is a small percentage of burnished pipes from the 17th century, which is normal for the city. Likewise the range and nature of the later pipes appear typical. The only area of uncertainty concerns the 18th-century armorial pipes. Very few of these have been adequately published from excavated contexts and there is no good comparative data for their use. While it might be expected that they would be particularly favoured amongst troops at a royal site this hypothesis remains to be tested.

Leather

The majority of the shoes dated to the 18th and earlier 19th centuries, the largest group coming from an 18th-century silty clay layer (3133) in trench 31. Four different welted constructions were represented, all of which were also seen on the post-medieval shoes recovered from Reading water-front sites (Mould 1997, 110 and fig 59 1a, 2a, 2b, 3a, 4a and 4c). The majority of the soles had a grain/flesh seam and the insoles an edge/flesh seam (Fig 104, 3) or raised rib seam (Fig 104, 4). One of the latter had the impression of bracing thread visible. Examples dating to the 18th century or later had the insole seam changing around the seat to accommodate the heel (ibid, fig 59 3a, 4a and 4c). Two constructions differed in having soles with a raised rib seam around the forepart and a grain/flesh seam to accommodate the attachment of the heel at the seat. The corresponding insoles were stitched around the seat but not around the forepart and had been, presumably, stuck in place (ibid, fig 59 4a and 4c).

The shoes had straight bottom units consisting of an insole and sole; some had middle packing. The heel was usually low (2 inches (51mm) or less) and made of separate heel lifts attached to the sole with wooden pegs. A 3/4-inch (19mm) wooden Louis heel that may date to the second half of the 17th, or the 18th, century was found in a clay layer (3193) of the latter date. The vamps and back-seamed two-part quarters were internally lined. Those sufficiently well preserved (eg, SFs74 and 86.1; Fig 141) had vamps extending up the instep, and quarters with either 'dog-leg' or sloping front seams extending into wide latchets which buckled across the instep. The majority had short, pointed toes. Two examples (SFs 91 and 92) curved upward in a pronounced 'kick' popular during the 1720s–30s. Square toes were also found, being more common in the later deposits.

A large fragment of calfskin sheet attached by a double row of iron nails to a rib of wood was also found in layer 3133. The sheet had been cut and torn before being discarded. No identifying features

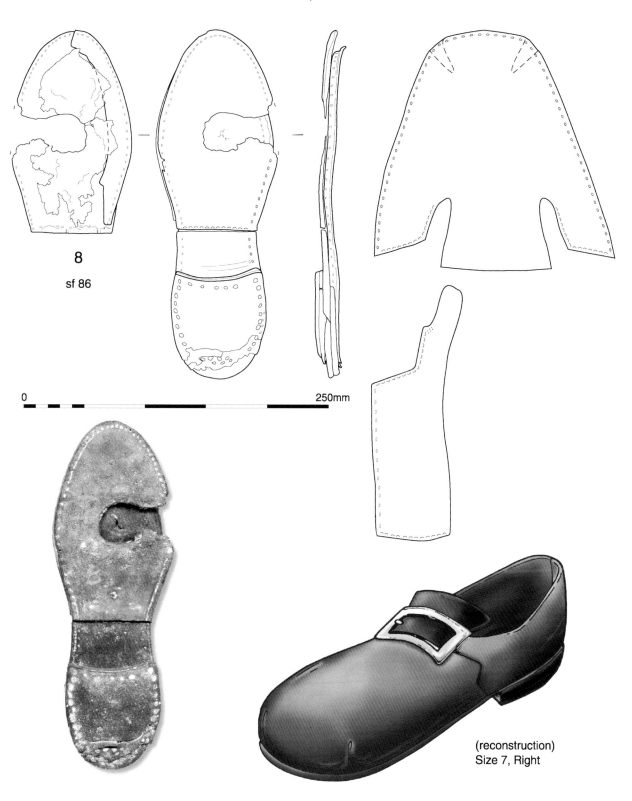

8

sf 86

0   250mm

(reconstruction)
Size 7, Right

Fig 141   Buckled shoe of welted construction, made straight, comprising sole, middle packing, insole, heel, welt, vamp, two-piece quarters and internal lining. Sole made in two pieces with grain/flesh seam, butt seamed across the waist, worn through at centre of the tread. Insole has an oval/square toe, wide tread, waist and seat with a raised rib seam around the perimeter. Large D-shaped heel ¼ inch high (6mm) with a single lift and top piece secured by wooden pegs, iron corrosion suggests nails also used. Three fragments of middle packing and three lengths of narrow welt. Vamp with square toe, fragmentary, Right of two-part quarters with dog-leg front seam extending into a buckle strap, junction of strap and front seam reinforced by a double line of stitching. Two pieces of internal lining whip stitched to the interior of the uppers and incorporated into the lasting margin. Upper of calfskin. Insole length 256mm, width tread 88mm, waist 60mm, seat 66mm. Height at centre back 86mm. Adult size 5, Adult size 7 with 10% allowance for shrinkage. SF 86, context 2850.

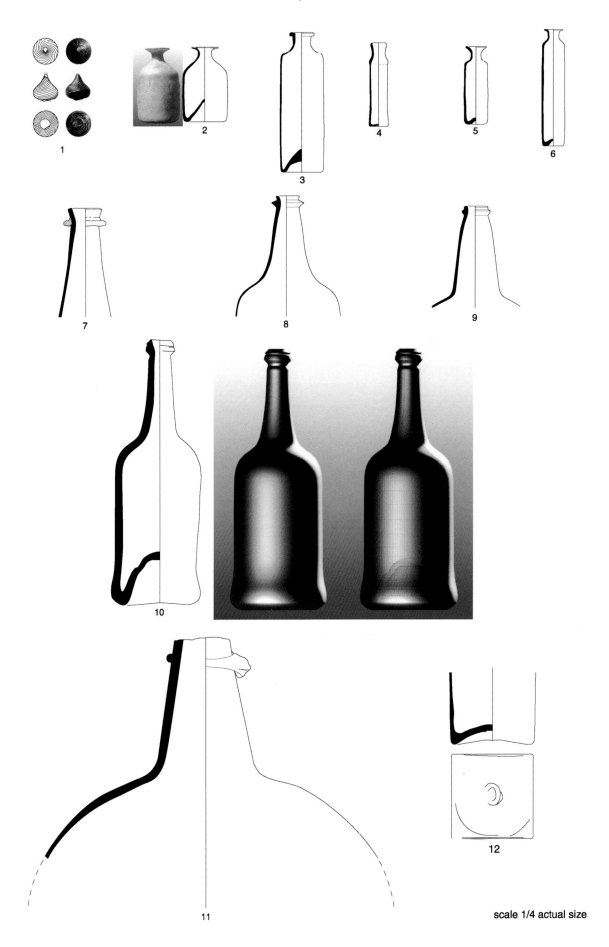

scale 1/4 actual size

remained but the combination of wood, nails and leather suggest furnishings or saddlery.

Glass (Fig 142)

The assemblage comprised a total of 395 fragments of glass. The three largest categories, in roughly equal proportions, were window glass, bottles and phials, with a few vessels and other glass objects also present. The glass ranges in date from the mid/late 17th to 20th centuries. Virtually all 17th-century glass was found in later contexts and so has been considered here rather than in Chapter 7. The 20th-century glass is not considered further here or in Chapter 10. A small selection of the assemblage has been illustrated; RPD in catalogue entries stands for Resting Point Diameter (the point of the base on which the bottle stands).

The window glass was all from plain glazing. The majority (56 per cent) came from the south-west causeway area and was predominantly of 19th-century and later date. Small fragments of 17th-century glass were found in later contexts in the south and west moats but constituted only 14 per cent of the group. Both crown (spun) and muff (cylinder-blown) glass were represented. A large fragment of 18th-century or early 19th-century crown glass came from layer 3133.

No more than 11 vessels were present with no significant distribution in terms of either date or area. Five fragments were undiagnostic. There were two possible beakers while the rest were wine or sherry glasses dating from the 17th and 18th centuries. The 'crizzled' knop of early crystal glass made with flint may be from the glass house of James Ravenscroft, a trader in Venetian glass who had established glass houses in the Savoy, London and at Henley-on-Thames in the 1670s. For a short time these made a new type of crystal glass from flint and fine sand, but this experimental period produced a poor-quality material that quickly crizzled, becoming dull and with a loss of glassy state. In 1676 river pebbles replaced the flint and, with a change in the treatment of stabilising salts, a more longstanding glass was produced (Charleston 1984, 110–14).

The handle (unillustrated) of a possible pouring vessel was found in trench 25, layer 2604. The handle was roughly made from an applied strip of blue glass decorated with two vertical ribs. The lower end curls away from the vessel body. It is probably of Bristol blue glass made during the 18th century (Newman 1977, 49–50).

A few glass objects were found, including a decorated stopper for a small flask or phial and a twisted rod. An eye bath was also recovered from test pit 68, probably dating from the 18th century. Phials were more numerous, with fragments of up to 16 being found. The majority came from the south-western causeway area. All were cylindrical, with a date-range covering the 18th century (Haslam 1984, 238–9). Two groups were represented, the first consisting of broader cylindrical types with a conical kick and the second of narrow cylindrical types with a slight basal indent. All had short necks and horizontal rims except one with a near-vertical fire-rounded rim. Rims were found from two further phials of the narrow cylindrical type.

Wine bottles made up the largest component of this assemblage. Typologically they were relatively comprehensive, with each significant change in shape represented up to the introduction of mechanised production at the turn of the 19th century. A small number of mid/late 17th-century shaft and globe types were present, followed by examples of onion bottles, mallet bottles and finally a large

Fig 142   Glass. 1: Tear-drop-shaped object with spiralling grooves in colourless glass. Possibly from a decorated stopper for a small flask or phial. Remains of broken stem on base. (17H, ctx.8133). 2: Wide-bodied phial, pale green. Rim D: 28mm, RPD: 40mm. Mid to late 18th C. 17E, ctx.3128. 3: Wide-bodied phial, colourless. Rim D: 26mm, RPD: 43mm. Late 18th C. 17E, ctx.3135. Other phials of this type came from 17D, ctx.2850, 17E, ctxs.3007, 3008, 3135, 17F*, ctx.6826. 4: Long-necked phial, slight green tint. Rim D: 15mm, RPD: 17mm, Hgt: 87mm. 18th C. 17E, ctx.3109. 5: Narrow-bodied phial, colourless. Rim D: 27mm, RPD: 20mm, Hgt: 80mm. Mid-late 18th C. (17H, ctx.8133). A second phial of this type came from 17E, ctx.3109 and 17H, ctx.8133. 6: Long-bodied phial, colourless. Rim D: 20mm, RPD: 19mm, Hgt: 120mm. Mid-late 18th C. (17E, 3187). A second long-bodied phial came from 17E, ctx.3128. 7: Shaft and globe, finish and neck, light green. Slightly flaring rim, string rounded c11mm below rim. Rim D: 36mm. Third quarter 17th C. Hume's Type 2 (Hume 1961, fig.3, no.2, 99). Residual in 18th-century layer 2821. 8: Mallet, finish and neck, quart size, light green. Vertical rim, uptooled string c5mm below rim. Rim D: 25mm. Early to mid-18th century (Banks 1997, fig.4.4, c1740 Jesus College Mallet, p.28). Layer 5606. A second quart-size mallet came from 17H, ctx.8311 and two larger pint-sized examples came from 17D, ctx.2850 and 17F*, 6824. 9: Mallet, finish and neck, light green. Uptooled string immediately below rim, flaring neck with indent beneath string from being tool-finished. Hume Type 15, Mid-18th C (Hume 1961, fig.4, no.15, 100). 17D, ctx.2849. Two further mallets came from 17E, ctx.3107 and 17F*, ctx.7116. 10: True cylindrical, complete, yellow-green. Downtooled rim, uptooled string immediately beneath, long, slightly tapering neck, sagged basal heel and high kick. Mid-18th C (Banks 1997, fig.4.4, c 1740 Magdalen College, p.28). 17E, ctx.3129. 11: Demijohn, finish, neck and shoulder, amber. Vertical rim, rounded string and rounded shoulder. Rim D: 60mm, Bore D: 40mm. Probably globular, ca.late-18th C. (www.antiquebottles.com). 17E, ctx.3165. 12: Square case bottle, base and lower body, pale green. Shallow domed kick with pronounced pontil scar. Moulded body, hand finished. Base: 90mm square. Late 18th C or early 19th C. 17E, ctx.3193.

181

proportion of true cylindricals dating from the late 17th to the mid/late 18th century. The top part of a large demijohn of amber glass from layer 3165 is of interest. Demijohns could hold up to 10 gallons of wine (or other liquid). This example would appear to be globular, probably dating to the 18th century (http://www.antiquebottles.com). It is slightly earlier than most of the finds from the context. Many other rims and bases from late 18th- to early 19th-century cylindrical bottles were also found.

Other types include 19th-century egg bottles that contained carbonised water or soda and small rectangular bottles with chamfered corners for household use dating to the 19th or early 20th centuries. One of these had an inscription indicating that it contained hair oil (context 3133). Two others from layers 3131 and 3128 (trench 31) may have been medicine bottles dating to the late 18th and early 19th centuries respectively. Both of these dates match well with other finds from the contexts.

Environmental evidence

Plant remains

The most numerous seeds and other macroscopic plant remains in the samples from the post-medieval part of the sequence from trench 31 were from edible fruits, flavourings and spices likely to have been derived from a drain. Some were probably from human sewage, such as grape (*Vitis vinifera*), apple (*Malus* sp.) or pear (*Pyrus* sp.), raspberry (*Rubus idaeus*), currant (*Ribes* sp.), blackberry (*R. fruticosus* agg.), fennel (*Foeniculum vulgare*), wild or alpine strawberry (*Fragaria vesca*), mulberry (*Morus nigra*), sweet cherry (*Prunus avium*) and fig (*Ficus carica*). Others such as black mustard (*Brassica nigra*) could either have been eaten or have grown as weeds on the site.

Supporting evidence for a sewage component in these sediments came from the occurrence of cereal bran, fragments of corn cockle (*Agrostemma githago*) and puparia of *Thoracochaeta zosterae* in most of the samples. Corn cockle was formerly a serious cornfield weed whose seeds commonly occurred as a contaminant of cereal grain and became ground with it when flour was made. *T. zosterae* is a fly whose larvae naturally feed on rotting seaweed but were also able to exploit the organic contents of medieval and early post-medieval latrines, in which it occurred in great profusion (Belshaw 1988). The many seeds of coriander (*Coriandrum sativum*) that occurred in the top of context 3132 and above might also have been derived from sewage. These samples, however, also contain many bracts and seeds of hop (*Humulus lupulus*). These are characteristic of brewing waste and it is thought likely that the coriander had been used along with hops to make a spicy 'winter warmer' type of beer. Other plant remains from context 3129, which contained the highest concentrations of sewage and brewing

waste, included some seeds of juniper (*Juniperus communis*), perhaps derived from their use as flavouring for food or gin, and some seeds of flax/linseed (*Linum usitatissimum*). A few seeds likely to be from sewage were found in post-medieval deposits in other trenches. They included dill (*Anethum graveolens*) from context 2834 in trench 27.

Pollen

In section A (2703; Fig 58) the upper 0.57m of the column sample lay within a thick layer of soil (2833) dated to the 17th–18th centuries. The lower 0.24m was characterised by a reduction in the derived pre-Quaternary and fern spores (*Dryopteris* type and *Pteridium aquilinum*). By contrast *Pediastrum* increased again to 60 per cent at 0.4m. Herbs remain similar to preceding zones, being diverse and dominated by Poaceae, which expands towards the top of the zone. There are some reductions of cereal types, including oats, and of *Cannabis sativa* type. Trees remain dominated by oak (*Quercus*) and hazel (*Corylus avellana*), with sporadic but interesting occurrences of Juniper (*Juniperus*), beech (*Fagus*), walnut (*Juglans*) and lindens (*Tilia*). Alder (*Alnus*) is absent. The top 0.33m of the column is characterised by higher values of Poaceae (to 64 per cent) and a sharp reduction of *Pediastrum* from 60 per cent to less than 10 per cent. There is a minor reduction in oak but increase of alder to 9 per cent.

In section C (3113; Fig 108), the upper 0.45m of the column (context 3133) is of 18th- to 19th-century date. In comparison with the medieval levels (Chapter 6), *Pediastrum* values are very markedly reduced (to less than 10 per cent and absence). Herb pollen remain dominant (85 per cent) with Poaceae (50–60 per cent) and cereal type (8–10 per cent) still important, though *Sinapis* type is reduced. Other changes include expansion of Fabaceae types, Chenopodiaceae and some Asteraceae types. There are also changes in tree and shrub pollen with expansion of oak (*Quercus*, to 15 per cent), alder (*Alnus*, 8 per cent) and hazel (*Corylus avellana*) type (10 per cent). There are more consistent records of lindens (*Tilia*) and interesting sporadic records of spruce (*Picea*), yew (*Taxus*) and hornbeam (*Carpinus*). Walnut (*Juglans*) and beech (*Fagus*) are reduced or absent.

A pollen column was also taken from trench 6, close to the point where the City ditch discharged into the moat during the medieval and post-medieval periods (Fig 143). The bottom 70mm comprised gravelly silt (context 630, probably medieval or early post-medieval although no finds were recovered). The overlying dark-grey to black silts (0.25–0.43m; context 629) were also undated but probably belonged to the post-medieval period. The subsequent buff-coloured organic sediments containing freshwater molluscs (0.05–0.25m; contexts 624–5) capped with a grey stony horizon (0–50mm; top of context 625) contained 18th-century pottery and clay pipes. The column therefore appears to cover a significant date-range but there were insufficient changes in the pollen spectra to justify sub-division of the profile into pollen zones.

Pollen was not as abundant as in sections A and C, perhaps due to the position relative to the City ditch. Nevertheless, the substantial numbers of *Pediastrum* cysts and the presence of some Hystrichospheres (especially at 0.2–0.3m) indicate a probable fresh-water environment (Fig 143). Poaceae dominate the pollen (50–60 per cent), with substantial numbers of cereal type as well. The herb assemblages are diverse, with many families (Chenopodiaceae, *Ranunculus* type, *Rumex conglomeratus, Vicia* type), including weeds of arable land/waste ground such as *Spergula* type, *Sinapis* type, Polygonaceae spp. and *Centaurea cyanus*. There are sporadic to high records of a number of tree/shrub types from regional or extra-regional sources. Oak and hazel are most important with slightly higher values at the top and bottom of the profile. Walnut, spruce and privet (*Ligustrum*) are significant as possible introductions to parks and gardens in or adjacent to the Tower.

Discussion of the pollen evidence

The post-medieval non-wetland pollen spectra appear broadly similar to those of the preceding era, but there are some characteristic differences. Oak and hazel remain the most consistent tree and shrub component and clearly derive from the region as a whole. Differences lie in the reduction of walnut, the sporadic presence of spruce and greater abundance of alder and lindens in section C. Spruce is not native in this interglacial, and has been noted at other London sites. Beech, elm (*Ulmus*), lindens and yew (*Taxus*) are poorly represented and are likely to be from local occasional growth.

The quantities of cereal pollen present are diminished in comparison with medieval levels, although it remains one of the most important constituents of the pollen assemblages. This may have been due to reduction in ordure and excrementitious material entering the moat from the latrines of the Tower or from streams entering the moat. Oats (*Secale cereale*) are absent from this later period, reflecting their greater importance during the medieval era. Overall, herb pollen assemblages remain the same with dominance (somewhat expanded) of wild grasses. Assemblages are again typical of urban surrounds and associated with cereals. The occurrence of more Asteraceae types including an unknown/as-yet-unidentified taxon represents one minor difference between the two periods.

Soil micromorphology

Post-medieval sediments in the western moat (trenches 27 and 31, Table A3.8) were generally strongly calcareous (more than 40 per cent carbonate), greyish yellow brown silt loams, with less calcareous (10.2 per cent carbonate) silty clays being present too (eg, context 3133). They also show marked variation in amounts of organic matter and total phosphate content (2.69–10.5 per cent LOI, 0.761–2.04mg g^{-1} respectively), magnetic susceptibility and χ_{conv}. In trench 27 coarse (0.5–5mm) *in situ* root traces were present (contexts 2937, 2852 and 2853), whereas in trench 31 coarsely bedded layers of burned shell and mortar debris were present (3133–3135). Coarse (15mm) wood charcoal occurred in context 3141. Cinders and pottery fragments were present in deposits showing various amounts of secondary micritic calcite and septaric gypsum formation. There were also variations in the numbers of mollusc (up to 9mm in size) and ostracod fauna present. There was evidence of coarse burrow mixing, together with occasional biogenic calcite (earthworm granules) and probable mineral excrements of earthworms. Many of these deposits showed positive residual total phosphate, high amounts of lead (eg, 3137, 260µm g^{-1}) and occasionally very high amounts of copper and zinc (3137, 543µm g^{-1} and 110µm g^{-1} respectively). Secondary iron phosphate staining was also in evidence.

These deposits were variable in character but overall indicated only moderately clean moat waters with both autochthonous calcium carbonate formation (eg, from outside the moat) and shell fauna. There had also been inputs of silts and clay of probably London Clay origin (dredged?) and anthropogenic materials. The latter included coarse materials (mortar, pottery, charcoal and cinders) and fine inputs of organic matter, phosphate (with positive residual) and heavy metals. For example, the highest amounts of zinc (110µg g^{-1}) and copper (543µg g^{-1}) occur in context 3137. The quantity of coarse detrital organic matter and *in situ* roots indicates plant growth on the moat sediments. Biogenic calcite, likely earthworm excrements and the formation of secondary calcite and gypsum indicate occasional and ephemeral drying out of the deposits. The depositional environment in the moat at this period clearly reflects some non-sedimentary processes, with calcium carbonate formation derived from off site alongside dumping of deposits rich in artefacts, rubbly material, phosphate and heavy metals. The moat sediments also become sub-aerially weathered and vegetated.

Post-medieval deposits of somewhat different character were found towards the east end of trench 27 at Section A (2833–6 and 2844). These deposits were dark greyish brown to brown calcareous (10.2–32.3 per cent carbonate) silty clays or silt loams. Generally they displayed the highest amounts of total phosphate (max. 2.97mg g^{-1}) in the Tower moat, with a marked positive residual. The deposits also showed some of the highest magnetic susceptibility readings (max. 62.3 × 10^{-8} m^3 kg^{-1}) and χ_{conv} (max. 13.0 per cent). The deposits were massive with fine lenses and crack microstructure. They also contained some of the highest amounts of lead (356µg g^{-1}), zinc (67µg g^{-1}) and copper (186µg g^{-1}).

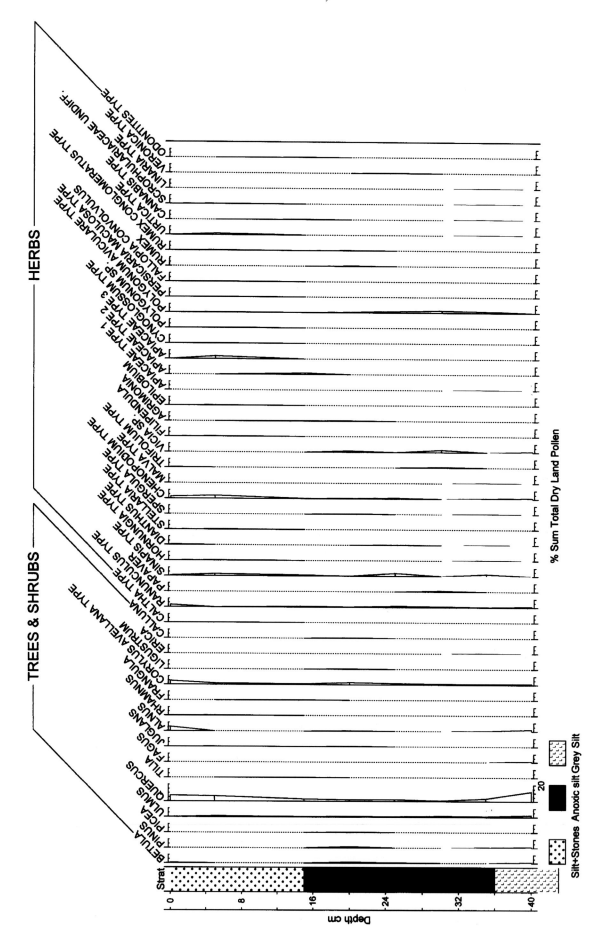

Fig 143   *Pollen diagram, trench 6.*

Chapter 8

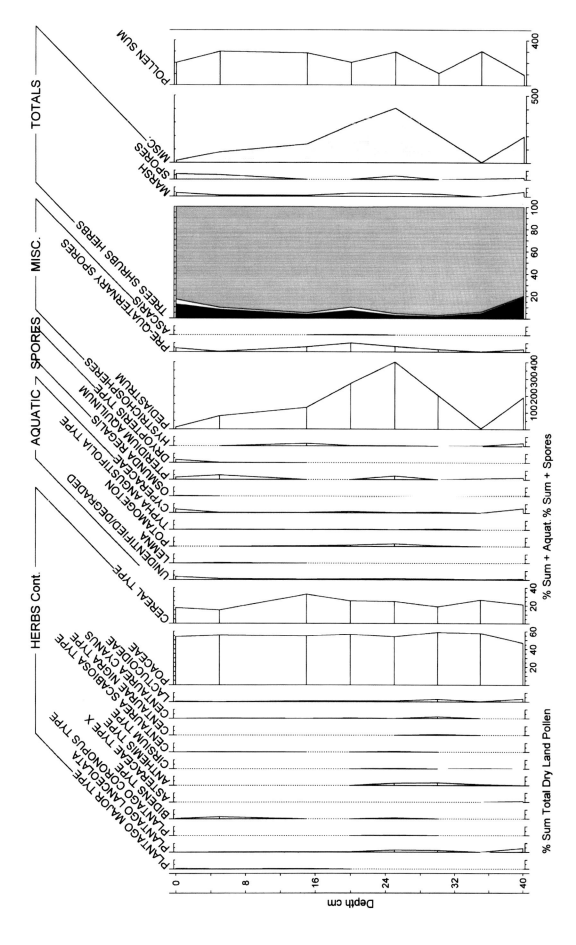

Fig 143   Pollen diagram, trench 6, continued.

185

A 0.4mm-thick lens of charcoal also occurred in layer 2833, a sediment marked by yellow staining, vivianite and carbonaceous spherules. These are indicators of high temperature industrial inputs.

These characteristics clearly reflect very high inputs of domestic and industrial waste, possibly influenced by the presence of the Mint and the Royal Ordnance. The former, in particular, was based in Mint Street on the other side of the outer curtain wall from the west moat. It is not difficult to imagine that mint waste was being thrown over the wall into the moat, despite some suggestion of orders to the contrary. The strong positive correlation between zinc and copper possibly indicates the manufacture of brass objects. These late post-medieval deposits were so strongly influenced by phosphate-rich cess that phosphate was precipitating out as vivianite and as associated amorphous and/or poorly crystalline iron-phosphate compounds. These stained some sediments with a yellowish colour. This and the evidence of rooting indicate periodic drying out of the moat sediments. It takes little imagination to infer that the moat environment was becoming increasingly unpleasant.

ANIMAL BONE

A total of 655 fragments of animal bone were recovered from moat deposits, of which 288 (43.97 per cent) post-medieval examples were identified to species. Nine fragments of indeterminate bird were recovered. A further 22.14 per cent were identified as either large (82) or medium-sized (63) mammal. Table 5 provides the full quantification of the post-medieval (and later) bones. A complete femur belonging to a large feline, probably lion or tiger, was the most interesting individual bone. The skull of a very large dog from a post-medieval deposit was also remarkable. The head of this animal is of a size not encountered in modern comparative material, but it conforms to the size and proportions of a large mastiff. The skull is complete and shows that the animal suffered an injury to the right eye socket. The one mole bone is probably intrusive.

Body part representation

The size of the post-medieval assemblage is too small to warrant detailed analysis of species and body part representation, but cattle and sheep dominate the assemblage and are almost equally represented according to both NISP and MNI (Table 6). Pig is poorly represented. The cattle and sheep remains are dominated by mandibles. A large number of cattle skull fragments are also present but, because of their fragile nature, this is probably a reflection of fragmentation. The major domesticates are represented by a few fragments belonging to most of the major limb bones although carpals, tarsals and phalanges are virtually absent. The ribs and vertebrae of both large and medium mammals are also present.

Table 5 Post-medieval and modern animal bone: species representation

	Post-medieval		Modern	
	No. frags	%	No. frags	%
Cattle	101	21	43	26
Sheep	115	23	40	24
Pig	22	4	4	2
Horse	3	1		
Dog	15	3	7	4
Cat	4	1	3	2
Deer			1	1
Rabbit	2			
Hare			1	1
Mole	1			
Large mammal	82	17	22	13
Medium mammal	63	13	22	13
Cormorant	1			
Goose	7	1		
Domestic fowl	9	2	1	1
Duck	1			
Bird indet.	9	2		
Cod	2			
Turbot	5	1		
Uid	50	10	19	12
Total	492	100	163	100

Ageing data

Few post-medieval bones provided ageing data, but epiphyseal fusion indicates that at least one cow was below two years old at the time of death. Almost all of the late fusing bones which could provide ageing data were unfused, indicating that some cattle were less than four years old at the time of death. Ageing information from tooth eruption and wear supports the fusion data. Again, at least one cow was below two years old at the time of death and at least two animals were below three years of age. The remainder were adult with at least three animals between three and six years, four between six and eight years and one between eight and ten years old at the time of death. There is no evidence for foetal/neonatal cattle nor the culling of animals below one year of age.

Epiphyseal fusion in sheep indicates that at least one animal was below two years and another below three and a half years of age at the time of death. The majority of ageable sheep bones, however, belonged to adult sheep. This is supported by data from tooth eruption and wear. There is no evidence for the presence of foetal/neonatal sheep. All the pig bones which could be aged were from immature animals.

Taphonomy

Many post-medieval bones displayed evidence of gnawing, mostly by canids (43) although four had been gnawed by rodents. Butchered bones had mostly been chopped (82), but 16 had cut-marks and three had been sawn. Cattle and sheep bones

Table 6 Post-medieval animal bone: body part representation of domestic mammals (NISP)

	Cattle	Sheep	Pig	Horse	Dog	Cat	Large mammal	Medium mammal
Horn core	2	2						
Occipital condyle		1			2			
Premaxilla	4							
Zygomatic	4							
Maxilla	9	1	1					
Skull frag	27	5			1		2	
Mandible	27	23				1		
Lower canine					1			
Lower incisor	1							
Lower molar	4	3		2				
Lower premolar		2						
Lower tooth	1							
Upper canine					1			
Upper molar	1	2						
Upper premolar	1				1			
Tooth	1							
Scapula	4	7	2		1			
Humerus	1	8	3		2	2		
Radius	2	10	2		1			
Ulna		6	1	1	1			
Pelvis	1	8	3					
Femur	6	5	5			1		
Tibia	1	13	3		1			
Calcaneum		1						
Intermediate		1						
Metacarpal		7						
Metapodial		1	2		1			
Metatarsal	2	5						
1st phalanx	1	3			2			
Cervical vert.							2	1
Thoracic vert.							4	4
Lumbar vert.							2	3
Vert.frag							7	2
Rib							29	21
Uid	1	1					36	32
Total	101	115	22	3	15	4	82	63
MNI	10	11	2					

displayed the most butchery marks, although one dog bone had been chopped and one domestic fowl bone was cut. Cut-marks were seen on only one cattle bone, whereas several sheep bones had been cut. One pig bone had been sawn. Both large and medium mammal remains also displayed significant butchery evidence. Forty-one animal bones had been burnt although burning was almost absent on the bird and fish remains.

Metrical analysis

Measurements were obtained from a number of post-medieval cattle and sheep bones. Where possible these have been compared with those held on ABMAP. Two cattle metatarsals provided comparative metrical data. Both were within the range seen for cattle from contemporary sites and were fairly close to the mean value. Most measurements on sheep bones fell within the range seen at contemporary sites. The only anomaly of note was a femur whose distal breadth was 7mm smaller than the contemporary range. Metrical comparisons were also made with individual post-medieval sites, showing that the measurements taken from post-medieval bones recovered from the Tower of London lay close to the mean of measurements taken at contemporary sites.

Discussion

The wide range of species present suggests that the occupants of the Tower of London consumed a varied diet that included beef, mutton, pork, rabbit, fowl and fish. By post-medieval times rabbit was an important minor component of the English diet (Davis 1987) and there is evidence that they were being bred in man-made warrens in some parts of southern England. The small size of the goose and duck suggests that wildfowl were being consumed and these were probably available locally. The more exotic cormorant would have been imported from the coast and may have been served at feasts, as was the case with seagulls during the medieval period (Hammond 1993). Cod could have been eaten either fresh or in a dried form. Turbot would also have been imported from the coast and is known to have been sold by London fishmongers during the medieval period (ibid).

In addition to the food animals, the remains of minor domestic species suggest that horse, dog and cat lived on or near the site. Horses would have provided transport and power (eg, for the horse mill in St Thomas's Tower). Dogs could have been kept for hunting, guarding or simply as pets. Alternatively their remains could represent the presence of stray dogs taking advantage of easy pickings. Similarly, the cat remains may represent strays, pets or animals kept to control pests.

The relatively large number of cattle and sheep mandibles is to some extent a reflection of density-related survival, but it also suggests that primary butchery waste was being disposed of in the moat. The recovery of major limb bone fragments and the remains of bird and fish further indicate that at least some kitchen waste was also discarded in the moat. The under-representation of cattle, sheep and pig phalanges in contrast to the survival of fragile skull fragments could be the result of the common practice of hoof removal along with the hide. The presence of a few first phalanges, however, suggests that this is more likely to be the result of recovery bias.

Ageing data indicate that the cattle comprised both sub-adult and adult animals. The bones of sub-adults probably represent animals slaughtered for meat arriving at the site as whole carcasses or joints of meat. The remains of adult animals suggest that older cattle, probably dairy cows that had become unproductive, were also being utilised for meat. These could have been kept on or near the site to provide a supply of milk. The sheep remains belonged primarily to adult animals, suggesting that wool production was more important than the production of prime mutton at this time. As would be expected for an animal kept primarily for meat, pork was derived from immature animals. There was no evidence for livestock rearing, which confirms that the inhabitants were generally consuming rather than producing food.

Evidence of gnawing indicates that bone refuse was deliberately given to dogs, left lying around or deliberately disposed of in a locality where it was available to both dogs and rodents. This probably occurred before it was gathered up and finally disposed of in the moat. The presence of gnawing on a rabbit bone supports the interpretation that these animals formed part of the diet, rather than their presence being of an intrusive nature. The considerable amount of butchery visible on the animal bone confirms the domestic nature of the deposits. The presence of a chop mark on the radius of a dog suggests that dog meat was of economic value. It may have been fed to other dogs or eaten by the local inhabitants. It is also possible that the fur was valued and that the lower limbs were removed before skinning. There was no evidence for the consumption of horse meat.

Comparison with contemporary sites

The post-medieval bones have been compared with groups from other contemporary sites of varying status and nature. Despite the small sample size of the moat assemblage, the same pattern of species representation is apparent. Cattle and sheep similarly dominated assemblages at Exeter (Maltby 1979), Launceston Castle (Albarella and Davis 1994) and Eynsham Abbey (Ingrem and Serjeantson 2003). Sheep may have been kept in greater numbers but cattle appear to have provided the majority of the meat. Pig seems to have become less important during this period: it was the least abundant of the major food species at all four sites. Pigs are generally slaughtered when immature, however, when their bones are still porous and therefore susceptible to degradation in the soil. They might be under-represented in the archaeological record. At Launceston the abundance of pig teeth has been explained as the result of poor survival of other parts of the carcass, which suggests that pig meat may have played a greater role in the diet than is indicated by the abundance of their bones. Deer accounted for only a small proportion of the assemblages from Launceston and Eynsham and were rarely recovered at Exeter. Rabbit contributed to the diet at the other post-medieval sites and horse, dog and cat were also generally present in small numbers.

The cattle remains from the moat included both sub-adult and adult animals but there was no evidence for the consumption of veal. In contrast, at Eynsham Abbey a large proportion of calves and cattle between 3 and 4 years of age were slaughtered. At Launceston, a marked change in the age of cattle was noted in the post-medieval period, when a greater proportion of juveniles were culled (Albarella and Davis 1994). At Exeter, an unusually high incidence of calves also suggested that veal had become important in the diet (Maltby 1979). According to Maltby (ibid) the rise in the importance of dairy farming during the post-medieval period was closely associated with the production of veal for towns.

At the Tower of London sheep remains belonged primarily to adult animals. At Launceston the preference appears to have been for those between the ages of two and six and this was also interpreted by the authors as indicating the consumption of mutton from sheep kept for wool (Albarella and Davis 1994). At post-medieval Exeter there was a big increase in the numbers of adult animals represented with few being slaughtered between 15 and 30 months. At Eynsham, nearly half were slaughtered between the ages of two and three years, but wool was still important as shown by the fact that a large proportion also survived past four years. The evidence therefore supports Trow-Smith's (1957) observation 'that although the demand for mutton was growing it had not yet overwhelmed the importance of wool'.

At Eynsham, Launceston and Exeter pigs were mostly immature and sub-adult when culled. This is to be expected from the most fecund farm animal which is exploited primarily for its young, although lard and skins were also valued (Maltby 1979). Documentary evidence shows that in certain areas of England the age of slaughter decreased from that of the medieval period. This was made possible by advances in pig husbandry, for instance in Leicestershire, where pigs were fattened in sties from the age of 9 to 12 months (Thirsk 1967, 194).

The varied nature of the household deposits at Exeter, where animals would have arrived on the hoof and then been slaughtered, suggests that most parts of the animal's skeleton were distributed along with the meat (Maltby 1979). At Launceston, by contrast, the small number of cattle teeth recovered was explained as perhaps representing a greater proportion of off-site butchery in the 16th and 17th centuries and changes in procurement strategy (Albarella and Davis 1994). The large proportion of mandibles recovered from the Tower of London suggests that here, as in Exeter, animals arrived on the hoof. Most parts of the carcass might have been distributed with the meat.

Chapter 9:   Six Hundred Years of Water Depth and Quality: 1240–1843

INTRODUCTION

It is surprisingly difficult to determine where the water level stood in the moat during its history. The drainage and backfilling (Chapter 10) occurred before the first edition large-scale Ordnance Survey map was published, but spot heights related to sea level might not have been provided for the moat water even if they had surveyed it before 1843. We therefore have to rely on two main strands of evidence: historical sources and data recovered directly from the archaeological excavations. This chapter begins with a brief overview of the historical information and then presents the information relating to water levels from the excavations. There is some (limited) relevant structural and stratigraphic information, rather more from the environmental analyses that have been carried out on the soils from the moat.

HISTORICAL INFORMATION

There is a general absence of detailed information in the primary documentary sources (eg, works accounts etc) regarding the exact water level, despite the often extensive and accurate surveys of the castle carried out in the post-medieval period. The plans drawn by Clement Lemprière in the early decades of the 18th century, for instance, are well known and extremely valuable for students of the Tower's development. They (and others) provide a wealth of detail regarding structures and spaces within and around the Tower, including its moat, but not about the water level in the latter. We must therefore consider alternative sources of information, which are—to a great extent—essentially artistic depictions of the site. Fortunately the basic accuracy of these can often be tested against surviving buildings and other structural details, although of course much has changed since the 19th century.

Firstly it needs to be stressed that most depictions pre-dating the 19th century are too schematic to be of serious value in assessing the water level. Such famous illustrations as that of the execution of Balmerino and Kilmarnock on Tower Hill in 1746 do show water in the moat (Impey and Parnell 2000, fig 121), but it is clearly impossible to suggest a level with anything approaching accuracy from this information. Perhaps the very obvious plant growth (reeds or grasses?) within the moat is more informative here. The same can be said for George Bryant Campion's painting of c1840 (ie, just before the moat was filled in), showing the castle from the same north-western perspective (Fig 144). Once again this shows water clearly enough, but also some vegetation and, in places, what appear to be mud banks around the outer edge. Unfortunately it is extremely difficult to assess the level of the water against existing structures such as Legge's Mount, and of course we cannot know how concerned the artist would have been to paint the level accurately anyway. Campion also depicts the weir or batardeau in the middle of the north-western arm of the moat, a structure which proved to be thoroughly elusive during the evaluation trenching (Chapter 8).

There are a few fixed points around the moat where a more accurate assessment of levels ought to be possible. The south-western entrance causeway is the most obvious one because of the wide central archway which, as we have seen in Chapter 8, was rebuilt in the 1780s. This makes earlier illustrations such as Paul Sandby's 1746–7 watercolour view of the Middle Tower (Fig 129) difficult to use, since not only the arch but also the entire upper part of the causeway was altered. We noted in Chapter 8 that Sandby possibly shows at least two of the original three arch positions. The Middle Tower gives a degree of orientation within the picture, and, as with the execution scene from the same period, Sandby shows vegetation (and mudflats) along the outer edge of the moat against the revetment wall. Sandby's work is especially valuable because he produced it to demonstrate his ability to work to the high standards of technical accuracy demanded by the Board of Ordnance. He would therefore have done his best to be faithful and accurate to the scene before him. Sandby went on to enjoy a distinguished career in their survey office, from where the Ordnance Survey itself grew. In very broad terms his watercolour suggests that the moat water was at a similar level to (or perhaps slightly higher than) the current grass here.

Early 19th-century views of the causeway area similarly imply that the water must have been at about the existing grass level. Bayley's *History and Antiquities of the Tower of London* (1821) includes a particularly good view from the west along the causeway to the Byward Tower (vol I, pl XXVI; Fig 145). There are many details which confirm the basic accuracy of the engraving, notably the stub of wall attached to the south face of the causeway just to the east of the arch. The archaeological significance of this feature (Chapter 5) could not have been apparent to Bayley's engraver, but the simple fact that they took the trouble to include it is important enough. To be fair the stub is shown slightly too far to the west, but the correspondence of its top with the crown of the central arch is true to life. The engraving clearly shows the water (at high tide) lying at the springing level of the arch, that is, approximately 2.5m OD (virtually the same as the current level to the north of the causeway).

Fig 144   View over the Tower moat from the north west in about 1840, in its last years as a water-filled feature, by George Bryant Campion (1796–1870). The outer edge is inaccurately shown, but the painting is interesting for its depiction of mud banks in the water, the late 18th-century weir, the latrine (or sentry post?) projecting from the north angle of the outer curtain wall, and the unusual view of the 17th-century Grand Storehouse, burnt in 1841. The rubble of the building was used in filling the moat in 1843–5.

An early 19th-century drawing (Fig 146) and Tugman's watercolour painting of the east side of the castle (including the moat) in 1826 (Fig 147) provide further valuable evidence for the water level. As noted in Chapter 5, both show the three turrets in their original form. In Tugman's painting the upper six courses of the battered foundation were exposed above the moat waters. The extent of the later 19th-century demolition makes it difficult to assess exactly where this sixth course would have lain, but it must have been quite close to the current grass level of about 2.9m OD. This would imply a water level somewhat higher than that suggested at the south-west entrance, where the crown of the arch lies at c3.4m OD.

STRATIGRAPHIC AND STRUCTURAL EVIDENCE

There was very little direct evidence for the original water level in the excavations. Nevertheless, on the west, north and east sides it was observed that the surface of the outer curtain wall was partially obscured by a film of concreted calcitic material in each trench where it was seen (eg, 12–14, 27, 81 and 83). The concretion was not present in the lowest courses of masonry, which would have been in permanent contact with water. The film was 0.13m

thick in places, but was often patchy over the wall surface. The top of the layer occurred at c2.24m OD in trench 12, 2.55m OD in trench 13 (with small isolated patches above this) and 1.06m OD in trench 14. The bottom lay at 0.5m OD in trench 12, 0.8m in trench 13 and 0.26m in trench 14 (Fig 148). In trench 27 the top and bottom were found at approximately 2.5m and 1m OD respectively (Fig 61).

Unusual accreted lime or calcitic deposits were also found against the various structures running laterally across the moat, especially on its east and west sides. In these cases, however, the deposit was more akin to the 'barnacle-like' encrustation noted by Peter Curnow in the east moat in 1960 (Fig 19). In trench 31, on the north side of the south-western entrance causeway (Fig 72), a band of this sort 1.3m wide and up to 70mm thick covered part of the late medieval/early post-medieval rebuild and was also evident on the original masonry to the west of the arch position (3157). The width of the band was fairly consistent along the length of wall exposed, but the thickness of accretion varied greatly and some areas were quite patchy. The accreted lime was recorded on the masonry only between the levels of 0–1.3m OD. In trench 25 at the south-eastern corner, the upper ashlar facing on the north side of the Iron Gate causeway displayed a thin layer of the barnacle-like encrustation. The truncation of this

Fig 145   View of the 13th-century Byward Tower, engraved and published in Bayley's History and Antiquities of the Tower of London of 1821 (vol I, plate xxvi), showing the moat at high tide. By 1821 the main drawbridge in front of the gatehouse had disappeared, but an 18th-century timber drawbridge to the Byward Postern (soon to be replaced by the existing cast iron contraption) still remained. Note also the guardhouse on the wharf, and the distant view of St Thomas's Tower. The gable windows immediately to the left of the Byward Tower belonged to the Stone Kitchen Tavern.

building in the 1680s made it impossible to assess the original extent of the film, but it was also noted further north in trench 83. Curnow had already recorded the presence of the 'barnacles' against the north face of the turret in 1960, and the 1997 excavation confirmed this. The top of the deposit lay at 2.2m OD (but more may have been present before the mid-19th-century truncation of the battered foundation) and it continued down to at least 0.5m OD.

Fig 146 An early 19th-century drawing of the east moat, showing the still-standing turret on the left and the continuous batter of the other two turrets. These were reduced to below turf level, probably when the moat was drained and backfilled. Compare with Tugman's painting in Figure 147.

It is difficult to determine precisely how these deposits formed. On the outer curtain wall it seemed to consist of calcitic material leached out either from the masonry itself or (more probably) from its mortar bonding. The 'barnacle-like' growth, by contrast, genuinely did appear to be 'fossilised' molluscan shells. In both instances, however, the crucial element was that the deposit was not ubiquitous on the masonry. There was a top and a bottom level for the film, although neither level was regular or consistent within trenches—let alone between them. It seems most likely that this was an effect caused by contact between the tidal flow and the masonry. Growth did not occur where the walls were permanently submerged but rather where they were in turns either above or below water according to the stage of the tidal cycle.

Taking due account of the variations in the top and bottom levels of the calcitic and barnacle layers, it can be suggested that the high- and low-water marks lay at around 2.5m and 0.5m OD respectively. Clearly these are unlikely to represent the full extent of the Thames's tidal regime—the difference between high and low water today is generally around 6m. Medieval water levels will certainly have been different to today's, of course, and from Edward I's time onwards (and probably Henry III's) the moat was separated from the river by dams or barriers. These would have restricted (deliberately) the tidal variation within the ditch, although the Thames will always have provided the bulk of the water supply irrespective of tidal influence as such. It is also important to remember that the base level of the moat would have risen gradually as silts accumulated there and were not removed during the periodic attempts to clean and dredge the ditch.

It seems reasonable to accept that the moat would have been filled to a level of around 2.5m OD. The historical evidence points towards such a height, and the determining level of the arch crown in the south-western entrance causeway shows that it cannot have been much higher without causing major problems for that structure. The archaeological evidence for such a level is also reasonably strong. The water point may have receded to a significantly lower level at the relevant point of the tidal regime. Alternatively the low-water point might in some way reflect drought conditions or deliberate drain-down (eg, for the periodic cleaning of the moat). In either circumstance it can be claimed with some confidence that all moat fills below a level of 2.5m OD could have formed in an essentially aquatic environment (though doubtless with non-aquatic influences as well). The microscopic scientific analysis of soil samples taken from the moat was very much directed towards the question of what that aquatic environment would have been like. The remainder of this chapter presents the results of the relevant analyses.

ENVIRONMENTAL EVIDENCE

Diatoms

A total of 125 diatom taxa were identified from sections A (Fig 25) and C (Fig 27). Given the low counting sum used, this indicates that the sediments are species-rich. Section A contained 119 diatom species (Figs 149, 150) and section C 85 diatom species (Figs 151, 152). In these sequences the rich diatom composition reflects both ecological factors, such as the presence of suitable environments for a diversity of diatom growth, and changes which take

Fig 147 A watercolour by J Tugman showing the Tower from the east in 1826 – a somewhat unusual but very valuable perspective. The east moat turrets are all shown, and this allows us to assess the water level at this point.

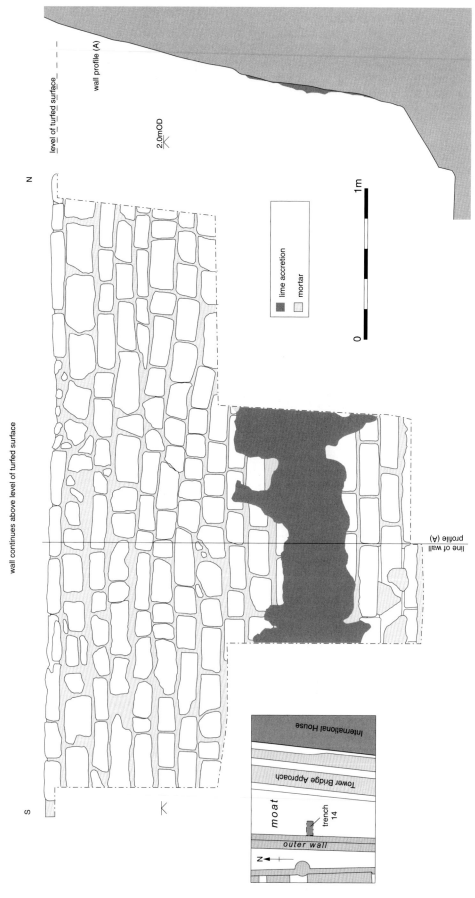

Fig 148   Elevation and profile of the outer curtain wall in trench 14 showing the calcareous concretion on the surface of the masonry.

196

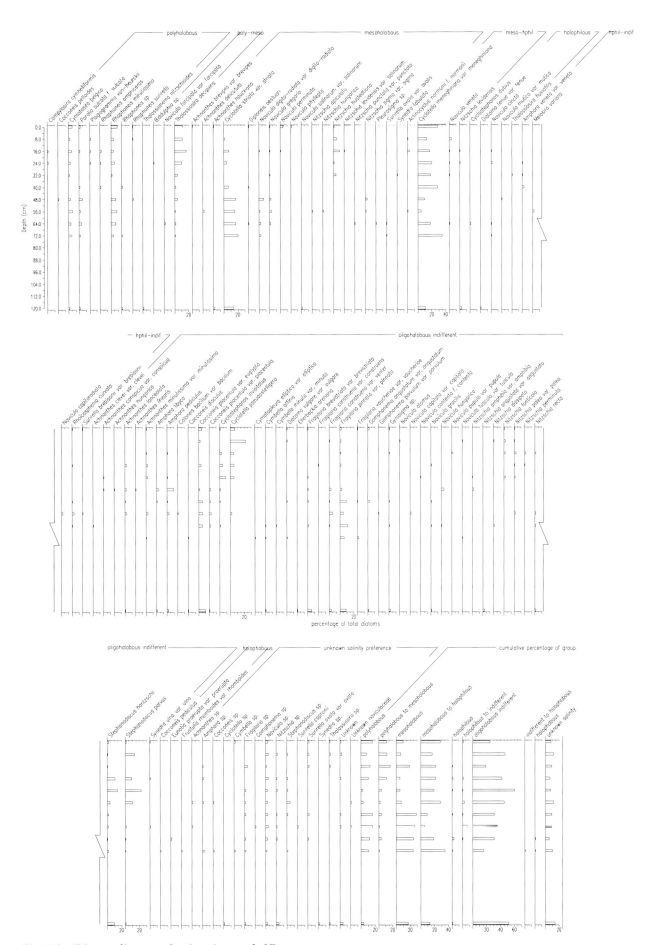

Fig 149   Diatom diagram, Section A, trench 27.

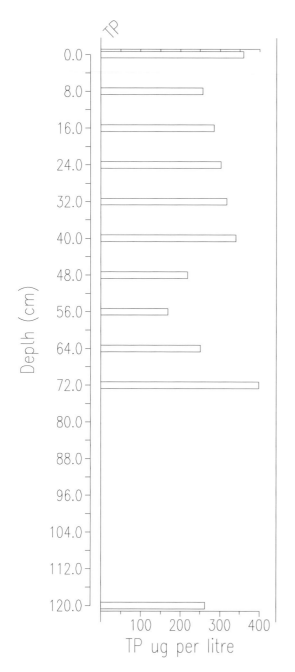

Fig 150   Total phosphorus diagram, Section A, trench 27.

life-cycle in open water. They are therefore easily transported upstream from their optimal environments for growth, on the coast (neretic spp.) or in the outer estuary. Discounting the unlikely possibility of the reworking of earlier estuarine sediments from within the moat, their presence, along with estuarine taxa, demonstrates unequivocally that the moat was in almost continuous contact with the tidal Thames during the periods of sediment accumulation (*see* below). However, it appears that the degree of contact was not uniform because there are noticeable trends in the percentages of both individual taxa (which have different salinity optima) and the cumulative percentages of taxa in the different aquatic groups. Exceptions to the clear evidence for contact with the Thames estuary are in C at 480mm and 560mm depth respectively. In these samples marine (polyhalobous) taxa are absent and only a low percentage of the estuarine (mesohalobous) species *Cyclotella striata* is present, whilst freshwater (oligohalobous indifferent) diatoms are dominant.

It is possible that, even where there are contiguous samples with estuarine taxa present, the estuarine contact was not continuous. It might appear to be so because of vertical mixing of sediment from periods of contact with sediment from periods of isolation from the estuary. Such vertical mixing could result from the activities of living organisms (bioturbation) or from physical mixing processes.

Cyclotella striata and other brackish water (mesohalobous) diatoms that would have grown in the tidal Thames in the vicinity of the moat are also present. *Cyclotella striata*, like the marine diatoms discussed, is a planktonic diatom carried on currents more easily than strongly attached benthic diatoms. This particular species is typical of the Thames estuary during the late Holocene up until and including the present time.

In general, for both sections A and C, freshwater and brackish water diatoms from the open-water (planktonic) habitat such as *Cyclotella*, *Stephanodiscus* and *Cyclostephanos* are common. Non-planktonic freshwater diatoms (eg, *Navicula*, *Cymbella*, *Achnanthes*, *Cocconeis*, *Gomphonema* and *Fragilaria*) form a smaller, though significant, component of the total assemblage. The same is true of the marine and marine-brackish diatom component where the majority of the diatoms are planktonic or semi-planktonic (ie, not firmly attached to surfaces). However, the dominance of planktonic diatoms within the saline component of the flora reflects the movement of life-forms that are more susceptible to long-distance transport. The marine species present are truly non-local because they would not have grown under conditions of freshwater or slightly brackish water.

The local (autochthonous) flora of freshwater to brackish diatoms is diverse, despite the numerical dominance of plankton. The assemblages are composed of a mixture of diatoms from different benthic, epiphytic and open-water sources. It therefore

place in the buried soils. The latter include the introduction of diatoms from distant habitats and variation through time in the suitability of conditions for diatom preservation. Mixed diatom assemblages reflect a number of disparate habitats and aquatic environments supplying diatoms to the fossil assemblage.

Estuarine species are represented in both sections A and C by marine (polyhalobous) diatoms which have been displaced from the outer Thames estuary, including *Rhaphoneis* spp., *Cymatosira belgica*, *Campylosira cymbelliformis*, *Paralia sulcata* and *Thalassiosira decipiens*. These diatoms are planktonic or semi-planktonic species which complete their

Fig 151   Diatom diagram, Section C, trench 31.

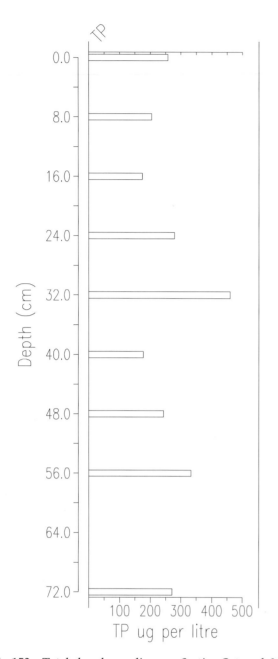

Fig 152 Total phosphorus diagram, Section C, trench 31.

as *Navicula mutica* and *Navicula atomus* are rare in both A and C.

The diatom flora suggests that, as well as being relatively shallow, the water in the moat was turbid and the sediments disturbed. There is little evidence for the epiphytic diatom growth found in water bodies with larger submerged or partly submerged plants (macrophyte beds). For example, common epiphytic diatoms such as *Cocconeis placentula* and *Fragilaria* spp. are relatively rare in these assemblages when they are compared with similar, but clearer water, bodies which would have allowed dense macrophyte growth at least in shallower water. This is congruent with pollen analytical evidence and plant macrofossil analysis, which indicate that aquatic macrophytes were not important in the moat.

Waste disposal, along with water currents from surface drainage, the City Ditch and the Thames, caused the introduction, mixing and resuspension of sediments. It is also likely that stocking the moat with fish would have increased organic pollution and turbidity. Further, it appears that for a large part of the year the moat remained turbid as a result of algal blooms and, specifically, diatom growth. The common freshwater planktonic diatoms *Stephanodiscus hantzschii* and *Stephanodiscus parvus* are both spring-blooming diatoms, whilst the cells of *Cyclotella meneghiniana* reach maximum concentrations during the summer. This might well have contributed to the deposition of the unusual calcitic and barnacle-like growths on walls in contact with the moat water.

Inferring the values of past aquatic phosphorus concentrations, or other chemical or environmental variables, from fossil diatom remains preserved in water-lain sediments involves two stages (eg, Cameron *et al* 1999). First the relationships between diatom abundances and contemporary phosphorus (or other variables) are modelled using a modern training or calibration set of surface sediment diatom samples and associated water chemistry. These relationships are used to derive a transfer function. The second stage is to use the transfer function to infer past phosphorus concentrations from the fossil diatom assemblages. In this case the most comprehensive existing diatom training set, derived from a wide geographical range of shallow, lowland water bodies (Bennion *et al* 1996), has been used to reconstruct the past nutrient status of the water bodies on the site.

In both sections, reconstructed nutrient levels for the moat were consistently high. In section A they varied from 168 μgl^{-1} to 398 μgl^{-1} and in 3112 from 174 μgl^{-1} to 460 μgl^{-1}. A relatively high percentage of the total fossil diatom assemblage of most samples is present in the TP (total phosphorus) calibration set. The percentage represented varies from 26 per cent to 95 per cent, but in over half of the samples is above 50 per cent (Table 7).

Given the difficulties of applying the TP transfer function in an environment directly influenced by

appears likely that the water depth in the moat, which may be reconstructed more accurately from other sources of evidence, was fairly shallow, perhaps in the range of one to two metres. Had the site of deposition been in deeper water, the plankton would have masked the presence of most non-planktonic species while in very shallow water non-planktonic diatoms would have been dominant (eg, Bradbury and Winter 1976). In these sequences, there is no evidence that the moat dried out completely at any time. If this were the case, it would be anticipated that there would be a greater number of poorly preserved valves and taxa capable of tolerating long periods of dryness (aerophilous taxa) in the assemblages. Desiccation-tolerant species such

Table 7 Percentages of the fossil diatom assemblages present in the TP calibration set

Core	Depth (mm)	Percentage of the diatom assemblage present in the TP calibration set
Λ	0	55
	80	60
	160	40
	240	67
	320	81
	400	83
	480	48
	560	53
	640	55
	720	53
	1200	62
C	0	32
	80	48
	160	48
	240	40
	320	38
	400	26
	480	95
	560	94
	720	52

estuarine waters it is unclear whether the apparent trends in nutrient levels are of significance. However, it is clear that the water was nutrient-enriched (eutrophic) and can be compared with lakes or ponds in the present day and in the past where there has been significant organic pollution from human action (OECD 1982; Birks *et al* 1995). Diatom analysis of sediments from the Bronze Age and the Roman period associated with archaeological sites in the Thames has suggested that there were elevated nutrient levels before the medieval period (unpublished reports on Bull Wharf and Vintry House, Tower Bridge). However, the maximum TP levels and types of diatom assemblage from these sequences in the Tower of London moat show that maximum TP levels were higher than those recorded at earlier sites.

Plant and mollusc remains

The plant and mollusc remains also provided valuable evidence for the moat's aquatic environment at various stages in its history. Context 1424, from the bottom of the newly excavated Edward I moat in trench 14, contained numerous shells of aquatic molluscs, including *Valvata piscinalis* and *Bithynia tentaculata*, which require relatively clean moving water. *Sphaerium corneum*, a bivalve mollusc which favours a muddy bed beneath slowly moving water, was present as well. These species also occurred in sediments of late 13th-century date in trench 31, although in much lower concentrations.

The moat appears to have been kept generally clear of aquatic vegetation during the early years of its use. However, context 2854 from trench 27 contained many seeds of annual weeds which grow on wet mud, particularly celery-leaved crowfoot (*Ranunculus sceleratus*), red goosefoot (*Chenopodium rubrum* gp.) and golden dock (*Rumex maritimus*). These plants probably flourished around the margins of the moat in the summer as the water level fell. It is possible that the banks of the moat were kept clear of tall vegetation because such plants were hardly represented amongst the seeds. This is broadly consistent with the 18th/19th-century illustrations (*see* above), which show relatively low-level growth on the outer edge at least.

The molluscs from late medieval sediments gave evidence for a change in conditions. The flowing-water species had been replaced by species tolerant of stagnant water, such as shells of *Gyraulus laevis*, which were very numerous. This freshwater to slightly brackish water gastropod is characteristic of permanent bodies of stagnant water (Ellis 1969, 127; Kerney 1999, 64). It is a rather uncommon species, although there are 20th-century records of it from Middlesex. *Lymnaea peregra*, another gastropod characteristic of stagnant water, was also well represented. The majority of the seeds, meanwhile, were again from the annual weeds of seasonally exposed mud that were found in the earlier deposits. Fully aquatic plants were represented only by a few seeds of horned pondweed (*Zannichellia palustris*). It is possible that the late medieval extension of the moat along the southern side of the Tower would have reduced the flow of the Thames around the moat system.

The onset of the post-medieval period was marked by a further change in its molluscan fauna, with the return of the flowing-water species *Valvata piscinalis*, *Bithynia tentaculata* and *Sphaerium corneum*. The transition was strongly marked, for example, in Context 31132 in trench 31. The recolonisation by flowing-water molluscs was perhaps the result of a minor stream being directed to feed the moat or an increased flow along the City Ditch, which flowed into the moat. Rather more aquatic plants seem to have grown in the moat, with seeds from watercress (*Nasturtium officinale*), fool's watercress (*Apium nodiflorum*) and pondweed (*Potamogeton* sp.) joining horned pondweed. A sample from trench 1 contained rhizome fragments resembling common reed (*Phragmites australis*) and culm fragments possibly of reed. However, remains of aquatic plants were not abundant and it is likely that the moat was mostly kept clear of weeds.

Seeds from a Bidentalia community, weeds of seasonally exposed mud, were present in most of the post-medieval samples. Celery-leaved crowfoot (*Ranunculus sceleratus*), red goosefoot (*Chenopodium rubrum* gp.) and golden dock (*Rumex maritimus*), which were well represented in the samples from the earlier periods, were joined by redshank (*Polygonum persicaria*), water pepper (*P. hydropiper*) and bur-marigold (*Bidens tripartita*). A celery seed (*Apium graveolens*), a wild saltmarsh plant as well as a cultivar, from context 3911 of trench 39 was as likely to have been from a plant growing on slightly brackish mud alongside the moat as to represent food remains. The general paucity of seeds of coarse herbaceous vegetation and developing scrub suggests that the environs of the moat continued to be kept clear of tall vegetation during the post-medieval period. However, the samples from trench 31 did contain some seeds from plants of disturbed or waste ground, including dyer's rocket (*Reseda luteola*) and dock (*Rumex* not *maritimus*). An example of death-watch beetle (*Xestobium rufovillosum*) from context 2833 (trench 27) was perhaps from an infestation in the large structural timbers of the Tower.

Although there was little evidence for the dumping of refuse in the moat (Chapter 8), a drain seems to have discharged organic effluent into it in the vicinity of trench 31. The samples from 18th-century context 31132 and above contained pupae closely resembling the trickling filter fly (*Psychoda alternata*). They were particularly abundant in context 3130 (19th-century, but pre-dating 1843). The larvae of Psychodidae feed on decaying matter, usually in water, and the common name of *P. alternata* has arisen because it is often abundant in filter beds at sewage works. Unlike other members of the genus, it favours dark habitats and also breeds in such places as drains and sink U-traps (Smith 1989, 37). The larvae of *P. alternata* are unlikely to have been able to flourish in the moat itself but are likely to have been washed into it from a drain.

The occurrence of both organic effluent and molluscs of relatively well-oxygenated moving water in the moat raises a problem of interpretation. There were sufficient shells to suggest that the flowing-water species were living in the moat rather than having been carried to it from a clean-water source. There was presumably a sufficient flow of water through the moat to dilute the discharge from the drain so that the water did not experience a complete oxygen deficit from the decay of suspended organic material.

Pollen

The earliest period represented by pollen is the backfill of Henry III's moat in trench 27, section A. This period was one of much disturbance caused by the excavation of Edward I's new moat while parts of the older one were being backfilled. The pollen zone displays a very substantial number of reworked Tertiary palynomorphs; excavation of the underlying London Clay was probably responsible for these fossils being in suspension. The presence of contemporaneous (medieval) pollen, however, suggests that these basal deposits need not represent mass dumping of clay but a dumping in combination with progressive sedimentation in muddy/turbid water. There are small numbers of *Pediastrum* along with

aquatic plants (*Potamogeton* type and *Myriophyllum* spp.) that indicate a largely freshwater habitat. Whether this is growth in the moat or input from the Thames is conjectural. Hystrichospheres may imply input from the river but other than the possible *Chenopodium* type there are surprisingly no marine or brackish water indicators. This contrasts with the diatom assemblages, which suggest regular/constant contact with the Thames. The basal grey silt in section C overlay gravel capping of piles dated to the late 1270s. Although only 80–100mm thick this unit perhaps correlates with the top of zone 1 (context 2840) in section A. It is thought that this basal sedimentary unit accumulated over a relatively short time-span of 10–25 years at the end of the 13th century.

There is a marked increase in *Pediastrum* in section A pollen zone 2 (contexts 2839, 2838 and 2844) and section C zone 2 (context 3136). There is also a reduction in palynomorphs in section A zone 2, while they are virtually absent from section C zone 2 (context 3136). This represents a change to more stable freshwater conditions, which seem to have pertained throughout the medieval period, represented by the peak in *Pediastrum* in section A zone 2.

The olive/buff-brown medieval sediments were sealed by post-medieval dark-grey to black anoxic silts which clearly represented a change in depositional environment from fresh water (?brackish water input occasionally) to stagnant waters. This seems to have been especially characteristic of the 18th century and probably the early 19th century as well. These levels are represented in the upper pollen zones in sections A (upper part of context 2833) and C (context 3133). *Pediastrum* is present, but with small values compared with the freshwater sediments of the medieval period. As with the latter, there is a surprisingly impoverished aquatic/marsh flora with only small numbers of Cyperaceae, *Potamogeton* type, and *Typha angustifolia/Sparganium* type. Perhaps this was as a result of high pollution levels or salinity from the Thames.

Soil micromorphology and related evidence

Very marked contrasts were evident in the 25 contexts sampled for soil analysis. Most of the properties showed a wide range of values, such as the proportion of sand (range 0.3–31.9 per cent), calcium carbonate (0.62–52.0 per cent), total phosphate (0.544–2.97 mg g^{-1}), magnetic susceptibility (χ_{conv}, 1.94–20.4 per cent) and copper (11–543 µg g^{-1}). The range of soil micromorphology included clayey, calcitic, shelly, laminated and massive. These findings clearly suggest that there had been substantial changes in the nature of the materials deposited as sedimentation occurred in the moat. Some of the changes had undoubtedly been affected by human activity.

The sediments are generally dominated by silts and clays, and the sands tend mostly to be fine (table A3.1). This is in keeping with a generally 'low energy' moat environment sited on London Clay, with refreshing of the moat during Henry III's reign occurring only at high tide when water levels rose above the south-west bank or dam that separated the moat from the Thames. Apart from the two samples of London Clay, all the contexts include appreciable concentrations of calcium carbonate, mostly from 10–30 per cent, but in six cases more than 40 per cent. Much of the carbonate appears to be well dispersed within the fine fraction of the sediments, often as microsparite. Although bivalve and ostracod shells and shell fragments were identifiable in many of the samples and some contexts contained mortar, the most likely source of the bulk of the carbonate would seem to be deposition from the water in the moat. If this assumption is correct, then the variable amounts of carbonate will largely reflect the relative rates of sediment input derived externally (or from the moat sides) and *in situ* carbonate deposition.

The presence of such high and variable concentrations is potentially significant in that the carbonate fraction is likely to have low total phosphate and heavy metal concentrations, and a low magnetic susceptibility. As a consequence the accumulation of carbonate will tend to 'dilute' the values of some of the key anthropogenic indicators. On the other hand, phosphate and heavy metals are less likely to be leached in a more alkaline, carbonate-rich environment. These factors need to be taken into account in interpreting the data.

The pH of some contexts is surprisingly low given their high carbonate content. For example, context 3136 has 52 per cent calcium carbonate, yet the pH is only 7.8 (a value of around 8.3 would be expected). During particle size analysis many of the samples tested positive for sulphate (table A3.2), reflecting the common presence of gypsum (calcium sulphate), which will increase the acidity through the formation of dilute sulphuric acid. In addition, iron sulphide (pyrite) is present in the London Clay mainly as an inherited mineral, and as neoformed minerals in sediments containing reworked London Clay (eg, post-1680 silts overlying the south-east causeway). Oxidation of the pyrite (along with other sulphides present in the predominantly oxygen-deficient environment of the moat) during air-drying of the samples may also contribute to the sulphate detected. In these circumstances, the pH data may be poorly representative of the original pH of the sediments. Many of the samples display quite high specific conductance values that might be associated with slightly saline conditions (eg, as a result of periodic inundation by brackish river water). However, the fact there is a negative (rather than a more usual positive) correlation between specific conductance and pH suggests that the values recorded are also influenced by the presence of sulphate. The pH and specific conductance data must therefore be interpreted with caution.

While the range in organic matter content (LOI 2.54–10.5 per cent) is not as great as for many of the other properties measured, thin humic laminations too fine to have been sampled separately for bulk analyses are evident in the thin sections of some contexts. These contain high quantities of detrital organic matter, much of which is charred (eg, thin section A, junction of 2833/2844). The small bulk samples may therefore considerably underestimate the true variability in organic matter content. Some degree of post-depositional organic decomposition will inevitably have occurred as well, particularly in the more aerobic, less-gleyed contexts. Organic matter inputs may have been derived from various sources, but plant growth within the moat or on (seasonally?) exposed deposits is demonstrated by *in situ* roots in some contexts (eg, thin section L, context 2576).

One striking feature of the data is the very high degree of correlation between LOI and two of the key indicators of human activity: total phosphate and the concentrations of the three heavy metals investigated. The very strong relationship with total phosphate ($r = 0.821$, $p < 0.001$) might to some extent reflect the presence of organic phosphate. Residual values from the regression line between total phosphate and LOI were calculated in order to identify those contexts which show phosphate enrichment beyond that anticipated from existing organic matter. These values are presented in table A3.2. Residual phosphate concentrations have been used successfully in this way at other archaeological sites (Crowther 1997), with high positive residual values providing the best indication of phosphate enrichment.

The strong positive correlations between LOI and the heavy metals (table A3.5) are unlikely to reflect a high metal content in the original organic matter (eg, in plant matter, faeces etc). However, chelates present in organic matter do form complexes with metal ions and the organic matter may therefore have picked up metals derived from other sources. Industrial processing (eg, from the Mint and the Royal Ordnance) and domestic waste, and even runoff from lead roofs (Prof W Burghadt pers comm) would all be likely sources. Lead was also used extensively to bond and waterproof major masonry structures in the moat and this might well have leached into the moat waters. The Henry III structure in the west moat, Edward I's south-west causeway and St Thomas's Tower are examples of structures where lead bonding has been found. Lead is present in the highest concentrations (mean 161 μg g^{-1}), followed by copper and zinc (88 and 41 μg g^{-1} respectively). There are significant correlations between all three metals, but the strongest is between copper and zinc ($r = 0.801$, $p < 0.001$), possibly inferring the manufacture/use of brass.

The magnetic susceptibility χ_{max} values largely reflect iron concentration within the sediments and are quite low but very variable (29.5–1280 x 10^{-8} m^3 kg^{-1}). This appears to reflect low χ_{max} values in the natural London Clay (table A3.3), the effects of gleying and the presence of high proportions of carbonate in some contexts. Not surprisingly, the lower values tend to occur in contexts that show evidence of gleying and/or contain high proportions of carbonate. Indeed, there is a significant correlation between χ_{max} and carbonate ($r = -0.749$, $p < 0.001$). None of the χ values are especially high (maximum 83.9×10^{-8} m^3 kg^{-1}) and χ is more closely correlated with χ_{max} than χ_{conv}. In these circumstances χ_{conv} (range, 1.94–20.4%) provides the most reliable measure of susceptibility enhancement, as might be associated with burning. Occasional silt-size rubified mineral matter of likely burned origin is ubiquitous in the upper part of section A in trench 27, where probable silt-size carbonaceous spherules of fossil fuel are also present (table A3.8). These could be windborne and reflect general conditions in London as well as those local to the Tower. Slag and cinders are also present in other post-medieval contexts, and the floor of the Rose Theatre, Southwark was strewn with cinders. The magnetic susceptibility results do, however, need to be interpreted cautiously, given the likelihood that some contexts may have been subject to post-depositional gleying and loss of iron, as iron movement is recorded in thin sections as void hypocoatings and as organic matter replacement (table A3.7). Contexts with χ values of greater than 50×10^{-8} m^3 kg^{-1} and a χ_{conv} of greater than 10.0 per cent are the ones which seem most likely to exhibit enhancement. The high χ_{conv} values recorded for the London Clay are difficult to explain, and merit further investigation. It is possible that these marine clays had been exposed to weathering since the Tertiary.

Later medieval deposits behind (north of) the Iron Gate causeway

The later medieval sediments (2581 and 2576) which accumulated against the Iron Gate causeway were massive, becoming finely but poorly laminated further upwards. They contained frequent building debris (mortar and sand grains), with frequent bivalve and ostracod shells (thin section L, context 2576; tables A3.7 and A3.8). Coarse wood charcoal, *in situ* roots and burrows and excrements of earthworms were present. The matrix was composed of microsparitic calcite crystals set in a weakly humic or peaty detrital organic mud. Tufa-like bodies were also present. This sediment was a highly calcareous (46.7 per cent carbonate) silty clay (28.7 per cent sand, 57.9 per cent silt, 13.4 per cent clay) with moderately high organic matter (8.92 per cent LOI) and total phosphate (1.17 mg g^{-1}) content. High specific conductance and sulphate content probably reflect the frequent allochthonous (non-local) and

etched gypsum, and the rare neoformed gypsum present. Gypsum can be precipitated from sea water and is present in the tidal mudflat deposits at the Rose Theatre site, but much of the gypsum here was probably reworked London Clay.

These shell-rich peaty deposits seem to have formed through gentle sedimentation behind the causeway, which acted as a dam. Very localised inwash of mortar debris was also apparent in the biogenic and inorganic carbonate deposits. The humic/peaty mud accumulated slowly, with plants growing on it. The mud was dry enough at times to permit earthworms to burrow. The relatively high total phosphate (1.17 mg g^{-1}) may reflect the biogenic nature of the sediment rather than a high cess input.

CONCLUSIONS

While disparities are apparent between the various strands of evidence, some conclusions can be drawn regarding the aquatic environment of the moat from the 13th to the 19th centuries. Firstly, the water level always seems to have been below c2.5m OD, with lower levels occurring at low tide, seasonally or under other circumstances (eg, during cleaning). The water depth seems to have been between 1m and 2m, with the suggested low-water mark perhaps pointing towards the greater depth. The river Thames was undoubtedly the major water source, but there were others such as the City Ditch and groundwater runoff. These made significant contributions, if not necessarily positive ones, to the aquatic environment, which was also affected by the dumping of cess, soil and refuse, with industrial waste being a significant factor locally.

The rate of water flow, and therefore the quality of the water itself, was variable. In general there seems to have been a relatively slow flow, decreasing at times to the point of stagnation. The margins of the moat were at least seasonally exposed and supported vegetation of various kinds, though apparently not major/tall plants. The various strands of evidence (historical as well as archaeological) point towards an environment which became steadily (if only slowly) less healthy as time wore on. Little change may have been apparent within one lifetime or even across several generations, but by the middle of the 19th century questions of water quality, pollution and disease had become important to the capital's inhabitants in a way not seen since the 14th century. The days of the wet moat were numbered.

Chapter 10: Period 6: The Moat 1845–2000

INTRODUCTION

The 19th century is a particularly interesting period in the Tower's history because we begin to hear many more than the official voices being raised. A relatively free and often critical press began to raise the concerns of the common people, and even the interests of the common soldiery started to come to the fore. It was perhaps inevitable that attention would focus more and more on the stinking morass of mud in the moat as metropolitan standards of hygiene and drainage became an ever greater cause for public (and official) concern. As with so many other aspects of the moat's history, the actions of this period—and particularly the draining of the moat—left a considerable mark in archaeological terms. This was not the end-point of our research, however, for the moat has continued to be affected by modern developments. These modern interventions (among which must be counted our excavations) are worthy of record in their own right, especially with respect to the Victorian works. This was the period, after all, when the Tower took on much of the physical aspect we see today.

DRAINING THE MOAT: DISCUSSIONS AND DECISIONS

The late 18th-century initiatives to cleanse the moat were followed by more than two decades of relative inactivity. Renewed proposals, however, were made in 1826–7. The Office of Works reported that:

the necessity to cleanse the moat is unquestionable, not only for the health of its inhabitants, but also for the purpose of admitting a sufficient flow of water for the machinery of the Mint and working the Wheel by which the inhabitants of the Tower are supplied with water (WO 44/131).

It was proposed to remove the sediment 'by operations of a backwater produced by constructing small temporary dams across the moat'. Presumably the idea was that the falling tide, concentrated at particular points, would sweep the silt out into the river.

Concern for the health of the Tower's inhabitants frequently recurred as a reason for cleaning the moat, and was indeed to be a decisive factor in the deliberations of the 1840s. The requirement of water for the Mint had also influenced the maintenance of the moat in the past, but the reference in 1826 needs some explanation, for the Mint had by then been established outside the Tower for 15 years. This time the water was required for the steam engines with which the Mint, in its new premises, had been equipped for the first time. The reference to the Tower's own water supply is a reminder that the water-powered pumps in St Thomas's Tower, successors to equipment first installed there in the 16th century, were still in use. They were only replaced by steam-powered machinery when the moat was drained.

To what extent these proposals were actually effected is not known, but it was only a few years later, in September 1830, that the last great attempt was made to restore the water-filled moat. Archival information is abundant, but perhaps less telling than the following account from the *Standard* of 15 October 1830:

The Duke of Wellington... having issued his orders for cleansing and deepening of the Tower moat, workmen are now busily employed in the process. The moat is to be deepened four feet all round the Tower. The water in the moat was allowed to run off; pieces of wood were laid across the bed at short distances, in the form of ratlins; upon this a railway in miniature is constructed; the mud, a thick rich compost, invaluable as manure, is collected into square boxes on wheels; these are pushed along the railway by labourers with very little trouble. The contents of the box are dropped into a barge, moored in front of the 'Traitor's Gate', the soil thus collected is taken up the river for the use of the rearers of Battersea plants and other agriculturalists.

In the event, however, the work was not as successful as the account suggests. A plan made after work had ceased in December 1830 notes that only a 'portion of the accumulated sediment' had been removed (WO 94/72/8. The plan accompanied Lord Beresford's Suggestions for the Defence of the Tower of 6 December 1830. Given the depth of water shown in the plan, it is presumed that the survey was prepared after the scouring was completed). A further 4,500 cubic yards of fill was ordered to be removed in the following year (WO 44/131). The stated reasons for this activity included all those cited in 1826, but the authorities were now also anxious to reinforce the Tower's defences, spurred on perhaps by the fall of the restored monarchy in France and agitation associated with the Reform Bill. Once again, the imagined threat was not an invading army but local unrest, with the wet moat and the iron railings at the top of the counterscarp both being cited as valuable obstacles to mob attack.

Operations at this time were not entirely confined to the moat itself. Renewed attention was paid to improving its perimeter, taking up the precedent set by the 1797 *Act for... improving and keeping in repair Tower Hill* (Tower Hill Improvement Act, 37 George

III, cap 87. For the preamble to the act, see Clayton and Leftwich 1934, 233–4). The counterscarp, enclosed by iron railings in 1828–9 (WO 44/133), was put down to ornamental gardens in 1837 (SO WP 2/203/60–6). This created the promenade around the moat's edge. The result was an early and interesting attempt to improve the surroundings of the Tower for reasons beyond the military and practical. A stern reminder of its ancient and more sinister role, however, is to be found in the Board of Ordnance's condition that 'no trees are planted, nor enclosure made that can afford cover'. The dense shrubberies and plane trees of today were clearly not the intention—the Tower was a fortress still.

Towards the final decision

The problems which eventually led to the draining and infilling of the moat had been apparent since the 13th century, but the decision was not taken lightly or quickly. Momentum towards infilling began within two years of Wellington's initiative of 1830, by which time the old problems, if they had ever abated, had returned with a vengeance. In 1832 the Constable was asked by the Secretary of St Katharine Docks, Sir John Hall, to build drains to carry the Tower sewage directly to the river (WP 2/200/34). This elicited the comment from the Royal Engineers' Office that the moat was nearly dry on the ebb tide and the recommendation that raking the reeking mud into the central channel should be discontinued in the summer months (WP 2/200/54*). Wellington's reaction was dismissive: the sewerage proposals were prohibitively expensive and unlikely to produce any benefit for years (WP 2/200/56*),while the smell would just have to be tolerated (WP 2/200/6*). He was persuaded that tidal action, properly managed, could be relied on to scour the moat and assured the Privy Council that this was so (WP 2/200/6*).

Wellington's opposition to further intervention on a grand scale prevailed until 1840–1, when a series of reports placed the blame for epidemics among the Tower inhabitants and garrison squarely on the stagnant moat (in particular the report of 25 May 1841 by J Johnson, Surgeon Major (WO 44/614) and the report of John Hunter, Apothecary to the Tower, of 5 June 1841 (WP 2/206/126*)).The crucial incident was an epidemic among the 1st Battalion of the Grenadier Guards, then stationed at the Tower. *The Times* of 14 May 1841 reported a number of deaths and 80 men in hospital, relating that the situation was attributed to the water supply. Two weeks later the Surgeon Major of the Guards explained that 'the bank of filthy mud which is exposed whenever the tide begins to ebb, impregnated with putrid animal and excrementitious matter, surrounded by rank vegetation… and emitting a most obnoxious smell… cannot fail to have a most prejudicial effect' (WO 44/614). He also cited the deplorable effect on the garrison's health of the previous attempt at cleansing in 1830.

Thus the health hazard posed by the moat had long been recognised, becoming more obvious as advances in metropolitan sanitation made its state more noticeable. In 1832, for example, the inhabitants of Trinity Square and Tower Hill had complained that 'a disease called cholera prevails to an alarming extent in the neighbourhood' and blamed it on the moat (WP 2/200/35. *Memorial of the undersigned inhabitants of Trinity Square, Tower Hill and its vicinity, to the Commissioners of the Central Board of Health, Whitehall, Westminster*, 17 July 1832). This time it was the garrison that had suffered, however, and a link with the moat (rightly or wrongly) became firmly established. Wellington was forced to take notice. Precisely what action was required was debated during the first months of 1841, the alternatives being renewed attempts at cleansing, or, as recommended by the Surgeon Major, John Hunter (Apothecary to the Tower) and others, the moat's conversion to a 'dry fosse'.

The final decision followed Wellington's receipt, in June 1841, of a note from the Royal Engineers' Office. They estimated that scouring and instituting a new management system would cost £4,630, whereas 'to convert the moat into a dry ditch and to build sewers therein to receive the soil and surface drainage' would only cost a small amount more (£4,775) (WO 44/614). It was proposed that the possibility of flooding the moat—presumably in the face of a military threat—was to be retained by keeping the sluices at Traitors' Gate. Within a few days Wellington wrote to the Master General of the Board of Ordnance. He accepted that scouring was an option, but noted that 'it must be observed however that the mass of mud would be very soon reformed in the ditch and would cost the same sum of money to remove it' (WO 44/614). His conclusion, while regretting the loss of the wet moat's defensive contribution, was to accept that 'it should be a dry ditch with a sewer and other works to carry off the water'.

Draining and infilling

The decision to transform the moat was more easily made than carried out. At a meeting of the Board of Ordnance on 15 July 1841 the Inspector General reiterated that 'the Duke of Wellington's observations respecting the health of the Garrison and inhabitants are of so paramount a character that it is incumbent to forego the defence of a wet ditch'. Equally, however, it was noted that no funds were to be forthcoming even in the following year, it not being 'intended to take any steps at present, in the contemplated work of draining the Tower moat' (WO 44/614—letter from the Commanding Engineer to the Inspector General of Fortifications, 1 July 1841, and memorandum on the above dated 15 July 1841).

The situation was exacerbated by divisions of authority. There was also opposition to expenditure on the moat when no funds had yet been set aside to repair or replace the recently burnt Grand Storehouse. The Board of Ordnance in 1842 (WO 49/166) noted the proposed expenditure of £5,359 whilst 'there is nothing for restoring the buildings of the Tower'. This comment interestingly reveals the initial intention was perhaps to restore rather than replace the Grand Storehouse: in November 1841, £180 had been spent on 'protecting the ruins'. There were vociferous objections from the Mint as well, who feared the loss of their main water source. In the end, work did not begin until March or April 1843. From then on, encouraged by a vicious campaign in the London press, it proceeded apace. A meeting of the Ordnance Board on 10 March finalised contractual arrangements for the work and agreed that a 10-horsepower engine, intended to replace the water wheels in St Thomas's Tower, should be ordered immediately (WO 49/167). On 21 April *The Times* reported that drainage works had already begun in the south moat, noting that 'the moat... is now in progress of being filled up, with a view to being converted into grounds for healthful recreation'. On 20 July the paper remarked that:

upwards of a hundred men are daily employed at the Tower in making preparations for filling up the moat. Extensive cuttings are being made in the soil for the purpose of effectually draining the swamp, and carrying off the numerous drainings which flow from the interior of the Citadel.

Exactly how the work was done, or in what order, is not always clear. After the initial draining of the moat and removal of unstable silts, the next step would almost certainly have been the building of the massive brick culvert running round three sides of the castle. This was placed within a trench dug down into earlier fills. Excavation has shown, however, that it was not inserted through the 1840s backfill but had rather been sealed in by the latter. The ordering and fixing of the cast iron downpipes to the Tower's outer wall in 1843 (WO 49/168; the suppliers were Messrs G Thompson and Sons), presumably linked to the culvert from the outset, suggests that this became operational very early on. At the same time, or immediately following, the massive task of deliberate infilling began. Trouble seems to have been taken to compact the fill, the upper levels containing carefully laid spreads of fine rubble and clinker. The grading of the surface was done with great skill, the ground level rising as much as 1.5m from south to north, approximately following the fall of the buried culvert. In spite of unforeseen difficulties encountered in 1844, the contractor being granted an additional £50 to overcome them (WO 47/2000, fols 3854–5), the main operation seems to have been complete by the end of 1845.

DRAINING THE MOAT: THE ARCHAEOLOGICAL EVIDENCE

Both the main culvert and several of the secondary ones which drained into it (Fig 153) were revealed during the 1996–7 excavations. The principal exposures of the main culvert were in trenches 25 (Fig 62), 27 (Fig 154), 30 and 31, while it was also seen in trenches 42, 81 and 83 and test pits 40, 41, 47 and 66. Secondary culverts were recorded in trenches 12, 27, 30 and 31, and in test pits 33, 36, 38, 50, 55 and 62. Water that accumulated in the main culvert was (and still is) allowed to drain out into the Thames at low tide through one or both of two penstocks in the south moat. The control mechanisms for these can still be seen. The western penstock (in the Bowling Green) was examined in test pit 34. This exposed the original Victorian brickwork of the manhole for the culvert. The upper courses of the manhole had been rebuilt at some point in the recent past with engineering bricks.

The construction of the culverts was clearly a massive engineering and structural project in its own right. A deep trench for the main drain was dug into the moat fills, with vertical sides for the bottom *c*2m. Evidence for shoring of this trench was found in trench 25 at the south-east corner, where several horizontal planks survived *in situ*. The excavations here also demonstrated that the construction gangs did not worry when they encountered historically significant structures such as the Iron Gate causeway. They simply tore a hole through the latter's masonry, leaving ragged edges to either side. The large ashlar facing blocks were dumped unceremoniously in the backfill of the construction trench. The same pattern was followed where the culvert passed through the central arch of the south-western entrance causeway. Here it was Edward I's foundation raft of beech piles which got in the way, but several individual timbers were simply dragged out and, again, dumped in the backfill. The ascription of these to Edward I's work was established dendrochronologically (Chapter 5).

The walls of the culvert's rectangular-sectioned chamber were built close against the face of the trench, with a gap of no more than 50mm in most places. This probably militated against the survival of more of the shoring. The upper part of the construction trench sloped outwards, typically at around 45°, to allow room for turning over the vault of the culvert. Straight joints in the brickwork at several points probably indicate gangwork or defined break points in the construction programme. The bricks themselves were typical mid-19th-century yellow and red stocks. The construction quality was fair, if somewhat crude, and mortar bonding was often absent. This may be due to leaching out or erosion by water seeping into or out from the drain. The effect was to create a very leaky drain.

The majority of the secondary culverts were of similar build to the main drain, but for the most part they were cylindrical. They were found coming through the outer curtain wall in the north and south moats, through the west side of St Thomas's Tower and through the revetment of the Lion Tower moat on the west side of the Bowling Green at the south-west corner of the moat. Perhaps surprisingly, no drains were noted coming through the late 17th-century revetment wall. At least one of the

Fig 153   A plan of the Tower moat drawn up in 1850 by or for the architect Anthony Salvin. The plan shows the drainage arrangements in the recently backfilled moat, including the new reservoir in its northern arm.

Fig 154   General view of trench 27 showing the Royal Engineers' culvert running across the excavation. Note also the outer curtain wall reflected in the water filling the centre of the trench – a reflected arrow-loop is also visible.

secondary drains had a straight joint in the brick-work like those seen in the main culvert. They generally discharged into the top part of the latter and appeared to have been built at the level from which the moat was backfilled.

A further feature associated with the new moat drainage was a reservoir dug into the centre of the north moat. A survey of *c*1850 recorded the capacity of the reservoir as 48,778 gallons (Fig 153), but its exact purpose is unclear. It probably acted as a settling tank for silt within the culvert and also to store excess water between the low tides when the culvert could be drained into the Thames. This showed up very clearly on the resistivity and ground-probing radar surveys undertaken during 1995 and 1996 (Fig 21); indeed the position of the reservoir is visible as a shallow depression in the grass. The south-western corner of the reservoir was examined in trench 42 during 1997 (Figs 155–7).

The structure had involved the excavation of a deep trench (5135) through the earlier moat fills from a level of 0.85m OD and into the London Clay. The bottom of 5135 lay beyond the safe depth of excavation, but it certainly lay well below 0m OD. This meant that only very small areas of pre-Victorian stratigraphy survived within the trench. Both the reservoir and the inspection chamber attached to its west side had been built up within 5135, using mostly unfrogged bricks measuring 230mm by 110mm by 70mm. A few frogged bricks were used as well; these were of the same dimen-

sions as the unfrogged ones. An equivalent inspection chamber is shown at the east end in a contemporary plan by Anthony Salvin.

The western face (4209) of the reservoir had evidently been constructed first, because the southern face (4258) had been crudely butted against it with a mortar joint rather than being keyed in. The western wall was slightly taller than the vault, topping out at 2.8m OD. It was probably at this point that the culvert (5110) was built, as its construction trench (5111) cut through the backfill of 5135. In all probability there would have been very little time-lapse between these processes. The vaulted roof (4259) also appears to have been a later addition, perhaps at the same time as the culvert. A section of the western face had to be cut away (4273) to allow the construction of the vault and again it had been mortared rather than keyed in. The top surface of the roof survived at a level of 2.65m OD.

THE AFTERMATH OF THE DRAINING: THE NORTH BASTION

The draining and backfilling of the moat undoubtedly had solid practical benefits for Tower authorities, but the perceived loss of defensive capability seems to have caused concern. The mid- to late 1840s therefore saw the last major reassessment of the Tower's defences, enforced by the imagined threat of the Chartist movement. This had been established

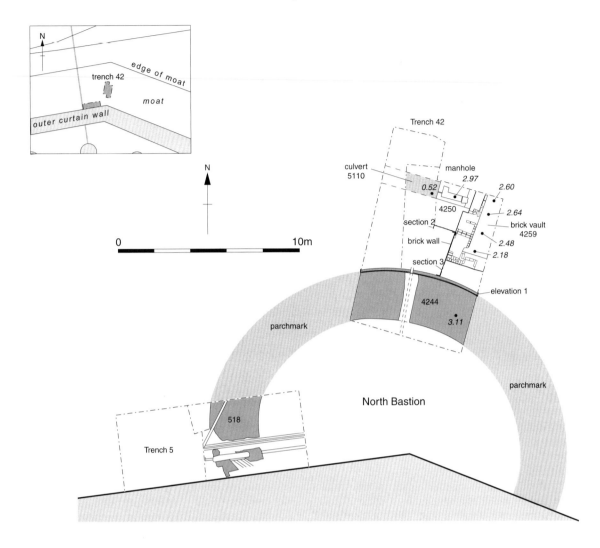

Fig 155 *Plan of trenches 5 (1995) and 42 (1997), showing the reservoir built in 1843–5 (top right-hand corner of trench 42) and the North Bastion built in 1848–52.*

in 1838 but was recognised as dangerous only between *c*1840 and 1848—especially in the context of the wave of European revolutions in the latter year. In 1846 a series of improvements were recommended and between 1848 and 1852 the western and northern ramparts overlooking the moat were modified for light artillery and musketry defence (*The Times*, 27 September 1850). The eastern wall was reinforced on similar lines in 1862 (Parnell 1995, 389), in a forlorn attempt to counter the threat of the dock buildings that had towered over it since 1829.

The most significant achievement took place with the building of the North Bastion in 1848. Built out into the filled moat at the break in alignment of the outer rampart, this was designed to provide artillery cover along the exposed faces of the wall to either side, along and over the moat, and over the approaches to the Tower from the north. Built of brick with a stone facing, it mounted three tiers of guns in casemates, with a fourth carried on the vaulted platform above (Fig 158). The foundations showed up very clearly on the geophysical and radar

surveys, and in dry conditions they can be identified as a parch-mark in the grass. The bastion presented interpretative problems for the reflooding scheme, so two trenches (5 and 42) were excavated in 1995 and 1997 respectively to examine it further (Figs 155–7). Only the upper surface of the wall was seen in trench 5, which is therefore not considered further here.

The construction trench (5115) for the semi-circular bastion (4244) had been cut vertically into dumped post-1843 fills 5125–8. The foundations were constructed in two stages. The first comprised concrete (mortar and limestone, 5113) which survived in good condition to 1.4m OD. The concrete had clearly been poured directly against the trench face and its bottom was not found within the excavation. The second stage (5112) comprised seven courses of red brick in English Bond, offset by 75mm. The top of the foundations lay at *c*1.8m OD. The bastion was faced with Kentish Rag limestone ashlar blocks (4241). The surviving masonry was in good condition (except for some cracks caused by bomb damage) and stood 1.12m high to *c*3m OD.

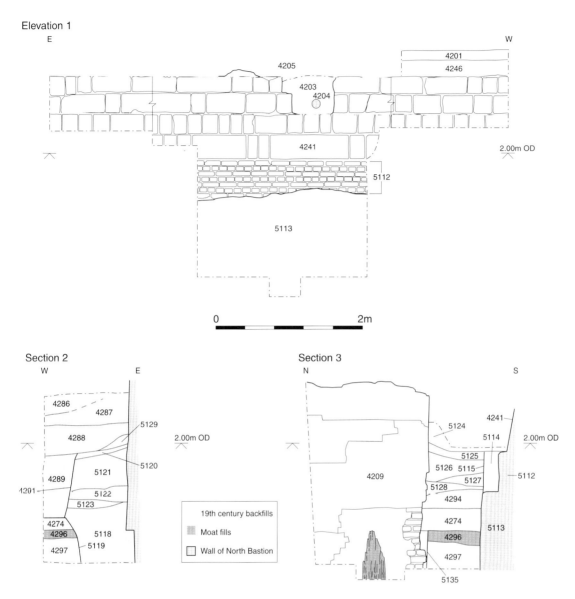

Fig 156   Sections against the Victorian reservoir and North Bastion (bottom), and elevation of the North Bastion (top), all in trench 42.

The masonry had a 20° battered face in keeping with the outer curtain wall. No stonework was identified on the interior face; instead this was constructed from red bricks (4243) bonded with greyish white mortar to a height of 3.05m OD. The brickwork was 2.3m wide (2.6m to the face of the ashlar). The interior of the bastion was not excavated in either trench 5 or 42.

THE LATER USES OF THE MOAT

Uses of the dry moat 1845–1996

Suggestions had been made as early as 1610 for making the best of the moat, or at least its perimeter, for recreation. This consideration surfaced again with the proposals for infilling the moat, public interest being stimulated by optimistic journalism.

A report in *The Times* of April 1841, for example, stated that the moat was being filled 'with a view to being converted into grounds for healthful recreation'. In July the same paper claimed that 'when work is completed, it is intended to lay out a considerable portion of the ground in ornamental gardens'; drawings exist setting out elaborate proposals. Other suggestions were equally unsuccessful, including the petition by Harrison, the works contractor, for a three-year lease of the newly reclaimed ground for growing mangel-wurzel. The application was declined, understandably, on the principle that 'possession of the Tower ditch should never be given to an individual unconnected with the Department' (WO 47/1986, fols 13, 922–4). By mid-1846 a decision had been taken—and effected—to put the whole area down to grass (*The Times*, 3 April 1846).

Fig 157   Trench 42 in the north moat was sited to examine the reservoir built in 1843–5 during the draining and backfilling of the moat, and the North Bastion, built within a few years of the completion of backfilling. The walls and vaulted chamber of the reservoir can be seen on the far side of the trench (the excavator with the planning board is standing on the chamber). The excavator holding the surveying staff is standing on the curving wall of the bastion.

Fig 158   Photograph of the North Bastion, seen from the west in 1900.

Since then the moat, or areas of it, has served a wide variety of functions. The open space was used for drilling by the Tower Garrison; in 1852 it was proposed that the space be made available to the Tower Hamlets Militia for the same purpose (WP 2/211/212). Cows which had previously been stalled inside the castle were removed to pasturage in the ditch in 1865; a painting of *c*1870 shows sheep grazing there (WO 94/58/14). In the 1880s the area to the south of the south-west causeway was used as vegetable gardens, probably extending along the whole of the south moat. A report of 1908 states that 'the southern moat is used as a garden by the Warders'. It added that 'the east and the adjacent half on the north side is grass and maintained by the bailiff of the Parks, the remaining half of the northern moat and the western moat are gravelled' (Works 14/224). A recently discovered photograph shows that soldiers were housed in temporary tents in the east moat (Fig 159). The exact date of the photograph is unknown, but it must post-date the early 1890s as Tower Bridge is visible in the background.

During the Second World War a larger area of the moat was turned over to allotments (Fig 160). Since then the moat has been used almost exclusively for recreation, access being confined to the military, Tower staff, their families and guests. New facilities have included a bowling green in the isolated area of former moat to the south of the Middle Tower causeway, a tennis court in its north-east corner and

a children's playground beside the Develin Tower. Occasional or one-off activities have included the spectacularly successful performance of *The Yeomen of the Guard,* directed by Anthony Besch (Peter Rice pers comm), staged during the London Festival of 1968, and the annual Tower Jog to raise funds for charity.

Fills of 1843–5

The backfilling of the moat presumably began as soon as the drainage was in place. A layer of mixed building rubble, clay and soil was dumped over the whole of the moat to a general depth of at least 1m. The infill was thinnest against the revetment wall, where the greatest depth of earlier fills survived, and thickest close to the outer curtain wall. Here the backfill was as much as 2m thick. Two quite clear horizons of fill were present. The lower one was predominantly clay and represented dredged material which had been dumped in the moat. Finds included pottery, clay pipes, brick and tiles, mostly of 19th-century date but including earlier material.

The horizon above this comprised an extremely compact series of mortar, sand and rubble lenses, again with predominantly 19th-century finds. This level incorporated earth and building rubble from the foundation trenches of the Waterloo Barracks, under construction in 1845 (*The Times*, 15 May 1845), and debris from the fire-damaged 17th-century Grand Storehouse which it replaced. *The Times* of

Fig 159 The east moat with tents pitched. The date of the photograph is uncertain, but the military uniforms suggest the late 19th century.

Fig 160   Digging for Victory: the south moat in use as a vegetable garden during the Second World War.

14 December 1844 reported that 'the military quartered at the Tower are now actively engaged in removing the rubbish from the ruins of the grand storehouse, and laying it down in the moat that surrounds this fortress'. Terracotta fragments found in trench 4 probably came from that building.

Access into the backfilled moat at the south-west entrance

Access into the newly backfilled moat was provided initially by a timber ramp along the north side of the causeway between the Middle and Byward Towers, starting from the latter and stopping in front of the central arch through the causeway itself (Fig 161). This decking was replaced in the later 19th century when the current ramp into the moat was built next to the Middle Tower. Traces of the original survived, however, in the form of a square arrangement of four stone pier bases (3183) against the Byward Tower (Figs 162, 163) and a massive stone slab (31104) in front of the arch. The sides of the square were 2m long. The four bases were all square in plan as well, with the sides being 0.48–0.55m long. The top edges

were chamfered and each had a central square recess at 1.91–1.95m OD. The distance between the outer edges of these recesses provides a maximum width for the ramp superstructure of c1.8m. They would have contained the timber uprights to support the decking as it joined the causeway. The southern two bases lay directly on the late 13th-century wall (3184) at the east end of the causeway, but the significance of this masonry was not recognised by the ramp-makers. The northern bases had their own brick foundations.

The slab was 2m long (the same distance as the sides of 3183) and 0.5m wide, with a rebate along the central 1.8m of its eastern upper edge. This provided the seating for the bottom of the ramp, which evidently rested at roughly 1.7m OD. This is approximately 0.8m below the existing grass level, showing that the upper part of the soil profile must date to the later 19th and 20th centuries.

Post-1845 fills

The upper metre or so of the soil profile in most parts of the moat comprised coarse rubble and soil, with at

Fig 161   A late 19th-century illustration of the access ramp next to the Byward Tower into the backfilled moat. Note that the Lion Tower has been demolished, while the Waterloo Barracks (for which the foundation stone was laid in 1845) can be seen to the left of the White Tower.

least one compacted gravel horizon. This may have been a deliberately laid surface. The rubble content ranged from broken and whole bricks, tiles and other building materials to large blocks of walling that had clearly come from demolitions. It was rarely possible to determine the exact context in which these had taken place, but candidates include dockland works, excavation and tunnelling operations on the London

Underground, and rebuilding in the post-war period after the blitz of 1940. These did not contain large quantities of finds.

Re-facing the Develin Tower

As described in Chapter 7, only three courses of the documented late 17th-century refacing of the tower

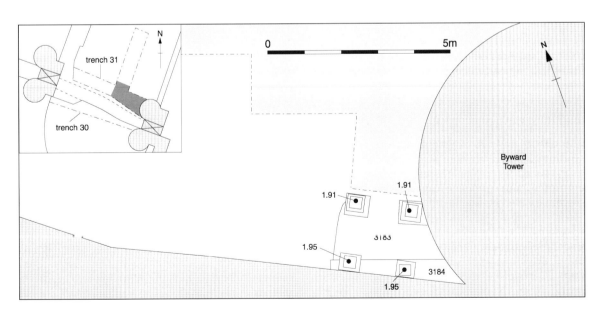

Fig 162   Plan of granite bases for the post-backfill access ramp into the moat next to the Byward Tower, as exposed in trench 31.

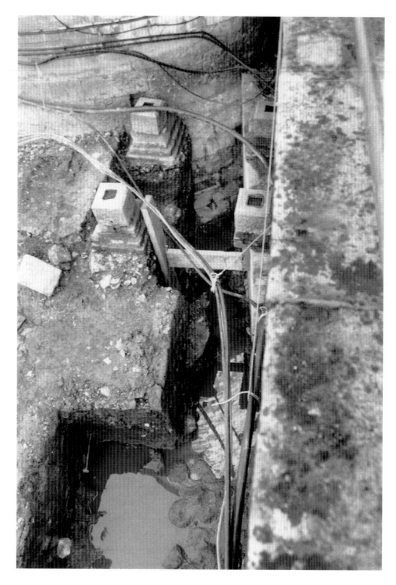

Fig 163   Detailed photograph of the granite bases for the access ramp, as exposed in trench 31.

survived, to just below current ground level. It is clear that this reconstruction must have happened after the moat was backfilled, leading to the survival of those lower three courses. The masonry had been completely rebuilt or at least refaced above this level, probably in the later 19th century (Fig 63). This is consistent with the major programme of works on the southern outer curtain wall and associated buildings, such as the Well Tower, under Anthony Salvin in c1879. This involved much refacing work, including the east face of the Develin Tower (Parnell 1993, 105). The distinctive tooling of the 17th-century ashlar seems to have been antithetical to the medieval 'ideal' which Salvin and his fellow architect John Taylor had in mind. Presumably this rendered it unusable elsewhere as well, at least in face work. Nevertheless similar blocks were found on the rear of the Victorian flank walls in front of Traitors' Gate in 1959 (Chapter 2). The original faces would not be visible here, of course. The same

drafting is visible on a number of facing stones on the riverside wall of the wharf where they are also clearly re-used. It would make sense if stones from the late 17th-century refacing of the Develin Tower had been re-used elsewhere.

THE SECOND WORLD WAR AND ITS AFTERMATH

Damage to the North Bastion and its surroundings

Late 19th- and early 20th-century deposits in trench 42 had been disturbed at c3.15m OD by the demolition of the North Bastion after the direct bomb hit on 5 October 1940 (Fig 164). The area enclosed by the bastion wall was covered with a 0.5m-thick layer of loose mortar (5132) containing 80 per cent Kentish Rag rubble. The deposit was too loose and uneven to have been an effective hard-core or make-up layer for the building's internal floor

216

Fig 164   The North Bastion in the aftermath of the direct bomb hit on 5 October 1940.

and is much more likely to have been demolition material. Several other buildings around the Tower also suffered damage during the Blitz. These included the Old Hospital Block and the late Victorian Main Guard. Although many of the buildings were repaired or restored the North Bastion was not, and the line of the outer curtain wall was restored in its place. Obviously the soils above 3.15m OD were of post-war date as well.

A wrought-iron gate was recovered from the post-war rubble in trench 42. It measured 1.8m by 1.37m and was found at 2.93m OD, approximately 0.6m below the surface. Late 19th/early 20th-century photographs clearly show several iron fences across the moat close to the North Bastion. One dating from 1898 also shows a gateway (Fig 158; John Stone, Birmingham Reference Library 147/29), and there is little doubt that the gate from trench 42 belonged to this.

Concrete blocks in trenches 14 and 25

Substantial blocks of concrete were found in two of the east moat trenches, 14 and 25. Structure 1416 ran roughly north–south across trench 14 (Fig 59) and may have been the capping for a service such as a ceramic drainpipe. The concrete (2569, in feature 2570) in trench 25 was much more substantial. It was not fully revealed within the trench in either plan (Fig 62) or section (Fig 119), but it appeared to be roughly square with sides at least 1.3m long. The top of the block lay at 1.84m OD and it continued down

for at least 1m. The north corner of the concrete was hard against the remains of the Iron Gate causeway and had evidently been poured against it, but fortunately no attempt had been made to cut into the historic masonry. The function of the block is not clear, but barrage balloons were tethered in the moat during the Second World War and the concrete may well have been one of the tethering points. It is conceivable that feature 1416 served the same function rather than being a service capping.

THE LATER 20TH CENTURY

Mains services were found in many of the trenches and test pits on all sides of the moat. Electricity, gas, water and drains were all represented. Most were found within the top metre of the soil profile, but a few were more deeply set. Fortunately they rarely caused serious disruption to the earlier moat fills.

A partial collapse of de Gomme's revetment wall in 1976

Part of the late 17th-century revetment wall to the east of the Postern Gate collapsed in 1976 because of a burst water main that flooded the unconsolidated fills behind the masonry (Fig 165). The latter was rebuilt with modern brick. The extent of foundation works for the rebuild was unknown prior to the 1995 and 1996 excavations. A stretch of the revetment running west from the north-east corner was rebuilt at about the same time, probably in association with

Fig 165   Part of the original late 17th-century revetment wall collapsed in the 1970s when a water main burst behind it. This photograph shows the rubble of the collapsed wall in the north moat.

the construction of a new subway under Tower Bridge Approach. There does not seem to have been an archaeological input to either project. These 1970s rebuilds were exposed in trench 6 (Fig 166), test pits 20 and 21 (western rebuild) and test pit 22 (eastern rebuild). The character of the foundations was so similar that they are described together here.

A substantial reinforced concrete foundation (613, 2010, 2107 and 2211) was sunk into the edge of the moat. The top of the concrete lay at about 2.7m OD, although there was an upstand at the southern edge some 3.5m from the revetment rising to 3.14m OD. This upstand had clearly been poured against steel shutters, the corrugated impressions of which were obvious on the southern edge of the structure. This continued down to at least 1.5m OD, and it seems likely that it would have penetrated to the under-lying natural London Clay. The ends of the foundation were exposed at the edges of the test pits, but their full depth could not be revealed because of health and safety constraints on the excavations. The concrete was at least 1.2m thick from its upper surface where it was exposed at the ends of the structure, and it seems likely that it was a solid mass down the full depth of the revetment. The latter had been rebuilt from the surface of the concrete upwards in modern brick (618, 2011, 2108, 2212), with a near-vertical face. This means that the battered de Gomme masonry projects forward from the modern work by 0.68m at the current ground level.

Temporary works in the moat for the Docklands Light Railway

The construction of the Docklands Light Railway (DLR) in the late 1980s and early 1990s affected the north-western revetment. Tunnelling operations at a depth of *c*15m below surface level along the line of the wall necessitated the insertion of supporting works in the moat to shore up the revetment for the duration of the construction programme. The excavations for the supporting works do not appear to have been monitored or recorded archaeologically.

Concrete was also used extensively for the temporary enabling works inserted into the north-west moat while the DLR tunnel was being bored under the north-west revetment. A concrete beam (309, 1911 and 2016) had been poured against the face of the wall. The concrete was up to 1.3m wide and 0.85m deep with an upper level of *c*2.9m OD in trench 3, 3.17m OD in test pit 19 and 3.18m OD in test pit 20. Concrete piles (six, not numbered individually in trench 3; three, group context 1912 in pit 19) were also found between 2.7m and 4m out (south) from the wall. The piles had been drilled at raking angles for stability; their depth could not be ascertained within the depth of the excavations. Photographs show that there was a concrete beam or series of pads capping the piles. These had been grubbed out (feature 307) after the DLR work had been completed.

218

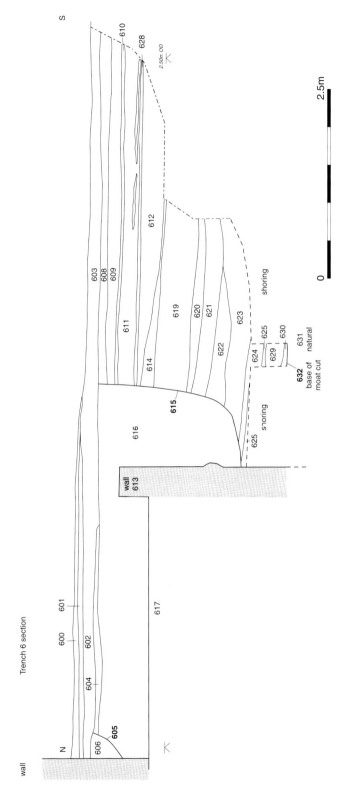

Fig 166   The eastern section of trench 6, excavated in 1995, showing the concrete foundation for the rebuilt revetment wall to the left.

FINDS

Pottery

Post-1843 contexts in trench 25 saw the appearance of 19th-century types such as refined earthenware. There was also a complete late stoneware blacking bottle. Earlier material was also present, however, and much of the pottery was clearly residual. Post-1843 contexts were not very productive in trench 27 but later 19th-century types such as transfer-printed ware and refined earthenware were present. Most were found in context 2859, although two complete redware paint pots, with their contents intact, were recovered from context 2821. The latest contexts contained very little pottery, but the majority belonged to the late 19th or 20th centuries. Most of this material came from context 2745, including two almost complete refined earthenware jam pots and several sherds of late English stoneware.

Similarly, most deposits containing pottery in trench 30 clearly post-dated the 1843 drainage programme. The finds include two complete London stoneware blacking bottles of late 19th- or early 20th-century date. Other late wares include red earthenware and refined earthenwares such as transfer-printed products and flowerpots. The earliest piece is a body sherd of Iberian coarseware, which is undoubtedly residual. There are other pre-1850 types, including red Border ware, red stoneware, Creamware, Cane ware and Pearlware, but these are all likely to be have been incorporated during the 1843 works, which probably involved the disturbance and redeposition of earlier deposits.

Post-1843 context 3165 in trench 31 contained almost exclusively Creamware and included some substantial fragments. This suggests that these finds may have been contemporary rather than residual. Other post-1843 contexts included high numbers of transfer printed ware and other refined earthenwares. Sunderland slipware, garden pottery and a Rhenish seltzer bottle are also late types. Earlier material was present too, including Black Basalt and tin-glazed earthenware. Once again, some degree of disturbance and redeposition is indicated.

The quantity of pottery is relatively low but there are some complete vessels or vessel profiles and deposition would appear to have been opportunist rather than the result of a continuous process of waste disposal.

ANIMAL BONE

One hundred and sixty three fragments of identifiable bone (15.27 per cent of the total assemblage) were recovered from Victorian/modern contexts (Table 5). The small size of the modern sample and uncertain origin of the animal bone prohibits detailed discussion and comparison with the post-medieval assemblage. Many context groups are likely to have been affected by significant degrees of residuality and the animal bone generally showed many similarities with the earlier phase. Cattle, sheep, pig and domestic fowl continued to be present and the varied nature of the diet is evidenced by the remains of deer and hare. Dog and cat were also present. The large size of some sheep bones may be an indication of post-medieval origin, but the majority of bones derived from animals similar in size to those found at other modern sites. Further details are available in the archive.

CONCLUSION: THE MOAT TODAY AND IN THE FUTURE

Following the completion of the excavations in 1997, the last trenches were backfilled and remaining spoil was taken away. Trenches were reseeded and today's visitors see little or no evidence that such an extensive campaign of excavations ever took place. An application to the Heritage Lottery Fund for financial assistance towards the reflooding was turned down in 1997 and there now seems to be little prospect of the project going ahead because of the very substantial costs involved. This report therefore draws the whole operation to a conclusion and the results of the archaeological project will now pass into the permanent archive housed at the Tower of London.

Appendix 1: The Pottery

by Duncan H Brown and Robert Thomson

The catalogue of ware and vessel types is set out with English wares described first followed by imported types, in chronological order. English wares are ordered according to increasing distance from London — thus London products are described before those from Surrey and so on. Imported wares are similarly arranged in order of increasing distance from London, with French wares followed by Low Countries and Rhenish products, and so on. The quantities of each ware are given by rim percentage (rp), weight in grams and sherd count. Detailed fabric descriptions are not necessary for most of the wares in this assemblage as they are familiar post-industrial types (eg, Creamware and transfer printed ware) or medieval and later types that have been described elsewhere.

ENGLISH WARES

Residual early pottery

Romano-British

47rp   467g   27 sherds

It is not surprising to find a small quantity of residual Romano-British material. This group includes black-burnished ware, mortaria, Samian and greyware.

Early medieval flint-tempered ware

0rp   4g   1 sherd

A single body sherd of a hand-built flint-tempered ware, of early medieval date, is a residual find in a 19th-century context.

Medieval English pottery

Shelly sandy ware

13rp   80g   2 sherds

This is an early medieval coarseware dating to the latter half of the 12th century and into the 13th. One rim sherd from a cooking pot or jar and a body sherd from a similar vessel occur in contexts that may be dated to the same period.

High medieval coarseware

0rp   61g   2 sherds

One body sherd and a base sherd represent two high medieval coarseware cooking pots or jars. The body sherd was recovered from a 13th-century context while the base is residual in a 15th-century deposit.

London-type ware

0rp   296g   7 sherds

Several London-type ware jugs are represented in this assemblage and all but one are from contexts dated to the high medieval period. The other is in a 19th-century deposit. London-type ware is another common find for high medieval London (Vince *et al* 1991) and it is no surprise to find it here.

Mill Green ware

0rp   36g   2 sherds

Mill Green ware was present in London from the end of the 13th century to around 1350. It is a redware, usually taking the form of white-slipped, green-glazed jugs. Both sherds here are residual, one in a 15th-century context and the other in a deposit dated to the 18th century.

High medieval greyware

0rp   21g   1 sherd

A single body sherd from a jug in a reduced sandy fabric occurs in a medieval context and is dated to the high medieval period (*c*1250–1350).

High medieval green-glazed redware

0rp   28g   1 sherd

The thumbed base of a jug in a sandy redware with a dark-green glaze occurs in a medieval context and has been dated to the high medieval period. This may be a fragment of Mill Green ware, which is one of the redware products of this period found most frequently in London.

Late medieval sandy wares

121rp   1512g   61 sherds

Fig A1.1 No 1

Late medieval sandy wares in broadly similar fabrics with quartz and iron inclusions are identifiable by the use of high firing temperatures and the sparse use of glaze. They occur here in a range of forms, including jars, handled cooking pots, bowls, jugs, mugs and a chafing dish. Some are residual in later contexts but many are from contexts dated to the 15th or early 16th centuries.

Kingston-type ware

12rp 85g 5 sherds

Kingston-type ware is a high medieval whiteware made at Kingston upon Thames and is a common find in medieval London (Pearce and Vince 1988). Two jugs are represented in 15th-century contexts, one by a rim and spout and the other by a slashed handle. Both vessels had an external copper-green lead glaze.

Coarse Border ware

73rp 1,509g 43 sherds

Fig A1.1 Nos 2–3

Coarse Border ware was produced at kilns on the Hampshire/Surrey border around Farnham and also further north towards Kingston upon Thames, from the late 13th century to *c*1500. This is a white earthenware with frequent coarse and medium quartz inclusions, often with a green glaze. Jars, bowls and jugs are all represented here. Some sherds appear to be in contexts that can be dated to the 15th century, although others are residual.

Surrey whiteware

39rp 104g 6 sherds

Surrey whiteware is a term applied, mainly by archaeologists working outside London, to the finer Hampshire/Surrey products that were made alongside Coarse Border ware and before Border ware. The date-range for this ware extends beyond 1500 (the end date for Coarse Border ware) up to the beginning of Border ware proper at around 1550. Two bowls, a jar or cooking pot and a jug are represented here.

Cheam whiteware

0rp 22g 1 sherd

Cheam whiteware is a late medieval product, with a date-range of around 1350 to 1500. The single body sherd present is from a 15th-century context.

Tudor Green

0rp 35g 2 sherds

Fig A1.1 No. 4

Tudor Green ware was the finest product made at the Hampshire/Surrey kilns in the 15th century. Cups, bowls and small jugs were the typical vessel types but the two sherds here are from a costrel and a money-box. Both are residual in later contexts.

Late medieval green-glazed whiteware

10rp 17g 1 sherd

The rim of a flanged bowl in a fine white fabric with a copper-green lead glaze is something of a curiosity. It occurs in an 18th-century context but is probably 15th- or early 16th-century in date. The form is unusual and the fabric suggests either Tudor Green ware or Beauvais whiteware.

Miscellaneous medieval sandy wares

12rp 53g 6 sherds

A number of small sherds in undistinguished wheel-thrown sandy fabrics have been grouped together as 'medieval', which signifies a date-range from the 13th to the 15th centuries. Two sherds came from deposits dated to the late medieval period. Four sherds occurred in 19th-century contexts.

Post-medieval English pottery

Post-medieval redware

1,839rp 34,419g 482 sherds

Figs A1.1–A1.6 Nos 5–34

Post-medieval redware is the most common ware group in the Tower moat assemblage. Early redware, which is essentially 16th-century in date, is represented by only five sherds. The majority of this group may therefore be dated to the 17th, 18th and 19th centuries, and mostly the latter. Plain, clear-glazed redware, fine redware and manganese-glazed redware are all represented, the latter by a single sherd from a mug. The range of forms includes jars, handled jars, paint pots, dishes, bowls, jugs, mugs, porringers and chafing dishes. The fabric is essentially a fine sandy ware that fires bright red. Some vessels have been identified as Hampshire products, from kiln sites around the South Downs in the area of Bishop's Waltham and Petersfield, but the origins of much of this material cannot be determined without more specific fabric and form analysis. Given the nature of the stratigraphy that yielded this assemblage, such an exercise would not be worthwhile, and such a project should be aimed at a more tightly dated and less disturbed group of finds.

Metropolitan slipware

25rp 152g 2 sherds

Fig A1.6 No. 35

Metropolitan slipware is one of the characteristic earthenware finds for 17th-century London but surprisingly little was present. This may reflect the late nature of most of the deposits in the Tower moat. A dish and a large bowl are the only vessels represented.

Surrey Border ware

359rp   4,296g   103 sherds

Figs A1.6–A1.7 Nos 36–42

Surrey Border ware, so-called because it was produced on the Hampshire/Surrey border at a number of kilns around Farnham, was one of the most common earthenwares supplied to London from the mid-16th to the end of the 17th centuries. It comprises just 4 per cent of the total assemblage weight at the Tower moat, and 5 per cent of the sherd count, which perhaps emphasises the 18th-century nature of most of the material. Surrey Border ware is a fine white earthenware often covered in a variety of glazes. Brown, green, olive-green and yellow-glazed types are all represented here, in a variety of forms that includes jars, pipkins, bowls, dishes, jugs, cups, chamber pots, money-boxes and also a bedpan.

Surrey Red Border ware

37rp   312g   3 sherds

Fig A1.7 No. 43

Surrey Red Border ware is much less common than the white version described above and extends in date to the end of the 18th century. Two jars are represented here, one of which is possibly a stool pot. There is also a base of an unidentified vessel.

English tin-glazed ware

595rp   3,631g   129 sherds

Fig A1.7 Nos 44–48

Tin-glazed ware was manufactured in England from the last half of the 16th century up to the end of the 18th. The majority of the tin-glazed ware here was probably made in London and most of the main types are represented. These include plain white, plain pale blue, blue-painted, blue-and-yellow-painted, dark blue on pale blue, manganese and sponged. Drug jars, ointment pots, bowls, handled bowls, chamber pots, condiments, plates and dishes are all represented.

Verwood-type ware

0rp   150g   2 sherds

The kilns at Verwood, near Ringwood on the fringes of the New Forest, were in production at least from the 17th century to the 20th. The sandy fabric is white or buff-coloured, usually with a pale-yellow to yellow-green lead glaze, although brown-glazed wares were also produced. The peak of production seems to have been in the 18th and 19th centuries and the two sherds present here, one from a bowl, are in contexts dated to the 18th century.

Post-medieval black-glazed ware

29rp   763g   15 sherds

Black-glazed earthenwares were in common use in England from the late 16th century and throughout the 17th. All but four of the sherds found in the Tower moat are from contexts dated to that period. Jars, bowls and mugs (including a tyg) are all represented.

Post-medieval yellow-glazed whiteware

0rp   24g   2 sherds

Two sherds from a single vessel in a whiteware with a clear yellow-coloured lead glaze cannot be located to a specific source. They occur with 18th-century pottery types but may be earlier in date.

English post-medieval earthenwares

24rp   482g   17 sherds

A small group of 17th- or 18th-century earthenwares cannot be associated with any specific production centre and have been classified together simply as 'English'. Six sherds are from jars, one from a bowl and another from a green-glazed money-box. There is also a large solid rod or cylinder, unglazed, 120mm long. This may represent a handle, or perhaps a foot, of a large vessel of unknown type.

English stoneware

2,141rp   18,579g   147 sherds

Figs A1.8–A1.9 Nos 49–53 and No. 55

Much of the English stoneware present here is of the grey or brown variety and most of it was probably made in London. The range of forms includes jars, bottles, jugs and mugs. Definite London stoneware products include Bartmann-style jugs, blacking bottles, a gorge or small cup and a measure. There are two sherds of white stoneware jars.

Nottingham stoneware

23rp   209g   8 sherds

Fig A1.8 No. 54

Two bowls and a tankard are represented in Nottingham stoneware, a distinctive brown type of 18th-century date. One unidentified body sherd came from a 19th-century context.

English porcelain

45rp   366g   9 sherds

English porcelain dates from the mid-18th century, although it is likely that these pieces are 19th-century in date. The sherds represent two bowls, a cup and a saucer.

Staffordshire wares

Midland purple

15rp   484g   14 sherds

Midland yellow

0rp   26g   1 sherd

Mottled brown-glazed ware

0rp   66g   3 sherds

Black-glazed ware

0rp   118g   4 sherds

Staffordshire redware

0rp   46g   2 sherds

Slipware

70rp   964g   24 sherds

Marbled slipware

8rp   41g   1 sherd

Marbled agate ware

18rp   126g   1 sherd

White salt-glazed stoneware

122rp   673g   42 sherds

White dipped stoneware

17rp   38g   1 sherd

Red stoneware

0rp   71g   1 sherd

Black basalt ware

35rp   151g   3 sherds

Cane ware

48rp   644g   27 sherds

Bone china

78rp   109g   11 sherds

Fig A1.9 No. 58

Creamware

1,420rp   5,329g   191 sherds

Fig A1.9 No. 56

Pearlware

503rp   998g   59 sherds

Fig A1.9 No. 57

Mocha ware

27rp   45g   3 sherds

Refined earthenware

415rp   3,563g   138 sherds

Transfer-printed ware

452rp   2,786g   135 sherds

A variety of 18th- and 19th-century Staffordshire products are present. These include earthenwares such as Midland purple, black-glazed ware and slipware; stonewares such as black basalt, cane ware; bone china; and refined earthenwares such as Creamware, Pearlware, transfer-printed and painted products. The most common Staffordshire products (Creamware, refined earthenware and transfer-printed ware) date to the industrial period and later. The last two types emphasise the 19th-century date of much of the assemblage.

Sunderland wares

44rp   705g   12 sherds

Sunderland products are relatively common finds in the south of England, a by-product of the extensive traffic in coal from the north east. Slipped redwares and transfer-printed lustreware are both represented here, the latter by one sherd (the base of a tankard) weighing 22 g. Slipware bowls and a jar are also present.

Early modern earthenware

0rp   362g   1 sherd

A single base sherd of a red earthenware jar with an internal brown glaze cannot be located to a particular source and has been designated as early modern earthenware, probably of southern English origin. It occurred in a 19th-century context.

Garden pottery

338rp   2,847g   56 sherds

Fig A1.9 Nos 59–61

Nearly all the sherds in this group are from flowerpots, including three complete vessel profiles. One of the flowerpots is in an unusual white fabric while the rest are in a red terracotta-type ware. There is also a dish, or flowerpot saucer, in the same redware type. It is suggested that the redware vessels were made in England, presumably in or close to London, but the origin of the white vessel is uncertain.

IMPORTED WARES

French wares

Yellow-glazed Beauvais whiteware

0rp   12g   1 sherd

Beauvais pottery was imported into England from the well-known production site just north west of Paris in the late 15th and early 16th centuries (Hurst *et al* 1986). This is a smooth, fine white ware, usually with green or yellow glazes. A single sherd of a mug handle occurs in context 3912, which may be 15th- or 16th-century in date.

Saintonge wares

0rp   56g   3 sherds

Two body sherds come from a 15th-century Saintonge whiteware jug. A small base sherd of post-medieval Saintonge ware was also found.

Post-medieval French earthenware

0rp   57g   1 sherd

There is a single base sherd in a fine, white, unglazed earthenware that is possibly northern French in origin, and probably 17th- or 18th-century in date.

French tin-glazed ware

0rp   66g   2 sherds

Two different types of French tin-glazed ware are represented. One is a small (3g) body sherd of faience, probably northern French, with the typical dark-brown exterior glaze and a white internal tin glaze. This is from an 18th-century context. There is also the base of a small ointment pot with a turquoise glaze from a 19th-century deposit. Similar vessels are known at Canterbury and have been identified as Parisian (J Cotter pers comm).

Low Countries wares

Low Countries redware

26rp   460g   11 sherds

Low Countries redware was a common import into England in the 15th to 17th centuries (Hurst *et al* 1986). Handled cooking pots, bowls and a frying pan are represented here, including a single sherd of a white-slipped redware bowl. Five sherds occur in contexts of 16th- or 17th-century date but the rest are likely to be residual finds.

Low Countries tin-glazed ware

0rp   22g   1 sherd

There is a single body sherd from an albarello or waisted drug jar in Low Countries tin-glazed ware. This piece occurs in an 18th-century context but could be residual, as tin-glazed ware production began in the 16th century in the Low Countries.

Werra-type slipware

14rp   60g   1 sherd

Werra-type slipware dates from the late 16th to the early 17th centuries. The fabric is a fine redware decorated with white slip lines, often in concentric circles. The piece here is from a bowl and had a green lead glaze.

Weser-type slipware

12rp   61g   1 sherd

Fig A1.10 No. 62

Weser-type slipware has a similar date-range to Werra-type slipware and is in the same tradition of white slip decorated red earthenwares. The complete profile of a bowl decorated with a polychrome slip motif was recovered from a context dated to the 18th century.

Rhenish wares

Siegburg stoneware

0rp   165g   4 sherds

Sherds from four Siegburg stoneware mugs in the distinctive 15th-century pale-grey fabric occurred in four different contexts. One of those is possibly 15th-century in date, but the rest are from the 17th, 18th and 19th centuries.

Langerwehe stoneware

0rp   1,161g   2 sherds

Fig A1.10 No. 63

Two Langerwehe stoneware jugs are represented by two base sherds. One of these may be Raeren rather than Langerwehe but in either case these vessels are of 15th- or early 16th-century date and occur in contexts of about that date.

Raeren stoneware

0rp   83g   2 sherds

The body and base sherds of two Raeren stoneware mugs are residual finds in 18th- and 19th-century contexts.

Frechen stoneware

73rp   871g   30 sherds

Frechen stoneware is a common import into England in the 16th and 17th centuries, usually in the well-known form of the bearded face jugs, or Bartmann (formerly called Bellarmine). All the sherds of Frechen stoneware here are from jugs although it is not possible to identify all of them as Bartmann-type vessels. Most finds are from 17th- or 18th-century contexts but there are some presumably residual fragments in 19th-century deposits.

Westerwald stoneware

400rp   1,083g   27 sherds

Fig A1.10 Nos 64–65

Westerwald stoneware, with its distinctive cobalt-blue decoration, was among the latest of the Rhenish stonewares to be imported in quantity into Britain. It dates from the end of the 16th century to the end of the 18th, but the peak of its importation seems to have been in the first quarter of the 18th century. Thereafter it is often difficult to distinguish true Westerwald from blue-painted grey English stoneware products. Jugs, tankards and chamber pots are typical forms and are all represented here, along with later seltzer bottles. All these finds occur in 18th- or 19th-century contexts.

Stoneware seltzer bottles

0rp   223g   2 sherds

The bases of two stoneware seltzer bottles were recovered from two 19th-century contexts. Seltzer, or mineral water, was a relatively common import—often from Austria and Germany—in the 19th century. It was carried in distinctive stoneware bottles, frequently marked with the brand of water, although neither of these sherds shows such evidence.

Iberian wares

Iberian coarseware

13rp   610g   10 sherds

This group includes a variety of thick-walled types that can be grouped together as Iberian coarseware. The predominant vessel form is the jar and four sherds—one rim and three body—are of Seville-type coarseware identified as 'Iberian Olive Jar' in the Museum of London system of nomenclature. In the same ware group are two body sherds from a large jar with combed decoration on the body and a body sherd from a flask. There is also a single sherd

of an Iberian redware jar with mica and quartz inclusions. All these types have a date-range from the 15th to the 18th centuries, although the two latter vessels are likely to be at the later end.

Iberian red micaceous ware

0rp   111g   1 sherd

Iberian red micaceous ware ranges in date from the 14th to the 17th centuries and this glazed body sherd, from a jug or a jar, was recovered from a 17th-century context.

Iberian tin-glazed ware

7rp   412g   8 sherds

Fig A1.11 No. 66

Three vessels—a jar and two bowls—are represented. One of the bowls has a blackened glaze and may be early in date, while the other two examples have blue-painted designs. All three vessels are likely to be 15th- or 16th-century in date but occur in 18th- or 19th-century contexts.

Italian and Mediterranean wares

North Italian marbled slipware

9rp   62g   5 sherds

North Italian marbled slipware is essentially a 17th-century product, although production continued into the 18th century. Two bowls and a lion's head costrel (Platt and Coleman-Smith 1975, no. 1363) are represented in 17th- or 18th-century contexts, while a fragment of a bowl and an unidentified body sherd are residual finds in later deposits.

Mediterranean earthenware

0rp   409g   2 sherds

There are sherds from two olive jars in fabrics that are likely to originate from the Mediterranean and are probably of 17th- or 18th-century date. Both came from contexts dated to the same period. Olive jars of this date are not unusual finds.

Miscellaneous imported tin-glazed ware

2rp   16g   1 sherd

A single small rim sherd of a dish in a tin-glazed ware with red inclusions has been identified as an import of unknown origin. It is probably Mediterranean, either Iberian or Italian. It was recovered from a context dated to the 18th century and may be a residual find.

Oriental wares

Chinese porcelain

203rp   850g   39 sherds

Figs A1.11–A1.12 Nos 67–70

Chinese porcelain was brought into England in vast quantities from the mid-17th century. Tea-bowls, cups and small plates are represented here, mainly in the common blue-and-white style, although there is one rim of a 'famille rose' cup.

CATALOGUE OF ILLUSTRATED POTTERY

1 Mug. Late Medieval sandy ware. Unglazed. Context 3130.
2 Jug. Coarse Border ware with external clear glaze. The interior is sooted. Context 2828.
3 Jug. Coarse Border Ware with overall dark green glaze on top half, glaze runs and splashes on lower half. Context 3141.
4 Money box. Tudor Green ware with all over external green glaze. Context 3620.
5 Cooking pot. Post-medieval redware with rich internal glaze. Heavy external sooting on the body. Context 3133.
6 Handled cooking pot with thumbing below rim. Post-medieval redware with partial glaze in and out. External sooting. Context 2850.
7 Tripod cooking pot. Post-medieval redware with rich internal and external clear glaze. Heavy sooting around external body, rim and handle. Context 2850.
8 Bowl. Post-medieval redware with internal clear glaze that is worn through use. External sooting on base. Context 2567.
9 Bowl. Post-medieval redware with internal clear glaze. External sooting on base. Context 2567.
10 Bowl. Post-medieval redware, internal and external clear glaze. Context 3007.
11 Bowl. Post-medieval redware with internal greenish-clear glaze heavily scored through use. Heavily sooted on the outer wall but not on the base. Context 3005.
12 Bowl. Post-medieval redware with internal and external greenish-clear glaze. Context 3128.
13 Bowl. Post-medieval redware, internal greenish-clear glaze, partially glazed exterior. Internal kiln scar. Context 31133.
14 Straight-sided bowl. Post-medieval redware with rich internal and external clear glaze. Some wear marks inside. Context 3141.
15 Bowl. Post-medieval redware, internal clear glaze with patches on the outer surface. The internal glaze is scored through use. Context 3703.
16 Paint pot. Post-medieval redware with rich internal clear glaze. Possibly Red Surrey Border ware? Patches and runs of black paint or pitch on internal and external surfaces. Context 3133.
17 Paint pot with internal residue. Post-medieval redware. Context 2821.
18 Paint pot with white and blue paint runs on the unglazed external surface. Internal clear glaze. Post-medieval redware. Context 2821.
19 Paint pot with external white paint residue and scoring of internal clear glaze. Post-medieval redware. Context 3133.
20 Pancheon. Post-medieval redware with thick internal clear glaze. Context 2850.
21 Dish. Post-medieval redware, internal clear glaze with dark brown streaks. Blobs of clear glaze on the outside. Context 2822.
22 Dish with owner's mark on the reverse. Post-medieval redware. Internal glaze abraded or worn from base. Context 31129.
23 Dish. Post-medieval redware. Internal glaze abraded or worn from base. Context 3809.
24 Dish. Post-medieval redware with internal clear glaze showing wear marks. Possible sooting on base. Context 3166.
25 Jug with incised lines. Post-medieval redware with rich clear glaze inside and out. Heavy kiln scars at the base. Context 3192.
26 Storage jar with thumbed bands below the flanged rim. Post-medieval redware, with internal and external clear glaze. An internal glaze run shows that the vessel was fired upside down. Context 2534.
27 Storage jar with a flange below the rim. Post-medieval redware with thick internal clear glaze. Context 2850.
28 Chamber pot. Post-medieval redware with rich internal and external clear glaze. Patches of lime-scale on the inside. Context 2822.
29 Chamber pot. Post-medieval redware with rich internal and external clear glaze. Context 3128.
30 Porringer. Post-medieval redware, possibly Red Surrey Border ware. Internal clear glaze with external green and clear glaze splashes. Context 5607.
31 Chafing dish. Post-medieval redware with internal clear glaze. Context 2631.
32 Fuming pot. Post-medieval redware with an external partial green glaze on the handle and body. Context 2850.
33 Base sherd with pre-firing mark incised into outer surface. The internal glaze is scored through use. Post-medieval redware. Context 3008.
34 Moneybox fragment, broken at the slot and the knob is missing. Post-medieval redware with an overall white slip under a green glaze. Context 2854.
35 Metropolitan slipware dish with white slip wavy line around rim. Unstratified.
36 Bedpan with a tubular handle. Surrey Border ware with internal all over, and external partial green glaze. Kiln scar on handle. Context 2534.
37 Handled bowl. Surrey Border ware with internal green glaze. Context 2604.

38 Bowl. Surrey Border ware with internal yellow (clear) lead glaze and external green glaze splashes. The exterior is sooted on the unglazed areas. Context 2534.

39 Bowl. Surrey Border ware with internal yellow glaze. Context 5607.

40 Bowl with horizontal handle. Surrey Border ware with internal yellow glaze and external green glaze. A partial kiln scar on the handle is from another vessel in a red fabric. Context 5607.

41 Dish. Surrey Border ware with internal and external yellow glaze. Context 2849.

42 Dish. Surrey Border ware with internal yellow glaze that has a green patch on the rim. The glaze is worn on the base. Context 5607.

43 Jar or stool pot. Red Surrey Border ware jar. External clear glaze, runs of glaze inside show the vessel was fired upside down. Context 3008.

44 Bowl, stained either in use or deposition. English white tinglazed ware. Context 3133.

45 Bowl. English tinglazed with blurred blue decoration on a light blue base. Context 3151.

46 Chamber pot with internal limescale and staining. English white tinglazed ware. Context 3133.

47 Drug jar. English white tinglazed ware, stained black all over, probably in deposition. Context 2611.

48 Pedestal jar. English pale blue tinglazed ware. Context 3133,

49 Bartmann-type jug. English stoneware. Context 31133.

50 Jug. English stoneware, dark brown on top half, lighter brown towards base. Traces of kiln scars. Context 3131.

51 Bottle, stamped 'Geo. Price'. Fulham stoneware. Context 3072.

52 Gorge or mug with a spread eagle medallion. London stoneware, probably Dwight. Context 3133.

53 Measure or blacking holder. London stoneware. Context 3007.

54 Bowl with roulette decoration. Nottingham stoneware. Context 3104.

55 Jar base with stamped lettering 'MALING, NEWCASTLE'. English white stoneware. Context 2745.

56 Teapot. Creamware with six rosettes painted in blue and orange. Context 3128.

57 Bowl. Pearlware with blue painted decoration. The glaze is crazed and black staining has penetrated the crazed lines on the base, both internal and external. Context 3151.

58 Teacup. White bone china with faded external lustre decoration. Context 3007.

59 Flowerpot. Red earthenware. Context 3005.

60 Flowerpot. Red earthenware. Context 3007.

61 Flowerpot. White unglazed earthenware. Context 3135.

62 Dish. Weser slipware, clear glaze with green patches, with feathered slip at the rim and brown slip lines on the outside. Context 2511.

63 Jug. Langerwehe stoneware, possibly Raeren. Glossy saltglaze. The side was dented prior to firing. Context 2937.

64 Tankard with 'GR' stamp. Westerwald blue and grey stoneware. Context 3151.

65 Seltzer bottle. Westerwald blue and grey stoneware. Context 2822.

66 Lid. Spanish tinglazed, with glaze decayed to black. Context 2850.

67 Tea bowl with blue decoration. Chinese porcelain with a maker's mark. Context 1407.

68 Tea bowl. Chinese porcelain. Context 2821.

69 Mug. Chinese porcelain with blue decoration and a brown line on the rim. Context 3151.

70 Fluted plate with blue decoration. Chinese porcelain. Context 6825.

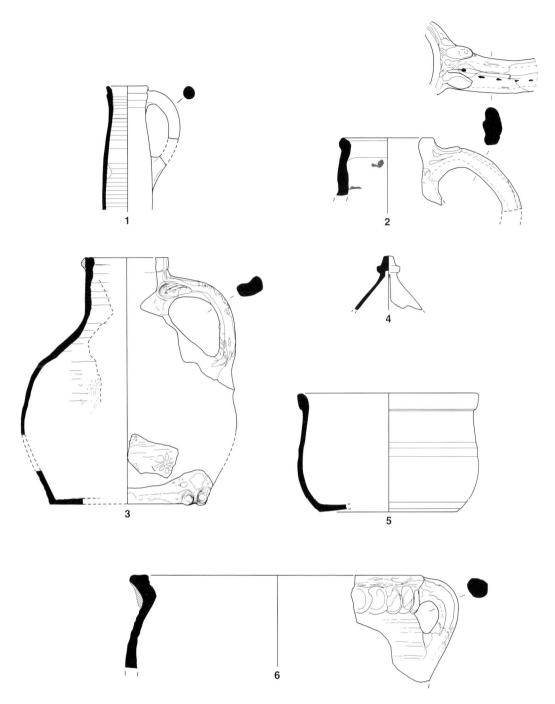

Fig A1.1 Late medieval wares and post-medieval redware. Scale 1:4.

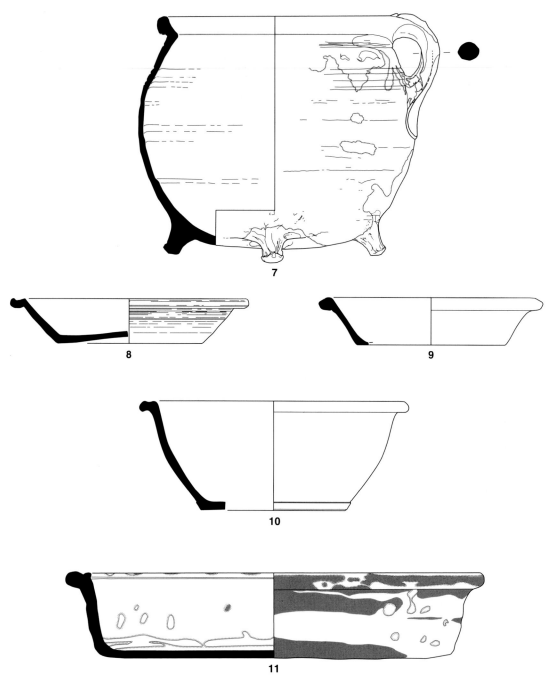

Fig A1.2   Post-medieval redware. Scale 1:4.

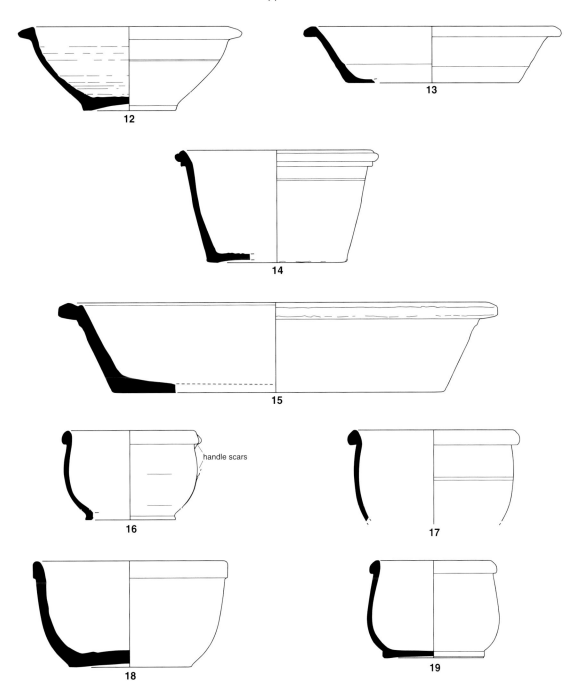

Fig A1.3   Post-medieval redware. Scale 1:4.

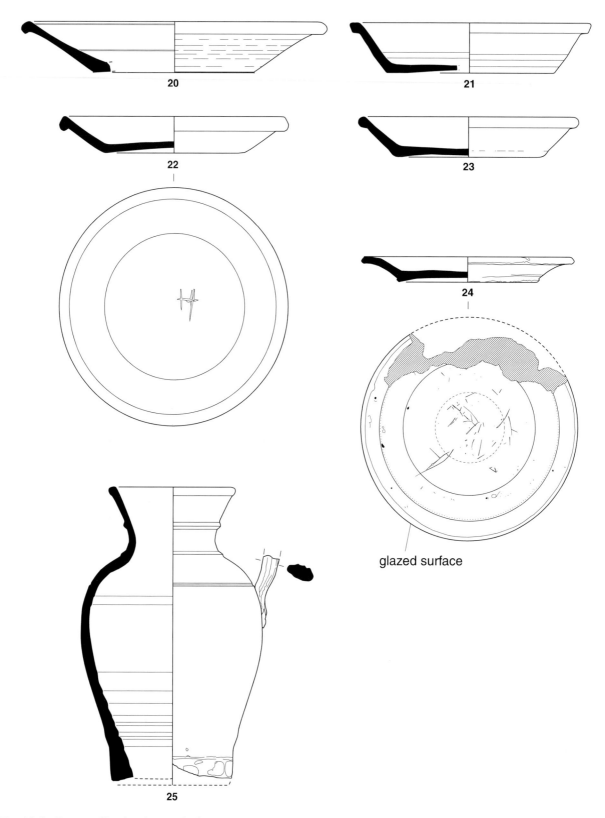

glazed surface

Fig A1.4   Post-medieval redware. Scale 1:4.

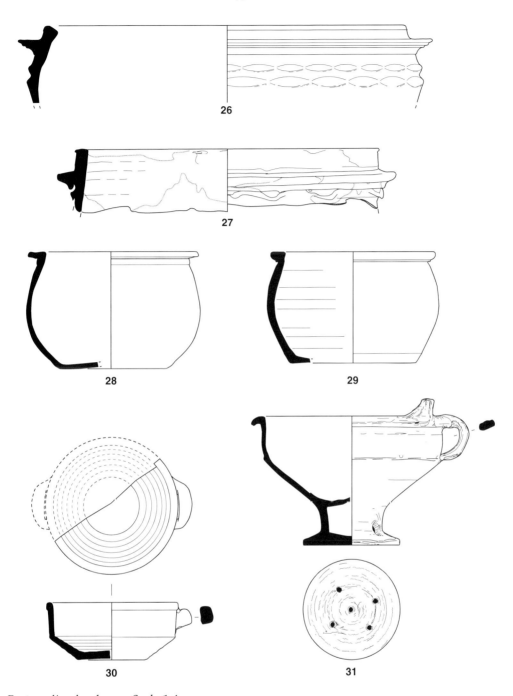

Fig A1.5   Post-medieval redware. Scale 1:4.

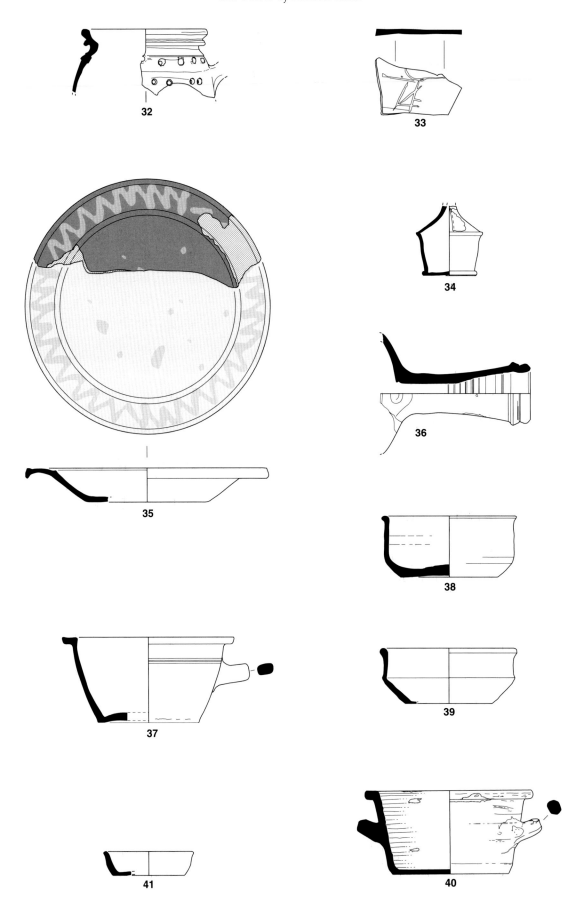

Fig A1.6   Post-medieval redware and slipped redware, Metropolitan slipware and Surrey Border ware. Scale 1:4.

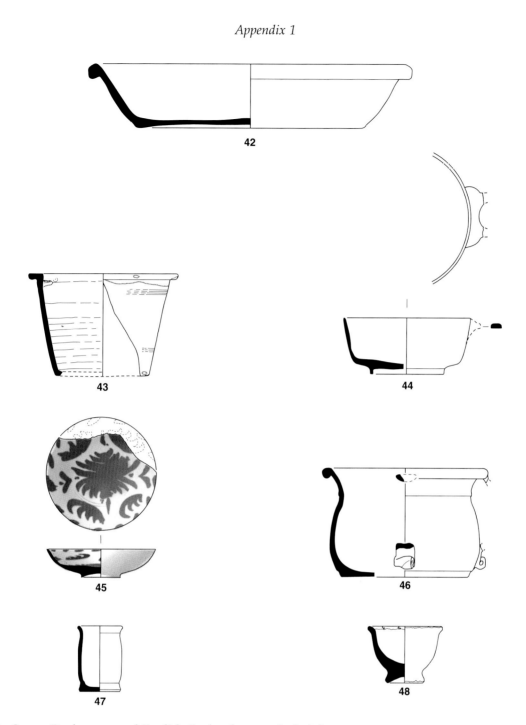

Fig A1.7 Surrey Border ware and English tinglazed wares. Scale 1:4.

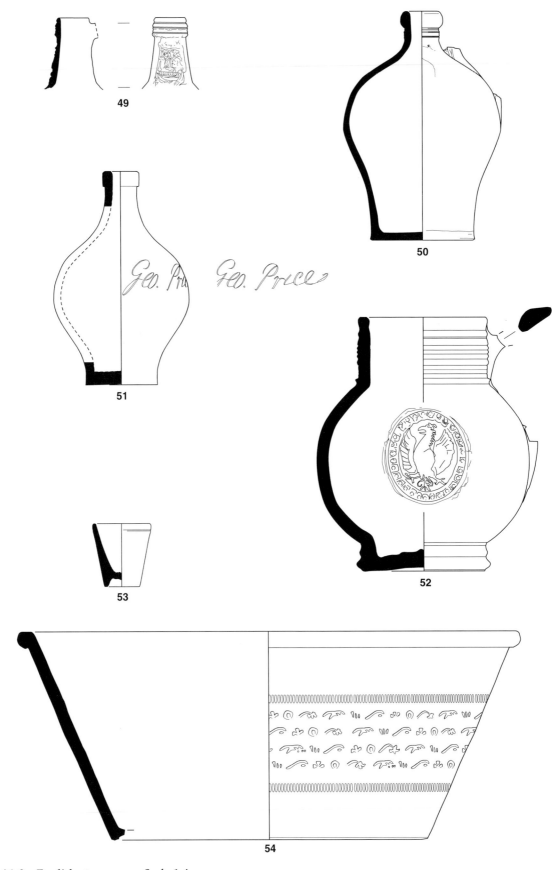

Fig A1.8   English stonewares. Scale 1:4.

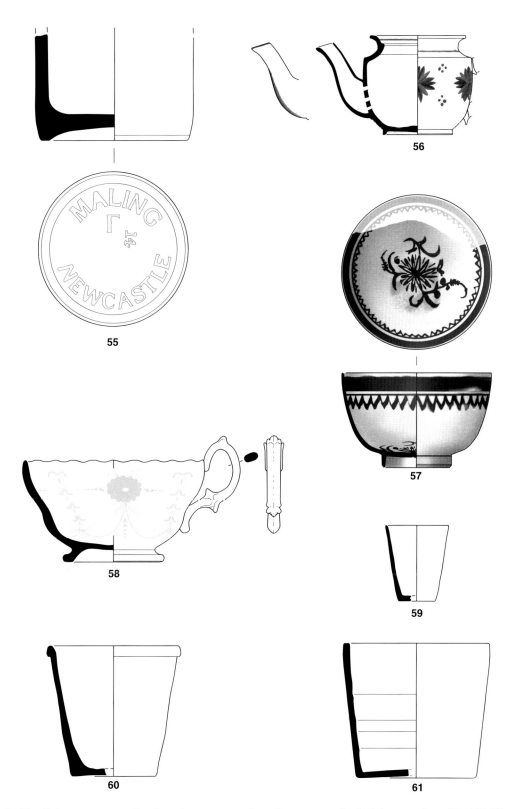

55

56

57

58

59

60

61

Fig A1.9   English stoneware, refined earthenwares and garden pottery. Scale 1:4, apart from Nos 55, 57 and 58, which are at scale 1:2.

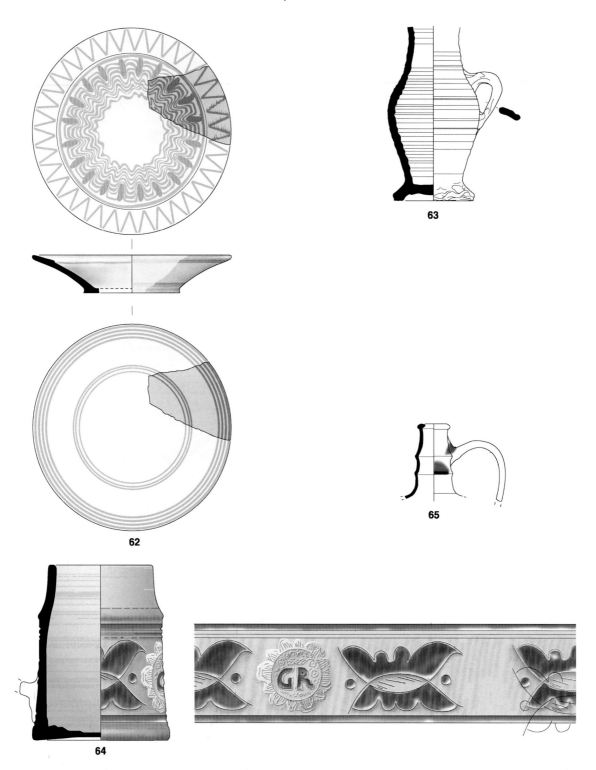

Fig A1.10 *Weser slipware, Langerwehe stoneware and Westerwald stoneware. Scale 1:4, apart from No. 64, which is at scale 1:2.*

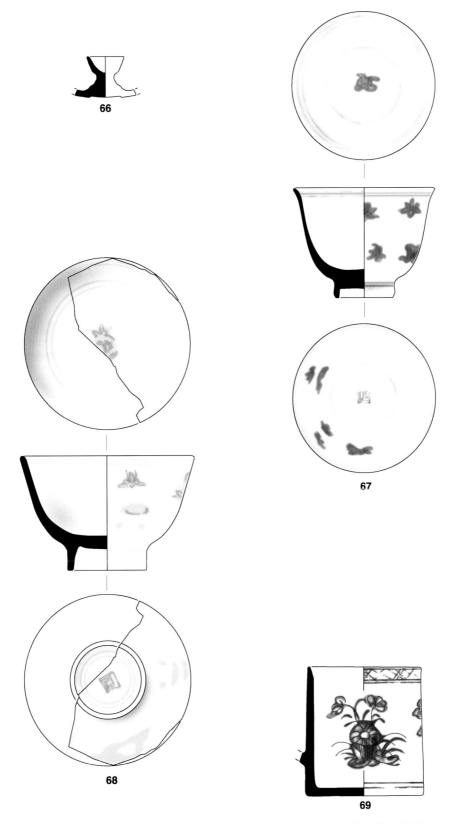

Fig A1.11   Spanish tinglazed ware and Chinese porcelain. Scale 1:2, apart from No. 66, which is at scale 1:4.

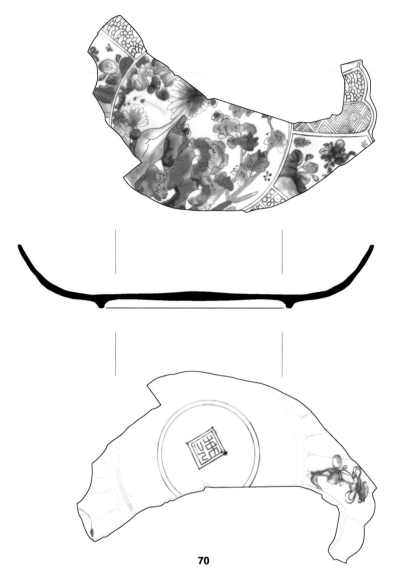

70

Fig A1.12   Chinese porcelain. Scale 1:2.

Appendix 2: The Clay Tobacco Pipes

by David Higgins

This appendix describes the clay tobacco pipes recovered during the moat excavations between 1995 and 1997. A selection have been illustrated and catalogued (Figs A2.1–5). Illustrated pipes are referred to by catalogue number in this report. The marked and decorated pipes are listed in Table A2.3.

THE BOWL FORMS AND MARKED PIPES

The Tower of London excavations included in this report have produced a total of 996 fragments of pipe, comprising 441 bowl, 537 stem and 18 mouthpiece fragments. These pipes are described and discussed collectively in the various sections below. These are followed by a section dealing with the relevance of the pipes to the archaeology of the site as a whole.

Bowl forms

None of the earliest styles of pipe, dating to c1580–1610, were encountered during the excavations. A small number of pipes of c1610–60 were recovered but the majority of the excavated pipes date from between the late 17th and mid-19th centuries. Almost all the bowls recovered are of typical London styles and would have been produced locally. Excavations in and around the City since the Second World War have produced many good groups of 17th- and 18th-century pipes, allowing a reliable typology of the standard forms to be produced (Atkinson and Oswald, 1969). In contrast, good deposits dating from around 1770 or later have proved to be surprisingly elusive in the archaeological record. The widespread use of hard surfaces, the collection of waste for disposal out of the urban area, the more fragile nature of post-1770 pipe styles and the destruction of later deposits through cellaring all appear to be contributory factors in this respect. The pipes from the Tower excavations are particularly important since they go some way towards filling this gap in the archaeological record. The soft silts of the moat provided ideal conditions for the preservation of the delicate pipe bowls and stems, while the filling of the moat in 1843–5 provides a valuable *terminus ante quem* for many of the pipe groups. Given that the earlier pipes from London are comparatively well documented, it is the late 18th- and early 19th-century material which has primarily been studied for this report.

In the following sections the pipes are described thematically according to the marks and decoration present on them. The accompanying illustrations clearly show the range of bowl forms which was being used from c1770 to 1845 (Nos 7–12; 18–38).

In the 1969 London typology there is a problem with the evolution of the heel form between c1770, when the Type 25 ends, and c1840, when the Type 29 starts. This gap is only partially filled by the Type 27, which has been dated to c1780–1820. This still leaves two gaps, 1770–1780 and 1820–1840, during which periods no heel types are recognised in the 1969 typology. The Tower of London finds provide good evidence for this period and clearly show that, as would be expected, a continuous range of heel forms was in use. These are based around the Type 27 form but with subtle variations as it evolved over time.

There are some large, thin-walled forms which usually have a trimmed base to the heel and which form a logical successor to the Type 25 form, for example, No. 48 (complete IB pipe). This example seems likely to date to c1770–1800 and so bridges the gap between the Type 25 and 27 forms in the London typology. From c1780 to 1820 the slightly shorter Type 27 form, as defined in 1969, becomes the most common type of pipe encountered although taller forms, such as No. 27, still occur. It is during this period that the trimming of the heel base as a finishing technique is discontinued. During the early 19th century heel bowls tend to become more compact and shorter, often with a less substantial and narrower heel (eg, No. 21). The later types are frequently decorated with flutes or other decorative schemes but the basic profile remains the same. Although the Type 27 bowl form occurs in a range of sub-types there is such an even gradation between the extremes as to make meaningful typological divisions based on profile alone impossible. This basic form continued to be produced right through the 1820s and 1830s, as can be seen from its general occurrence in the pre-1845 moat deposits and from the identifiable marked pieces. Although there were clearly a range of variants, the basic Type 27 form remains a valid distinction. The main revision that is necessary is to extend its overall date-range so that it now becomes c1770–1845. This bridges the gaps in the 1969 typology and accords with the evidence of marked pipes and sealed groups from the Tower moat excavations.

Alongside the Type 27 heel bowls a range of spur types was also produced (London Type 28). These are much less common and more restricted in range than the heel types. They are usually plain and are most common around 1820–40, although some examples may have been made later. Examples from the moat excavations are Nos 9–12. This form clearly continued in use later (see Context 7109 below) and the low numbers represented in this sample may be partly due to the 1840s cut off date for the majority of the excavated deposits.

The 1843–5 filling of the Tower moat sealed the earlier silt deposits and marks an abrupt change in the pattern of artefact deposition in the excavated areas. Despite this, a few later deposits did contain pipes and these show a different range from those in the moat silts. The rather funnel-shaped Type 27 bowl with its large heel was replaced by a new form, Type 29. This is characterised by a somewhat egg-shaped bowl with a much smaller heel. Context 7109 produced a good group of such bowls (Nos 41–43). This group is particularly important since it appears to be associated with the demolition of buildings around the Lion Tower in the early to mid-1850s. This not only provides a good date for the introduction of this new form but also shows how rapid and complete was the change in styles from the previous decade. Alongside the Type 29 bowls, and contemporary with them, a new spur form appears. This is essentially a shortened version of the Type 28 form with a slightly chunkier spur. Examples from the 7109 group are illustrated (Nos 39–40). This appears to have been a standard London form of *c*1840–80 and needs to be added to the London typology.

The only other forms of note are three pieces that are certainly imports to the capital. One of these is a John Hunt pipe of *c*1660–90 from the Bath or Bristol area (No. 3) and another is a Birchall pipe from Chatham of *c*1780–1820 (No. 18). Both are discussed more fully below. The other example is an unstratified find from trench 47 (No. 45). This dates from the 19th century and is an unusual piece made of white clay with a surface coating of red clay. The bowl has zones of decoration including fronds or feathers and a series of lion's head masks. This is likely to be an import from mainland Europe, possibly France or Italy. These three pieces represent just 0.68 per cent of the 441 bowl fragments recovered and show that imports never formed a significant proportion of the pipes in everyday use at the Tower.

Discussion of the stamped pipes

Eighteen of the 441 bowl fragments had stamped marks on them (4 per cent), details of which are provided in Table A2.1. Only a small proportion of London pipes were ever stamped and the numbers recovered are typical of the proportions that would be expected from the capital. The majority of the stamped marks date from *c*1680 to1845, reflecting the period of silting between the last major refurbishment of the wet moat and its final filling.

Most of the stamped pipes are of typical London styles and would have been produced locally. There are two possible exceptions. The first is a WW mark on a bowl of *c*1660–80 (No. 2). Although this bowl form could have been produced in London, it is rather more chunky and barrel-shaped than is normal. Furthermore, the bowl is finely burnished, a technique not often employed on London pipes but typical of other areas. Finally, the neat lettering

within a beaded border and flanked by dots and pierced sexfoils is very similar to the mark used by William Pemerton of Guildford in Surrey (Higgins 1981, fig 6). Pemerton is an interesting maker who produced unusually fine pipes, often beautifully burnished, and who appears to have come from Eton in Buckinghamshire. The form, finish and mark of the WW pipe suggest links between the two makers and it may be that the WW pipe was produced in the Eton area and traded to London.

The other imported piece is the John Hunt pipe from the Lion Tower (TOL 80 context 4, No. 3). The Hunt family were prominent West Country pipemakers during the 17th and 18th centuries. They appear to have started pipemaking in Norton St Philip, to the south of Bath (Lewcun 1985). John Hunt I was born there in 1628 and purchased his freedom in Bristol in 1651. He was a founder member of the Bristol Pipemakers Guild in 1652 and took an apprentice in 1653 but there is no further record of him in Bristol after this date (Lewcun 1985, 17–18). Despite this he seems likely to have worked in the town for a while since quite a wide range of mid-17th-century pipes bearing his name are known from Bristol (Jackson and Price 1974). The archaeological evidence provided by his later products suggests that he subsequently moved to the Bath area. An example of one of the Bath pipes is illustrated by Lewcun (1985, fig 16) but it differs from the London example in that the name is stamped in two lines as opposed to three.

The attribution of the John Hunt pipes is complicated by the fact that there were at least two later members of the family with the same name. These two makers took their freedoms in Bristol in 1689 and 1694 (Jackson and Price 1974, 47) and at least one of them was producing pipes at that centre until well into the 18th century. There is also a record of a John Hunt in London who took the Oath of Allegiance in 1696 as a journeyman pipemaker (Oswald 1975, 138). It is possible that this was one of the Bristol makers who had moved to seek work in the capital.

Many different variations of the John Hunt mark are known and they have a wide distribution. Examples have been recorded from various places on the English coast from the Wirral (Meols) to London as well as in Ireland at Dublin Castle and in Scotland at Edinburgh Castle (Oswald, unpublished research notes; Gallagher and Sharp 1986). This is an unusually wide distribution pattern and suggests that the maker or makers producing these pipes operated on quite a large scale. Some of the material clearly belongs to the mid-17th-century Bristol workshops but it is hard to find good parallels for the combination of mark and bowl form represented by the Lion Tower find.

The example from the Lion Tower is not the first John Hunt pipe to be recorded from London but it adds to the large and complex distribution pattern of known examples. It was probably made in the Bristol or Bath area around 1660–90 but how it

Table A2.1   Stamped marks with details of context, small find number (SF), bowl form, moulded mark (mm), stamped mark (Stamp), date and illustration catalogue number (No.) for each piece

Context	SF	Form	mm	Stamp	Date	No.	Comments
17C 96 2632		10v		'sun'	1630–1660	1	Heel stamped with an incuse 'sun' mark.
17D 97 8079		–		WW	1660–1680	2	Heel stamped with a relief WW mark.
80 99 4		17v		IONH HVNT	1660–1690	3	West Country style bowl with incuse heel stamp reading IOHN/HVNT. John Hunt probably worked in the Bristol/Bath area.
17E 96 3193		20		IB	1680–1710	4	Bowl with the same heart-shaped relief stamp reading IB on both the bowl and heel.
17E 96 3133		21v		WB	1680–1710	5	Relief WB stamp on the bowl. Same pipe mould and die stamp as an example from 3193.
17E 96 3193		21v		WB	1680–1710		Relief WB stamp on the bowl. Same pipe mould and die stamp as an example from 3133.
17E 96 3193		25	ER	ER	1730–1770	6	Moulded initials ER on heel, incuse stamped mark ER on bowl.
17E 96 3166		27	IH	HEDGES	1780–1820		Heel with moulded mark IH, bowl stamped HEDGES. John Hedges recorded at North St, Pentonville, 1817–1819.
17E 97 u/s		27	IJ	JONES	1780–1820	7	Heel with moulded initials IJ, bowl with incuse stamp reading JONES.
17E 96 3066		27	IW	London Arms	1780–1820		Two fitting fragments with IW moulded on heel and the London Arms stamped on the bowl.
17D 97 2859		27	IF	FORD	1800–1830	8	Heel with moulded initials IF; bowl with incuse stamp reading FORD
17F* 97 7403		28v		BALME MILE END	1820–1840	12	Bowl with incuse stamped, shield-shaped mark reading BALME/MILE/END. Various Balmes worked at Mile End in the C19th.
17E 97 3130		28	IF	FORD STEPNEY	1820–1840	9	Initials IF moulded on spur with FORD/STEPNEY stamped on bowl.
17E 97 u/s	215	28	TS	London Arms	1820–1840	10	Moulded initials TS on spur with London Arms stamped on the bowl.
17E 96 3005		28	JS	SMITH....G	1820–1840		Moulded spur mark JS with stamped bowl mark [S]MITH/...G.
17D 96 2859		27/28	**	WILLIAMS LONDON	1820–1850		Moulded star on either side of heel, incuse stamp reading WILLIAMS LONDON on bowl, leaf seam away from smoker only.
17F* 97 7310		28	BL	B.LEACH	1830–1850		Spur with moulded mark BL, bowl stamped B.LEACH. Benjamin Leach recorded at Whitechapel Road 1840–47.
17 95 619		28	RO	OSBORNE & Co LONDON	1830–1850	11	Spur with moulded mark RO; bowl with stamped mark OSBORNE & Co, LONDON

came to be in London is still not clear. Isolated examples of an individual pipemaker's work are occasionally found some distance from their source but this example appears to form part of a more consistent distribution pattern. It could simply be that these pipes were readily available in Bristol and that they were used and lost by sailors during the course of their travels. Alternatively, it could be that the distinctive form and finish of these pipes made them marketable in other areas and that the pipes reflect more organised trading patterns. It is interesting to note that examples have been found in at least three fortified sites—Dublin and Edinburgh Castles and at the Tower of London. Until there has been more study of the trade and marketing of pipes it is hard to say whether this is fortuitous or whether it is the result of some other mechanism, for example, the movement of troops, the provision of supplies or the demand for specific styles of pipe at a high-status site.

Mould-marked pipes

In addition to the stamped marks a total of 179 of the 441 bowl fragments (40.6 per cent) had moulded marks on them, examples of which are illustrated (Nos 6–44). The use of moulded initials was adopted by the London makers during the late 17th century and remained the standard method of marking pipes thereafter. These marks are often difficult to identify with any certainty because of the duplication of the same initials amongst the numerous London pipe-makers. The description, illustration and cataloguing of marked pipes from London is gradually making this easier, especially as distribution patterns of particular marks become apparent. The recovery of this sizeable group from the Tower makes an important contribution to this process. During the early 19th century the maker's full name and address was often moulded on the stem of the pipe, making positive identification much easier. All the marked pipes, whether stamped or moulded, are listed alphabetically together with the decorated pipes in Table A2.3.

The recovery of a good range of pipes spanning the period *c*1680–1860 from the Tower has allowed the relative frequency of bowl forms, marks and decoration to be compared. A summary of this information is provided in Table A2.2. This breakdown reveals a considerable amount about the changing fashions in pipes during this period.

There were four principal styles of pipes (Types 19–22) being produced by the London makers from about 1680 to 1710. The proportions of these were, however, markedly different. Of the 121 attributable examples 61 per cent were Type 22 pipes, 27 per cent Type 20, 11 per cent Type 21 and there was only one Type 19 pipe. The Type 22 pipe was clearly more than twice as popular during this period than its nearest rival. None of these types were decorated but 16 examples (13 per cent) were marked. The distribution of these marks was not even, ranging from 23 per cent of the Type 21 pipes down to just 3

per cent of the Type 20 pipes. This suggests that, during this period, the style of the bowl was a significant factor in determining whether or not a particular pipe should be marked. This has profound implications for any debate on why marks were used. It can be demonstrated that manufacturers produced a range of different styles to meet the requirements of the market. This being the case, any simplistic model of makers either choosing or being required to mark their products falls down. The contemporary perception of the pipe was clearly bound up with its form and style, so any consideration of the use and meaning of marks takes on another level of complexity.

Similar patterns can be observed amongst the 18th-century pipes, when two forms (Types 25 and 26) dominated the London market. Of the 110 examples of these forms, 96 per cent were of Type 25 and just 4 per cent of Type 26. Just over half of the Type 25 pipes were marked and yet only 1 per cent were decorated. In contrast, 75 per cent of the Type 26 pipes were marked and 50 per cent of them decorated (though of course the actual numbers involved are very small). This shows that Type 26 pipes were much rarer but that, when they did occur, they were much more likely to be marked and decorated. Once again, there appears to be a relationship between the bowl form and the style of marking and decoration that was used. From the late 18th century the number of marked pipes rises to well over 90 per cent for all types of bowl while the number of decorated pipes rises from *c*50 per cent around the turn of the century to over 80 per cent by the second half of the 19th century.

Analysing the percentages of marked and decorated pipes by bowl form and looking at these changes over time provides a much more dynamic and complex picture of the London pipemaking industry than has been apparent from previous studies. Not only can the relative frequency of different bowl styles be seen but also the different

Table A2.2   Numbers of plain, marked and decorated pipes by bowl type for the period c1680–1860

Form	Date	No mark (plain)	No Mark (dec)	Marked (plain)	Marked (dec)	Total	% marked	% dec
20	1680–1710	32	0	1	0	33	3	0
21	1680–1710	10	0	3	0	13	23	0
20/22	1680–1710	1	0	0	0	1	0	0
22	1680–1710	62	0	12	0	74	16	0
19	1690–1710	1	0	0	0	1	0	0
25	1700–1770	47	4	54	1	106	52	1
26	1740–1800	1	0	1	2	4	75	50
25/27	1770–1820	1	0	11	0	12	92	0
27	1770–1850	0	2	26	25	53	96	51
27/28	1820–1850	0	0	3	5	8	100	63
28	1820–1850	0	1	11	15	27	96	59
28/29	1830–1860	0	0	0	2	2	100	100
29	1840–1860	0	0	1	6	7	100	86
Total		155	7	123	56	341		

attributes of marking and decoration that they possessed. In broad terms the percentage of marked pipes shows a gradual increase from around 13 per cent in the late 17th century to around 90 per cent in the late 19th century. Similarly, the percentage of decorated pipes rises from 0 per cent to around 100 per cent over the same period. Within this broad evolution, however, specific forms clearly had particular attributes that may well have reflected the cost and social context within which they were used. Once these attributes are more fully comprehended and, in particular, when comparative inter-site date is available, a more detailed interpretation should be possible.

MOULD-DECORATED PIPES

Although there are isolated examples of decorated 17th-century pipes it was only during the 18th century that moulded decoration became a regular feature of the pipemaker's production range. The London makers were amongst the earliest to experiment with moulded decoration in this country and small numbers of such pipes were in circulation by the second quarter of the 18th century. The popularity of decorated pipes increased steadily during the third quarter of the century so that, by the last quarter, they formed a significant part of the overall production range. For most of the 19th century the majority of London pipes were decorated in some way. The Tower excavations have produced a good range of decorated pipes covering the styles being used between the early 18th century and c1845. The principal types of decorative motif are discussed thematically below.

Armorial pipes

Pipes depicting the Royal Arms or the Prince of Wales Feathers were amongst the earliest of the mould-decorated designs and, although they were never particularly common, they are the most frequently encountered of the early designs. These motifs continued to be used right through the 19th and into the 20th century but the later versions were far outnumbered by other decorative varieties. The Tower excavations have produced one of the best assemblages of armorial pipes to have been recovered from a controlled excavation in this country. A total of 11 armorial bowls were recovered, eight of them dating to c1730–90 and the remaining three to c1820–45. These pipes provide a rare opportunity to consider a diverse group of armorial pipes within a larger excavated assemblage.

The only substantial body of excavated evidence relating to armorial pipes appears to derive from colonial Williamsburg, in Virginia. At that site 76 examples bearing the Royal Arms have been recovered, all but four from sites with tavern-keeping associations (Noël Hume 1970, 146). Unfortunately, no absolute figures for other classes of pipes are given and so it is not known what percentage of the tavern

pipes had armorial decoration or, indeed, what percentage of all pipes were recovered from taverns as opposed to other classes of site. It does seem, however, that in Williamsburg there was an association between this type of pipe and taverns. It is also interesting to note that only two pipes with the Prince of Wales feathers were recovered from Williamsburg. Such a heavy bias in favour of the Royal Arms is certainly not typical of these pipes in England and it serves as a reminder that the supply and use of pipes in the colonies differed from that in the domestic market.

The armorial pipes from the Tower excavations were recovered from trenches 1, 6, 7, 25, 27, 30 and 31. The Stone Kitchen tavern stood just inside the south-west entrance to the Tower (ie, near trenches 30 and 31) but the distribution pattern of the armorial bowls suggests that these pipes were in general use rather than being particularly associated with the tavern. Furthermore, only two of the pipes were produced in the same mould and a variety of different designs and makers' marks occurs on the others. This shows that the pipes were coming from a range of sources and that they are not the product of one particular commission or order to supply the Tower with pipes. There are three pipes with the Royal Arms, six with the Prince of Wales Feathers and one depicting both designs, although the Royal Arms is the principal motif. This suggests that, at the Tower, there was no particular preference between these two motifs.

In terms of the frequency with which this type of pipe occurs, it is useful to consider the two different groups. The earlier group of eight bowls, manufactured around 1730–90, date from a period when other forms of decorated pipe were rarely produced. There are four pipes with the Hanoverian Arms as the principal motif, the two complete examples of which are illustrated (Nos 13–14). There is also a damaged bowl very similar to No. 14 but with a different scheme of decoration on the mould seam (not illustrated). This appears to be almost identical to, if not the same as, an example illustrated by Atkinson and Oswald (1980, pl 3.12), described as a gauntlet holding a rose and thistle. They date this to 1760–80 with examples recorded from Tower Bridge, Southwark and Putney. The fourth Hanoverian Arms pipe is even more fragmentary, but similar to No. 14 except that it has an undecorated seam facing away from the smoker. The base of the bowl is completely missing but the surviving profile suggests it would have been a Type 26 pipe. There are also four examples with the Prince of Wales Feathers as the principal motif. Two are from the same mould (No. 15), the other two being Nos 16 and 17.

The bowl forms represented by these eight pipes are London Types 25 and 26, or variants of them, which are heel and spur forms respectively. These two forms were current from about 1700 and 1740 and were used almost exclusively by the London makers for the majority of the 18th century. They do not, however, occur in equal proportions. Of some 123 identifiable examples from the Tower excavations 118 were of Type 25 (96 per cent) but only five of

Type 26 (4 per cent). This strong bias in favour of the Type 25 form seems to be typical of pipe assemblages from London although no inter-site comparisons have been carried out to see how consistent this figure is. The eight armorial bowls from this earlier group make up just 6.5 per cent of the Type 25 and 26 pipes but they are not equally distributed between the two bowl forms. Five occur on Type 25 bowl forms, of which they represent just 4.2 per cent, while three are on Type 26 forms, of which they represent 60 per cent. This shows that decorated bowls were still relatively scarce during this period and that, when they did occur, they were particularly associated with the Type 26 bowl form. Particular bowl forms have been shown to have been associated with specific stem lengths (Higgins 1987, 432–5) and it may be that the elaborately decorated Type 26 bowls were more expensive items that might also be expected to have longer than average stems. Until complete examples have been recovered it will be impossible to test this hypothesis.

With regard to the nature of the decoration, in four examples the Royal Arms was the primary motif while in the other four it was the Prince of Wales Feathers. Despite the distinctive nature of these designs there does not seem to have been any particular desire by the makers to identify their work. Of the five Type 25 bowls only one (No. 13) has a maker's mark. This consists of the crowned initials WM, which can be attributed to William Manby of Limehouse, recorded working from 1719 to 1763 (Oswald 1975, 142). The Manbys were a prominent pipemaking family with a substantial export trade. A similar WM armorial pipe has been recovered from Williamsburg, Virginia (Noel Hume 1970, pl VI A), but differences in detail show that the American example was produced in a different mould. The fact that Manby needed at least two virtually identical armorial moulds hints at the scale of his production. A WM armorial pipe has also been recorded from Chiswick (Atkinson and Oswald 1980, 368).

Only two of the Type 26 spurs survived, both of them marked. One was damaged but possibly read WB while the other was marked NA (No. 14). Armorial pipes marked WB have been recorded from Southampton, Winchester and London, while examples marked NA come from Williamsburg in Virginia, Bankside Power Station in London and Steyning in Sussex. (Atkinson and Oswald 1980, 364–7). Atkinson and Oswald suggest local makers in Southampton and Chichester for these two marks although, given the paucity of other imported pipes from London, it would seem more likely that the Tower finds were produced by two as yet unidentified London manufacturers. Overall, only three of the seven surviving armorial heels or spurs were marked (43 per cent). This is rather less than the 57 per cent of all Type 25 or 26 bowls which had makers' marks on them and shows that, despite their striking design, there was no particular effort made to identify the makers of these pipes. Further work is

clearly needed to explore the contemporary perception of these pipes and the circumstances under which they were used. Given that the Tower was a Royal site it would also be interesting to compare the percentage of armorial pipes found here with other classes of site in London.

The later group of armorial pipes dates from c1820 to 1845 (Nos 19–21). By this date styles had changed and the majority of the pipes were both marked and decorated. The three bowls combine the use of the Prince of Wales Feathers with a range of masonic emblems and are remarkable for their similarity, particularly Nos 20 and 21, where the details of the design and execution are so close as to suggest that the same hand designed both moulds. The moulded initials and partial stem mark on No. 20 clearly show that this pipe was made by James Russell, who is recorded working at Wapping from 1822 to 1834. This date fits perfectly with both the style of the bowl and the nature of the decorative motifs employed. The JS pipe (No. 21) can likewise be attributed to a John Smith of Wapping, recorded working from 1844 to1862. The recorded dates appear to be too late for this style of pipe and it seems likely that Smith was, in fact, working from the 1820s or 1830s. The similarity of these three examples, all produced by different makers, makes it clear that this particular pattern was popular in London around 1820–45. It does not appear to have been recorded before and makes an important addition to the previously identified range of pipes bearing the Prince of Wales Feathers (Le Cheminant 1981).

Masonic pipes

Four pipes bearing masonic designs were recovered from the excavations. Three of these were also decorated with the Prince of Wales Feathers and have been described above. The fourth is an unusual bowl since it combines the maker's initials, GB, with the moulded lettering BIRCHALL/CHATHAM around the bowl rim (No. 18). Rim lettering was most frequently employed in the Lincolnshire area although it was occasionally adopted by makers in other parts of the country as well (Walker and Wells 1979, fig 9). Oswald and Le Cheminant (1989, 6) give a date of approximately 1803–40 for George Birchall of Chatham but the style of this bowl would seem to suggest a date in the late 18th century rather than the early 19th for this piece. Having said that, it may have been that a particular bowl form became associated with this type of masonic pipe and that it remained in use long after other fashions had changed. A French pattern book produced by the firm of Fiolet in 1846 shows a very similar bowl, described as an *Anglaise maçonique*. The Tower example is also of interest since it represents a rare import to London from the surrounding counties. The style of the masonic decoration is closely matched by that on a heel bowl, also marked GB, from Ewell in Surrey (Higgins 1981, fig 31.10).

Leaf-decorated seams

Perhaps the most common and widely employed form of decoration on pipes consists of leaf-decorated seams. The origin of this motif appears to lie in the elaborate foliage designs found on the armorial pipes described above. By the late 18th century this had been reduced to a more uniform but still relatively long and widely spaced line of leaves, such as those seen on the Birchall armorial pipe (No. 18). It also became quite common to alternate the leaf motif with a plain line or spike. Around 1810–30 the leaves tended to become more compact and serrated, often with a sharply curved line between each pair of leaves. This motif can be clearly seen on some of the early 19th-century fluted bowls (Nos 27–29). During the period c1820–60 this line usually became a short, straight spike, after which it was often omitted altogether. Another variant, popular from c1840 to 1880, showed alternating oak leaves and acorns, which were often used on one seam in conjunction with a plain line of leaves on the other (eg, Nos 41–42). Leaves were also used to decorate the seams or sides of the stem, as can be seen in Nos 31–34. Although most of the illustrated examples have other motifs on the bowl sides there were many otherwise plain bowls with just leaf-decorated seams. Overall, 50 of the Type 27–29 bowls had leaf-decorated seams. This averages 52 per cent of all these types, although the proportion of just the later forms with leaf-decorated seams (Types 28 and 29) rises to 73 per cent, showing that leaf decorated seams became increasingly common during the course of the century.

Fox and grapes pipes

Pipes decorated with a fox and grapes design were popular around the second quarter of the 19th century and four examples were recovered from the Tower excavations. The three complete bowls are Nos 22–24. These are of variable quality, with one example (No. 23) having particularly poorly moulded decoration. The fourth bowl (damaged) shows a seated fox, similar to No. 22 but with a line representing the ground beneath it. It has the moulded initials IF on the heel. The fox and grapes design appears to have been particularly associated with London although this pattern also occurs in surrounding counties, such as Surrey (Higgins 1981). It was also produced in France with several versions, including both the standing and the seated fox varieties, occurring in a pattern book produced by the firm of Fiolet in 1846. The Fiolet catalogue places this design amongst a number of other English styles, suggesting both that this pattern was probably English in origin and that their production of it may have been intended primarily for the export market.

Fluted decoration

Fluted decoration was introduced during the second half of the 18th century and became the first relatively common and widespread decorative design to be used on pipes. During the 18th century the flutes tended to be broader and more curved, often with a line above and other decorative motifs, such as foliage or dots. A good example of this type can be seen in No. 26. Alternating thick and thin flutes were especially popular during the late 18th or early 19th century, often occurring on pipes with leaf-decorated seams as well. During the 19th century flutes tended to become increasingly narrow and uniform in width. A typical range of these pipes, many of them associated with heel and stem marks, are Nos 27–35.

THE COMPLETE PIPES

Stems and mouthpieces were surprisingly rare given that the soft moat silts appear to have provided ideal conditions for the preservation of substantially complete pipe fragments. Some 441 pipe bowls were recovered from the excavations but only 18 mouthpieces. Despite this, it was still possible to reconstruct three complete pipes. There are only around 100 complete pipes dating from before 1850 known from the whole of the British Isles and so these three make an important contribution to this corpus.

The earliest complete pipe has a London Type 18 bowl and dates to c1660–80 (Nos 47 and 50). The stem is only broken in one place and the pipe was probably discarded intact. Unbroken pipes are occasionally recovered from silty deposits or rubbish pits, suggesting that they were of so little value as to be regarded as disposable on occasions. This style of pipe was particularly common in Restoration London and the Tower example is of typical form and finish. The stem is 275mm long and is basically straight, save for a slight warping to one side. The mouthpiece is simply cut without any visibly surviving evidence for a tip coating. Six contemporary complete pipes from England were recorded during a survey in 1987 (Higgins 1987, 64) and another six have come to light since. These range from around 260mm to 320mm in length and show that the Tower example was towards the shorter end of the average range for the pipes of this period.

The other two complete pipes both have typical London bowl forms of late 18th- or early 19th-century date and seem likely to represent examples of the everyday pipes of this period. The earlier of the two has a large, thin-walled bowl marked IB and probably dates to c1770–1800 (Nos 48 and 51). It has a gently curved stem with a length of 357mm, a simple cut mouthpiece without any surviving evidence of a tip coating and a trimmed heel. The second pipe is marked WS and probably dates to c1780–1820 (Nos 49 and 52). It has a gently curved stem with a length of 364mm and a simple cut mouthpiece without any surviving evidence of a tip coating. The heel has not been trimmed. The similarity of stem length between these two examples may indicate that this form was associated with a specific stem length, as has been observed amongst earlier pipes (Higgins 1987, 423–44). It was certainly the case that pipes were produced in a variety of lengths (*see* Manufacturing and finishing techniques, below) and it seems probable that these two examples represented the same type or length of pipe.

These pipes are exceptional because no complete examples bridging the gap between the 18th-century London Type 25 and early 19th-century forms had been recovered previously. The 18th-century forms had much thicker, straight stems that normally seem to have ranged from around 300mm to 390mm in length. The Tower finds have stem lengths towards the upper end of this range but are markedly different in form. Their bowls and stems are much thinner and, in particular, the stems of both examples are curved. This provides the earliest firm evidence for pipes with curved stems and suggests that this feature was adopted as part of a package, together with the new bowl form and thinner stem. Only five complete early 19th-century pipes are recorded nationally and these have stems with lengths of around 350mm to 450mm. The Tower examples clearly fit into a pattern of pipe development for everyday pipes being used in this country. They are towards the upper stem length range for the earlier pipes but towards the lower end of the range for later pipes. As such, they form part of a steady trend towards increasing average stem length that can be traced back to the late 16th century. Perhaps more importantly, they appear to mark the point at which the traditional straight stem, which had been current for two centuries, was replaced by the curved stem that became the standard form for all later long-stemmed pipes.

MANUFACTURING AND FINISHING TECHNIQUES

There are a few points to note with regard to the manufacturing and finishing of these pipes, the most significant of which concerns the form of the complete pipes and their handling in the workshop when freshly moulded. The complete pipe of *c*1660–80 is a heel form and many of the early papers on pipes suggest that the spur or heel was used to stand the pipe so as to prevent the hot bowl from burning furniture. This suggestion, however, is not borne out by early paintings, which invariably show pipes either being held while smoked or lying on one side when not in use. Furthermore, the complete pipe from the Tower, despite having a low, flat heel, will not stand upright unsupported. This characteristic has been noted amongst other complete early pipes and clearly demonstrates that these objects were never intended to be stood in this way.

The other point of note regarding the 1660–80 pipe is that the stem is slightly uneven, curving slightly to the right when held as smoked. Such warping can arise either during the drying of the pipe or as it is fired. As already noted, this pipe will not stand upright unsupported and, if it is held this way, the stem makes contact with a flat surface only at the very tip. The same applies if the pipe is laid on its right-hand side (as smoked). On its left-hand side the pipe lies fairly comfortably, with most of the stem, but not the tip, in contact with a flat surface. The best contact, however, is made with the bowl hanging upside down over the edge of a flat surface. In this position the pipe sits slightly to one side but with nearly the full length of the stem in contact with the surface. This suggests that, after moulding, the pipe was most probably laid inverted on a flat surface with its bowl hanging over the edge. There is a small nick in the clay at the top of the bowl/stem junction which may have been caused by laying the soft pipe over such an edge. In the same way, the two complete pipes of *c*1770–1820 will not lie 'comfortably' on either side and must have been laid upright or inverted on some type of former to produce the stem curve after moulding. One of these also has a small indentation at the bowl/stem junction.

Detailed probate inventories and other records of pipemakers' tools dating from the 17th century onwards often include 'grates' amongst the equipment. Peacey (1995) has identified these as wooden frames, the later examples of which had angled slats arranged in an arc so as to produce a curved stem. These appear to have been made to take standard lengths of pipe—for example, 10, 12, 15, 18 or 24 inches—and an example survives amongst the Pollock collection of pipemaking equipment in the Museum of Science and Industry in Manchester. The physical evidence from the Tower suggests that, from at least the 1680s, the standard manufacturing process in England involved laying the pipes in an inverted position on drying grates. This contrasts with the Dutch system, where pipes were placed upright in specially shaped wooden trays to dry.

Other evidence of manufacturing processes provided by the Tower finds relates to the polishing or burnishing of the pipe surface while in a leather-hard state. Only six bowls and two stems were burnished, ranging in date from *c*1610 to 1710. Burnishing virtually died out in London after *c*1710 and was never particularly common before that. The small numbers of burnished pipe fragments recovered simply reflect the paucity of earlier material from these excavations and they are insufficient to draw any meaningful conclusions. It is worth noting, however, that three of the six bowls also had stamped marks on them (Nos 2–4). The John Hunt pipe has a poor burnish but the other two are finely finished and all three would have been more expensive than ordinary pipes.

Internal bowl marks were confined to the Type 25 bowls, 17 out of 106 of which (16 per cent) exhibited them. These were all in relief and provided the following examples (as viewed from above with the bowl facing away from the smoker): one with a single horizontal bar; two with a single vertical bar; one with an eight-arm star (bowl marked IM); one with a diagonal line with two bars across it (marked ?RR);

two with a cross arranged as an 'x' (one marked with crowned harps); and ten with a cross arranged as a '+' (one marked ?AG, one marked ER, one marked RW and two with a crowned WM mark). About half of the examples with internal bowl marks (8 out of 17) were also maker-marked. This is the same proportion of marked examples as found amongst all Type 25 bowls and shows that there was no correlation between the use of internal bowl marks and the moulded makers' marks.

No detailed information with regard to heel trimming was collected, although it was noted in passing that the majority of the Type 27 bowls did not have trimmed heels. The use of trimming was almost universal on all heel pipes before the end of the 18th century. The introduction of the new Type 27 bowl from the 1770s may have been associated with this change in finishing technique. At the same time the introduction of mould-decorated seams ended the necessity for trimming this part of the pipe. There is some documented opposition from the pipe-trimmers at about this time, worried about job losses as a result of these less labour-intensive finishing methods.

ACKNOWLEDGEMENT

I am grateful to Peter Hammond of Nottingham for access to his provisional list of post-1750 London pipemakers from his current research (1999).

SUMMARY

The pipes from the 1995–7 Tower Excavations provide a good sample of London pipes, especially for the period from *c*1670–1845. The combination of soft silts and tightly documented historical events has produced a well preserved and closely datable body of evidence. This has provided much new information about the production and changing styles of pipes in London as well as shedding light on their supply and use at the Tower. The nineteenth century groups are particularly valuable since good excavated deposits of this date are extremely rare in London. The recovery of three complete pipes has filled gaps in the evolution of stem lengths as well as suggesting a date for the introduction of curved stems. Two new bowl forms that should be added to the London typology have been identified, as has a new variant of the Prince of Wales feathers motif. An analysis of the bowl form and mark data has shown the relative frequencies with which these attributes occur and has shown that, during the eighteenth century, some 6.5% of the Tower pipes had armorial decoration. The use of internal bowl marks has been shown to be unconnected with the use of moulded makers' marks but it has been shown that there is a significant correlation between bowl form and the use of marks. In this respect the mark can be seen to be an integral element of a pipe's design and style.

CATALOGUE OF ILLUSTRATED PIPES

The illustrated pipes are described below. Where die types have been identified in the National Clay Tobacco Pipe Stamp Catalogue being compiled by the author the unique die number is quoted (eg, Die No 1786). Makers have been identified with reference to Oswald's 1975 list and the draft list provided by Hammond (1999). Pipes 1–49 are at 1:1 with the stamp details for Nos 1–12 at 2:1. The complete pipes, Nos 50–52, are shown at a reduced scale.

1 Bowl of *c*1630–1660 with an incuse-stamped 'sun' mark on the heel (Die No 1786). Not milled but a plain groove all around the rim. Stem bore 8/64". TOL 17C 96 2632.

2 Bowl of *c*1660–1680 with the relief-stamped mark WW on the heel. Neat bulbous heel form—not closely matched in London typology—with a finely burnished surface. Stem bore 8/64". TOL 17D 97 8079.

3 West Country style bowl of *c*1660–1690 with the incuse-stamped mark IOHN HVNT on the heel (Die No 1790). John Hunt probably worked in the Bristol/Bath area. There is a poor burnish on the bowl but the stem does not appear to have been burnished. The rim is bottered and the stem bore is 6/64". TOL 99 4.

4 Bowl of *c*1680–1710 with the relief-stamped mark IB on both the bowl and heel (Die No 1787). The bowl is finely burnished, it has an internally trimmed, bottered and fully milled rim and the stem bore is 6/64". TOL 17E 96 3193.

5 Bowl of *c*1680–1710 with the relief-stamped mark WB on the bowl facing the smoker (Die No 1788). The rim is bottered but was probably not milled (a small section is chipped away) – the stem bore is 6/64". TOL 17E 96 3133. There is another example made in the same mould and marked with the same die from TOL 17E 96 3193, which also has a stem bore of 6/64".

6 Bowl of *c*1730–1770 with the moulded initials ER on heel and an incuse-stamped ER mark on the bowl (Die No 1789). The rim is cut and wiped rim; stem bore 4/64". TOL 17E 96 3193.

7 Bowl of *c*1780–1820 with the moulded initials IJ on the heel and an incuse stamp reading 'JONES' on the bowl (Die No 1757). A John James is recorded at Bow in 1794 and Mile End New Town in 1799 and a James Jones is recorded at 11 Whutecross St, St Lukes in 1799 and at 56 Featherstone St, St Lukes from 1802–39. Stem bore 4/64". A James Jones is also recorded at Toppings Wharf, Tooley Street, Borough in 1832. TOL 17E 97 U/S

8 Bowl of *c*1805–1865 with the moulded initials IF on the heel and an incuse stamp reading 'FORD' on the bowl (Die No 1758). Probably John Ford of Stepney, working 1805–65. Stem bore 4/64". TOL 17D 96 2859.

9 Bowl of *c*1820–1840 with the initials IF moulded on spur and 'FORD/STEPNEY' as an incuse

stamp on the bowl (Die No 1759). John Ford of Stepney is recorded from 1805–65. See also No. 40. Stem bore 4/64". TOL 17E 97 3130.

10 Bowl of *c*1820–1840 with the relief-moulded initials TS on the spur and the London Arms incuse-stamped on the bowl (similar to Die Number 1269). Most likely Thomas Henry Scourfield, Whitechapel Rd, 1805–39 or, possibly, Thomas Shipway, Bermondsey, 1832–68 (see also No. 39). Stem bore 4/64". TOL 17E 97 U/S (SF 215).

11 Bowl of *c*1830–1850 with the relief-moulded initials RO on the spur and the incuse-stamped 'OSBORNE & Co, LONDON' on the bowl (Die No 1756). Robert Osborne is listed in directories at 19 Webb Square, Shoreditch in 1836 and in Bethnal Green Road from 1840–45. A William Thomas Osborne was trading as 'Osborne & Co' as late as 1913. Stem bore 4/64". TOL 17 95 619.

12 Bowl of *c*1820–1840 with the incuse–stamped mark 'BALME/MILE/END' on the bowl facing the smoker (Die No 1755). There were various Balmes working at Mile End during the nineteenth-century. Stem bore 3/64". TOL 17F* 97 7403.

13 Bowl of *c*1730–1780 with the relief-moulded mark WM (crowned) on the sides of the heel and the Hanovarian Arms on the bowl. Made by William Manby of Limehouse, who is recorded from 1719–1763. Stem bore 4/64". TOL 17C 96 2511.

14 Bowl of *c*1740–1780 with the relief-moulded mark NA (or possibly HA) on the sides of the heel with the Hanovarian Arms and Prince of Wales Feathers on the bowl. Christian initial N has a bar cut over it in the mould, possibly intended to change it to an H. There are no currently documented London makers with either the initials HA or NA. Stem bore 4/64". TOL 17D 96 2875.

15 Bowl of *c*1740–1780 depicting the Prince of Wales Feathers. This is a composite drawing made from two identical examples recovered from TOL 17C 96 2541 and TOL 17 95 715. The stem bores of both examples are 4/64".

16 Bowl of *c*1740–1770 depicting the Prince of Wales Feathers. The base is badly damaged but appears to have been an unmarked heel form. Stem bore 6/64". TOL 17C 96 U/S.

17 Bowl of *c*1740–1790 depicting the Prince of Wales Feathers and with a pattern of dots on either side of the heel. Stem bore 5/64". TOL 17F* 97 7109.

18 Bowl of *c*1800–1840 with the relief-moulded initials GB on the spur and BIRCHALL/ CHATHAM moulded around the rim. Stem bore 4/64". TOL 17E 97 3129 (SF 220).

19 Bowl of *c*1780–1820 with the relief-moulded mark WR on the sides of the heel. The surname initial appears to have been altered in mould and it was possibly an H originally. Stem bore 4/64". TOL 96 23.

20 Bowl of *c*1820–1840 with the relief-moulded initials JR on the heel and RUSS[ELL]/ [WA]PPING on the stem. John Russell is recorded at 24 Green Bank, Wapping, from 1822–32. Stem bore 4/64". TOL 17E 96 3008.

21 Bowl of *c*1820–1850 with the relief-moulded mark JS on the sides of the heel and SMIT[H]/ [WA]PPING on the stem. A John Smith is recorded at Wapping from 1844–62. Stem bore 4/64". TOL 17E 96 U/S (SF 218).

22 Bowl of *c*1810–1840 with the relief-moulded mark TD on the sides of the heel and fox and grapes decoration on the bowl. Probably either Thomas Davis, Westminster 1827/8 or Thomas Duggan, Smithfield, 1805–32. Stem bore 4/64". TOL 17E 96 3007.

23 Bowl of *c*1810–1840 with the relief-moulded mark IE on the sides of the heel and fox and grapes decoration on the bowl. Probably John Edwards of Wapping and Aldgate, 1784–1812. Stem bore 4/64". TOL 17F 96 4107.

24 Bowl of *c*1810–1840 with the relief-moulded mark HC on the sides of the heel and fox and grapes decoration on the bowl. The initials appear to have been altered in the mould with the original surname perhaps being an E. Possibly either Hannah Clark, 1835–5 or Henry Cox, 1837–50, both of High Holborn. Stem bore 4/64". TOL 17E 97 U/S.

25 Stem fragment of *c*1840–1880 with the relief-moulded mark I.ELLIOTT [L]AMBETH WLK among the stem. A pipemaker called C. J. Elliott was recorded at Tyler St, Lambeth from 1857–71. Stem bore 4/64". TOL 17F* 97 7407.

26 Scalloped bowl of *c*1780–1820 with the relief-moulded mark IW on the sides of the heel. The surname initial W is unusual in that it has been moulded sideways on heel. There were several makers with these initials during this period. Enclosed flutes and dots on bowl with foliage decoration along the stem. Stem bore 4/64". TOL 96 20.

27 Fluted bowl of *c*1790–1830 with relief-moulded stars on the sides of the heel. Another example made from the same mould as this one was found in the same context but with the stars deleted from mould. Both examples have stem bores of 4/64". TOL 17E 96 3007.

28 Fluted bowl of *c*1780–1820 with the relief-moulded mark WS on the sides of the heel. There were several makers with these initials during this period. Stem bore 4/64". TOL 96 23. See No. 49 for another WS pipe. There is also a bowl from TOL 96 3133 with the same profile and decoration as No. 28 but with the initials IF on the heel (not illustrated). The form and style of decoration of these two examples is so similar that they were probably designed by the same mould-maker.

29 Fluted bowl of *c*1820–1840 with the relief-moulded mark TF on the sides of the spur.

Probably made by one of the Thomas Fords, working between 1835 and 1890. Stem bore 4/64″. TOL 17E 97 3128.

30 Bowl of *c*1780–1830 with the relief-moulded mark IM on the sides of the heel. There are 13 flutes on each side of bowl but none on the mould seams themselves. There were several makers with these initials during this period. Stem bore 5/64″. TOL 17F 96 3801.

31 Fluted bowl of *c*1820–1850 with the relief-moulded stars on either side of heel and 'T.WOOTTEN.No 12/PARK STREET BORO' on the stem. Thomas Wootten was recorded at this address from 1822–48. See also Nos 32–34. Stem bore 4/64″. TOL 17F 96 3811.

32 Fluted bowl of *c*1790–1840 with the relief-moulded mark TW on the sides of the heel, possibly for Thomas Wootten (see Nos 31, 33 and 34). Stem bore 4/64″. TOL 17E 96 3165.

33 Stem fragment of *c*1810–1840 with the relief-moulded mark /O.12?/ /PAR/ along the stem. This is almost certainly part of a mark reading 'T WOOTTEN No 12 / PARK STREET BORO' (*cf* No. 31). Stem bore 4/64″. TOL 17E 96 3109.

34 Fluted bowl of *c*1820–1850 with relief-moulded stars on heel and 'T.WOOTTEN/[PARKS]TREET BORO' on the stem. Thomas Wootten was recorded at this address from 1822–48 (see also Nos 31–33). Stem bore 5/64″. TOL 17E 96 3008.

35 Fluted bowl of *c*1810–1850 with the relief-moulded mark JC on the sides of the heel. There were several makers with these initials during this period. Stem bore 4/64″. TOL 17E 96 3109.

36 Stem fragment *c*1820–1860 decorated with leaves and stars. Stem bore 4/64″. TOL 17 95 706.

37 Bowl of *c*1800–1840 with the relief-moulded mark TF on heel and 'T.FORD.CANNON/ STREET.LONDON' moulded along stem. Thomas Ford is recorded at 41 Cannon Street Road from 1835–40. Stem bore 4/64″. TOL 17E 97 3164 (SF 210) with an identical example from TOL 96 3133.

38 Bowl of *c*1780–1820 with the relief-moulded stars on the sides of the heel. There are faint striations on bowl sides as if mould has been altered to remove flutes. Stem bore 4/64″. TOL 17E 97 3128.

39 Two joining bowl of *c*1820–1860 with the relief-moulded mark TS on the sides of the spur. See No. 10 for possible makers. Stem bore 4/64″. TOL 17F* 97 7109.

40 Bowl of *c*1820–1860 with the relief-moulded mark IF on the sides of the spur. Stem bore 4/64″. Possibly John Ford of Stepney, who is recorded from 1805–65 (see No. 9), although there were several other makers with these initials during this period. TOL 17F* 97 7109.

41 Bowl of *c*1840–1880 with the relief-moulded mark WW on the sides of the heel. There were several makers with these initials during this period. Stem bore 3/64″. TOL 17F* 97 7109.

42 Bowl of *c*1840–1880 with relief-moulded shields on the sides of the heel. Stem bore 4/64″. TOL 17F* 97 7109.

43 Decorated bowl of *c*1840–1880 with the relief-moulded mark WB on the sides of the heel. There were several makers with these initials during this period. Stem bore 4/64″. TOL 17F* 97 7109.

44 Two fitting fragmants from a small heel bowl of *c*1840–1880 with an unusual bird mark moulded on either side of the heel. Stem bore 4/64″. TOL 96 8.

45 Unusual nineteenth-century pipe bowl made of white clay but with a red surface finish—possibly a southern European import, perhaps southern France or Italy. There are various decorative elements on the bowl, including a raised band with three lion masks on either side of the bowl and a foliage motif on each seam. The pipe has been made in a two piece mould and it has a cut rim. Stem bore 4/64″. TOL 17F 96 U/S (SF 52).

46 This bowl form occurs regularly in London but is not included in the London Typology (Atkinson & Oswald 1969). The form can be dated to *c*1660–90 and this example is particularly important since it was recovered from the construction trench for a new revetment wall of *c*1670–1683, which provides firm support for the suggested date range. The rim is bottered and three-quarters milled. Stem bore 6/64″. TOL 17A 96 2226.

47 Bowl of *c*1660–80 with a joining stem and mouthpiece fragment that make up a complete pipe with a stem length of 275mm (No. 50). Rim bottered and half-milled; mouthpiece simply formed by a cut end. Stem bore 6/64″. TOL 17D 96 2851.

48 Bowl of *c*1770–1800 with the relief-moulded mark IB on the sides of the heel. There were several makers with these initials during this period. Fitting fragments making up a complete pipe with a curved stem of 357mm in length (No. 51). Cut mouthpiece; stem bore 4/64″. TOL 17E 96 3128 (SF 82).

49 Bowl of *c*1780–1820 with the relief-moulded mark WS on the sides of the heel. Joining fragments making up a complete pipe with a curved stem of 364mm in length (No. 52). Cut mouthpiece; stem bore 4/64″. There were several makers with these initials during this period. TOL 17E 97 3131. See also No. 28.

50 Complete pipe of *c*1660–80 with a stem length of 275mm. See No. 47 for detail of bowl. TOL 17D 96 2851.

51 Complete pipe of *c*1770–1800 with the relief-moulded mark IB on the sides of the heel and a stem length of 357mm. See No. 48 for bowl detail. Stem bore 4/64″. TOL 17E 96 3128 (SF 82).

52 Complete pipe of *c*1780–1820 with the relief-moulded mark WS on the sides of the heel and a stem length of 364mm. See No. 49 for bowl detail. Stem bore 4/64″. TOL 17E 97 3131.

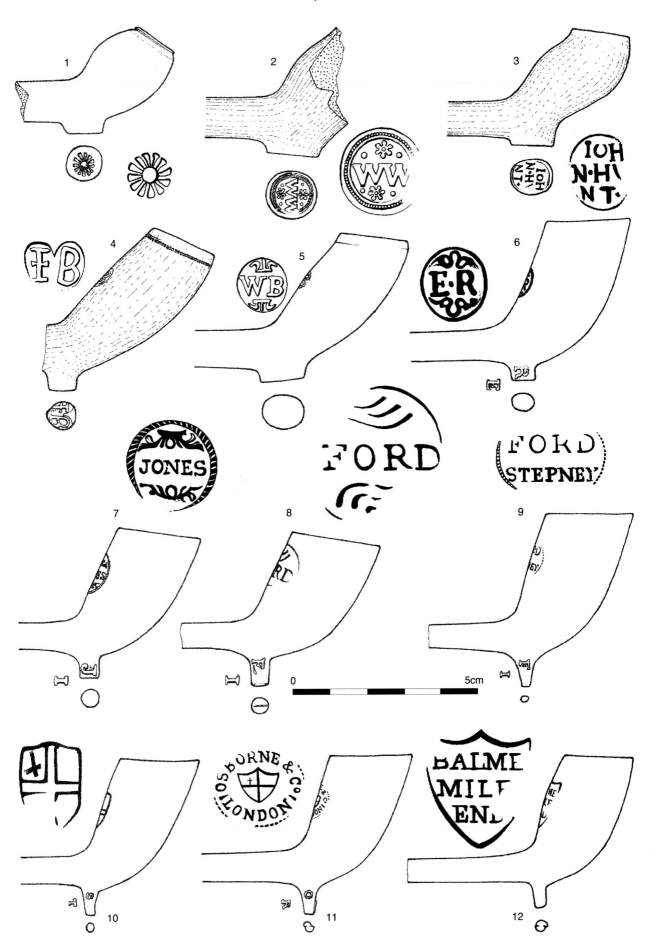

Fig A2.1   Clay pipes Nos 1–12.

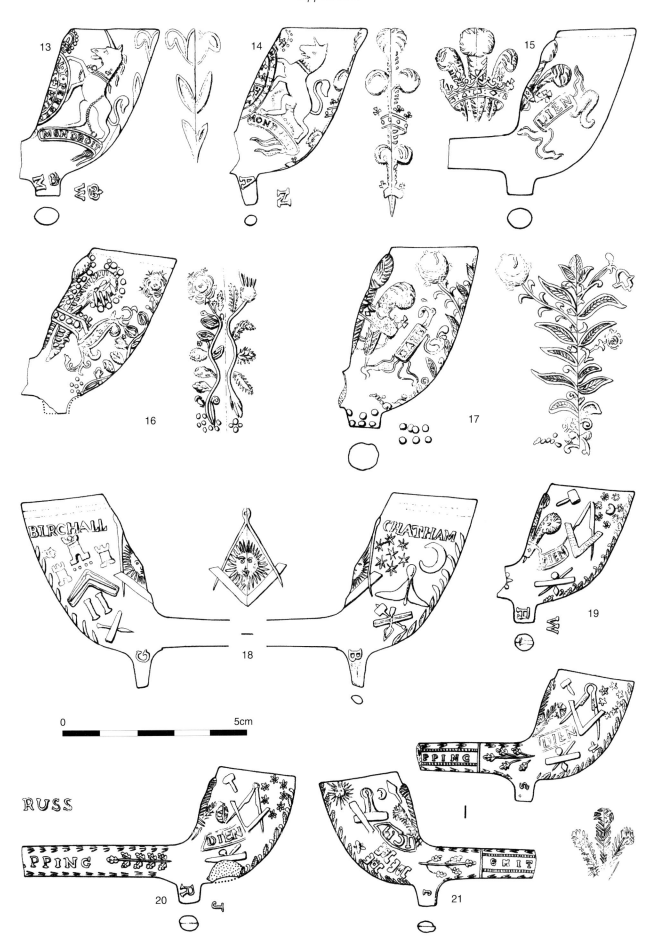

Fig A2.2   Clay pipes Nos 13–21.

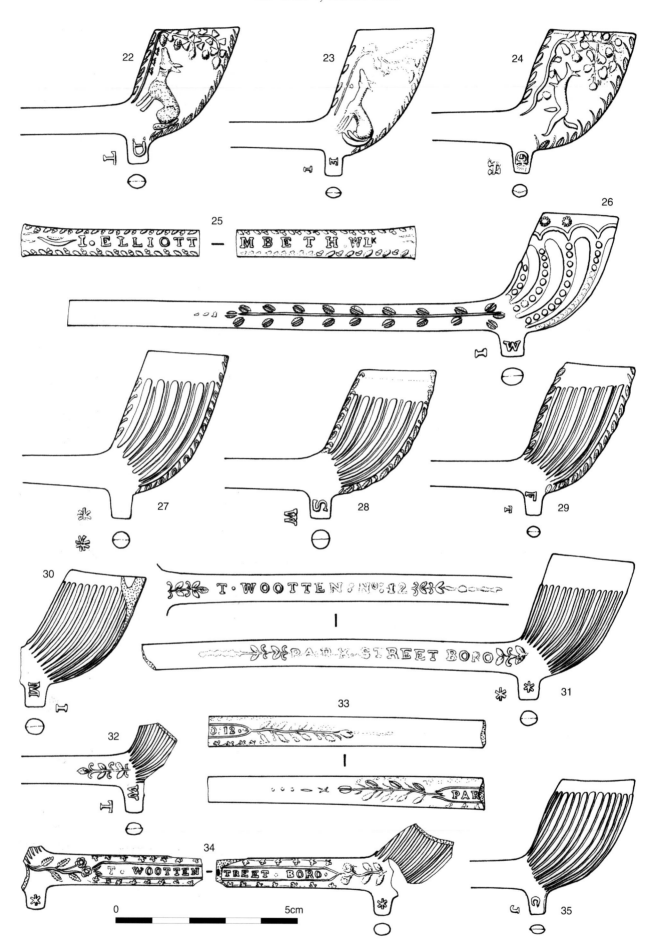

Fig A2.3   Clay pipes Nos 22–35.

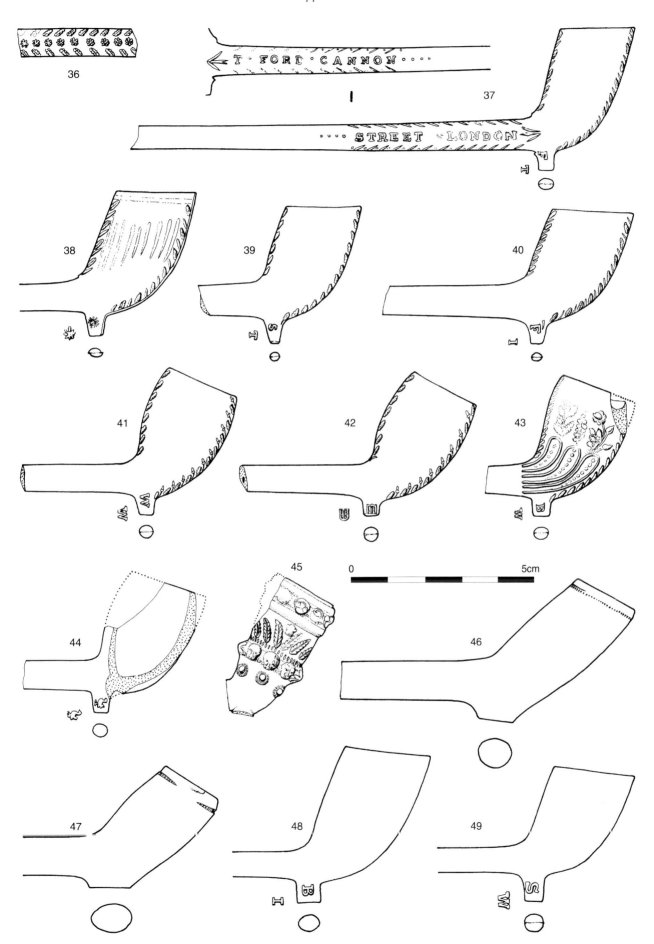

Fig A2.4   Clay pipes Nos 36–49.

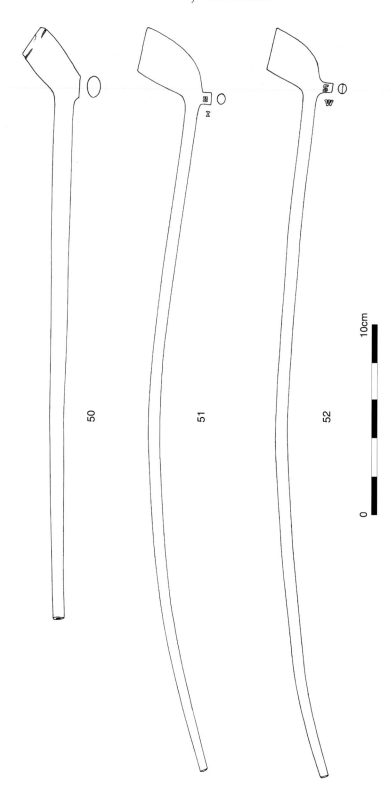

Fig A2.5   Clay pipes, three complete pipes, Nos 50–52.

MARKED AND DECORATED PIPES

Table A2.3 provides an alphabetical list of the pipes with moulded marks, followed by details of any decorated pipes without marks. These pipes have varying combinations of moulded initials on the heel or spur, moulded marks along the stem and stamped marks. To simplify the entries, the information from these three types of mark has been amalgamated in the description. The columns provide the following information: details of the context for each fragment; the number of joining bowl (B), stem (S) and mouthpiece (M) fragments making up each piece; Christian name information (CN); surname information (Surname) and any other details (including a note of crowned initials); the position of the mark(s) (HS = heel sides, SS = spur sides, BF = bowl facing the smoker, BS = bowl sides, SL = mark along the stem sides); the type of mark (T) where I = incuse and R = relief; the method used to make the mark (M) where M = moulded and S = stamped; the main decorative motifs, if any (LDS = Leaf Decorated Seams, POWF = Prince of Wales Feathers); the date of the fragment; and any figure number and comments.

Table A2.3 Marked and decorated pipes

Area	Tr	Yr	Cxt	SF	B	S	M	Form	CN	Surname	Other	P	T	M	Decoration	Date	Cat No	Comments
17	4	95	419		1			25	A	A	(crowned)	HS	R	M		1700–1750		Christian initial damaged, could be an A.
17B	14	96	1423		1			25	A?	A		HS	R	M		1700–1770		
17D	27	96	2875		1			26	N/H	A		HS	R	M	Royal Arms, POWF, etc	1740–1780	14	Christian initial N had a bar over it, possibly intended to change it to an H.
17E	30	96	3005		1			27v	W	A		HS	R	M	LDS, flutes	1800–1840		Damaged bowl Very fine flutes and poorly formed leaves.
17E	31	96	3133		1			22	M	A/H?		HS	R	M		1680–1710		Very faint initials, especially the surname which is very unclear.
17F*	73	97	7323		1			–	H	B		HS	R	M		1760–1800		Probably Henry Blundell, recorded at Borough 1745–64.
17E	31	96	3128	82	1	3	1	27v	I	B		HS	R	M		1770–1800	48/51	Fitting fragments making up a complete, straight-stemmed pipe.
17E	31	96	3193		1			20	I	B		H/BF	R	S		1680–1710	4	Bowl with an identical IB stamp on both the bowl and heel.
17E	30	96	3007		1			27v	S	B		HS	R	M	LDS	1800–1840		
17E		97	u/s		1			27v	S	B		HS	R	M	LDS	1780–1820		
17E	31	96	3133		1			21v	W	B		BF	R	S		1680–1710	5	
17E	31	96	3193		1			21v	W	B		BF	R	S		1680–1710		
17F*	71	97	7109		1			29v	W	B		HS	R	M	LDS, flutes, foliage, etc	1840–1880	43	
17C	25	96	2534		1			25	I?	B?		HS	R	M		1700–1740		
17	6	95	619		1			26	W?	B?		SS	R	M	Royal Arms	1740–1780		Damaged bowl with very faint and damaged initials, possibly WB.
17F*	74	97	7403		1			28v		Balme	Mile End	BF	I	S		1820–1840	12	Bowl with incuse stamped, shield-shaped mark reading BALME/MILE/END. Various Balmes' at Mile End in C19th.

						28v	G	Birchall	Chatham	SS/BS	R	M				
17E	31	97	3129	220	1	28v	G				R	M	LDS, masonic	1800–1840	18	Initials GB moulded on spur with BIRCHALL/CHATHAM moulded around the rim. Previously unrecorded maker.
17E		97	u/s		1	27	H	C		HS	R	M	Fox and grapes	1810–1840	24	Initials appear to have been altered in the mould. The original surname was perhaps an E.
17E	3	96	20		1	28	J	C		SS	R	M	LDS	1810–1840	35	
17E	31	96	3109		1	27v	J	C		HS	R	M	Flutes	1810–1850		
17F*	71	97	7102		1	28/29	J	C		SS	R	M	LDS	1830–1890		
17F*	71	97	7109		1	28/29	J	C		HS	R	M	LDS	1820–1880		
17E	78	98	8517		1	28v	J	C		SS	R	M		1820–1840		
17F*	74	97	7401		1	28	T	C		SS	R	M	LDS	1820–1840		
17E	30	96	3005		1	28v	H	D		SS	R	M	LDS (front seam only)	1810–1850		
17F	37	96	3703		1	25	I	D		HS	R	M		1700–1770		The Christian name initial is formed as a capital I but it also has a dot above it.
17E	31	97	3130		1	27	L	D		HS	R	M	LDS, fox and grapes	1780–1820	22	
17E	30	96	3007		1	27v	T	D		HS	R	M		1810–1840		
17F	41	96	4107		1	27v	I	E		HS	R	M	Fox and grapes	1810–1820	23	
17E	31	97	3109		1	27/28	W	E?		HS	R	M	Fox and grapes	1800–1840		Surname initial unclear-possibly E but could also be D, B or F.
17F*	74	97	7407		1	–	I	Elliott	[L]ambeth	SL	R	M	LDS	1840–1880	25	Stem fragment with moulded lettering reading I.ELLIOTT/[L]AMBETH.WLK? C J Elliott recorded at Tyler St, Lambeth, 1857–71.
17E	30	96	3073		1	27v	I	F		HS	R	M	Fox and grapes	1800–1840		
17E	31	96	3133		1	27v	I	F		HS	R	M	LDS	1780–1830		
17E	31	96	3133		1	27v	I	F		HS	R	M	LDS, flutes	1780–1830		
17F*	71	97	7109		1	28v	I	F		SS	R	M	LDS	1820–1860		
17F*	71	97	7109		1	29v	I	F		HS	R	M	LDS	1840–1880	40	
17E	31	97	u/s		1	28	I	F		SS	R	M	LDS	1820–1860		
17E		97	u/s		1	27v	I	F		HS	R	M	LDS	1800–1840		

Table A2.3 (continued)

Area	Tr	Yr	Cxt	SF	B	S	M	Form	CN	Surname	Other	P	T	M	Decoration	Date	Cat No	Comments
17E	31	96	3108		1			28v	T	F		SS	R	M	LDS	1810–1850		
17E	31	97	3128		1			28v	T	F		SS	R	M	LDS, flutes	1820–1840	29	Alternating thick and thin flutes.
17F*	71	97	7116		1			27/28	T?	F		HS	R	M	LDS, flutes	1780–1830		Surname initial unclear could be H, R, P or F.
17E	30	96	3005		1			27/28	I	F?		HS	R	M	LDS	1810–1850		
17F*	71	97	7116		1			27v	I	F?		HS	R	M		1780–1820		
17D	27	96	2859		1			27	I	Ford		HS/BF	R/I	M/S		1805–1865	8	Heel with moulded initials IF; bowl with incuse stamp reading FORD
17E	31	97	3130		1			28	I	Ford	Stepney	SS/BF	R/I	M/S		1820–1840	9	Initials IF moulded on spur with FORD/STEPNEY stamped on bowl.
17E	31	96	3133		1			27/28v	T	Ford	Cannon St	HS/SL	R	M	LDS	1835–1853		Heel marked TF, stem marked T.FORD.CANNON/STREET.LONDON. Thomas Ford recorded at Cannon St Rd 1835–53.
17E	31	97	3164	210	1			27/28	T	Ford	Cannon St	HS/SL	R	M	LDS and stem dec	1800–1840	37	TF moulded on heel and T.FORD. CANNON/STREET. LONDON moulded along stem.
17D	27	96	2766		1			25	A?	G		HS	R	M		1700–1770		
17B	14	96	1407		1			22	M	G		HS	R	M		1680–1710		
17E	31	96	3193		1			22	M	G		HS	R	M		1680–1710		
17E	31	96	3129		1			25/27	W	G		HS	R	M		1760–1800		Different mould to the example from Context 3132.
17E	31	96	3192		1			25/27	W	G	(crowned)	HS	R	M		1760–1800		One of two bowls from the same mould in this context.
17E	31	96	3192		1			25/27	W	G	(crowned)	HS	R	M		1760–1800		One of two bowls from the same mould in this context.

Fabric	No. 1	No. 2	Cat. no.	Count	Qty	Type	First	Surname	HS	R	M	LDS	Date	Fig.	Notes
17E	31	97	31147	217	1	22v	W	G	HS	R	M		1680–1710		Probably made by William Goulding of Stepney, recorded in 1712.
17C	3	96	20		1	27v	I	H	HS	R	M	LDS	1800–1830		
17E	25	96	2602		1	27v	I	H	HS	R	M	LDS	1810–1850		
17E	31	97	3109		1	27	I	H	HS	R	M		1780–1820		
17E	31	96	3128		1	25/27	I	H	HS	R	M		1760–1800		
17F	36	96	3620		1	28	J	H	HS	R	M		1820–1840		
17E	31	96	3166		1	27	I	Hedges	HS/BF	R/I	M/S		1780–1820		Heel with moulded mark IH, bowl stamped HEDGES. John Hedges recorded at North St, Pentonville, 1817–1819.
	80	99	4		1	17v	IOHN	HVNT	H	I	S		1660–1690	3	West Country style bowl impressed with a mark reading IOHN/HVNT. John Hunt probably worked in the Bristol/Bath area.
17E	31	96	3133		1	27v	I	I	HS	R	M		1780–1810		
17	1	95	u/s		1	27	I	I	HS	R	M		1780–1820		Dot moulded to right of Christian name initial.
17F*	71	97	7109		1	29v	B	J	HS	R	M	LDS	1840–1880		Attributed to Benjamin Jacobs, recorded at Portman Place, Mile End 1862–4 and Clark St, Commercial Rd E., 1874–85.
17E		97	u/s		1	27	I	Jones	HS/BF	R/I	M/S		1780–1820	7	Heel with moulded initials IJ, bowl with incuse stamp reading JONES.
17E	31	97	3132		1	27	M	K	HS	R	M		1780–1820		A Michael Keens is recorded at 15 York Place, Limehouse Fields, in 1836.
17C	25	96	2601		2	25	I	K?	HS	R	M		1700–1770		Two fitting fragments—surname initial damaged.

Table A2.3 (continued)

Area	Tr	Yr	Cxt	SF	B	S	M	Form	CN	Surname	Other	P	T	M	Decoration	Date	Cat No	Comments
17F*	73	97	7310		1			28	B	Leach		SS/BE	R/I	M/S		1830–1850		Spur with moulded mark BL, bowl stamped B.LEACH. Benjamin Leach recorded at Whitechapel Road 1840–47.
17	7	95	715		1			25	–	M		HS	R	M		1700–1770		Damaged heel so uncertain if initials are crowned or not; Christian initial could possibly be R or M.
17C	25	96	2633		1			22	–	M		HS	R	M		1680–1710		Damaged heel with Christian initial missing
17	6	95	625		1			25	I	M	(crowned)	HS	R	M		1700–1770		One of two IM pipes from different moulds in this context.
17E	31	96	3193		1			25	I	M		HS	R	M		1700–1750		
17E	31	96	3193		1			25	I	M		HS	R	M		1700–1750		One of two IM pipes from different moulds in this context.
17F	38	96	3801		1			27	I	M		HS	R	M	Flutes	1780–1830	30	13 flutes on each side of bowl; none on mould seams.
17E	31	96	3133		1			25	R	M		HS	R	M		1700–1770		
17F	69	96	6915		1			25	R	M		HS	R	M		1700–1770		
17	5	95	501		1			22	R?	M	(crowned)	HS	R	M		1680–1710		
17	7	95	708		1			25	W	M	(crowned)	HS	R	M		1700–1770		
17	7	95	708		1			25	W	M	(crowned)	HS	R	M		1700–1770		
17	7	95	708		1			25	W	M	(crowned)	HS	R	M		1700–1770		
17	7	95	715		1			21	W	M	(crowned)	HS	R	M		1680–1710		Christian initial partially missing but almost certainly a W.
17	7	95	715		1			25	W	M	(crowned)	HS	R	M		1700–1770		
17	7	95	719		1			22	W	M		HS	R	M		1680–1710		
17	7	95	719		1			22	W	M		HS	R	M		1680–1710		
17B	14	96	1409		1			22	W	M	(crowned)	HS	R	M		1680–1710		
17C	25	96	2551		1			25	W	M	(crowned)	HS	R	M	Royal Arms	1730–1780	13	Complete Armorial bowl.
17C	25	96	2541		1			22	W	M	(crowned)	HS	R	M		1680–1710		
17C	25	96	2631		1			22	W	M	(crowned)	HS	R	M		1680–1710		

17C	25	96	2631	1	22	W	M	(crowned)	HS	R	M	1680–1710	WM mark with device above—possibly intended as a crest or fleur-de-lys rather than a crown.
17C	25	96	2631	1	25	W	M	(crowned)	HS	R	M	1700–1770	
17D	27	96	2849	1	25	W	M	(crowned)	HS	R	M	1700–1770	
17D	27	96	2859	1	25/27	W	M		HS	R	M	1760–1800	Very thin bowl and stem.
17E	31	96	3193	1	25	W	M	(crowned)	HS	R	M	1700–1770	Different mould from another crowned WM pipe found in the same context.
17F	53	96	5314	1	25	W	M	(crowned)	HS	R	M	1700–1770	
17F	53	96	5314	1	25	W	M	(crowned)	HS	R	M	1700–1770	Different mould from another crowned WM pipe found in the same context.
17F	56	96	5606	1	27	W	M		HS	R	M	1780–1820	Thick bowl form.
17	7	95	715	1	25	R	M?		HS	R	M	1700–1770	
17E	31	96	3109	1	28	R	O		SS	R	M	1810–1840	
17	6	95	619	1	28	R	Osborne	& Co London	SS/BF	R/I	M/S	1830–1850	11 — Spur with moulded mark RO; bowl with stamped mark OSBORNE & Co, LONDON
17C	25	96	2511	1	25	T	P		HS	R	M	1700–1770	
17D	27	96	2850	1	25	W	P		HS	R	M	1700–1770	
17H	83	97	8366	1	25v	W	P		HS	R	M	1690–1740	
17C	25	96	2603	1	25	E	R		HS	R	M	1700–1770	
17E	31	96	3128	1	25	E	R		HS	R	M	1700–1770	
17E	31	96	3193	1	25	E	R		HS/BF	R/I	M/S	1730–1770	6 — Moulded initials ER on heel. stamped mark ER on bowl.
17F	59	96	5900	1	25	E	R		HS	R	M	1700–1770	
17F	68	96	6824	1	25	E	R		HS	R	M	1700–1770	
17H	83	97	8371	1	25	M	R	(crowned)	HS	R	M	1700–1750	Possibly Mary Robins, recorded in 1686.
17B	14	96	1409	1	25	R	R		HS	R	M	1700–1750	
17B	14	96	1409	1	25	R?	R		HS	R	M	1700–1770	
17E	31	96	3128	1	25/27	T	R		HS	R	M	1760–1800	
17E	31	96	3133	1	25/27	T	R		HS	R	M	1760–1800	One of three examples from the same mould in this context.

Table A2.3 (continued)

Area	Tr	Yr	Cxt	SF	B	S	M	Form	CN	Surname	Other	P	T	M	Decoration	Date	Cat No	Comments
17E	31	96	3133		1			25/27	T	R		HS	R	M		1760–1800		One of three examples from the same mould in this context.
17E	31	96	3133		1			25/27	T	R		HS	R	M		1760–1800		One of three examples from the same mould in this context.
17H	81	97	8120		1			25	T	R		HS	R	M		1700–1770		
	3	96	23		1			27	W	R		HS	R	M	LDS, POWF, masonic	1780–1820	19	Surname initial appears to have been altered in mould, possibly H originally.
17E	31	96	3128		1			27	W	R		HS	R	M		1780–1820		
17E	31	96	3193		1			27	W	R		HS	R	M		1770–1820		
17E	30	96	3008		1			27v	J	Russ[ell]	[Wa]pping	HS/SL	R	M	LDS, POWF, masonic	1820–1840	20	Heel initials JR, moulded stem mark RUSS//PPING for John Russell, recorded at 24 Green Bank, Wapping, 1822–32.
17	7	95	u/s		1			25	A	S	(crowned)	HS	R	M		1700–1770		
17F*	73	97	7309		1			27/28	I	S	(I over W)	HS	R	M		1800–1850		Christian name initial I appears to have been engraved over a deleted W, suggesting mark was originally WS.
17A	15	96	u/s		1			25	I	S		HS	R	M		1700–1770		
17F*	71	97	7109		2			28	T	S		SS	R	M	LDS	1820–1860	39	Two joining bowl fragments.
17E	31	97	u/s	215	1			28	T	S	London Arms	SS/BF	R/I	M/S		1820–1840	10	Moulded initials TS on spur with London Arms stamped on the bowl.
	3	96	20		1			27	W	S		HS	R	M		1780–1820		
	3	96	23		1			27	W	S		HS	R	M	LDS, flutes	1780–1820		
17E	31	96	3107		1			27	W	S		HS	R	M		1780–1820	28	Large, thin-walled bowl with altered initials, the surname having been changed to an S cut upright on the heel.
17E	31	97	3131		1		1	27	W	S		HS	R	M		1780–1820	49/52	Joining fragments making up a complete pipe with a curved stem of 365mm in length.

Context			Find	Qty	Ct	Ref	In1	In2	Maker	Stem	Form	R/I	M/S	Decoration	Date	Fig	Comments
17E	31	97	3133	1		27v	W	S			HS	R	M		1780–1820		Another unstratified example marked WS from Trench 31 is from a different mould.
17	3	95	u/s	1		27	W	S			HS	R	M		1780–1820		
17E	31	97	u/s	1		27	W	S			HS	R	M		1780–1820		
17E	31	97	u/s	1		27	W	S			HS	R	M		1780–1820		Another unstratified example marked WS from Trench 31 is from a different mould.
17E		97	u/s	1		27	W	S			HS	R	M		1780–1820		Unclear initials, first probably I or T, second possibly an S.
17D	27	96	2822	1		26	I/T?	S?			HS	R	M		1740–1790		
17E	30	96	3005	1		28	J		Smith		SS/BF	R/I	M/S		1820–1840		Moulded spur mark JS with stamped bowl mark [S]MITH/…G.
17E	31	96	u/s	1	218	27v	J		Smith	Wapp.ng	HS	R	M	LDS, POWF, masonic	1820–1850	21	Heel marked JS and stem SMIT[H]/[WA]PPING. A John Smith is recorded at Wapping from 1844–62.
17F	37	96	u/s	1	1	–			Smith	Foo[tball pipe]	SL	I	M		1880–1920		Stem with moulded mark [S]MITHS/FOO[TBALL PIPE]. Attributed to Richard Smith.
17E	31	97	3132	1		27v	–	T			HS	R	M		1780–1820		135mm of curved stem survives, heel damaged.
17E	3	96	23	1		27	I	T			HS	R	M		1780–1820		Pipe mould rim appears to have been raised by c5mm in height at some point.
17E		97	u/s	1		27/28	I	T			HS	R	M		1780–1830		
17E	3	96	23	1		27	J	T			HS	R	M		1780–1820		Surname W moulded sideways on heel. Enclosed flutes and dots on bowl, complete foliage dec on stem survives.
17E	30	96	3005	1		28v	W	T			SS	R	M	LDS	1820–1840	26	
17E	3	96	20	1		27	I	W			HS	R	M	LDS, flutes, foliage	1780–1820		

Table A2.3 (continued)

Area	Tr	Yr	Cxt	SF	B	S	M	Form	CN	Surname	Other	P	T	M	Decoration	Date	Cat No	Comments
17E	30	96	3066		2			27	I	W	London Arms	HS/BF	R/I	M/S		1780–1820		Two fitting fragments with IW moulded on heel and the London Arms stamped on the bowl.
17D	27	96	2822		1			25	I?	W		HS	R	M		1700–1770		
17E	31	96	3129		1	1		25/27	P	W		HS	R	M		1770–1800		Bowl and fitting stem.
17D	27	96	2822		1			25	R	W		HS	R	M		1700–1770		
17	1	95	u/s		1			25	R?	W		HS	R	M		1700–1750		Early Type 25 form.
17E	31	96	3166		1			27	S	W		HS	R	M		1780–1820		
17E	31	96	3165		1			27v	T	W		HS	R	M	Flutes, foliage on stem	1790–1840	32	
17E	30	96	3007		1			–	W	W		HS	R	M		1810–1850		
17F*	71	97	7109		1			29v	W	W		HS	R	M	LDS	1840–1880	41	
17D	27	97	8079		1			–	W	W		H	R	S		1660–1680	2	Neat bulbous heel form-not closely matched in London typology.
17H	81	97	8133		1			25	W	W	(crowned?)	HS	R	M		1700–1770		Faint initials with some sort of symbol moulded above each, possibly crowns.
17D	27	96	2859		1			27/28	*	Williams	London	HS/BF	R/I	M/S	LDS	1820–1850		Moulded star on either side of heel, incuse stamp reading WILLIAMS LONDON on bowl, leaf seam away from smoker only.
17E	30	96	3008		1			27v	T	Woott[en]	[Park St]reet Boro	HS/SL	R	M	Flutes	1820–1850		Stars on heel, T.WOOTT[EN]/[PARK ST]REET BORO moulded on stem. Tho Wootten recorded there 1822-48.
17E	30	96	3008		1			27v	T	Wootten	[Park St]reet Boro	HS/SL	R	M	Flutes	1820–1850	34	Stars on heel, T.WOOTTEN/[PARK ST]REET BORO moulded on stem. Tho Wootten recorded there 1822-48.

Appendix 2

Site	Context	Year	No.	Qty	Drawing	T	Wootten	No 12 Park Street Boro	HS/SL	R	M	Decoration	Date	Fig	Comments
17F	38	96	3811	1	27					R	M	Flutes, foliage on stem	1820–1850	31	Stars on either side of heel and T.WOOTTEN. No 12/PARK STREET BORO or stem. Tho Wootten recorded there 1822–48.
17F*	71	97	7109	1	28	J	–		SS	R	M	LDS	1820–1850		Surname initial damaged.
17	7	95	715	1	25	R?	–		HS	R	M		1700–1770		Thick bowl form.
17	7	95	715	3	25v	R	.		HS	R	M		1750–1790		Three fitting fragments with single dot on RHS of heel.
80	80	99	4	1	28	*	*		SS	R	M	LDS	1810–1850		Fragmentary bowl with a small star moulded on either side of the spur. Different mould from a similar example in TOL 80 99 12.
80	80	99	12	1	28v	*	*		SS	R	M	LDS	1810–1850		Leaf decorated seams and a star moulded on each side of the spur. Different mould from a similar example in TOL 80 99 4.
30	30	96	3007	1	27	*	*		HS	R	M	LDS, flutes	1790–1830	27	Thin heel with stars in deep relief. An example from the same context has had stars deleted from mould.
31	31	97	3109	1	27	*	*		HS	R	M	LDS	1780–1820		Two fitting fragments giving 185mm or surviving stem—curved.
31	31	97	3109	1	28	*	*		SS	R	M	LDS and	1820–1840		Faint striations on bowl sides as if mould altered to remove flutes.
31	31	97	3128	1	27v	*	*		HS	R	M	?flutes	1780–1820	38	
31	31	96	3133	1	28v	*	*		SS	R	M	LDS	1820–1850		Poor quality bowl with unclear dot or star on either side of the spur.
31	31	96	3193	1	25	*	*		HS	R	M		1700–1750		Moulded spur mark on heel—presumed to have occurred both sides although left hand side chipped away.

Table A2.3 (continued)

Area	Tr	Yr	Cxt	SF	B	S	M	Form	CN	Surname	Other	P	T	M	Decoration	Date	Cat No	Comments
17F*	71	97	7106		2			28?	*	*		SS	R	M		1820–1850		Two joining bowl fragments.
17F*	71	97	7109		1			28	*	*		SS	R	M	LDS	1820–1840		Heel with neat star mark—bowl missing but traces of decoration survive.
17	5	95	u/s		1			–	*	*		HS	R	M	Traces only	1820–1880		
17	7	95	715		1			25v	.	.		HS	R	M		1750–1790		Single dot on either side of heel.
17D	27	96	2823		1			25/27	.	.		HS	R	M		1760–1800		Moulded dot on each side of heel
	3	96	8		2			29v			birds	HS	R	M		1840–1880	44	Two fitting frags from a small heel bowl with an unusual bird mark moulded on either side of the heel
17B	14	96	1422		1			25	?	?		HS	R	M		1700–1770		Illegible heel mark.
17C	25	96	2541		1			25	?	?		HS	R	M		1700–1770		Illegible mark.
17C		96	u/s		1			25v	?	?					POWF, rose and thistle	1740–1770	16	Almost certainly an unmarked heel type (heel badly damaged); crude POWF, etc, dec.
	3	96	20		1			27/28	–	–					LDS	1800–1830		Spur or heel missing.
17E	30	96	3005		1			27/28?	–	–					LDS	1820–1840		Foliage decoration on both sides of a stem fragment.
17F*	71	97	7109			1		–	–	–					Foliage dec on stem	1820–1880		
17F*	71	97	7109		1			28/29?	–	–					LDS	1820–1880		Bowl fragment only.
17F	47	96	u/s	52	1			–	–	–					Lion heads, feathers, etc	1800–1900	45	Very unusual bowl. Possibly a southern European import, perhaps southern France or Italy.
17	1	95	u/s		1			26?	–	–					Royal Arms	1730–1780		Damaged bowl with heel or spur missing but almost certainly a spur type. Traces of initials (illegible).

Context			SF no	No.	No.	Plate	/O.:2?//PAR/	Symbol	SL	R	M	Leaves, etc	Date	No.	Notes
17E	31	96	3109	1			–						1810–1840	33	Part of a decorated stem with moulded mark, almost certainly 'T WOOTTEN No 12/ PARK STREET BORO'.
17C	25	96	2631		2	25		crowned flowers	HS	R	M		1700–1770		Joining fragments with crowned flower mark on either side of heel
17D	27	96	2761		1	25		crowned harps	HS	R	M		1720–1780		
17D	27	96	2829		1		–	crowned harps	HS	R	M		1690–1710		
17E	31	96	3193		1	25		crowned harps	HS	R	M		1700–1770		Crowned harps on both sides of heel, the first being preceded by a dot.
17	3	95	u/s		1	25		crowned harps	HS	R	M		1700–1770		
17C	25	96	2567		1	25		crowned harps?	HS	R	M		1700–1770		Unclear symbol marks, probably crowned harps on either side of heel.
17F	56	96	5607		1	25		crowned sun	HS	R	M		1700–1770		Crowned sun or flower mark on either side of the heel.
17D	27	96	2822		1	25		flowers	HS	R	M		1700–1770		A single flower or sun symbol on either side of heel.
17C	25	96	2567		1	25		harp? and crown	HS	R	M		1700–1770		First symbol mark unclear but probably a harp with single crown on other side.
17F*	71	97	7109		1	29v		rings	HS	R	M	LDS	1840–1880		Serrated ring motif moulded on each side of heel.
17F*	71	97	7109		1	29v		shields	HS	R	M	LDS	1840–1880	42	Shield moulded on each side of heel.
17C	25	96	2632		1	10v		'sun'	H	I	S		1630–1660	1	
17E	30	96	3006		1		–					Claw and egg	1860–1920		
17	5	95	u/s	1	1		–					Claw design	1860–1920		Bowl fragment only.
17F	36	96	3621	1	1		–					Foliage	1810–1850		Spray of foliage moulded on stem sides.
17	5	95	u/s	1	1							Foliage	1820–1860		
17E	31	97	3128		1	28v	–					LDS	1820–1840		

Table A2.3 (continued)

Area	Tr	Yr	Cxt	SF	B	S	M	Form	CN	Surname	Other	P	T	M	Decoration	Date	Cat No	Comments
17E	30	96	3007		1			27							LDS, flutes	1790–1830		Same mould as another example from this context but without the star marks on the heel.
17	7	95	706			1		–							LDS, stars	1820–1860	36	
17	7	95	715		3			25v							POWF	1740–1780	15	Three fitting fragments. Same mould as an example from TOL 17C 96 2541.
17C	25	96	2541		1			25v							POWF	1740–1780	15	Same mould as an example from TOL 17 95 715.
17F*	71	97	7109		1			25/26							POWF, foliage, dots	1740–1790	17	Large bowl form with the body of a Type 26 but the heel of a Type 25.

Appendix 3: Soil Micromorphology Data

Table A3.1   Particle size of the various contexts

Context	Coarse sand (%)	Medium sand (%)	Fine sand (%)	Silt (%)	Clay (%)	Texture class*
London Clay (#6)	0.2	0.1	3.5	36.8	59.4	C
London Clay (#7)	0.2	0.4	1.6	38.0	59.8	C
2576	6.5	8.9	13.3	57.9	13.4	ZL
2604	2.2	2.8	5.1	50.3	39.6	ZyCL
2833	0.1	0.3	1.6	60.0	38.0	ZyCL
2834	0.4	1.7	9.4	66.2	22.3	ZL
2835	0.4	1.1	2.7	71.5	24.3	ZL
2836	2.0	2.9	4.0	59.4	31.7	ZyCL
2838	0.1	0.1	0.3	49.1	50.4	ZyC
2839	0.1	0.2	1.7	35.7	62.3	C
2840	0.1	0.1	0.4	49.7	49.7	ZyC
2841	<0.1	0.1	0.2	45.9	53.8	ZyC
2842	0.1	0.2	0.6	43.7	55.4	ZyC
2844	3.7	7.0	4.9	44.3	40.1	ZyC
2852	2.1	2.2	6.1	74.6	15.0	ZL
2853	0.2	0.5	1.4	81.0	16.9	ZL
2937	0.9	1.8	8.8	71.1	17.4	ZL
2964	6.5	3.3	3.4	54.4	32.4	ZyCL
2965	0.5	0.5	1.4	50.9	46.7	ZyC
2966	0.9	0.8	5.6	50.6	42.1	ZyC
2967	2.5	2.8	11.4	56.3	27.0	ZL
3133	0.2	0.2	1.4	53.1	45.1	ZyC
3136	0.8	3.2	14.7	62.5	18.8	ZL
3137	9.3	13.2	9.4	29.0	39.1	CL
3141	1.3	4.5	12.5	60.9	20.8	ZL

* Texture class: C = Clay, CL = Clay loam, ZL = Silt loam, ZyC = Silty clay, ZyCL = Silty clay loam.

Table A3.2   Chemical properties of the various contexts

Context	CaCO$_3$ (%)	pH (1:2.5, water)	Specific conductance (μmho cm^{-1} @ 25°C)	LOI (%)	Phosphate-P (mg g^1)	Residual phosphate-P¶ (mg g^{-1})	Sulphate†
London Clay (#6)	0.62	7.0	2080	2.54	0.544	−0.11	+++
London Clay (#7)	1.22	7.7	765	2.82	0.847	0.13	+++
2576	46.7	7.6	1440	8.92	1.17	−0.97	+++
2604	11.3	7.5	1640	9.43	2.35	0.09	+++
2833	10.2	7.6	2170	9.11	2.97	0.78	+++
2834	29.4	7.8	1690	7.84	2.65	0.76	+++
2835	29.4	7.7	1750	9.62	2.80	0.49	++
2836	32.3	7.8	1560	5.50	1.54	0.20	++
2838	10.5	7.7	1840	5.62	1.39	0.02	++
2839	5.76	7.7	2310	5.58	1.23	−0.13	++
2840	14.6	7.9	1670	4.85	1.13	−0.06	++
2841	9.42	7.8	1800	4.58	0.918	−0.21	+++
2842	11.3	7.8	2210	4.67	1.08	−0.07	+++
2844	15.8	7.8	1870	4.65	1.17	0.02	++
2852	45.7	7.8	1070	7.89	1.99	0.09	++
2853	48.7	7.8	1184	7.89	2.04	0.14	+++
2937	40.0	7.7	1450	10.5	1.85	−0.66	+++
2964	26.3	7.9	1520	3.04	1.12	0.35	+++
2965	15.4	8.1	718	4.14	1.18	0.15	+
2966	15.1	8.1	602	4.28	0.983	−0.08	+
2967	33.9	8.3	508	2.69	0.761	0.07	+

Table A3.2   (continued)

Context	CaCO$_3$ (%)	pH (1:2.5, water)	Specific conductance (μmho cm^{-1} @ 25°C)	LOI (%)	Phosphate-P (mg g^{-1})	Residual phosphate-P[¶] (mg g^{-1})	Sulphate[†]
3133	10.2	7.7	1170	7.29	1.79	0.03	+++
3136	52.0	7.8	1200	5.90	1.18	−0.26	+++
3137	13.2	7.6	1300	5.69	0.845	−0.54	+++
3141	40.0	7.8	1270	4.34	0.872	−0.20	+++

¶ Residual value of phosphate-P based on regression between phosphate-P and LOI: phos = 0.060+0.234 LOI.

† Qualitative assessment of based on BaCl$_2$ test in particle size analysis: +++ = 'high', ++ = 'moderate', + = 'low'.

Table A3.3   Magnetic properties of the various contexts

Context	χ (10^{-8} m^3 kg^{-1})	χ$_{max}$ (10^{-8} m^{-3} kg^{-1})	χ$_{conv}$ (%)
London Clay (#6)	44.6	219	20.4
London Clay (#7)	44.6	243	18.4
2576	4.2	66.5	6.32
2604	83.9	689	12.2
2833	54.4	680	8.00
2834	52.0	399	13.0
2835	62.3	533	11.7
2836	29.1	452	6.44
2838	31.5	533	5.91
2839	32.1	723	4.44
2840	34.0	620	5.48
2841	40.8	535	7.63
2842	24.3	539	4.51
2844	31.8	564	5.64
2852	1.6	29.5	5.42
2853	10.5	96.2	10.9
2937	2.4	58.5	4.10
2964	22.5	292	7.70
2965	22.0	213	10.3
2966	24.2	247	9.81
2967	20.1	122	16.5
3133	24.8	1280	1.94
3136	6.3	83.8	7.52
3137	20.6	274	7.51
3141	4.8	92.0	5.22

Table A3.4   Heavy metal concentrations of the various contexts

Context	Pb (μg g^{-1})	Zn (μg g^{-1})	Cu (μg g^{-1})
London Clay (#6)	10	33	17
London Clay (#7)	11	27	16
2576	117	39	299
2604	421	77	96
2833	271	67	77
2834	298	53	140
2835	356	61	186
2836	95	24	25
2838	43	30	17
2839	58	36	22
2840	49	28	16
2841	58	61	55
2842	65	29	19
2844	114	29	19
2852	209	65	69
2853	145	23	44
2937	169	33	51
2964	67	23	11
2965	93	20	13
2966	182	21	13
2967	280	18	12
3133	164	42	39
3136	175	50	388
3137	260	110	543
3141	306	21	22

Table A3.5   Pearson product moment correlation coefficients for relationships between properties of the various contexts. All coefficients shown are significant at p < 0.05 (i.e. 95% confidence level)

	pH	Cond	LOI	Phos-P	χ	χ$_{max}$[†]	χ$_{conv}$[†]	Pb	Zn[†]	Cu[†]
Carb	ns	ns	ns	ns	−0.606	−0.749*	ns	ns	ns	ns
pH		−0.581	ns	ns	ns	ns	ns	ns	−0.470	ns
Cond			ns	ns	ns	0.496	ns	ns	ns	ns
LOI				0.821*	ns	ns	ns	0.536	0.553	0.639
Phos-P					0.417	ns	ns	0.580	0.459	0.402
χ						0.702*	0.426	ns	ns	ns
χ$_{max}$[†]							ns	ns	ns	ns
χ$_{conv}$[†]								ns	ns	ns
Pb									0.445	0.499
Zn[†]										0.801*

† Variables log transformed to improve parametricity.

* Correlation significant at $p < 0.001$ (i.e. 99.9% confidence level).

ns Not significant.

Table A3.6   Summary of results from individual contexts

Ctxt	Key features*	Interpretation
Trench 25: SE causeway – post-1680 silting		
2604	Predominantly silts and clays; moderate $CaCO_3$ content; high LOI, phosphate P (but only small +ve residual), χ, χ_{max}, χ_{conv}, Pb and Zn; and moderate Cu.	The texture indicates deposition in a lower energy environment than 2576. Very strong evidence of anthropogenic inputs (cf. 2576), probably from cess and domestic/industrial waste, and of some of the sediments having been subject to burning.
Trench 25: SE causeway – 13th century (?) silting		
2576	High silt content; lowest clay content; relatively high sand content; high LOI and Cu; moderate phosphate-P (but −ve residual), χ_{conv}, Pb and Zn; and low χ and χ_{max}.	The texture suggests deposition in a relatively high-energy environment and/or sediment sources that are deficient in clays. Apart from the high Cu concentration there is little evidence of anthropogenic inputs.
Trench 27 ("barbican" area): Eastern end – Full sequence of 13th century to post-medieval silting		
2833	Mostly silts and clays, with very little sand; high LOI, phosphate-P (highest, and with +ve residual), χ and χ_{max} (though $\chi_{conv} < 10\%$), Pb and Zn; and moderate $CaCO_3$.	Distinguished from underlying context by its very low sand content, and much lower carbonate concentration. Slightly less evidence of burning than in 2835 (below). Otherwise very similar in terms of anthropogenic indicators, though this is against a background of a lower carbonate concentration (i.e. there is less 'dilution').
2834	As 2835 (below), but with a higher proportion of (mostly fine) sands; and a slightly lower silt content, LOI and χ_{max}.	As 2835 (below).
2835	High silt content; and high $CaCO_3$, LOI, phosphate-P (with high +ve residual), χ, χ_{max}, χ_{conv}, Pb, Zn and Cu.	This context shows signs of a strong anthropogenic input, particularly in view of the relatively high carbonate content: high phosphate and heavy metal concentrations, and high magnetic susceptibility. These characteristics seem likely to be attributable to the incorporation of cess and domestic/industrial waste, the latter including material that has been subject to burning. In view of the obvious anthropogenic input it seems likely that cess and other organic wastes contribute to the high LOI.
2836	Higher proportion of silts than clays; sands present (not as sandy as 2844); high $CaCO_3$; moderate LOI and phosphate-P (higher than underlying contexts and with +ve residual); and low χ, χ_{max}, χ_{conv}, Pb, Zn and Cu.	Distinguished from underlying contexts by higher silt content, which may indicate a change in the source/character of sediments and/or deposition in a slightly higher energy fluvial environment; and by a much higher carbonate content. The latter may reflect an increased rate of carbonate deposition from the water in the moat relative to other sediments, the presence of more shell material, or the incorporation of mortar. The increased phosphate-P suggests a possible increase in cess-type input, though there is no evidence of burning or of enrichment in heavy metals.

Table A3.6 (continued)

Ctxt	Key features*	Interpretation
2844	Mostly silts and clays, but with 15.6% sand; moderate $CaCO_3$, phosphate-P, χ, χ_{conv} and Pb; and low LOI, Zn and Cu.	Presence of coarser material and a lower proportion of clays distinguish it from the underlying contexts. Levels of carbonate, LOI and phosphate-P are similar to those in 2842 (below) and probably of similar origin. The slightly higher Pb concentration possibly suggests a greater anthropogenic input, though levels of Zn and Cu remain low. Little evidence of burning.
2838	As 2842 (below), but with slightly higher LOI and phosphate-P.	As 2842 (below)
2839	As 2842 (below), but with less $CaCO_3$ and slightly higher LOI and phosphate-P.	As 2842 (below)
2840	As 2842 (below), but with slightly lower proportion of clay.	As 2842 (below)
2841	As 2842 (below)	As 2842 (below)
2842	Clay-rich; moderate $CaCO_3$ and phosphate-P (but −ve residual); and low LOI (though higher than in London Clay), χ, χ_{conv}, Pb, Zn and Cu.	Similar texture and low heavy metal concentrations as London Clay samples, which suggests that this context may be largely derived from this source. However, the presence of moderate carbonate and phosphate concentrations, and a higher LOI, indicates the incorporation of sediments from other sources. Although some of the carbonate may be derived from mortar (cf. context 2843, below) and/or shells, it seems likely that there has been substantial deposition from the water in the Moat. The higher LOI and phosphate concentration might be attributable to plant growth within the moat and/or some degree of cess-type input. The magnetic susceptibility data provide no evidence of burning within this context.
2843	No bulk sample supplied	Described as soft, rubbly mortar foundation, containing shelly sand material in initial assessment report.
LC(#6)	Clay-rich; high χ_{conv}; low Cu; and lowest $CaCO_3$, LOI, phosphate-P and Pb.	Natural London Clay, very similar to #7 (below)
LC(#7)	Clay-rich; high χ_{conv}; and low $CaCO_3$, LOI, phosphate-P, Pb, Zn and Cu.	Natural London Clay, with no evidence of organic accumulation or anthropogenic input. The high χ_{conv} is difficult to explain and merits further investigation.
Trench 27 ("barbican" area): Western end – post-medieval silting		
2937	Very similar to 2853, but with a higher LOI (the highest recorded) and a lower phosphate-P concentration (with a high −ve residual)	As 2853 (below), but with less evidence of a phosphate-rich cess input.
2852	Very similar to 2853, but slightly more sandy and less silty, and with a stronger indication of heavy metal contamination.	As 2853 (below), but possibly with a rather higher domestic/industrial component.
2853	Very silty, with low clay content; high $CaCO_3$, LOI, phosphate-P (with small +ve residual) and χ_{conv}; moderate Pb and Cu; and low χ, χ_{max} and Zn.	High carbonate content, which is presumed to be mostly derived from the deposition from water in the moat, suggests the context developed under

Table A3.6   (continued)

Ctxt	Key features*	Interpretation
		conditions in which there was limited inwash into the moat of minerogenic sediments, which could also account for the higher LOI. The very high silt content clearly includes a significant proportion of carbonates. The high phosphate and the moderate concentrations of Pb and Cu (particularly in view of the 'dilution' due to the high carbonate content) may indicate inputs of cess, with some domestic/ industrial inputs. The low χ_{max}, which is indicative of a low Fe content, suggests that the sediments may be heavily gleyed. If this is the case, then the magnetic properties provide an unreliable basis for assessing the extent to which components of the sediment have been subject to burning.

Trench 31: SW causeway – medieval to post-medieval silting

Ctxt	Key features*	Interpretation
3141	Predominantly silts; relatively high sand content; high $CaCO_3$ and Pb; and low LOI, phosphate-P, χ, χ_{max}, Zn and Cu.	Apart from the high Pb concentration, which is difficult to explain, there is little evidence of anthropogenic input. The relatively high carbonate content suggests slow sedimentation. The low χ_{max} is perhaps attributable to gleying.

Section 2717: 13th century "barbican" – silting below timbers

Ctxt	Key features*	Interpretation
2964	Predominantly silt and clay, but with quite a high sand content (including coarse sands); high $CaCO_3$ and sulphate; moderate specific conductance, pH, phosphate-P (with +ve residual), χ, χ_{max} and χ_{conv}; and low LOI, Pb, Zn and Cu.	This context shares some of the properties of the underlying context 2965, and there are signs of similarly low levels anthropogenic input. In this case it is less clear as to whether the context is water-lain. Thus, while the very low LOI suggests not, the higher conductance and sulphate content suggests that it might be. In the latter case, much of the carbonate may be derived from the moat waters or mollusc shells, rather than from mortar.
2965	As 2966, except slightly higher phosphate-P (with small +ve residual).	As 2966, though the higher phosphate concentration may possibly reflect the incorporation of some cess-type material.
2966	Very similar to 2967, except less sandy and with a lower (moderate) $CaCO_3$ content.	As 2967, except that the slightly different texture and lower carbonate content perhaps indicate less incorporation of mortar.
2967	Predominantly silt, but with a relatively high sand content; high $CaCO_3$, pH, χ_{conv} and Pb; moderate χ and χ_{max}; and low LOI, phosphate-P, specific conductance, sulphate, Zn and Cu.	The texture and high carbonate content suggests that this context is not purely redeposited/disturbed London Clay. However, the low phosphate and low concentrations of Zn and Cu (though not of Pb) indicate a limited anthropogenic input; and the low LOI (similar to the London Clay samples) indicates that this context might not have accumulated by normal fluvial sedimentation processes.

Table A3.6   (continued)

Ctxt	Key features*	Interpretation
		The high pH, low conductance and sulphate would appear to support this interpretation. One possible interpretation would be that this deposit comprises largely London Clay, intermixed with mortar. The high χ_{conv} value is in keeping with the results recorded in the London Clay (#6 and #7). This is difficult to explain, and cannot necessarily be assumed to reflect burning, particularly in view of the low χ value.

Section 3112: SW causeway – 13th century and post-medieval silting

Ctxt	Key features*	Interpretation
3133	Mostly silts and clays, with low sand content; high χ_{max} (highest recorded); moderate $CaCO_3$, LOI, phosphate-P (with slight +ve residual), Pb and Zn; and low Cu.	The very high χ_{max} indicates a higher Fe content than the other contexts, which is possibly of anthropogenic origin. The context shows more sign of phosphate enrichment, though less of heavy metal enrichment, than the underlying context.
3136	High silt content and relatively high (mostly fine) sand content; high $CaCO_3$ (highest recorded), Zn and Cu; moderate LOI, phosphate-P (but with −ve residual) and Pb; and low χ and χ_{max}.	Clearly distinguished from underlying and overlying contexts (3137 and 3133) by very high carbonate content. The high silt fraction includes carbonates, which presumably were largely precipitated from the moat waters. The is high heavy metal contamination (particularly in view of 'dilution' caused by carbonate), which may be indicative of industrial sources, but little evidence of phosphate enrichment (as might be associated with cess inputs). The low χ_{max} suggests that the context is quite heavily gleyed.
3137	Relatively high sand content (highest recorded) and low silt content; high Pb, Zn and Cu (highest recorded); moderate $CaCO_3$, LOI, χ, χ_{max}, χ_{conv}; and low phosphate-P (with −ve residual value).	The high sand content suggests a relatively sandy source and/or deposition in a relatively high-energy environment. The high heavy metal contamination may be indicative of industrial sources, but no there is evidence of phosphate enrichment or magnetic susceptibility enhancement (as might be associated with cess inputs and burning).

*Footnotes:

1. The terms 'high', 'moderate' and 'low' are used relative to the distribution of values in the present data set.

2. The residual value cited for phosphate-P is the residual from the regression line for the relationship between phosphate-P and LOI (Table 2).

Table A3.7 Soil micromorphology of sediments (counts)

Bulk Sample (context)	Site Context/Period/Feature	Period	Thin section	Microfabric/Facies Type	Relic pyritised wood	Pyrite	Gypsum	Vivianite	Root trace	Root channels	Iron eplaced OM and staining	Laminated	Massive	massive micrite	Heterogeneous	Micro-sparite	Earthworm features	Coarse shell (molluscs)	Shell (Ostracods?)	Detrital organic matter	Anthropogenic inclusions	Mortar	Burrows
x2833	Trench 27	Post-Med.	A-upper	7			aaaa		a	a	aa	f	ffff		fff					aaaaa	a		
x2834	Section 2702	Post-Med.	A-lower	7			a	a	a	a	a	fff	ff	f	f	a			aaa	aaaaa	aa		
x2834	ditto	Post-Med.	B-upper	7			a		a	a	aa	ff	fffff		ff	a		a	aaa	aaaaa	aa		
x2835	ditto	Post-Med.	B-lower	7			a	a			aa	ff	ffff		ff			a	a	aaa	aa		
x2844	ditto	13thC	B-lower	4			aa				aa	ff	ffff		f			a	a	aaa	a		
x2838	ditto	13thC	E-upper	4			aa						ffff					aa	a	aaa	a		
x2839	ditto	13thC	E-lower	4			a						ffff					a	a	aa	a		
x2840	ditto	13thC	G-upper	4			aa		a	a			ffff			a		a	a	aa	a		
x2841	ditto	13thC	G-lower	4			aaa		a	a	a		fffff			a		a		aa	a		
x2841	ditto	13thC	H-upper	4			aaa		a	a	a	fffff	fffff		a	a				aa	a		
x2842	ditto	13thC	H-lower	4			aaa		a	a	aa	fffff			a	a				aa	a		a
(x6)	ditto	London Clay?	J	1a			aaa		a	a	aa	fffff		a	ffff								
(x7)	ditto	London Clay?	K	1b	aaa		a		a		aa	f			f								
x2576	Trench 25	13thC	L	3			a		aca	aaa	a	fffff	ff		f	a	aa	aaa	aaaaa	aaa	aaa	aa	aa
x2604	Trench 25	post-1680	M	5		aa	aaa		a	a	a		fffff		ff			aa	aaa	aaaa	aaa	a	
x3141	Trench 31	Post-Med.	N	6		aa			a			ff	fffff		ff			aa		aaa			
x2937	Trench 27	17th C	O-upper	6			aa		aa	aa		fff	fffff					a		aaaa			aa
x2852	Trench 27	17th C	O-lower	6					aa	aaa			fffff					a		aaa			
x2852	Trench 27	17th C	P-upper	6					aa	aa			fffff							aaa			
x2853	Trench 27	17th C	P-lower	6					aa	aa			fffff							aaa			
x2964	Section 2717	13th C	Q-upper	2b		aa				a		ffff	ff	fff	ff	a				aaa			
x2965	Section 2717	13th C	Q-lower	2b		aa				a		fffff		fff	f				a	aa			
x2966	Section 2717	13th C	S-upper	2a			?		a	a	aa	fffff	fffff	ffff	f	aa				aa			
x2967	Section 2717	13th C	S-lower	2a		a			aa	aa	aaaa	fffff	fff	fff		aa				aaa			
x3133	Section 3112	post-med	T-upper	6								ff	fff		ff	aa	a	a	aa	aaa	aa	aa	
x3136	Section 3112	post-med	T-lower	6					aa	aa		ff	fff		f		a	aa	aa	aa	aaa	aaa	a
x3136	Section 3112	post-med	U-upper	6			a				a		fff		ffff			aa	aa	aa	aaa	aa	aaa
x3137	Section 3112	post-med	U-lower	6					aa	aa		ffff	ff	fff	f	aa	aa	aa	aa	aa	a	aa	aa

* - very few 0–5%, f - few 5–15%, ff - frequent 15–30%, fff - common 30–50%, ffff - dominant 50–70%, a - rare <2%, aa - occasional 2–5%, aaa - many 5–10%, aaaa - abundant 10–20%, aaaaa - very abundant >20%.

Table A3.8 Facies Types (soil microfabric types and associated data)

Material	Sample Number examples	Soil Micromorphology (M), Bulk Data (BD), Microprobe (Probe) and Elemental Map (EM)	Interpretation and Comments
Facies 1a / Soil Microfabric Type 1a	**J** x6	SM: Massive with relic fine bedding (1mm thick clay and fine silt beds and clay and coarse silt beds; crack microstructure; 10–15% voids, very dominant moderately well accommodated very fine to medium (100μm–0.5mm) cracks, and very few fine channels; Mineral – Coarse:Fine, limit at 20μm, C:F, 40:60, Coarse, very dominant, generally coarse silt-size quart, with very few micas, fresh glauconite and opaques; few coarse 0.4 by 0.8mm rounded nodular concretions of black pyrite (brassy under OIL); Fine speckled and dotted yellowish brown to dark yellowish brown (PPL), medium interference colours (open to close porphyric, uni-strial b-fabric, XPL), yellowish brown, with black and reddish flecks (OIL); few darkish brown (PPL), with low interference colours (XPL), dark yellowish brown (OIL), variants; Organic – many relic fine blackened and brown amorphous organic matter fragments; occasional possible relic roots; Pedofeatures – many fine to coarse (80–800μm) gypsum, with occasional septaric gypsum (roses); occasional ferruginous impregnation, poor pseudomorphic replacement of organic matter; rare fine (800μm) burrow infills, with ferruginous hypocoatings of burrows and channels. BD: Clay (3.8% sand, 36.8% silt, 59.4% clay); very poorly calcareous (0.62% CaCO₃, very low organic matter (2.54% LOI) and low phosphate-P (0.544mgg⁻¹); moderately high magnetic susceptibility (44.6 × 10⁻⁸ m³kg⁻¹) and high χ_{conv} (20.4%); high sulphate, and very low Pb, Zn and Cu.	Natural London Clay (Trench 27, Section 2702): finely bedded clay with fine and coarse silt and very little fine sand that contains nodular pyrite/ pyritised wood concretions; most relic organic replaced by iron; major impregnation by secondary gypsum.
Facies 1b / Soil Microfabric Type 1b	**K** x7	SM: as F1a, but heterogeneous mixture of F1a variants, and common patches of coarse silt and very fine sand; pyritised wood is not in evidence. BD: Clay (2.2% sand, 38.0% silt, 59.8% clay); very poorly calcareous (1.22% CaCO₃), very low organic matter (2.82% LOI) and moderate phosphate-P (0.847mgg⁻¹); moderate magnetic susceptibility (44.6 × 10⁻⁸ m³Kg⁻¹) and high χ_{conv} (18.4%); high sulphate and very low Pb, Zn and Cu.	Disturbed natural London Clay (Trench 27, Section 2702), with fabric heterogeneity, with pyrite and gypsum not evident in the thin section although sulphate present in bulk sample; deposit is possibly slightly more "weathered"
Facies 2a / 2966–2967 Soil Microfabric Type 2a	**S** 2966 2967	2966: SM: (10 degree sloping) greyish brown massive with patches of grey; massive and crack microstructure; 25% voids, very dominant moderately well-accommodated fine (0.5–1mm) curved planes; C:F, 05:95, very dominant silt size quartz and fine sand size and silt-size rounded gypsum?; Fine – highly speckled yellowish brown to greyish yellowish brown (PPL), very high interference colours (open porphyric, crystallitic b-fabric, XPL), grey with many very fine black specks (OIL); very abundant amorphous fine (and 200μm) and blackened / charred organic fragments; Pedofeatures – many microsparitic crystal infills of vughs; occasional ferruginous staining an impregnation of amorphous plant material/root traces. BD: Silty clay (7.3% sand, 50.6% silt, 42.1% clay); moderately calcareous (15.1% CaCO₃), low organic matter (4.28% LOI) and moderate phosphate-P (0.983mgg⁻¹ P); moderate magnetic susceptibility (24.2 × 10⁻⁸ m³kg⁻¹) and moderate χ_{conv} (9.81%); high Pb, but low sulphate, Zn and Cu.	13th century silting below barbican timbers (Trench 27, Section 2717) Basal deposits below 13th century timbers; massive, very finely humic calcareous silty clay (partly originating from constructional mortar deposits and humic moat silty clay, including very fine charcoal and likely fragments from 2967; all deposited under mainly water logged conditions, with occasional subaerial ex posure allowing secondary microsparite to form in voids; over and developing from

278

Lowermost basal deposits (2967): Sub-aerial cyclical silting of calcareous silt loam, of a constructional lime/ash origin, and their slight weathering (faunal burrowing and algal activity); all followed by humic calcareous silt deposition, and its fine rooting; sub-aerial weathering also leading to pelletty micrite becoming massive micrite and the localised formation of microsparite in voids. First two cycles of sediment became rooted by medium rooted plants and as the site got wetter, microbiological activity gave rise to ferruginous replacement of organic matter and associated pyrite framboid formation. High levels of Pb could be associated with the practice of lead bonding of stone-work of the lowermost foundations here.

Trench 27, Section 2717) Basal deposits below 13th-century timbers; steeply sloping very thin calcareous silty clay loam laminae composed of calcareous silts and small amounts of detrital organic matter layers, with rare "shelly fauna".

2967:

SM: 10 degree sloping, microlaminated (1–2mm), with white and brown laminae; vugh (spongy), crack and channel microstructure; 20% voids, common fine (200–400μm) open vughs (white pelletty layers), frequent poorly accommodated fine cracks (brown layers) and few medium (1–1.5mm) channels; Mineral – C:F, 10:90, Coarse, poorly sorted fine silt to fine sand-size quartz; rare fine fragments of London Clay Fine, layers of i) spongy micritic calcite – cloudy grey to cloudy yellowish grey (PPL), high interference colours (open porphyric, crystallitic, XPL), grey (OIL); occasional to many relic amorphous and rare tissue organic matter and yellow stains (associated Fe replacement and pyrite formation – see below); ii) brown stained micrite – cloudy, greyish brown (PPL), low to medium interference colours (open porphyric, crystallitic, XPL), greyish brown to orange (OIL); many relic (max. 800μm) plant fragments – rounded as root sections? or as long tissues; rare channel edge root traces; abundant relic amorphous organic matter and rare fine charcoal.; iii) massive micritic calcite (as i); Pedofeatures, rare patches many loose micro sparite infills (in iii); patches of many pyrite (in i); abundant ferruginisation of organic matter (especially in ii); very abundant pelletty/thin excremental fabric in i and ii.

BD: Silt loam (16.7% sand, 56.3% silt, 27.0% clay); highly calcareous (33.9% $CaCO_3$), very low organic matter (2.69% LOI) and moderate phosphate-P (0.761mgg^{-1}); moderate magnetic susceptibility (20.1 × 10^{-8}m^{3}kg^{-1}) and moderate χ_{conv} (16.5%); high Pb, but low sulphate, Zn and Cu.

2964

SM: As SMT 2965, but more massive and coarsely (1–5mm) bedded, more poorly sorted with occasional sand-size quartz; frequent thin (2mm) layers of spongy calcareous SMT 2967; common layers of fragmented organic matter (as SMT 3/2965); rare secondary calcite (microsparite); occasional pyrite framboids.

BD: Silty clay loam (13.5 sand, 54.4% silt, 32.4% clay); strongly calcareous (26.3% $CaCO_3$), low organic matter (3.04% LOI) and phosphate-P (1.12mgg^{-1}); moderate magnetic susceptibility (22.5 × 10^{-8}m^{3}kg^{-1}) and χ_{conv} 17.7%); low sulphate, Pb, Zn and Cu.

2965

SM: As SMF 2/2966, 45 degree sloping, very finely (100μm) laminated, within more coarse (0.5, 1 and 4 mm) laminae (i – calcareous bards and ii – calcareous bands with included organic matter); <5% voids (also 10% planar voids), fine vughs; two laminae contain 0.5–2.0mm size shell; rare fragments of gypsum crystals; rare fine layers of organic matter/charcoal lengths; i) dotted cloudy grey (PPL), high interference colours (open porphyric, crystallitic b-fabric, XPL), grey with black dots (OIL); occasional amorphous and rare charred organic matter; ii) cloudy grey with fine (<200μm) brown patches (PPL), (open porphyric, crystallitic b-fabric, XPL), grey with yellowish brown patches and very fine black specks (OIL); abundant small fragments of amorphous organic matter/tissues and rare fine charcoal (occasional layers with many charcoal); occasional pyrite framboids.

BD: Silty clay (2.4% sand, 50.9% silt, 46.7% clay); calcareous (15.4% $CaCO_3$), organic matter (4.14% LOI) and phosphate-P (1.18mgg^{-1}); moderate magnetic susceptibility (22 × 10^{-8}m^{3}Kg^{-1}) and χ_{conv} (10.3%); low sulphate, Pb, Zn and Cu.

Facies 2b/
2964–2965
Soil
Microfabric Type 2b

Q
2964
2965

Table A3.8 *(continued)*

Material	Sample Number examples	Soil Micromorphology (M), Bulk Data (BD), Microprobe (Probe) and Elemental Map (EM)	Interpretation and Comments
Facies 3/2576 Soil Microfabric Type 3	**L** 2576	SM: massive with some fine, poorly formed laminae of intercalated detrital organic matter and calcitic sediment; C:F, 40:60, moderately poorly sorted with common bivalve and ostracod shells, frequent sand to gravel-size mortar, some suffering dissolution, frequent etched gypsum crystals? and sand-size quartz and flint; large (10mm) size charcoal and elongate (25mm) *in situ* roots present; pale yellowish cloudy grey (PPL), very high interference colours (open porphyric, crystallitic b-fabric/microsparitic, XPL), grey with dark brown specks (OIL); pale yellowish organic staining (peaty) with many amorphous and tissue fragments of organic matter; many weak dissolution of mortar and etching of gypsum?; many secondary micritic (around mortar), tufa like growths and microsparitic (in voids/around plant remains) calcite formation; rare gypsum; occasional but coarse (8mm) likely earthworm burrows containing mammilated excrements BD: silt loam (28.7% sand, 57.9% silt, 13.4% clay); highly calcareous (46.7% CaCO$_3$), moderately high organic matter (8.92% LOI) and moderate phosphate-P (1.17mgg^{-1}); low magnetic susceptibility (4.2 × 10^{-8}m^{3}kg^{-1}) and low χ$_{conv}$ (6.32%); high sulphate, and high Pb and Cu, and low Zn.	13th century (Edward I) shelly and "peaty" mud deposition with *in situ* rooting and earthworm burrowing at times; in puts of mortar, which has undergone small amounts of dissolution (from organic acids/subaerial weathering) and recrystalisation.
Facies 4/2838–2839–2844 Soil Microfabric Type 4	**E (B lower)** 2838 2839 2844	2844 SM: as SMT 4/2841 BD: Silty clay (15.6% sand, 44.3% silt, 40.1% clay); moderately calcareous (15.8% CaCO$_3$), low organic matter (4.65% LOI) and high phosphate-P (1.17mgg^{-1}); moderate magnetic susceptibility (31.8 × 10^{-8}m^{3}kg^{-1}) and low χ$_{conv}$ (5.64%); moderate sulphate, and Pb, and low Zn and Cu. 2838 SM: as SMT 4/2841 BD: Silty clay (0.5% sand, 49.1% silt, 50.4% clay); moderately calcareous (10.5% CaCO$_3$), low organic matter (5.62% LOI) and high phosphate-P (1.39mgg^{-1}); moderate magnetic susceptibility (31.5 × 10^{-8}m^{3}kg^{-1}) and low χ$_{conv}$ (5.91%); moderate sulphate, and low Pb, Zn and Cu. 2839 SM: as SMT 4/2841 BD: Clay (2.0% sand, 35.7% silt, 62.3% clay); moderately poorly calcareous (5.76% CaCO$_3$), with low organic matter (5.58% LOI) and high phosphate-P (1.23mgg^{-1}); moderate magnetic susceptibility (32.1 × 10^{-8}m^{3}kg^{-1}) and low χ$_{conv}$ (4.44%); moderate sulphate, and low Pb, Zn and Cu.	Edward I: Trench 27, Section 2702; continued clay and silty clay deposition, with increasing amounts of phosphate-P and small increases in organic content and shell indicative of likely plant and cess inputs.

Facies 4/2840–2841 Soil Microfabric Type 4	**G** 2840 2841	**2840** SM: as SMT 4/2841 with occasional large molluscs present, massive and very finely laminated with frequent brown, greyish brown (PPL) laminae, moderately high to high interference colours (moderately open porphyric, speckled and crystallitic b-fabric, XPL), brown and grey with many fine red and black specks; abundant fine amorphous and charred organic matter. BD: Silty clay (0.6% sand, 49.7% silt, 49.7% clay); moderately calcareous (14.6% $CaCO_3$) with low organic matter (4.85% LOI) and moderate phosphate-P (1.13mgg^{-1}); moderate magnetic susceptibility (34×10^{-8}m^{3}kg^{-1}) and low χ_{conv} (5.48%); high sulphate, and low Pb, Zn and Cu. **2841** SM: as SMT 4/2841 with gypsum and ferruginous hypocoatings; rare shelly fauna.	Edward I: Trench 27, Section 2702; becoming more laminated with calcitic laminae and shell upwards, with London Clay still continuing to supply relic pockets of sand.
Facies 4/2840–2842 Soil Microfabric Type 4	**H** 2840 2842	**2840** SM: As SMF 4/2842, but at the 2840/2842 junction many impregnative ferruginous mottling and hypocoatings on vughs and cracks, and often associated occasional concentrations of abundant gypsum crystals. BD: Silty clay (0.4% sand, 45.9% silt, 53.8% clay); moderately calcareous (9.42% $CaCO_3$) with low organic matter (4.58% LOI) and moderate phosphate-P (0.918mgg^{-1}); high magnetic susceptibility (40.8×10^{-8}m^{3}kg^{-1}) and moderately low χ_{conv} (7.63%); high sulphate, and low Pb, Zn and Cu. **2842** SM: Massive, crack microstructure; 30% voids, very dominant fine to medium (0.5–2mm) well accommodated planar voids and few fine vughs; C:F, 10:90, very dominant silt and sand size quartz; and very few calcite and mica; Fine—speckled yellowish to dark yellowish brown (PPL), low interference colours (moderately open porphyric, speckled and crystallitic b-fabric, XPL), brown and grey with many fine red and black specks; abundant fine amorphous and charred organic matter; occasional micritic infilling of finest vughs; occasional ferruginous hypocoatings of medium size vughs. BD: Silty clay (0.9% sand, 43.7% silt, 55.4% clay); moderately calcareous (11.3% $CaCO_3$) with low organic matter (4.67% LOI) and moderate phosphate-P (1.08mgg^{-1}); moderate magnetic susceptibility (24.3×10^{-8}m^{3}kg^{-1}) and low χ_{conv} (4.51%); high sulphate, and low Pb, Zn and Cu.	Edward I: Trench 27, Section 2702; initial 13th century silty clay moat sedimentation that is strongly influenced by the London Clay substrate, including pockets of fine sand relic of the London Clay, and many gypsum formation.
Facies 5/2604 Soil Microfabric Type 5	**M** 2604	SM: massive, with moderately well-accommodated crack structure; C:F, 45:65, common silt-size quartz and calcite, frequent sand-size quartz, with chalk, mortar, and frequent coarse (4×8mm) bivalve shell; rare black (PPL) and red (OIL) slag and cinder, rare coprolitic bone (1mm); heavily speckled and dotted greyish brown (PPL), moderate interference colours (open porphyric, crystallitic b-fabric, XPL), greyish yellowish brown with many black and occasional reddish specks (OIL); very abundant fine charred with amorphous organic matter; many gypsum and occasional pyrite. BD: Silty clay loam (10.1% sand, 50.3% silt, 39.6% clay); calcareous (11.3% $CaCO_3$) with moderately high organic matter (9.43% LOI) and very high phosphate-P (2.35mgg^{-1}); moderately high magnetic susceptibility (83.9×10^{-8}m^{3}kg^{-1}) and moderate χ_{conv} (12.2%); high sulphate, and high Pb, Zn and Cu.	Post 1680; humic and charcoal-rich silts, with mortar and rare slag/cinder and coprolitic bone inclusions; much secondary gypsum and pyrite.

Table A3.8 (continued)

Material	Sample Number examples	Soil Micromorphology (M), Bulk Data (BD), Microprobe (Probe) and Elemental Map (EM)	Interpretation and Comments
Facies 6/3141 Soil Microfabric Type 6	N 3141	3141 SM: as SMT 6/2937, but with many fewer detrital organic matter, but very few coarse inclusions of mortar (2mm), pottery (3mm) and wood charcoal (6mm); fine chalk and charcoal; shelly fauna (bivalves and ostracods). BD: Silt loam (18.3% sand, 60.9% silt, 20.8% clay); very strongly calcareous (40.0% $CaCO_3$) with low organic matter (4.34% LOI) and moderate phosphate-P (0.872mgg^{-1}); very low magnetic susceptibility (4.8 × 10^{-8}m^{3}kg^{-1}) and χ_{conv} (5.22%); high Pb and low Zn and Cu.	Trench 31, Southwest Causeway: medieval and Post-Medieval; calcareous silting with traces of building debris and high lead input.
Facies 6/3133–3136 Soil Microfabric Type 6	T 3133 3136	3133 SM: as M, with fine laminae within massive, and with occasional coarse (5mm) heavily burned cinder; post 1680-like dark brown sediments BD: Silty clay (1.8% sand, 53.1% silt, 45.1% clay); calcareous (10.2% $CaCO_3$) with moderately high organic matter (7.29% LOI) and high phosphate-P (1.79mgg^{-1}); moderate magnetic susceptibility (24.8 × 10^{-8}m^{3}kg^{-1}) and very low χ_{conv} (1.94%); high sulphate, and moderately high Pb, and moderate Zn and Cu. 3136 SM: massive with some coarse bedding at top; C:F, 10:90, with frequent sand-size quartz and dominant ostracods and shell; occasional to many coarse charcoal, occasional coarse plant fragments, rare bone and likely biogenic (earthworm) calcite and possible biogenic micritic infills; top 15mm of mainly mortar, mortar debris showing some weak decalcification, and likely burned shell.; fine fabric as L.	Trench 31: Section 3112 below late post-medieval layer that include likely inputs of reworked London Clay-rich moat sediments, with calcareous and detrital organic matter rich laminae. Post-medieval shelly waterlain calcareous sediments, with likely dump of mortar limestone, tufa with an earthworm granule.
Facies 6/3136–3137 Soil Microfabric Type 6	U 3136 3137	3136 SM: as below, but poorly sorted and heterogeneous with building (mortar/limestone) debris, coarse charcoal, flint and limestone; burrowed mixing of occasional thin organic layers; phytoliths present; rare yellowish Fe/P? staining; rare gypsum. BD: Silt loam (18.7% sand, 62.5% silt, 18.8% clay); extremely calcareous (52.0% $CaCO_3$) with moderately organic matter (5.9% LOI) and high phosphate-P (1.18mgg^{-1}); low magnetic susceptibility (6.3 × 10^{-8}m^{3}kg^{-1}) and moderate χ_{conv} (7.52%); high sulphate, and high Pb, very high Cu. 3137 SM: As L, with molluscs up to 9mm in size; and becoming more massive in upper 15mm; occasional fine burrows, moderately thin excrements and likely calcite pseudomorphs of fine (0.4mm) roots. BD: Clay loam (32.9% sand, 29.0% silt, 39.1% clay); calcareous (13.2% $CaCO_3$) with moderately low organic matter (5.69% LOI) and moderate phosphate-P (0.845mgg^{-1}); moderately high magnetic susceptibility (20.6 × 10^{-8}m^{3}kg^{-1}) and moderate χ_{conv} (7.51%); high sulphate, and high Pb and Zn, very high Cu.	Trench 31: Section 3112; post-medieval burrowed mixture of organic and building debris-rich calcareous sediments, becoming more finely laminated and massive with shelly fauna with depth.

Facies 6/2937–2852 Soil Microfabric Type 6	O	2937 2852	**2937** SM: similar to SMT 6/2852, but more heterogeneous, finely burrowed; massive with relic laminae; C:F, 05:95, silt and sand size quartz and subangular etched and weathered fragments of gypsum; few small shelly fauna; speckled cloudy greyish and yellow pale brown (PPL), high interference colours (crystallitic b-fabric, XPL), pale greyish brown (OIL); abundant to very abundant tissue and amorphous organic matter fragments; occasional coarse (5mm) root traces and fragments; one lamination with a series (3) of coarse (2–5mm) size gypsum septaric nodules (roses); BD: Silt loam (11.5% sand, 71.1% silt, 17.4% clay); very strongly calcareous (40.0% CaCO$_3$) with high organic matter (10.5% LOI) and high phosphate-P (1.85mgg^{-1}); very low magnetic susceptibility (2.4 × 10^{-8}m^{3}kg^{-1}) and χ_{conv} (4.1%); high sulphate, moderate Pb, Zn and Cu. **2852** SM: as Facies 6/2852, but with large 5mm shell/root casts.	Trench 27, post-Medieval: higher inputs of detrital organic matter but rather lower amounts of heavy metal and phosphate from cess. Finely laminated with coarse detrital organic matter fragments, *in situ* coarse roots with associated secondary micritic coatings; and secondary gypsum.
Facies 6/2852–2853 Soil Microfabric Type 6	P	2852 2853	**2852** SM: Massive, with crack, channel and chamber microstructure; 15% voids, frequent moderately poorly accommodated fine (<1mm) planar voids and medium (2–3mm) chambers and (root) channels; C:F, 05:95, with very few sand-size fragments of gypsum crystals; dark yellowish cloudy grey (PPL), high interference colours (micritic/microsparitic – crystallitic b-fabric), yellowish grey with fire specks (OIL); abundant fine amorphous and tissue organic matter; few 0.5–2mm size root traces (in channels); BD: Silt loam (10.4% sand, 74.6% silt, 15% clay); very strongly calcareous (45.7% CaCO$_3$) with moderately high organic matter (7.89% LOI) and high phosphate-P (1.99mgg^{-1}); very low magnetic susceptibility (1.6 × 10^{-8}m^{3}kg^{-1}) and low χ_{conv} (5.42%); high sulphate, Pb, Zn and Cu. **2853** SM: As SMT 4/2853, but with rare small 2mm size microsparitic ghost of septaric and acicular vivianite. BD: Silt loam (2.1% sand, 81.0% silt, 16.9% clay); very strongly calcareous (48.7% CaCO$_3$) with moderately high organic matter (7.89% LOI) and high phosphate-P (2.04mgg^{-1}); low magnetic susceptibility (10.5 × 10^{-8}m^{3}kg^{-1}) and moderate χ_{conv} (10.9%); high sulphate, Pb, Zn and Cu.	Post Medieval; western end of Trench 27; massive highly calcareous silts, with gypsum as included clasts, and occasional ghosts of vivianite present; homogenised and rooted. The high phosphate and the moderate concentrations of Pb and Cu (particularly in view of the 'dilution' due to the high carbonate content) may indicate inputs of cess, with some domestic/industrial inputs.
Facies 7/2833–2834 Soil Microfabric Type 7	A	2833 2834	**2833** SM: basal boundary between 2833 and 2834 is marked by a thin (0.4mm) black, charcoal dominated lamination; above as 2834, but more heterogeneous and massive, and much less shelly, and marked by abundant secondary gypsum crystal impregnation and occasional ferruginous staining of the matrix. BD: Silty clay loam (2% sand, 60.0% silt, 38.0% clay); calcareous (10.2% CaCO$_3$) with moderately high organic matter (9.11% LOI) and high phosphate-P (2.97mgg^{-1}); moderate magnetic susceptibility (54.4 × 10^{-8}m^{3}kg^{-1}) and moderate χ_{conv} (8.0%); high sulphate, Pb, Zn and Cu.	High inputs of burned debris, heavy metals and cess.

283

Table A3.8 (continued)

Material	Sample Number examples	Soil Micromorphology (M), Bulk Data (BD), Microprobe (Probe) and Elemental Map (EM)	Interpretation and Comments
		2834 SM: as SMT10/2835, but with a basal 3mm thick sandy/weathered mortar (plaster) lamination (rounded medium quartz and glauconitic sand, with shell and sparse calcitic matrix and very few ferruginised plant remains); heavily dotted and speckled dark greyish brown to blackish brown (PPL), medium to low interference colours (open porphyric, crystallitic b-fabric), brownish grey to brown with very abundant brown and black, with red specks (OIL); very abundant charred and amorphous organic matter; shelly fauna; occasional to many silt-size fragments of organic matter; occasional fine charcoal; occasional to many planar voids loosely infilled with micrite and coarse biogenic? calcite also rarely present; rare patch (5mm long) of yellow amorphous (Fe/P?) impregnation of mortar (see above), with rare associated vivianite. BD: Silt loam (11.5% sand, 66.2% silt, 22.3% clay); moderately calcareous (29.4% $CaCO_3$) with moderately high organic matter (7.84% LOI) and high phosphate-P (2.65mgg^{-1}); moderate magnetic susceptibility (52×10^{-8}m^{3}kg^{-1}) and moderate χ_{conv} (13%); high sulphate, Pb, Zn and Cu.	
Facies 7/2834–2835 Soil Microfabric Type 7	**B** 2834 2835	**2834** SM: As 2835, with greater heterogeneity, less well-preserved bedding; includes very few and size fragments of mortar, plaster and "greensand" (from local geology); rare inclusions with possible carbonaceous spherules (10–20µm); rare patches of vivianite; occasional ferruginous replacement of organic matter and hypocoatings staining into surrounding matrix; rare clayey intercalations. BD: Silt loam (11.5% sand, 66.2% silt, 22.3% clay); moderately calcareous (29.4% $CaCO_3$) with moderately high organic matter (7.84% LOI) and high phosphate-P (2.65mgg^{-1}); moderate magnetic susceptibility (52×10^{-8}m^{3}kg^{-1}) and moderate χ_{conv} (11.7%); high sulphate, Pb, Zn and Cu. **2835** SM: massive with fine, medium and coarse (0.5, 2 and 6mm) laminae; 15% voids, very dominant fine to medium moderately well accommodated planar voids and few medium channels; C:F, 10:90 (microsparitic matrix), silt and fine sand-size quartz, gypsum and in places very dominant shell; speckled greyish brown and heavily speckled and dotted dark brownish grey – organic laminae (PPL), high to moderate interference colours (open porphyric, crystallitic b-fabric, XPL), pale brownish grey and brown, with abundant black and red specks (OIL); many and abundant amorphous, tissue and charred fine organic matter; rare root traces, many plant fragments, and many shelly fauna; intercalatory-like features at the base of some fine beds; occasional gypsum and fine (0.1mm) amorphous yellow infills. BD: Silt loam (4.2% sand, 71.5% silt, 24.3% clay); moderately calcareous (29.4% $CaCO_3$) with moderately high organic matter (9.62% LOI) and high phosphate-P (2.80mg g^{-1}); moderate magnetic susceptibility (62.3×10^{-8}m^{3}kg^{-1}) and moderate χ_{conv} (11.7%); high sulphate, Pb, Zn and Cu.	Post-medieval muddy deposition of calcareous deposits, many shell-rich, with anthropogenic inclusions, and evidence of re-wetting and fluctuating water tables. Deposition of fine calcareous muds.

Bibliography

Acott, T G, Cruise, G M and Macphail, R I 1997. 'Soil micromorphology and high resolution images'. In S Shoba, M Gersimova and R Miedema (eds) *Soil Micromorphology: Diversity, Diagnostics and Dynamics*, Moscow-Wageningen: International Soil Science Society, 372–8

Adovasio, J M 1977. *Basketry Technology. A Guide to Identification and Analysis*. Chicago: Aldine.

Albarella, U and Davis, S 1994. *Medieval and Post-Medieval Mammal and Bird Bones from Launceston Castle, Cornwall: 1961–1982 Excavations*. Anc Mon Lab Rep **18/94**, London

Alexander, J S 1996. 'Masons' marks and stone bonding'. In T Tatton-Brown and J Munby (eds) *The Archaeology of Cathedrals*, Oxford University Committee for Archaeology Monograph **42**, 219–36, Oxford

Andersen, S T 1970. 'The relative pollen productivity and pollen representation of North European trees, and correction factors for tree pollen spectra'. *Danm. Geol. Unders.* **2/96**, 1–99

Andersen, S T 1973. 'The differential pollen productivity of trees and its significance for the interpretation of a pollen diagram from a forested region'. In H J B Birks and R G West (eds) *Quaternary Plant Ecology*, Oxford: Blackwell Scientific, 109–115

Atkinson, D R and Oswald, A 1969. 'London clay tobacco pipes'. *Journal of the British Archaeological Association* **XXXII**, 171–227

Atkinson, D R and Oswald, A 1980. 'The dating and typology of clay pipes bearing the Royal Arms'. In P J Davey (ed) *The Archaeology of the Clay Tobacco Pipe* III, BAR Brit Ser **78**, 363–91, Oxford

Avery, B W and Bascomb, C L (eds) 1974. *Soil Survey Laboratory Methods*. Soil Survey Technical Monograph **6**, Harpenden

Baillie, M G L and Pilcher, J R 1973. 'A simple crossdating program for tree-ring research'. *Tree Ring Bulletin* **33**, 7–14

Baker, C A, Moxey, P A and Oxford, M 1978. 'Woodland continuity and change in Epping Forest'. *Field Studies* **4**, 645–69

Ball, D F 1964. 'Loss-on-ignition as an estimate of organic matter and organic carbon in non-calcareous soils'. *Journal of Soil Science* **15**, 84–92

Banks, F 1997. *Wine Drinking in Oxford 1640–1850*. BAR Brit Ser **257**, Oxford

Bateman, N 1998. 'Public buildings in Roman London: some contrasts'. In B Watson (ed) *Roman London: Recent Archaeological Work*, Journal of Roman Archaeology Supplementary Series **24**, 47–57, Oxford

Bayley, J 1821. *History and Antiquities of the Tower of London*. London: Cadell

Bell, M, Caseldine, A and Neumann, H 1999. *Prehistoric Intertidal Archaeology in the Welsh Severn Estuary*. Council for British Archaeology: York

Belshaw, R 1988. 'A note on the recovery of *Thoracochaeta zosterae* (Haliday) (Diptera: Sphaeroceridae) from archaeological deposits'. *Circaea* **6**, 39–41

Bennett, K D, Whittington, G and Edwards, K J 1994. 'Recent plant nomenclatural changes and pollen morphology in the British Isles'. *Quaternary Newsletter* **73**, 1–6

Bennion, H, Juggins, S and Anderson, N J 1996. 'Predicting epilimnetic phosphorus concentrations using an improved diatom-based transfer function and its application to lake eutrophication management'. *Environmental Science and Technology* **30**, 2004–7

Bentley, D 1984. 'A recently identified valley in the City'. *The London Archaeologist* **5.1**, 13–16

Bethell, P and Máté, I 1989. 'The use of phosphate analysis in archaeology: a critique'. In J Henderson (ed) *Scientific Analysis in Archaeology*, Oxford University Committee for Archaeology Monograph **19**, 1–29, Oxford

BGS (British Geological Survey) 1993. *North London: England and Wales Sheet 256, Solid and Drift Geology, 1:50,000.*

Biddle, M (ed) 1990. *Object and Economy in Medieval Winchester*, Winchester Studies **7.ii**. Oxford: Clarendon

Biddle, M and Barclay, K 1990. 'Sewing pins and wire'. In M Biddle (ed) *Object and Economy in Medieval Winchester*, Winchester Studies **7.ii**, 560–71. Oxford: Clarendon

Biddle, M and Cook, L 1990. 'Buttons'. In M Biddle (ed) *Object and Economy in Medieval Winchester*, Winchester Studies **7.ii**, 571–81. Oxford: Clarendon

Birks, H J B, Anderson, N J and Fritz, S C 1995. 'Post-glacial changes in total phosphorus at Diss Mere, Norfolk inferred from fossil diatom assemblages'. In S T Patrick and N J Anderson (eds) *Ecology and Palaeoecology of Lake Eutrophication*. Proceedings of a workshop held at Salten Skov, Slikeborg, Denmark, 14–18 May 1994, Service Report **7**, 48–9, Geological Survey of Denmark

Blair, J 1991. 'Purbeck marble'. In J Blair and N Ramsey (eds) *English Medieval Industries*, London: Hambledon, 41–56.

Boesneck, J A 1969. 'Osteological differences between sheep (*Ovis aries* Linne) and goat (*Capra hircus* Linne)'. In D R Brothwell and E S Higgs (eds) *Science in Archaeology*, London: Thames and Hudson, 331–58

Bond, C J 1988. 'Monastic fisheries'. In M Aston (ed) *Medieval Fish, Fisheries and Fishponds*, BAR Brit Ser **182** pt I, 69–112, Oxford

Bone, D A 1999. 'The London Clay formation (early eocene) at Southleigh landfill site, near Emsworth, Hampshire (with a note on Lidsey landfill site, near Bognor Regis, West Sussex)'. *Tertiary Research* **19**, 91–9

Bradbury, J P and Winter, T C 1976. 'Areal distribution and stratigraphy of diatoms in the sediments of Lake Sallie, Minnesota'. *Ecology* **57**, 1005–14

Brett, D W 1978. 'Dendroclimatology of elm in London'. *Tree Ring Bulletin* **38**, 35–44

Brigham, T 1990. 'The late Roman waterfront in London'. *Britannia* **21**, 99–183

Brigham, T 1998. 'The port of Roman London'. In B Watson (ed) *Roman London: Recent Archaeological Work*, Journal of Roman Archaeology Supplementary Series **24**, 23–34, Oxford

Brooke, C N L and Keir, G 1975. *London 800–1216*. London: Secker and Warburg

Bullock, P, Fedoroff, N, Jongerius, A, Stoops, G and Tursina, T 1985. *Handbook for Soil Thin Section Description*. Wolverhampton: Waine Research Publications

Cameron, N G 2000a. 'Diatom Analysis of Middle Bronze Age Sediments from TWE98'. Unpublished archive report

Cameron, N G 2000b. 'No.1 Poultry (ONE94): Diatom Analysis and Aquatic Environmental Reconstruction Using Transfer Functions for Total Phosphorus and pH'. Unpublished archive report

Cameron N G et al 1999. 'Surface-sediment and epilithic diatom pH calibration sets for remote European mountain lakes (AL:PE project) and their comparison with the Surface Waters Acidification Programme (SWAP) calibration set'. *Journal of Paleolimnology* **22**, 291–317

Charles, F W B and Charles, M 1995. *Conservation of Timber Buildings*. London: Donhead Publishing

Charleston, R J 1984. *English Glass*. London: Allen and Unwin

Clark, A J 1990. *Seeing Beneath the Soil*. London: Batsford

Clayton, P and Leftwich, B R 1934. *The Pageant of Tower Hill*. London

Cleve-Euler, A 1951–55. 'Die Diatomeen von Schweden und Finland'. *Kungliga Svenska Vetenskaps Handlingar Ser.* **4** 2(1) 3–163; **4**(1) 3–158; 4(5) 3–255; 5(4) 3–231; 3(3) 3–153

Colvin, H M (ed) 1963–76. *The History of the King's Works*. Vols I–V. London: HMSO

Cook M, 1998. *Medieval Bridges*. Shire Archaeology Series **77**, Princes Risborough

Cooper, L and Ripper, S 1994. 'The medieval Trent bridges at Hemington Fields, Castle Donington'. *Leicestershire Archaeology and History Society Transactions* **68**, 153–61

Courty, M A, Goldberg, P and Macphail, R I 1989. *Soils and Micromorphology in Archaeology*. Cambridge: Cambridge University Press

Cronne, H A and Davis R H C (eds) 1968. *Regesta Regum Anglo-Normannorum*. Vol 3. Oxford: Clarendon

Crowther, J 1997. 'Soil phosphate surveys: critical approaches to sampling, analysis and interpretation'. *Archaeological Prospection* **4**, 93–102

Crowther, J and Barker, P 1995. 'Magnetic susceptibility: distinguishing anthropogenic effects from the natural'. *Archaeological Prospection* **2**, 207–15

Dalton, R and Hamer, S H 1910–1918 (reissued 1967). *The Provincial Token Coinage of the 18th Century.*

Davis, S 1987. *The Archaeology of Animals*. London: Batsford

Davison, B K 1967. 'Three 11th-century earthworks in England: their excavation and implications'. *Château Gaillard* **2**, 39–48

Denys, L. 1992. *A Check List of the Diatoms in the Holocene Deposits of the Western Belgian Coastal Plain with a Survey of their Apparent Ecological Requirements, I: Introduction, Ecological Code and Complete List*. Service Géologique de Belgique Professional Paper **246**, Berchem

Dick, W A and Tabatabai, M A 1977. 'An alkaline oxidation method for the determination of total phosphorus in soils'. *Journal of the Soil Science Society of America* **41**, 511–14

Driesch, A von den 1976. *A Guide to the Measurement of Animal Bones from Archaeological Sites*. Peabody Museum Bulletin **1**, Cambridge, MA

Dyakowska, J 1947. 'The pollen rain on the sea and coasts of Greenland'. *Bull Internat Academy Polonaise* **B**, 25–33

Edlin, H 1971. *Wayside and Woodland Trees, A Guide to the Trees of Britain and Ireland*. London: Warne

Egan, G and Pritchard, F 1991. *Medieval Finds from Excavations in London, 3: Dress Accessories c1150–c1450*. London: HMSO

Ellis, A E 1969. *British Snails* (2nd edn). Oxford: Clarendon

English Heritage, 1998. *Dendrochronology: Guidelines on Producing and Interpreting Dendrochronological Dates*. London: English Heritage

Gallagher, D B and Sharp, A 1986. *Pypis of Tabaca*. Edinburgh: City of Edinburgh Museums and Art Galleries

Getty, R 1975. *Sisson and Grossman's The Anatomy of the Domesticated Animals*. Philadelphia: Saunders

Goodall, I H 1983. 'Iron objects'. In P Mayes and L Butler (eds) *Sandal Castle Excavations 1964–1973, A Detailed Archaeological Report*, Wakefield: Wakefield Historical Publications, 240–52

Goodall, J 2000. 'Little Wenham Hall, Suffolk'. *Country Life*, 6 July, 126–31

Goodburn, D 1992. 'Woods and woodland: carpenters and carpentry'. In G Milne (ed) *Timber Building Techniques in London c900–1400: An Archaeological Study of Waterfront Installations and Related Material*, London and Middlesex Archaeological Society Special Paper **15**, 106–30, London

Graham, I D G and Scollar, I 1976. 'Limitations on magnetic prospection in archaeology imposed by soil properties'. *Archaeo-Physika* **6**, 1–124

Grant, A 1982. 'The use of toothwear as a guide to the age of domestic ungulates'. In R Wilson, C Grigson and S Payne (eds) *Ageing and Sexing Animal Bones from Archaeological Sites*, BAR Brit Ser **109**, 91–108, Oxford

Greig, J R A 1981. 'The investigation of a medieval barrel-latrine from Worcester'. *Journal of Archaeological Science* **8**, 265–82

Greig, J R A 1982. 'The interpretation of pollen spectra from urban archaeological deposits'. In A R Hall and H Kenwood (eds) *Environmental Archaeology in the Urban Context*, CBA Res Rep **43**, 47–65, York

Greig, J R A 1989. 'From lime forest to heathland – five thousand years of change at West Heath Spa, Hampstead, as shown by the plant remains'. In D Collins and A Lorimer (eds) *Excavations at the Mesolithic Site on West Heath, Hampstead 1976–1981*, BAR Brit Ser **217**, 89–99, Oxford

Greig, J R A 1992. 'The deforestation of London'. *Review Palaeobotany and Palynology* **73**, 71–86

Greig, J R A 1995. 'Archaeobotanical and historical records compared – a new look at the taphonomy of edible and other useful plants from the 11th to the 18th centuries AD'. *Circaea* **12**, 211–47

Grew, F and de Neergaard, M 1988. *Shoes and Pattens. Medieval Finds from Excavations in London*, 2. London: HMSO

Grimm, E C 1991. *TILIA and TILIA-GRAPH*. Springfield, IL: Illinois State Museum

Groves, C forthcoming. 'Tree-ring Analysis of Softwood Timbers from Excavations in the Tower of London Moat, Tower Hamlets, London'

Groves, C and Hillam, J 1997. 'Tree-ring analysis and dating of timbers'. In J D Hurst, *A Multi-period Salt Production Site at Droitwich: Excavations at Upwich*, CBA Res Rep **107**, 121–6, York

Hall, J 1996. 'The cemeteries of Roman London: a review'. In J Bird, M Hassall and H Sheldon (eds) *Interpreting Roman London*, Oxbow Monograph **58**, 57–84, Oxford

Halstead, P 1985. 'A study of mandibular teeth from Romano-British contexts at Maxey'. In F Pryor, C French and D Crowther (eds) *Archaeology and Environment in the Lower Welland Valley, Vol 1*, East Anglian Archaeol Rep **27**, 219–82, Cambridge

Hamond, F W 1983. 'Phosphate analysis of archaeological sediments'. In T Reeves-Smyth and F W Hamond (eds) *Landscape and Archaeology in Ireland*, BAR Brit Ser **116**, 47–80, Oxford

Hammond, P W 1993. *Food and Feast in Medieval England*. Stroud: Alan Sutton

Harding, P and Newman, R 1997. 'The excavation of a turf-sided lock at Monkey Marsh, Thatcham, Berkshire'. *Industrial Archaeology Review* **XIX**, 31–48

Harvey, J 1948. 'The western entrance to the Tower of London'. *Transactions of the London and Middlesex Archaeological Society* **9**, 20–35

Harvey, Y 1975. 'The small finds catalogue'. In C Platt and R Coleman-Smith (eds) *Excavations in Medieval Southampton 1953–1969* ii, Leicester: Leicester University Press, 254–95

Haslam, J 1984. 'The glass'. In C Halpin and T Hassall (eds) 'Excavations in St. Ebbe's, Oxford, 1967–1976, part II: post-medieval domestic tenements and the post-dissolution site of the Greyfriars'. *Oxoniensia* **XLIX**, 232–49

Haslam, J 1988. 'Parishes, churches, wards and gates in eastern London'. In J Blair (ed) *Minsters and Parish Churches: The Local Church in Transition 950–1200*, Oxford University Committee for Archaeology Monograph **17**, 35–43, Oxford

Hearne, T 1720. *Textus Roffensis*. Oxford

Hendey, N I 1964. *An Introductory Account of the Smaller Algae of British Coastal Waters. Part V, Bacillariophyceae (Diatoms)*. Ministry of Agriculture, Fisheries and Food Series **IV**, London

Higgins, D A 1981. 'Surrey clay tobacco pipes'. In P J Davey (ed) *The Archaeology of the Clay Tobacco Pipe*, VI, BAR Brit Ser **97**, 189–293, Oxford

Higgins, D A 1987. *The Interpretation and Regional Study of Clay Tobacco Pipes: A Case Study of the Broseley District*. Unpublished PhD Thesis, University of Liverpool

Higgins, D A 1994. 'Clay tobacco pipes'. In J Hiller and G D Keevill (eds) 'Recent archaeological work at the Tower of London'. *Transactions of the London and Middlesex Archaeological Society* **45**, 147–81

Higgins, D A and Davey, P J 1994. *Draft Guidelines for Using the Clay Tobacco Pipe Record Sheets*. Unpublished

Hillam, J 1979. *Tree-ring Dating in London: The Mermaid Theatre Site (THE79) Interim Report*. Anc Mon Lab Rep **3008**, London

Hillam, J 1992. 'Tree-ring analysis of oak timbers'. In K Steedman, T Dyson and J Schofield (eds) *Aspects of Saxo-Norman London*, III: *The Bridgehead and Billingsgate to 1200*, London and Middlesex Archaeological Society Special Paper **14**, 143–73, London

Hillam, J, Morgan, R A and Tyers, I 1987. 'Sapwood estimates and the dating of short ring sequences'. In R G W Ward (ed) *Applications of Tree-ring Studies*, BAR Int Ser **333**, 165–85, Oxford

Hodgett, G A 1971. *Cartulary of Holy Trinity Aldgate*. Leicester: London Record Society

Howard, R E, Laxton, R R and Litton, C D 1998. *Tree-ring Analysis of Timbers from Chicksands Priory, Chicksands, Bedfordshire*. Anc Mon Lab Rep **30/98**, London

Hume, I N 1961. 'The glass wine bottle in Colonial Virginia'. *Journal of Glass Studies* **III**, 90–117

Hurst, J, Neal, D and van Beuningen, H J 1986. *Pottery Produced and Traded in North-west Europe 1350–1650*, Rotterdam Papers **VI**, Rotterdam

Hustedt, F 1930–66. 'Die Kieselalgen Deutschlands, Oesterreichs und der Schweiz unter Berucksichtigung der ubrigen Lander Europas sowie der angrenzenden Meeresgebeite'. In Dr L Rabenhorst's *Kryptogamen-Flora von Deutschland, Oesterrech und der Schweiz* 7, Parts 1–3. Leipzig: Akademische Verlagsgesellschaft

Hustedt, F 1953. 'Die Systematik der Diatomeen in ihren Beziehungen zur Geologie und Okologie nebst einer Revision des Halobien-systems'. *Sv. Bot. Tidskr* **47**, 509–19

Hustedt, F 1957. 'Die Diatomeenflora des Fluss-systems der Weser im Gebiet der Hansestadt Bremen'. *Ab. naturw. Ver. Bremen* **34**, 181–440.

Impey, E 1997. 'The western entrance to the Tower of London, 1240–1241'. *Transactions of the London and Middlesex Archaeological Society* **48**, 59–75

Impey, E and Keevill, G 1997. *The Tower of London Moat: A Summary History of the Tower Moat, Based on Historical and Archaeological Research Undertaken for the Tower Environs Scheme.* London: Historic Royal Palaces

Impey, E I and Parnell, G 2000. *The Tower of London: The Official Illustrated History.* London: Merrell Publishers in association with Historic Royal Palaces

Ingrem, C 2003. 'The post-dissolution occupation'. In A Hardy, A Dodd and G D Keevill, *Aelfric's Abbey: Excavations at Eynsham Abbey, Oxfordshire, 1989–92,* Oxford Archaeol Thames Valley Landscapes Mono **16**, 406-27

Jackson, R G and Price, R H 1974. *Bristol Clay Pipes.* Bristol City Museum Research Monograph **1**, Bristol

Jenkins, J G 1974. *Nets and Coracles.* London: David and Charles

Jennings, S and Smythe, C 1982. 'A preliminary interpretation of coastal deposits from East Sussex'. *Quaternary Newsletter* **37**, 12–19

Jessop, O 1996. 'A new artefact typology for the study of medieval arrowheads'. *Medieval Archaeol* **40**, 192–205

Keay, A 2001. *The Elizabethan Tower of London: The Haiward and Gascoyne plan of 1597.* London Topographical Society Publication No. **158** with Historic Royal Palaces and The Society of Antiquaries of London

Keevill, G 1997. 'The Tower of London'. *Current Archaeology* **154**, 384–7

Kerney, M P 1999. *Atlas of the Land and Freshwater Molluscs of Britain and Ireland.* Colchester: Harley Books

Kooistra, M J 1978. *Soil Development in Recent Marine Sediments of the Intertidal Zone in the Oosterschelde, the Netherlands: A Soil Micromorphological Approach.* Wageningen: Soil Survey Institute

Larking, L B 1859. 'The fabric roll of Rochester Castle'. *Archaeol Cantiana* **2**, 111–32

Lawson, G 1990. 'Jew's harp'. In M Biddle (ed) *Object and Economy in Medieval Winchester.* Winchester Studies **7.ii**, 724–5. Oxford: Clarendon

Laxton, R R and Litton, C D 1989. 'Construction of a Kent master chronological sequence for oak, 1158–1540 AD'. *Medieval Archaeol* **33**, 90–8

Le Cheminant, R 1981. 'Clay pipes bearing the Prince of Wales' feathers'. In P J Davey (ed) *The Archaeology of the Clay Tobacco Pipe* VI, BAR Brit Ser **97**, 92–101, Oxford

Lewcun M, 1985. 'The Hunt family identified'. *Society for Clay Pipe Research Newsletter* **8**, 14–21

Lipman, V D 1978. 'The jurisdiction of the Tower authorities outside the walls'. In J Charlton (ed) *The Tower of London: Its Buildings and Institutions,* London: HMSO, 144–52

Long, A J, Scaife, R G and Edwards, R J 1999. 'Pine pollen in intertidal sediments from Poole Harbour, UK; implications for late-Holocene sediment accretion rates and sea-level rise'. *Quaternary International* **55**, 3–16

Luard H R (ed) 1876. *Matthaei Parisiensis Monachi Sancti Albani Chronica Majora.* Rolls Series, Vol 3. London

Luard H R (ed) 1890. *Flores Historiarum,* Vol 2. Rolls Series. London

MacGregor, A 1985. *Bone, Antler, Ivory and Horn: The Technology of Skeletal Materials since the Roman Period.* Beckenham: Croom Helm

Macphail, R I 1994. 'Soil micromorphological investigations in archaeology, with special reference to drowned coastal sites in Essex'. *SEESOIL* **10**, 13–28

Macphail, R I nd. 'Assessment of Rose Theatre Sediments'. Unpublished archive report

Maloney, J 1983. 'Recent work on London's defences'. In J Maloney and B Hobley (eds) *Roman Urban Defences in the West,* CBA Res Rep **51**, 96–117, York

Maltby, J M 1979. *Faunal Studies on Urban Sites: The Animal Bones from Exeter 1971–1975.* Sheffield: Department of Prehistory and Archaeology, University of Sheffield

Margeson, S 1993. *Norwich Households: The Medieval and Post-Medieval Finds from Norwich Survey Excavations 1971–1978.* East Anglian Archaeology Rep **58**, Norwich

McNeill, T 1997. *Castles in Ireland.* London: Routledge

Melville, R V and Freshney, E C 1982. *British Regional Geology: The Hampshire Basin and Adjoining Areas* (4th edn). London: HMSO

Milne, G 1985. *The Port of Roman London.* London: Batsford

Milne, G 1992. *Timber Building Techniques in London c. 900–1400: An Archaeological Study of Waterfront Installations and Related Material.* London and Middlesex Archaeological Society Special Paper **15**, London

Mitchiner, M 1988. *Jetons, medalets and tokens.* Vol 2. London: Seaby

Moore, P D and Webb, J A 1978. *An Illustrated Guide to Pollen Analysis.* London: Hodder and Stoughton

Moore, P D, Webb, J A and Collinson, M E 1991. *Pollen Analysis* (2nd edn) Oxford: Blackwell

Morris, R K 1979. 'The development of later Gothic mouldings in England, *c*1250–1400, Part II'. *Architectural History* **22**, 1–48

Mould, Q A 1993. 'Leather'. In J W Hawkes and M J Heaton (eds) *A Closed-Shaft Garderobe and Associated Medieval Structures.* Wessex Archaeological Report **3**, 62–7

Mould, Q A 1997. 'Leather'. In J W Hawkes and P J Fasham (eds) *Excavations on Reading Waterfront Sites, 1979–1988,* Wessex Archaeological Report **5**, 108–41, Salisbury

Murphy, C P 1986. *Thin Section Preparation of Soils and Sediments.* Berkhamsted: A B Academic Publishers

Nayling, N 1991. *Dendrochronology Report on Timbers from Thames Exchange, City of London.* MoLAS Dendro Rep **07/91**, London

Newman, H 1977. *An Illustrated Dictionary of Glass.* London: Thames and Hudson

Nichols, G 1999. *Sedimentology and Stratigraphy.* Oxford: Blackwell

Noël Hume, A 1970. 'English clay tobacco pipes bearing the Royal Arms from Williamsburg, Virginia'. *Post-medieval Archaeol* **4**, 141–6, pls IV–VIII

OECD 1982. *Eutrophication of Waters: Monitoring, Assessment and Control.* Paris: Organization for Economic Cooperation and Development

Oswald, A 1975. *Clay Pipes for the Archaeologist.* BAR Brit Ser **14**, Oxford

Oswald, A 1978. 'New light on some 18th-century pipemakers of London'. In J Bird and H Chapman (eds) *Collectanea Londiniensia: Studies in London Archaeology and History Presented to Ralph Merrifield*, London and Middlesex Archaeological Society Special Paper **2**, 346–75, London

Oswald, A and Le Cheminant, R 1989. 'Regional variations of clay pipe markings in eastern England'. *Society for Clay Pipe Research Newsletter* **24**, 6–11

Parnell, G 1982. 'The excavation of the Roman city wall at the Tower of London and Tower Hill, 1954–76'. *Transactions of the London and Middlesex Archaeological Society* **33**, 85–133

Parnell, G 1983a. 'The western defences of the Inmost Ward, Tower of London'. *Transactions of the London and Middlesex Archaeological Society* **34**, 107–50

Parnell, G 1983b. 'Excavations at the Salt Tower, Tower of London, 1976'. *Transactions of the London and Middlesex Archaeological Society* **34**, 95–106

Parnell, G 1983c. 'The refortification of the Tower of London 1679–86'. *Antiquaries Journal* **63**, 337–52

Parnell, G 1985. 'The Roman and medieval defences and later development of the Inmost Ward, Tower of London: excavations 1955–77'. *Transactions of the London and Middlesex Archaeological Society* **36**, 1–79

Parnell, G 1993. *The Tower of London.* London: English Heritage/Batsford

Parnell, G 1995. 'Getting into deep water?' *The London Archaeologist* **7.15**, 387–90

Payne, S 1973. 'Kill-off patterns in sheep and goats: the mandibles from Asvan Kale'. *Anatolian Studies* **23**, 281–303

Payne, S 1985. 'Morphological distinctions between the mandibular teeth of young sheep, *Ovis*, and goats, *Capra*'. *Journal of Archaeological Science* **12**, 139–47

Peacey, A 1995. 'Grates: an old problem revisited'. *Society for Clay Pipe Research Newsletter* **45**, 25–8

Pearce, J and Vince, A 1988. *A Dated Type-Series of London Medieval Pottery Part 4: Surrey Whitewares*, London and Middlesex Archaeological Society Special Paper **10**, London

Pierpoint, S 1986. '41–42 Trinity Square'. *The London Archaeologist* **5.6**, 164

Platt, C and Coleman-Smith, R 1975. *Excavations in Medieval Southampton 1953–1969, i, The Excavation Reports, ii, The Finds.* Leicester: Leicester University Press

Ponge, J F 1999. 'Horizons and humus forms in beech forests of the Belgian Ardennes'. *Soil Science Society of America Journal* **63**, 1888–1901

Potter, G 1991. 'The medieval bridge and waterfront at Kingston upon Thames'. In G L Good, R H Jones and M W Ponsford (eds), *Waterfront Archaeology, Proceedings of the Third International Conference on Waterfront Archaeology held at Bristol 1988.* CBA Res Rep **74**, 137–49, York

Rackham, O 1990. *Trees and Woodland in the British Landscape* (2nd edn). London: Dent

Reineck, H E and Singh, I B 1986. *Depositional Sedimentary Environments.* Berlin: Springer-Verlag

Renn, D 1997. *Caerphilly Castle.* Cardiff: CADW

Rigold, S E 1975. 'Structural aspects of medieval timber bridges'. *Medieval Archaeol* **19**, 48–91

Robinson, M 1995. *Macroscopic Plant and Invertebrate Remains from the 1995 Excavations in the Tower of London Moat.* Unpublished archive report

Robinson, M 1996. 'Macroscopic plant and invertebrate remains'. In G D Keevill and C Bell (eds) 'The excavation of a trial trench across the moat at Hampton Court Palace'. *Transactions of the London and Middlesex Archaeological Society* **47**, 151–3

Robinson, M 1998. *Macroscopic Plant and Invertebrate Remains from the 1996 and 1997 Excavations in the Tower of London Moat.* Unpublished archive report

Robinson, M and Hubbard, R N L B 1977. 'The transport of pollen in bracts of hulled cereals'. *Journal of Archaeological Science* **4**, 197–9

Rogers, Col. H C B 1960. *Weapons of the British Soldier.* 5, 146–7. London: Seeley

Rowsome, P 1998. 'The development of the town plan of early Roman London'. In B Watson (ed) *Roman London: Recent Archaeological Work*, Journal of Roman Archaeology Supplementary Series **24**, 35–46, Oxford

Ruddock, T 1979. *Arch Bridges and Their Builders.* Cambridge: Cambridge University Press

Salzman, L S 1997. *Building in England Down to 1540, A Documentary History.* Oxford: Clarendon

Sankey, D 1998. 'Cathedrals, granaries, and urban vitality in late Roman London'. In B Watson (ed) *Roman London: Recent Archaeological Work.* Journal of Roman Archaeology Supplementary Series **24**, 100–6, Oxford

Scaife, R G 1982a. 'Pollen analysis of urban medieval sediments'. In P Mills (ed) 'Excavations at Broad Sanctuary, Westminster'. *Transactions of the London and Middlesex Archaeological Society* **33**, 360–5

Scaife, R G 1982b. *Pollen Analysis of Roman Peats Underlying the Temple of Mithras, London.* Anc Mon Lab Rep **3502**, London

Scaife, R G 1986 'Pollen in human palaeofaeces: a preliminary investigation of the stomach and gut contents of Lindow Man'. In I M Stead, J B Bourke and D Brothwell (eds) *Lindow Man: The Body in the Bog*, London: British Museum Press, 126–35

Scaife, R G 1990. 'Yaxley Manor Farm, Cambs. Pollen Assessment of the Moat Fills'. Unpublished archive report

Scaife, R G 1995a. 'The Tower of London Moat: A Preliminary Pollen Analysis of the Moat Fills'. Unpublished archive report

Scaife, R G 1995b. 'Pollen analysis of the Lindow III food residues'. In R C Turner and R G Scaife (eds) *Bog Bodies. New Discoveries and New Perspectives*, London: British Museum Press, 83–5

Scaife, R G 1996. 'Pollen samples'. In G D Keevill and C Bell (eds) 'The excavation of a trial trench across the moat at Hampton Court Palace'. *Transactions of the London and Middlesex Archaeological Society* **47**, 153–4

Scaife, R G 1999. 'Falcon House: Pollen Analysis of the City of London Medieval Ditch Fills'. Unpublished archive report

Scaife, R G, Blake, N and Mauquoy, D 1997a. 'The Tower of London Moat Auger Survey'. Unpublished archive report

Scaife, R G, Blake, N and Clapham, A J 1997b. 'Tower of London Moat Survey: East Side: December 1997'. Unpublished archive report

Schweingruber, F H 1988. *Tree Rings*. Dordrecht: Reidel

Scollar, I, Tabbagh A, Hesse, A and Herzog, I 1990. *Archaeological Prospecting and Remote Sensing*. Cambridge: Cambridge University Press

Serjeantson, D 1996. 'The animal bones'. In S Needham and T Spence (eds) *Runnymede Bridge Research Excavations, Volume 2 – Refuse and Disposal at Area 16 East Runnymede*, London: British Museum Press, 194–233

Sidell, J, Wilkinson, K, Scaife, R G and Cameron, N forthcoming. 'Palaeoenvironmental Investigation of Sediments along the New Jubilee Line Extension, East London'.

Simpson, I A 1997. 'Relict properties of anthropogenic deep top soils as indicators of infield land management in Marwick, West Mainland, Orkney'. *Journal of Archaeological Science* **24**, 365–80

Smith, K G V 1989. *An Introduction to the Immature Stages of British Flies*. Royal Entomological Society Handbooks for the Identification of British Insects **10** pt 14, London

Stace, C 1991. *New Flora of the British Isles*. Cambridge: Cambridge University Press

Stanley, E A 1969. 'Marine palynology'. *Oceanography and Marine Biology Annual Review* **7**, 177–92

Stevenson, J (ed) 1875. *Radulfi de Coggeshall Chronicon Anglicanum*. Rolls Series. London

Stubbs, W (ed) 1882. *Chronicles of the Reigns of Edward I and Edward II*: vol 1. Rolls Series. London

Tatton Brown, T 1974. 'Excavations at the Custom House site, City of London, 1973'. *Transactions of the London and Middlesex Archaeological Society* **25**, 117–219

Tatton-Brown, T 1975. 'Excavations at the Custom House site, City of London, 1973 – part 2'. *Transactions of the London and Middlesex Archaeological Society* **26**, 103–70

Taylor, A J 1996. *The Jewel Tower, Westminster*. London: English Heritage

Thirsk, J 1967. 'Farming techniques'. In J Thirsk (ed) *The Agrarian History of England and Wales Volume, IV, 1500–1640*, Cambridge: Cambridge University Press

Tite, M S 1972. 'The influence of geology on the magnetic susceptibility of soils on archaeological sites'. *Archaeometry* **14**, 229–36

Tite, M S and Mullins, C E 1971. 'Enhancement of magnetic susceptibility of soils on archaeological sites'. *Archaeometry* **13**, 209–19

Trow-Smith, R 1957. *A History of British Livestock Husbandry to 1700*. London: Routledge and Kegan Paul

Tyers, I 1996. 'Appendix 1: Dendrochronology on shipping from London, twelfth to seventeenth centuries'. In P Marsden (ed) *Ships of the Port of London: Twelfth to Seventeenth Centuries*, English Heritage Archaeological Report **5**, 193–7, London

Tyers, I 1998. *Tree-Ring Analysis and Wood Identification of Timbers Excavated on the Magistrates Court Site, Kingston upon Hull, East Yorkshire*. ARCUS Rep **410**, Sheffield

Tyers, I 1999. *Dendrochronological Spot-dates of Timbers from the Millennium Foot Bridge Sites (MBC98) and (MFB98) London*. ARCUS Rep **521**, Sheffield

Tyers, I 2000. *Tree-ring Analysis of Timbers from the Tower of London Moat, Tower Hamlets, London*. ARCUS Rep **293**, Sheffield

Tyers, I 2001. 'Tree-ring analysis of the Roman and medieval timbers from medieval London Bridge and its environs'. In B Watson, T Brigham and T Dyson, *London Bridge: 2000 years of a river crossing*, MoLAS Mon Ser **8**, 180–90 London

Tyers, I and Boswijk, G 1996. *Dendrochronological Spot-dates for 82 Timbers from Suffolk House, City of London, Three Ways Wharf, City of London, Guys Hospital, Southwark, Lafone St, Southwark, Jacob's Island, Southwark, and Atlantic Wharf, Tower Hamlets*. ARCUS Rep **286**, Sheffield

Tyers, I and Hibberd, H 1993a. 'Tree-ring dates from Museum of London Archaeology Service: List 53'. *Vernacular Architect* **24**, 50–4

Tyers, I and Hibberd, H 1993b. *Dendrochronology, Wood Identification, and Wattle Analysis for the Fleet Valley Developer's Report*. MoLAS Dendro Rep **03/93**, London

Vince, A 1990. *Saxon London: An Archaeological Investigation*. London: Seaby

Vince, A (ed) 1991. *Aspects of Saxo-Norman London, II: Finds and Environmental Evidence*. London and Middlesex Archaeological Society Special Paper **12**, London

Walker, I C and Wells, P K 1979. 'Regional varieties of clay tobacco pipe markings in eastern England'. In P J Davey (ed) *The Archaeology of the Clay Tobacco Pipe* I, BAR Brit Ser **63**, 3–66, Oxford

Watson, B 1992. 'The Norman fortress on Ludgate Hill in the City of London, England, recent excavations 1986–1990'. *Château Gaillard* **15**, 335–45

Watson, B (ed) 1998. *Roman London: Recent Archae-ological Work*. Journal of Roman Archaeology Sup-plementary Series **24**, Oxford

Watson, J 1992. 'Basketry'. In C A Butterworth and S J Lobb (eds) *Excavations in the Burghfield Area, Berkshire. Developments in the Bronze Age and Saxon Landscapes*. Wessex Archaeology Report **1**, 115, Salisbury

Werff, A van der and Huls, H 1957–74. *Diatomeeënflora van Nederland*, 1–10. De Hoef, The Netherlands

Wheatley, A forthcoming. 'The White Tower in myth and legend'. In E Impey (ed) *The White Tower*, Historic Royal Palaces

Wheeler, A 1969. *The Fishes of the British Isles and North West Europe*. London: Macmillan

Wheeler, A 1979. *The Tidal Thames*. London: Routle-dge and Kegan Paul

Whipp, D 1980. 'Excavations at Tower Hill 1978'. *Transactions of the London and Middlesex Archae-ological Society* **31**, 47–67

Worssam, B C and Tatton-Brown, T 1994. 'Kentish Rag and other Kent building stones'. *Archaeol Cantiana* **112**, 93–125

Wright, D 1959. *Baskets and Basketry*. London: Batsford

www.antiquebottles.com

Index

Note: Page numbers in *italics* refer to illustrations.